Faulkner's MGM Screenplays

Faulkner's MGM Screenplays

EDITED WITH AN INTRODUCTION

AND COMMENTARIES BY

Bruce F. Kawin

THE UNIVERSITY OF TENNESSEE PRESS / KNOXVILLE

OTHER BOOKS BY BRUCE KAWIN

Telling It Again and Again: Repetition in Literature and Film
Faulkner and Film
Mindscreen: Bergman, Godard, and First-Person Film
To Have and Have Not (ed.)
The Mind of the Novel: Reflexive Fiction and the Ineffable

Special Consultant for Film Studies for The University of
Tennessee Press
Neil D. Isaacs

Turn About (filmed as *Today We Live*) copyright © 1933 by Metro-
Goldwyn-Mayer Corporation, renewed 1960 by Metro-Goldwyn Mayer
Inc.
*The College Widow, Manservant, Honor, Lazy River, Absolution, Flying
the Mail, War Birds,* and *Mythical Latin-American Kingdom Story*
copyright © 1982 by Metro-Goldwyn Mayer Film Co.
Plates 16 through 29 inclusive copyright © 1933 by Metro-Goldwyn-Mayer
Corporation, renewed 1960 by Metro-Goldwyn-Mayer Inc.

Library of Congress Cataloging in Publication Data.

Faulkner, William, 1897-1962.
  Faulkner's MGM screenplays.

  Bibliography: p.
  Includes index.
  Contents: Manservant—The college widow—Absolution—[etc.]
  1. Faulkner, William, 1897-1962—Manuscripts—Facsimiles. 2. Moving-picture
plays. 3. World War, 1914-1918—Drama. I. Kawin, Bruce F., 1945- . II. Title. III.
Title: Faulkner's M.G.M. screenplays. IV. Title: M.G.M. screenplays.
PS3511.A86A6 1982   791.43'75   82-1915
ISBN 0-87049-351-5   AACR2

Contents

Illustrations

Faulkner in the Hollywood Hills, c. 1936. Used by permission of Mrs. Meta Wilde.

Preface

This book contains facsimiles of every surviving manuscript William Faulkner wrote for MGM studios (1932–33), with the exceptions of *Louisiana Lou* (released as *Lazy River*) and the third draft of *Turn About* (released as *Today We Live*). Related materials such as the first version of *Turn About*, a second version of *The College Widow*, and the treatment for *War Birds* are not extant. The four treatments and three screenplays reproduced here should prove a significant addition to the Faulkner canon, and I have done my best to indicate throughout the ways they enlarge on the characteristic themes of his fiction, build on or anticipate many aspects of his other screenplays and books, and succeed or fail on their own terms as professional screenwriting. I have also attempted in the Introduction to establish the true story of Faulkner's first year in Hollywood.

The genesis of this volume over a six-year period is a story in itself, and since I am greatly indebted to the help of many friends and colleagues, I will try to acknowledge their aid in something better than a list of names.

While I was researching my book *Faulkner and Film* in Los Angeles, I met Herbert S. Nusbaum, a diligent and congenial MGM lawyer with a serious commitment to the preservation and scholarly examination of the studio's extraordinary holdings. Mr. Nusbaum authorized a Vault search that netted *The College Widow*, *Flying the Mail*, the second draft of *Turn About*, *War Birds*, and the *Mythical Latin-American Kingdom Story*. About a week later, he discovered the only copy of *Absolution*; *Manservant* remained among the missing. The late Jim Powers, of the American Film Institute's (AFI) Center for Advanced Film Studies, put me in touch with director Howard Hawks, who spoke to me at length about his long association with Faulkner: their friendship, their disagreements, and the films they made together—the first of which was *Today We Live* (1933), from Faulkner's *Turn About*. With this material, I went back to Colorado to write *Faulkner and Film*, keeping in mind the suggestions of several members of my family, especially Hershel Toomim, that at some point I should attempt to see at least the MGM scripts cleared for publication.

A few years later, I met several members of Faulkner's family at a conference organized at the University of Mississippi by Evans Harrington and Ann Abadie, and one of them, Victoria Black, offered to approach Jill Faulkner Summers on behalf of the publication project. In the meantime, my former agent, Joan Gilbert, had been trying to interest publishers in the venture but had found that such a volume was not expected to sell widely enough to merit further consideration. Late in 1979, however, the University of Tennessee Press (suggested by Mr. Nusbaum in the light of their volume on *Intruder in the Dust*), under the direction of Carol Orr, decided to go ahead with the book. Mrs. Summers, Faulkner's daughter, generously agreed to approve publication, and Wendy Schmalz of Harold Ober Associates was prompt in drawing up a contract. Ernest Callenbach, film editor at University of California Press, queried Michael Millgate, Carolyn Porter, Marvin Klotz, Irving Malin, and James Meriwether as to what they would like to see in such a volume and made their letters available to me. At that point, the University of Colorado's Council on Research and Creative Work granted me a year off to work on the book; I want to express my special thanks to Jane Roberts of CRCW and to my department chairman, Jim Kincaid, for facilitating this Faculty Fellowship.

I returned to Los Angeles, and this time Mr. Nusbaum arranged for me to go into the Vault myself. *Manservant* had been mysteriously returned. *War Birds* had been misfiled, but I found it a few days later. The file on the *Mythical Latin-American Kingdom Story* turned out to include Faulkner's original typescript. The *Honor* file included a huge manuscript that for a while appeared to be Faulkner's. The file on *Today We Live* was crammed with fourth carbons that proved to unravel the knotty question of which scenes in *Today We Live* were written by whom. In these searches I was greatly helped by the Vault supervisor, Susie Battle, who allowed me to share her work space for nearly a month, and by the staff of the Script Department, especially Paula Larrabure, Marian Kidd, and Rose Perechov. In the Copy Department, Keith Carson and Betty Reed made many suggestions and devoted considerable time to making these facsimiles the best possible, despite the fact that the originals were in desperate shape. Bonnie Rothbart of the Research Department tracked down several stills and some obscure information about 1930s studio practice. Dore Freeman, head of the Publicity Department and a lifelong collector of Joan Crawford memorabilia, let me have many rare stills from *Today We Live*, as well as a photo of what is apparently the only extant lobby card for that picture, from his private collection. Faulkner collector Carl Petersen shared copies of some of the letters and telegrams he acquired for his collection on *Lazy River*. And Sam Marx talked with me at length about MGM's relations with its writers in the 1930s and shared many reminiscenses about Faulkner, Hawks, Irving Thalberg, and many of the writers involved in the generation of these screenplays.

Anne Schlosser, librarian for the AFI, put me in touch some years ago with Mrs. Meta Doherty Wilde, in connection with an edition I was preparing of Faulkner's script for *To Have and Have Not*. Though she had not known Faulkner during his time at MGM, Mrs. Wilde helped me sort through various MGM scripts in search of examples of his handwriting; she also provided several unpublished photographs of Faulkner in Los Angeles in 1935–37. Joseph Blotner sent me a copy of *Night Bird* and went back into his extensive files for materials not included in his Faulkner biography, especially in regard to *Honor* and *A Ghost Story*. I am grateful to Jim Palmer, Michel Gresset, and Anna Catalana for their enthusiasm, feedback, and personal support.

I particularly want to acknowledge the contribution made to this undertaking by my editorial assistant, Sherri Hallgren. During the crucial period when the manuscripts were being authenticated and copied (1980), she worked with tireless precision; much of the retouching of the copies was done by her, and she helped conduct the interviews with Sam Marx and Mrs. Wilde.

Throughout this project I have worked on the assumption that anything Faulkner wrote is of some interest, and it is extremely gratifying to find at least one press, out of the more than twenty that were approached, with the resources and conviction to bring these scripts forward; the credit here goes to Carol Orr at Tennessee and to her readers, especially Neil D. Isaacs, special consultant for film books published by the University of Tennessee Press. Jill Faulkner Summers deserves special thanks for allowing these scripts to be published in spite of her concern that they might not measure up to the standards of the published fiction. For arranging MGM's publication permission, for his dedication to the project since its first conception, and for his invaluable assistance at every stage, the man who most richly merits my thanks, and those of readers who may find this book interesting and valuable, is Herbert Nusbaum.

Bruce F. Kawin

April 1982

MGM Studios, front entrance, 1934. Used by permission of Marc Wanamaker, Bison Archives.

Inside the MGM lot, mid-1930s. (c) MGM.

Introduction
Faulkner at MGM

The Story Department Files at MGM occupy one end of the basement of the Thalberg office building. Sometimes called the Vault, this large concrete room contains a long bookcase with copies of every book to which the studio ever bought rights, close ranks of open shelving filled with current television and movie scripts, and toward the back another series of quiet shelves—so dusty that file personnel are issued cotton gloves—packed with synopses, treatments, screenplays, and cutting continuities for nearly every property MGM (and some of its pre-1924 antecedent companies) either released or worked on in hopes of eventual production. One can find there, in a yellowed binding augmented by a rubber band, the fragile carbon of Erich von Stroheim's original continuity for *Greed*; Herman J. Mankiewicz's first treatment for *The Wizard of Oz*; the voluminous narrative for *2001* and a shooting script that varies significantly from the film as released; eight accordion files for a Jean Harlow script called *Today is Tonight*; F. Scott Fitzgerald's *Infidelity*, complete with a memo explaining his rationale for treating adultery as "theft," and in another file his handwritten manuscript for *The Women*—and among these thousands of numbered properties rest also the treatments and screenplays written by William Faulkner between May 1932 on the MGM lot and May 1933 at his home in Oxford, Mississippi.

It is ironic that a writer to whom dust was such a vital metaphor for the interrelatedness of success and defeat, tradition and modernity, should with the facsimile publication of these scripts be accorded a qualified victory in the dust. The MGM vaults have their own aura of past glory, inseparable from the memory of that time when Metro was the most prestigious studio of the thirties; thanks to Faulkner's own sometimes humorously falsified or embittered accounts of his time in Hollywood (1932–54), there is also about his first scripts the aura of frustration and defeat. It has seemed until now that the only benefit Faulkner received from his time at Metro, besides his much-needed salary, was the beginning of his long and successful association with director Howard Hawks, for whom he later worked on *The Road to Glory, Air Force, To Have and Have Not, The Big Sleep, Land of the Pharaohs,* and such unproduced properties as *Sutter's Gold, Battle Cry,* and *Dreadful Hollow.* Now that the MGM scripts are finally available, readers can make their own judgments about the value of some of the work Faulkner actually did in Hollywood, much of which is intriguingly related to his fiction, some of which is terrible by any standard, and some of which, I think, can stand on its own as good screenwriting.

This work needs to be placed in two contexts: how screenplays were written and what Faulkner had published by the time he arrived at MGM. The latter included some of the best work he was ever to achieve, and his screenwriting of course pales before *The Sound and the Fury, As I Lay Dying, Sanctuary,* and *Light in August.* It does not look so inadequate in comparison with *Soldiers' Pay, Mosquitoes, Flags in the Dust, Dr. Martino and Other Stories,* or *These 13,* and it doubtless surpasses his poetry, the allegory *Mayday,* the play *Marionettes,* and lesser unpublished prose. Some of the awkward rhetoric, grand gesturing, and sentimentality of *Soldiers' Pay,* his first novel, is complemented by that in *War Birds,* for instance, which suggests that some of the deficiencies of the screenplays can be attributed to Faulkner's being a beginner in the medium, rather than to drunkenness and a nervous contempt for Hollywood. There is certainly little trace of these problems in *To Have and Have Not* (1944), for example. It is significant that Faulkner was at times passively and at others actively involved in MGM's attempts to acquire some of his best stories: "Honor," "Ad Astra," and "All the Dead Pilots." It is also true that the first treatment he showed them, *Manservant,* was a reworking of a minor failure called "Love." Some of his scripts have the virtues of his better short stories; most are interesting for the skeletal way they reveal Faulkner's sense of tragic form or for their abbreviated indications of some of the ways he saw love, honor, sacrifice, and sublimated incest. Readers who value *Flags in the Dust* and *The Unvanquished* will find in *War Birds* a missing link, a way out of the Waste Land; they will also learn much from the ways Faulkner reworked "All the Dead Pilots," which at the time he considered his best story, and "Ad Astra" into motion picture terms. The author of *Sanctuary* is present, too, in a treatment one MGM reader considered "an evil, slimy thing, absolutely unfit for screen production"—*The College Widow.* And *Turn About* has several important connections with *The Sound and the Fury,* besides serving as the skeleton for Hawks's unfortunately forgotten *Today We Live,* an intermittently powerful exercise

Faulkner, 1936. Used by permission
of Mrs. Meta Wilde.

Faulkner at Hollywood's Garden of Allah, 1935.
Used by permission of Mrs. Meta Wilde.

in restrained melodrama that proved the only film MGM produced from any of these scripts. (*Lazy River*, as released, includes none of Faulkner's writing.)

Screenplays cannot be read the way one might read published prose. Most of them are continuing drafts of work in progress, and not even the Final, or shooting script, is final, since it is subject to further emendation by the director, the actors, and even the writer if s/he happens to be on the set. The film is the finished text, and not even the director is always guaranteed a say in those changes by the editor and producer that determine the ultimate content and structure of the work. The fact that these scripts offer the reader a look at early unpolished drafts by an author who meticulously revised what he published as fiction should not be held against them. Because much of the polishing of *Turn About* was done by other hands, I have deliberately selected the earliest surviving draft (the second of three) that appears to reflect Faulkner's view of the story, even though he went on to compile a script that salvaged some of the second draft while incorporating extensive work by Dwight Taylor, Edith Fitzgerald, and Hawks himself.

The standard procedure for generating a screenplay at MGM in the early thirties (substantially the same at other studios) was as follows. A property or idea was brought to the attention of the head of the Story Department—in this case (1930–37) Sam Marx, who has said that at that time he kept track of four hundred stories a week, from optioned novels to intriguing paragraphs in the newspapers. Marx might have a reader work up a synopsis of the story and then circulate that among producers or directors who might be interested in pursuing it, or discuss the story with Irving Thalberg, the top production executive (succeeded by Louis B. Mayer after Thalberg's death in 1936, and occasionally filling in when Thalberg's health failed). Once a story was approved, Marx would assign a writer to the project (sometimes the producer would request a specific author). The writer would first compose a *treatment*, a short prose outline of the proposed film, usually broken up into major scenes or numbered plot developments and sometimes containing dialogue. If the writer originated the story (as opposed to receiving it on assignment), s/he would usually begin with a treatment and see whether it would be approved for further work. In this volume, *Flying the Mail* is a treatment from previous work by others, while *Manservant* and *Absolution* are originals not approved for production and therefore presented here in their first and only drafts. (There appears to have been a second draft of *The College Widow*, but it has been lost.) The

Mythical Latin-American Kingdom Story is unusual in that it was written as a complete screenplay with no treatment or studio consultation whatever.

Once the treatment was approved, the writer (or another writer) would prepare a *temporary screenplay,* sometimes called a *dialogue continuity.* There were often first, second, third, and even subsequent versions. In this volume, *Turn About* is a Second Temporary (though it was not so labeled by the Script Department; most of these scripts were simply called continuities). These usually contained completely realized scenes with full dialogue; the scenes were almost never broken down into shots, since that was left to the director, nor were there indications of camera placement. For this reason, not even a shooting script can be taken as more than a general guide to the *cinematic* talents or intentions of the writer; we cannot know what levels of montage Faulkner may have envisioned for *Turn About,* for instance, since it was part of his job to leave all that to Hawks. There are moments in his scripts, however, when he forgets this rule and makes it possible for us to generalize about his visual imagination—notably, the newspaper montage at the beginning of the *Mythical Latin-American Kingdom Story* (hereafter *MLAK*) and the smashed-window/star fadeout at the climax of *War Birds*. Each of these temporary screenplays would be typed, mimeographed, and distributed by the Script Department, which would put on the front cover the date copying had been completed. Although the interested director or producer would have seen the script as it was written (the writer's typed or handwritten sheets were turned in to the Script Department almost daily, then typed and returned; the writer would then make any changes or corrections and pass them on to the producer, while assembling a complete draft for final copying), the whole Temporary might then be sent back for rewrite, often at the hands of a different author, who might be able to concoct an interesting variation or some good scenes that could be incorporated into a final version. Each such draft was often emended in part; new pages—marked "Changes" with the date of composition or in some cases the date of copying—would be interleaved in their proper places.

At each stage, there was an opportunity to evaluate the project and proceed or cancel. Many stories were abandoned by the producers when it seemed unlikely that the writers would be able to come up with adequate screenplays; even after buying rights and charging writers' time to a property, producers would suffer only a small loss by calling a halt at this stage, compared with the cost of mounting a full production. If a property got to the *final screenplay* or *shooting script* stage, it was often the case that a director had been lined up and actual production scheduled. The Final, like the earlier versions, was usually broken not into shots but into scenes; it contained what was at the time intended to be the complete dialogue and action of the picture. (There are no Finals in this volume, but a reader interested in seeing a Faulkner shooting script can consult my edition of *To Have and Have Not*.[1]) If a script was stopped at this point, it would be shelved, perhaps to be synopsized and evaluated by a reader at some later time; there are MGM reader reports on some of Faulkner's scripts well into the forties. If a script went into production, the Final was used as the director's and actors' working copy; most on-the-set changes were kept track of by the script supervisor and passed along to the editor. When the film had been shot and had gone from rough cut to final cut, the editor or an assistant would write a *cutting continuity*, which contained a complete and precise record of the film shot-by-shot, including camera placement and every audible bit of dialogue—even in crowd scenes.

From the synopsis stage to the cutting continuity, and no matter how many copies were distributed, a "File Copy" and a "Vault Copy" of each manuscript were placed in the Story Department Files; the File Copy might circulate, but the Vault Copy (often the original or best) would not. Sometimes when a property was completed or else abandoned, both copies went to the vaults. For a variety of reasons, including the cost of storage, the impracticality of keeping variant drafts of properties likely never to be produced, and the fact that most of these materials were not copyrighted (the films were copyrighted, but the writer's work was bought outright, usually for salary), many of these manuscripts were destroyed during periodic housecleanings, although an attempt was made to retain Vault Copies of the most useful or significant documents. The first draft of *Turn About*, the treatment for *War Birds*, and Faulkner's pages for *Lazy River (Louisiana Lou)* are among the missing, and several of the manuscripts included here were for years among the misfiled.

The scripts in this volume are, wherever possible, Vault Copies. Without altering the text in any way, we have slightly retouched the facsimiles to mask blemishes, tears, and punch holes. The insertion of footnote numbers in the original scripts has been decided against in the interest of textual integrity, so the reader will find at the end of each introductory editorial chapter a section of notes keyed to the scripts' original page numbers. *MLAK* is presented in Faulkner's

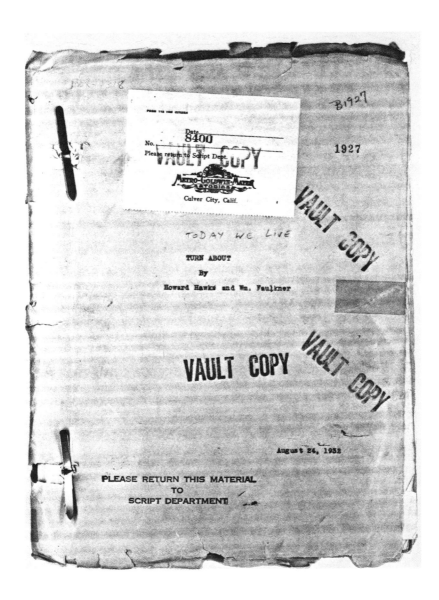

The Vault Copy of Turn *About*.

BPWDEN--- Put it on.

OTTO (takes magneto)---They're going to let us use it, are they? Going to let us take a littl hop in our own ship, huh?

BOWDEN--- Come on. Get it on the ship.

OTTO climbs aboard. LIEUTENANT is watching BOWDEN.

LIEUT---Your bags are already aboard, senor.

BOWDEN--- Thanks. Good of you.

LIEUT---It seems that you did not need them last night, anyway.

BOWDEN---Are you asking me? (to OTTO) Want any help?

OTTO---No. (He emerges carrying crank) O.K. What do we do now?

BOWDEN--- Get set with the crank.

OTTO---Sure I';; get set with it. You just keep him looking at you a minute longer. I'll get it set into him and take a couple of turns

BOWDEN--- Get set there. (To LIEUTENANT) One may depart, senor?

LIEUT--- Why not, senor?

BOWDEN approaches, mounts, OTTO sets the crank.

LIEUT--- A pleasant journey.

BOWDEN---Thanks. (To OTTO) Clear. (OTTO begins to turn crank. The LIEUT watches BOWDEN)

LIEUT---And a safe and quick return.

BOWDEN---Thanks.I hope it will se safe. anyway.

LIEUT---It will be, if it is also quick.

es.oOTTO enters ship, engine increases and gh DISSOLVE to

diminishes above pass, sound dies away.

89

Example of an unretouched page (*Mythical Latin-American Kingdom Story*, p. 89). (c) MGM.

original typescript (of which there had been no file record but which I discovered in July 1980) and *Turn About* in a typed version prepared by Hawks's office; the others are Script Department mimeographs, many of them faint impressions on badly aging low-quality paper. The photographs from *Today We Live* are not frame enlargements but production stills taken on the set by a staff photographer; although posed, they generally capture the blocking and lighting of their respective scenes.

* * *

"The truth is," he later said, "that I was scared. I was scared by the hullabaloo over my arrival, and when they took me into a projection room to see a picture and kept assuring me it was all going to be very very easy, I got flustered."—*Faulkner: A Biography*[2]

The story of Faulkner's career at MGM begins long before he reported to Sam Marx on Saturday, 7 May 1932, at the age of thirty-four. With the exceptions of *Manservant, The College Widow*, and *Lazy River*, every script he wrote for MGM was centrally concerned with aviation, usually in the context of World War I, and flying was one of the avocations he shared with Hawks (who told me he was responsible for the suggestion that Faulkner write *Pylon*). In that sense, the work for these scripts began in 1918 in Toronto, where Cadet Faulkner trained at the RAF School of Aeronautics and where he apparently learned to fly a Curtiss "Jenny" and became fascinated with (as Blotner puts it) the "glamorous and fatal" Sopwith Camel, one of which he used to say he had crashed upside down in the top of a hangar. To qualify for the RAF, Faulkner posed as a British subject and developed an uncanny British accent, the traces of which are evident in the stilted dialogue of *Turn About*. When he found, like the embittered cadet at the opening of *Soldiers' Pay*, that "they had stopped the war on him," he developed something of a fixation on the glories of aerial combat. In addition to spreading stories that he had been injured in action, he appears to have given World War I almost as important a role as the Civil War in his heroic imagination, taking the former as an emblem for the Waste Land—but not in quite the same way as Pound or Eliot, because although he shared much of their perspective on the shattering of the old order and the possibilities of modernism, he differed in finding the Great War an ideal field for his heightened sense of romantic possibility. The infusion into this romanticism not only of his personal disappointments but also of his growing understanding of toughness, despair, and self-destructiveness led to his best work on the timeless, hopeless limbo of Waste Land consciousness ("Ad Astra," "All the Dead Pilots," *Flags in the Dust*, *War Birds*, *The Road to Glory*, and even *Soldiers' Pay*) as well as to the hard-edged investigations of honor, amorality, and damnation in the postwar world ("Honor" and *Sanctuary*). *A Fable* demonstrates that the war remained a crucial imaginative resource even in later years, his World War I stories and scripts amounting—after the Yoknapatawpha corpus—to the second major cycle in his work. The many World War II scripts he wrote for Warner Brothers, such as *Life and Death of a Bomber* and *The De Gaulle Story*, are a minor addition to this cycle; involved more with politics than with existential absolutes, they are on a different track.

In 1929 he married Estelle Oldham shortly after her divorce, and in 1930 they and her children moved into Rowan Oak, a sizable estate. By the end of the thirties he had become the sole support of an extended family, and between 1929 and 1950, when he won the Nobel Prize, he experienced a serious need for money. In 1931 his agent—Ben Wasson, who was with the prestigious Leland Hayward agency—introduced him to several studio representatives during a visit to New York. At that time Tallulah Bankhead, who was under contract at Paramount and MGM, suggested he write a screenplay for her. This idea evidently excited him and he began work on a treatment that may have been related to *Sanctuary* and may even have been *Night Bird* (perhaps in a longer version that has not survived), which later served as the basic outline for *The College Widow*. Although Faulkner eventually went to Hollywood to work on *Flesh* rather than on a property for Bankhead, this indirect connection with Paramount may have prepared the way for their buying the rights to *Sanctuary*, which they released in 1933 as *The Story of Temple Drake*. It is more likely, however, that the executive most responsible for this acquisition was Paramount's Meritt Hubbard, who (as Blotner notes) "had been an editor at *The Saturday Evening Post*. Hubbard later said that he had encouraged [Faulkner] in the writing of the book and had promised that Paramount would buy it."[3]

Sam Marx remembers Irving Thalberg as "an ardent reader and a great respecter of good writing."[4] As the head of the Story Department, Marx had "carte blanche from Thalberg to go after and try to sign up any good, accomplished writer that might show." In 1932, *Fortune* had half-seriously observed that a larger group of writers worked under Marx than had composed the King James Version of the Bible. Although Thomas Wolfe, Noel Coward, and Eugene O'Neill gracefully turned him down, Marx had on his staff such accomplished screenwriters as Frances Marion, Anita Loos, and Jules Furthman; authors such as Fitzgerald, P. G. Wodehouse, and Ben Hecht, who were known in literary circles; and in the Reading Department, before she became well-recognized, even Lillian Hellman. Marx kept track of the respective strengths and credits of the writers to whom he had regular access but was also open to the possibility that new talents "on the literary horizon might bring something unusual to the screen"; when he found promising writers, he "reached out for them." Although Marx would instruct new "book-writers" in the special requirements of screenwriting, he was clearly interested in the possibility of their making an original and creative contribution rather than bent on turning them into formulaic "hacks." So when Leland Hayward—whom Marx respected as an aggressive and reliable agent whose clients were consistently "top flight"—told him about Faulkner during a 1931 trip to Los Angeles, Marx was interested in signing him up.

By 15 April 1932 the deal had been arranged. Faulkner was to be paid $500 a week for six weeks, beginning 7 May; he was also to receive round-trip train fare, and the contract could be extended for up to thirty days at the discretion of the studio if he were in the middle of a project at the time of expiration. Otherwise, there were "no options," and it was clearly a trial contract, even shorter than the norm of thirteen weeks. "Obviously if he had worked out well we would have *landed* on him," says Marx, "to try to keep him there and work on other things—that happened all the time." Typically, a junior writer was given "a three months' deal with options that could run three, five, or seven years, always at mounting salaries." It is likely, then, that Faulkner declined the options, not that Marx withheld them. The property to which Marx wanted to assign Faulkner was *Flesh*, a wrestling picture starring Wallace Beery that was intended as a box-office follow-up to Frances Marion's major hit *The Champ*, in which Beery had of course starred as a prizefighter. It was specifically *Flesh* and not *Sanctuary* that Faulkner went to MGM to write, and the odds are that he or at least his agent knew it beforehand.

Nevertheless, he made quite a spectacle when he arrived, particularly in regard to the prospect of working on a Beery vehicle. As Marx remembers it, Faulkner walked into his office with a "bloody gash" on his forehead. He said he had been hit by a cab while changing trains in New Orleans—but since the cut was still bleeding and

Louisiana was three or four days away by train, Marx considers it likely that Faulkner had been injured more recently: "There was no doubt he was doing some heavy drinking, and that was none of my business. We had a lot of heavy drinkers, and as long as they didn't get drunk around my office that was up to them. So whether he got into a fight in New Orleans, whether he got into a drunken spree and fell on his face, I don't really know." Marx said, "We're going to put you on a Wallace Beery picture," and Faulkner said, "Who's he?" Marx then arranged for Faulkner to see a print of *The Champ*, and while they were waiting for the projectionist to set up, the two had a short conversation. Faulkner said he did not like big cities, that he had not liked New Orleans and did not expect to like Los Angeles. He was sorry to hear he had been assigned to a Beery picture because "I would like to work on a newsreel or Mickey Mouse, because those are the kind of movies I like." "I took that seriously," says Marx; "I was looking at a man I didn't know, from a small town in Mississippi, so my estimation was that he was dead on-the-level." He was glad that *Flesh* was not going to demand oversophistication and sent Faulkner off in the company of an office boy, telling him to come back after the screening, when they would set him up with an office. He assured Faulkner that they would give him all the help he might need, including a practiced screenwriter as collaborator if he so desired. "We know the story we want," he said; "we're looking for it to be broken into scenes. Rest assured that whatever you want, we will make available."

The office boy was back in about twenty minutes. Marx asked where Faulkner was, and the boy said, "He's left, he's gone out of the studio. He didn't want to look at the movie; he was talking all the time." Among the things he had said to the boy was "Do you own a dog?" The boy did not, and Faulkner said, "Every boy should have a dog." (This further confirmed Marx's sense that he was dealing with "a farm boy come to the big city.") Soon Faulkner had asked, "How do you stop this thing?" When the boy had the projectionist stop the film, Faulkner said there was no point watching any more because he knew how it would come out, then asked how he could get out of the studio. The boy pointed in the direction of the main gate, and Faulkner went through it. Expecting never to see Faulkner again, Marx assigned Moss Hart to *Flesh* (directed by John Ford in 1932) and sent notice to Hayward that the contract had been abrogated.

On Monday, 16 May, Faulkner walked into Marx's office and said he was ready to work; he had been wandering in Death Valley during part of the interim. Marx had no property to assign him at that point but gave him a few pointers on screenwriting and encouraged him to write some original treatments. Among these standard instructions was the reminder that he would have to appeal to the eye more than to the other senses and that he could not, like a novelist, describe the scent of a woman's perfume or—and this was obviously important to Faulkner—a character's thoughts. Faulkner declined the offer of a collaborator and began work on *Manservant*, which may have been intended as a property for John Gilbert.[5] By 23 May, the payroll department had put him back on salary as of 10 May, and at that point Faulkner began turning his manuscripts in to the Script Department for copying. *Manservant* was copied by 25 May, *The College Widow* by 26 May, and *Absolution* by 1 June. By that time Marx had assigned him to *Flying the Mail*, another Beery vehicle, and Faulkner's treatment for that property was copied by 3 June.

The story of Faulkner's erratic behavior on 7 May had gotten around the studio, from "Who's he?" to Mickey Mouse, and Marx found that most of the producers did not want to work with Faulkner, that they considered him unreliable if not incompetent. Only Hawks proved to have some special interest in him several months later, but even with *Today We Live* (released 21 April 1933) as testimony that Faulkner could be a reliable worker, Marx was unable to interest any producer even in reading *MLAK*, which he considered a fine property. So by the time Faulkner was ready to take Hollywood seriously, he had acquired a reputation that ruled out *his* being taken seriously.

The much-debated question of Faulkner's attitude toward writing for films has been complicated by his later statements that he was only a "script doctor" modifying others' work (something he really did only on *Flying the Mail*, at least at MGM) and that he worked in Hollywood simply for the money it brought him. Faulkner's stories about himself were often cagey and inaccurate, from the steel plate he said he had in his skull as the result of a war injury, to his sometime insistence that he had not read *Ulysses*. Marx's impression is that Faulkner considered fiction his major medium, that he knew little or nothing about film when he started at MGM, and that he had no interest in doing anything in the film business beyond writing—but also that Faulkner was "sincere" about his studio work, that he wanted to "*earn* his salary," and that he was disappointed when his scripts were not approved for production. Considering the quality of the screenplays in this volume, I think Marx's view of the case is reliable.

Faulkner spent the last days of his first contract (23–26 June) working on *Turn to the Right*, in Marx's words "one of those terrible things that happens to a studio every once in a while." A Broadway play that had been made as a silent picture, it had "a noble 'turn to the right' sort of theme" and was at one time or another assigned to "probably every writer on the staff. Any time you had an available writer there was an outside chance somebody would come up with a good notion and you could save it." Faulkner attended several story conferences but apparently told Marx he could do nothing with it. Except for the silent cutting continuity, all materials on *Turn to the Right* were discarded and the property was written off as a tax loss, so there is no way to be sure whether Faulkner did write anything for it. On 25 June Marx was notified, in response to a query memo to F. L. Hendrickson (Personnel and Legal), that Faulkner's contract was "not to be extended." Then the studio apparently changed its mind and allowed Marx to offer Faulkner a one-year contract at $250 a week. Faulkner refused, partly because he was irritated at the way his agency had handled the studio negotiations and partly because Paramount had optioned *Sanctuary* on 16 June, auguring a future in which he might be in a sufficiently secure financial position not to have to accept a demeaning 50 percent cut in salary.

While he was off the MGM payroll, he met Howard Hawks. Hawks's brother William, an agent, had read "Turn About" when it appeared in *The Saturday Evening Post* (5 March 1932) and had considered it promising. Howard, William, and an unknown "third party" paid $5,000 for the story (Faulkner received $2,250), which as of 8 October 1932 they were still attempting to sell to MGM for $7,500 (according to a memo from the Legal Department). In the meantime, Hawks decided to go ahead with *Turn About* as an independent producer and asked Faulkner to talk with him.

This is the way Hawks later described their meeting:

> He came in. I said, "My name's Hawks," and he said, "I saw it on a check." He lit a pipe and I said, "Well, I'd like to have you do your story, 'Turn About.'" And he didn't say a damn word and I began to get mad, you know. So I talked for 45 minutes about what I wanted to do, and said, "That's it." He got up. I said, "Where are you going?" "Going in to write. I'm going to write it." So I said, "When will I see you again?" He said, "About five days." I said, "Mr. Faulkner, it shouldn't take you five days to get started and then come back and talk to me," and he said, "No, I can *write* it in five days."

Hawks then told Faulkner that he had been greatly impressed by *Soldiers' Pay* and had followed his work ever since, even making a point of telling some of his literary friends in New York that they

Howard Hawks, 1932. (c) MGM. From the Wisconsin Center for Film and Theater Research.

ought to read him; this had apparently had something to do with the small but favorable reception accorded *The Sound and the Fury*, which was newly on the shelves at the time Hawks was praising *Soldiers' Pay*.

> So, Bill said it would take him five days to do the script. And I said, "Okay, would you like a drink?" He said, "Yes." Well, we woke up in a motel in Culver City the next morning. He was fishing cigarette stubs out of a mint julep glass. And in five days he came in with the script. And we became good friends—we liked to fish, we liked to hunt. When he needed money, he always used to call me and say, "Do you have anything for me to do?" and if I didn't, I'd make up something.[6]

Along with their mutual enjoyment of hunting, fishing, and drinking, the two men had much in common. Both were reserved and private, gentlemanly and soft-spoken. Each was a perfectionist in his chosen field. Hawks had been born in 1896, Faulkner in 1897. Both liked to fly. As readers, they shared an admiration for Conrad and Hemingway. They even wore similar tweeds, and each lost a younger brother to a freak plane crash. They went on to enjoy for more than twenty years an effective working relationship based on mutual respect, as well as that special intimacy that sometimes arises between two people whom others regard as aloof and closed but who open themselves to each other. Hawks even began to take Faulkner along on the "dove hunts," about which he used to tell a misleading story that appears in virtually every discussion of Faulkner and Hollywood (including my own *Faulkner and Film*[7]). The story goes that Clark Gable, Faulkner, and Hawks were driving out to the Imperial Valley to go dove hunting; the subject of conversation turned to literature, and Gable asked Faulkner who were the best modern writers. Faulkner listed several, including himself. Gable asked, "Do you write, Mr. Faulkner?" and he replied, "Yes, Mr. Gable; what do you do?" Hawks told the story because it was funny, not because it was entirely true; he especially enjoyed the irony of the two men's (feigned?) ignorance of each other's reputations. Although the conversation may have occurred as described, the rest of the story is that the "dove hunts" were wild weekends in rented bungalows and that no one participated in them who was not well known to the others.[8] So another similarity between Hawks and Faulkner is that each enjoyed recreating his past in the interest of telling a good story and often used such anecdotes as a smokescreen. The account of Faulkner's career at MGM presented here repeats such stories only when they have checked out. The story that Faulk-

TURN ABOUT   By WILLIAM FAULKNER

ILLUSTRATED BY ALBIN HENNING

The Boat Rushed in Those Furious, Slewing Turns. He Didn't Hear the Boy Speak. He Just Felt the Boat Straighten Out

THE American—the older one—wore no pink Bedfords. His breeches were of plain whipcord, like the tunic. And the tunic had no long London-cut skirts, so that below the Sam Browne the tail of it stuck straight out like the tunic of a military policeman beneath his holster belt. And he wore simple putties and the easy shoes of a man of middle age, instead of Savile Row boots, and the shoes and the putties did not match in shade, and the ordnance belt did not match either of them, and the pilot's wings on his breast were just wings. But the ribbon beneath them was a good ribbon, and the insigne on his shoulders were the twin bars of a captain. He was not tall. His face was thin, a little aquiline; the eyes intelligent and a little tired. He was past twenty-five; looking at him, one thought, not Phi Beta Kappa exactly, but Skull and Bones perhaps, or possibly a Rhodes scholarship.

One of the men who faced him probably could not see him at all. He was being held on his feet by an American military policeman. He was quite drunk, and in contrast with the heavy-jawed policeman who held him erect on his long, slim, boneless legs, he looked like a masquerading girl. He was possibly eighteen, tall, with a pink-and-white face and blue eyes, and a little dull gold mustache above a mouth like a girl's mouth. He wore a pea-coat, buttoned awry and stained with recent mud, and upon his blond head, at that unmistakable and rakish swagger which no other people can ever approach or imitate, the cap of a Royal Naval officer.

"What's this, corporal?" the American captain said. "What's the trouble? He's an Englishman. You'd better let their M.P.'s take care of him."

"I know he is," the policeman said. He spoke heavily, breathing heavily, in the voice of a man under physical strain; for all his girlish delicacy of limb, the English boy was heavier—or more helpless—than he looked. "Stand up!" the policeman said. "They're officers!"

The English boy made an effort then. He pulled himself together, focusing his eyes. He swayed, throwing his arm about the policeman's neck, and with the other hand he saluted, his hand flicking, fingers curled a little, to his right ear, already swaying again and catching himself again. "Cheerio, sir," he said. "Name's not Beatty, I hope."

"No," the captain said.

"Ah," the English boy said. "Hoped not. My mistake. No offense, what?"

"No offense," the captain said quietly. But he was looking at the policeman. The second American spoke. He was a lieutenant, also a pilot. But he was not twenty-five and he wore the pink breeches, the London boots, and his tunic might have been a British tunic save for the collar.

"It's one of those navy eggs," he said. "They pick them out of the gutters here all night long. You don't come to town often enough."

"Oh," the captain said. "I've heard about them. I remember now." He also remarked now that, though the street was a busy one—it was just outside a popular café—and there were many passers, soldier, civilian, women, yet none of them so much as paused, as though it were a familiar sight. He was looking at the policeman. "Can't you take him to his ship?"

"I thought of that before the captain did," the policeman said. "He says he can't go aboard his ship after dark because he puts the ship away at sundown."

"Puts it away?"

"Stand up, sailor!" the policeman said savagely, jerking at his lax burden. "Maybe the captain can make sense out of it. Damned if I can. He says they keep the boat under the wharf. Run it under the wharf at night, and that they can't get it out again until the tide goes out tomorrow."

"Under the wharf? A boat? What is this?" He was now speaking to the lieutenant. "Do they operate some kind of aquatic motorcycles?"

"Something like that," the lieutenant said. "You've seen them—the boats. Launches, camouflaged and all. Dashing up and down the harbor. You've seen them. They do that all day and sleep in the gutters here all night."

"Oh," the captain said. "I thought those boats were ship commanders' launches. You mean to tell me they use officers just to ——"

"I don't know," the lieutenant said. "Maybe they use them to fetch hot water from one ship to another. Or buns. Or maybe to go back and forth fast when they forget napkins or something."

"Nonsense," the captain said. He looked at the English boy again.

"That's what they do," the lieutenant said. "Town's lousy with them all night long. Gutters full, and their M.P.'s carting them away in batches, like nursemaids in a park. Maybe the French give them the launches to get them out of the gutters during the day."

"Oh," the captain said, "I see." But it was clear that he didn't see, wasn't listening, didn't believe what he did hear. He looked at the English boy. "Well, you can't leave him here in that shape," he said.

Again the English boy tried to pull himself together. "Quite all right, 'sure you," he said glassily, his voice pleasant, cheerful almost, quite courteous. "Used to it. Confounded rough paré, though. Should force French do something about it. Visiting

---

"Turn About," page 1, *The Saturday Evening Post* (5 March 1932).

ner asked to work "at home" and then returned to Oxford, for instance, appears to have been dreamed up by a studio publicist; though it is in fact true that Faulkner did much of his MGM writing in Mississippi, the circumstances were quite different. It seems particularly important to clear up the "dove hunt" story because it has so often been used to demonstrate Faulkner's ignorance of and alienation from the Hollywood "scene," while the real story seems to demonstrate the opposite.

Faulkner wrote the first draft of Turn About before any contract or pay arrangement had been settled on. In a letter to Ben Wasson (September 1932) he said, "I would have made this script for nothing, being interested in the story."[9] Hawks took the Temporary to Thalberg, his brother-in-law (they had married the Shearer sisters). "Close your door and start looking this over," he said. After reading it, Thalberg said, "I feel as if I'd make tracks all over it if I touched it. Shoot it as it is." Marx was authorized to rehire Faulkner, and on 26 July he went back on payroll at $250 a week. Although there was no contract, it was understood that Faulkner would report primarily to Hawks and that Turn About would be produced by MGM, details to be arranged. Faulkner was proud of negotiating this deal himself and refused to pay the Selznick-Joyce Agency the 10 percent they requested from his Turn About money; he maintained his working relationship with Wasson at the Hayward Agency and put up with the necessity of paying William Hawks as an additional agent. As he described this deal in a letter to Wasson (November 1932), "Hayward sold Hawks TURN ABOUT, I saw Hawks and I myself arranged with Marx to have $250.00 a week, without any signed contract at all, to work on TURN ABOUT alone and no interference from any Jew in California, with the privilege of returning to Oxford to do the work—thus accomplishing an arrangement which my so-called agents either could not or would not attempt."[10] In a later letter to Wasson (12 February 1933), he compared this arrangement to "that of a field hand; either of us (me or M.G.M.) to call it off without notice, they to pay me by the week, and to pay a bonus on each original story."[11] Working in Oxford, however, had not been part of his deal with Marx; it was arranged later, among the two of them and Hawks, when Faulkner received word of his father's death on 7 August.

In the meantime, Thalberg had told Hawks that Turn About would have to be rewritten to include a starring role for Joan Crawford. MGM made three or four Crawford pictures a year at that time, and when she or a comparable star was ready for an assignment and no tailor-made scripts were in the works, it was customary to make a

Faulkner and his friend John Crown imitating musclemen at the beach,
c. 1936. Used by permission of Mrs. Meta Wilde.

Faulkner, c. 1936. Used by permission of Mrs. Meta Wilde.

place for her in an ongoing production. (The ins and outs of this casting decision will be discussed in the chapter on that script.) Although Hawks's usual working method was to outline each scene in detail before the screenwriter composed it and often to call for subsequent revisions, it seems that much of *Turn About* was written by Faulkner on his own—the first draft in those five days, and much of the second (the first with Crawford) in Mississippi. He was out of town from 10 August, with Hawks's approval, until 3 October, when he reported to Hawks to perform revisions on the script. While in Oxford, he had completed the second draft (filed by the Script Department on 24 August) and proofread *Light in August*. During October he completed the third draft, still called *Turn About* and copied by 25 October. The Paramount deal for *Sanctuary* was finalized on 17 October; he was paid over $6,000. On 22 October he went off payroll and returned to Oxford, with the understanding that he was to work on Harry Behn's adaptation of his story "Honor."

It is not at all clear how much work Faulkner did on *Honor*, if any. The story of John and Bayard Sartoris, however, was very much on his mind. On his own, he began writing a story called "With Caution and Dispatch" as well as a short biography of John Sartoris, extending the family history he had begun in 1926–27 as *Flags in the Dust* (published as *Sartoris* in 1929 after extensive cutting). He wrote a treatment for Hawks—apparently lost—called "Faulkner Story No. 2," which became the basis for *War Birds*. MGM owned a property called *Diary of the Unknown Aviator* that had been published anonymously in *Liberty* magazine under the title *War Birds*, and to this Faulkner added material from "Ad Astra" and "All the Dead Pilots." ("Honor" involved some of the same characters as "Ad Astra.") According to the MGM payroll cards, his time was charged to *War Story* for the week ending 28 November, at $600 a week. From 28 November to 20 February 1933, his time was charged to "continuity and dialogue" on *Honor*, though another card notes that for the week ending 22 February he worked three days on *Honor* and three days on *War Story*. (Although Harry Behn was normally associated with King Vidor, it is possible that *Honor* was being written for Hawks; much of Jules Furthman's later draft of *Honor* is echoed in *Only Angels Have Wings*.) For the weeks ending 1, 8, and 15 March, Faulkner's time was charged simply to *Honor*, and as of 15 March he was back at work on *War Story*. On 18 March, with Faulkner's approval, his salary was cut to $300 a week. By now, Thalberg was away from the studio, recovering from a heart attack, and Louis B. Mayer had taken over as temporary head of production;

The first installment of *War Birds* in *Liberty* magazine (14 August 1926).

Mayer, Marx, and Hawks worked out the new salary arrangement, but it was clearly Hawks who was primarily responsible for keeping Faulkner on the payroll. *War Birds* was copied by the Script Department before 12 January 1933. Faulkner's typescript, bearing the title *A Ghost Story*, is not in MGM's possession.[12] (*Honor* exists in several drafts dated between January and late March of 1933; the question of Faulkner's collaboration on those scripts will be taken up in the chapter on *Honor*.)

It is not of course certain that Faulkner's output corresponded with what appeared on payroll cards thousands of miles away. If anything, those cards reflect what MGM was told by Hawks's office, and Hawks had told Mayer (according to a memo of 2 February from the head of the Legal Department, M. E. Greenwood) "that Hawks was thoroughly convinced that Faulkner at $600.00 per week was a good investment if for nothing else than that we would have first call on stories written by Faulkner." It is likely that Faulkner wrote little that was not for MGM during this period, since he seems to have taken seriously the clause in his contract that signed over as studio property whatever he might write during his employment, and he was not about to start work on a novel that he would not own. So while it is possible that he was working on *Honor* and *War Birds* by turns, it is also possible that he had begun work on *MLAK* and even that he was taking a rest.

In the meantime, the Legal Department at MGM was trying to decide what to do about *War Birds*. A series of memos from Greenwood, written between 14 January and 3 March 1933, reveals the following story. Faulkner wanted $2,500 each for "Ad Astra" and "All the Dead Pilots" should MGM decide to go ahead with production on *War Birds*. As of 12 January, when the script had been copied, Hawks had it "for reading" and had told Marx that he wanted Faulkner kept on salary. Mayer decided to let the matter "ride for a couple weeks." On 2 February, Greenwood reported the conversation between Hawks and Mayer quoted above, and on 16 February, Greenwood again asked Mayer what he wanted to do about Faulkner. Mayer said to "continue Faulkner on salary for another period of 4 weeks and then bring the matter to his attention." In a long memo of 16 January, Greenwood noted that his reading of the script synopsis and the two stories had convinced him that there was insufficient overlap to warrant paying "$2,500.00 each for these two stories even if his combined script was acceptable to us." A copyright attorney researched the publication data on the stories and concluded that neither was in the public domain; on 17 February, Faulkner wrote

Marx a letter to the same effect, in response to a studio query. On 3 March, Greenwood wrote Marx, "I understand that Howard Hawks thinks Faulkner's story might be worked out if Faulkner would come to the studio and work on it with Hawks' supervision and cooperation and that Howard intends to take this phase up with Faulkner when Howard has completed his present picture." The 50 percent salary cut was negotiated between then and 18 March. *Today We Live* had its advance premiere in Oxford on 12 April; it had been previewed and reviewed in a longer version on 16 March, was previewed again on 18 April, and was finally released on 21 April, thus freeing Hawks to work on *War Birds* and raising the question of Faulkner's return to the studio. It is not at all clear why Hawks and Faulkner did not proceed with *War Birds*, but Faulkner's reluctance to return to Hollywood may have made the difference. Perhaps he was waiting for his $5,000.

By the end of March, Faulkner's time was being charged to *MLAK*, an original that had not been cleared in advance with Marx or Hawks. He continued to work on it until he was finally taken off the payroll on 13 May. In the meantime, the studio had begun production on *Lazy River*, at that time called *Louisiana Lou*, and Marx felt that Faulkner, as a southerner, ought to be assigned to the project. Faulkner was instructed to report to director Tod Browning (*Dracula* and *Freaks*) in New Orleans. The two met on 26 April and spent most of the next week or so traveling back and forth between the bayou location set and the Hotel Roosevelt in New Orleans. Despite Faulkner's colorful version of these events (that the boat trips were so long they only had time for lunch on the set before returning, etc.), he did in fact write much of a 62-page script for Browning at this time—but as it was never delivered to MGM and the only copy (actually a 28-page fragment) is in the hands of a private collector who has declined to release it for publication, that script is not included in this volume.

Marx and Browning exchanged wires on Faulkner's progress. Browning's read in part, "Party referred to in your wire brilliant capable man but had unfortunate start. . . . He will not go to Culver City to finish dialogue until after birth of child due in June but wishes to write at his home in Oxford." Marx then wired Faulkner, "Owing to necessity Browning script being completed here at studio and your inability to return here I believe it best we relieve you of your assignment. Many thanks for all you have done. Studio feels the system of working is not feasible consequently we will be most happy to continue you on staff here at any time you advise us you will come to California. I have asked Howard Hawks to write you and plan out some deal for the future."[13] He had been taken off payroll on 6 May and reinstated by 8 May—evidently at Browning's request—but on 13 May he was definitely fired. A letter from Hawks seems to have been involved in this, but one can only speculate as to its contents. My best guess is that Hawks decided for some reason not to go ahead with *War Birds* but to do *Viva Villa* (MGM, 1934, from a Ben Hecht script) instead. When I met Hawks in 1976, he still had a copy of what he called Faulkner's "ghosts from the past" story; he especially liked the part about the boy's discovery that the man who had taken him hunting had killed his father (John Sartoris) in the war, and the image of John's ghostly plane. So it is possible that Hawks simply laid *War Birds* aside for a while—perhaps till Faulkner would be ready to return to the studio—and then lost interest in it. The next time Faulkner came to Hollywood, it was to work for Hawks on *Sutter's Gold* (July 1934) at Universal.

In any case, on 13 May, Marx sent a wire to Oxford, where Faulkner had been for several days: "Dear Bill: I held up Howard Hawks letter as Tod needed you this extra week. However letter is going forward and week is up today. Please send work you have done to Browning at New Orleans. Many thanks again. Regards, Sam Marx."[14] Whatever the contents of that letter, its "going forward" marked the end of Faulkner's employment. On 14 May, Faulkner sent Browning pages 34–62 of his script together with Marx's telegram and the following letter:

Dear Tod:
    Just received the enclosed, which explains itself. I am going ahead with the dialogue, though. They want to can me, and I am ready to quit, so just let it ride as it lays; you need not even tell them that I have not finished, and I'll get the rest of it done in another week.
    I have left plenty of margin, so you can jot down corrections etc., and fire it back to me. I would have had a bigger batch of mss. ready, but I held back to get your new synopsis today, and I had to back up and make some changes. I'll get the rest of it done by next Sat., and in the meantime dont say anything more to the studio about keeping me on. Just let it go.
    My most respectful devoirs to Mrs Browning, and best regards to yourself.
                                                                    Bill

p.s. You might drink a bottle of beer for me. I'm reduced to hard whiskey now, being in a prohibition state.[15]

Sometime between then and June, Faulkner finished *MLAK* and sent it to Marx. His daughter Jill was born on 24 June. On 22 June,

Marx wrote to Hendrickson, "Mr. Faulkner is asking for the right to novelize this story and I would like to have you draw up papers granting this right. In the papers you might refer to it as the mythical Latin-American kingdom story. I find that the script he did is very unsatisfactory and hope that if he novelizes it we may find a better basis for a motion picture in it." Up until then the property had been untitled. Marx later developed a more favorable opinion of *MLAK* and even now, in 1980, is still attempting to interest the studio in revising and producing it. By 27 June, the novelization was authorized, though Faulkner never went on to write it. The Legal Department insisted on receiving Faulkner's assignment of rights on *Honor, War Story,* and *Louisiana Lou* as well as "a general assignment covering the period November 28, 1932 to May 13, 1933." On 19 July, Faulkner wrote to Marx that he had done no work on *Honor* but that he understood he might be entitled to bonuses for the rights to use "Honor," "Ad Astra," and "All the Dead Pilots." "I know you all are too busy to write idle letters," he continued, "but I would like to know how Tod is coming with LOUISIANA LOU. I was getting pretty steamed up over it when I got the air. He's a fine fellow. Give him my best when you see him, and Howard Hawks too. I'm going to write Howard a note some day. Remember me to everyone."[16] On 18 August, Marx paraphrased Faulkner's remarks to Hendrickson and added, "As we are not proceeding with these stories, I don't think we can reasonably request his assignment without paying him something for them. Do you agree with me on this?" Hendrickson penciled "Yes" on the memo, and the result was not payment but the dropping of the attempt to obtain rights to the three stories.

Back in the bayou country, Browning had been having his own troubles. The head of the B-picture unit, Lucien Hubbard, had found fault with the dailies Browning was sending in from New Orleans and had decided to turn the picture over to one of his regular directors, George B. Seitz, and to write a new script himself. So when Marx sent the assignment contracts (for *MLAK, Louisiana Lou,* and the period from November to May) to Faulkner on 24 August, he let him know Browning had been taken off the picture and added, "So you see he got the air, too." Before he retired, Browning was to make only three more films, all of them for MGM.

The rest of the story is readily summarized. *MLAK* had been copied by 26 August, but Marx found no producer—Mayer in particular—willing to read it. It was a relatively inactive period at the studio with Thalberg away. Faulkner went back to writing fiction, including a revision of the story on which *Manservant* had been based, "Love." In a mid-July letter to Harrison Smith he said, "I have turned out three short stories since I quit the movies, so I have not forgot how to write during my sojourn downriver."[17] By February 1934, he had begun *Absalom, Absalom!* Soon he would be back in Hollywood to revise Eisenstein's *Sutter's Gold* for Hawks, and by the end of 1935 he would begin work at 20th Century-Fox, where he would meet Meta Doherty and write much of *The Road to Glory.* Sometime in the late thirties, MGM went on to pay $25,000 for the rights to *The Unvanquished*—not because they necessarily wanted to make it, but because they needed some leverage in their negotiations with David O. Selznick. Selznick owned *Gone with the Wind* and wanted to cast Clark Gable. Gable was under contract to MGM, which had passed up an opportunity to buy the novel before it had become such a success; now they wanted Selznick to let them release the picture in exchange for Gable's services. Ed Knopf or Sam Zimbalist (not Sam Marx, despite Bennett Cerf's account) reached Cerf at Random House and optioned *The Unvanquished.* MGM's intention was to threaten Selznick that "if he didn't let them make *Gone with the Wind* they were going to make a *Gone with the Wind* of their own" (in Faulkner's words). Selznick agreed to let MGM release the film, though it is likely that Gable had more to do with his decision than *The Unvanquished* did. In September 1946, Mayer vetoed a reissue of *Today We Live.* On 12 October 1949, after watching the world premiere of MGM's *Intruder in the Dust* in Oxford, Faulkner wrote to Marx.

> Dear Sam:
>   Ever since our mild fiasco of twenty years ago, I have felt that accounts between me and MGM were not at balance, and my conscience hurt me at times. But since seeing Clarence [Brown]'s 'Intruder in the Dust' here last night, the qualms have abated some. I may still be on MGM's cuff, but at least I am not quite so far up the sleeve.
>   Yours,
>   Bill[18]

Faulkner's final sense of his time at MGM, then, was not that he had been exploited but that he had not given them their money's worth, and that with the rights to *Intruder* he had at last given them something fine. Many of Faulkner's readers have taken the hint and considered his fiction his only significant contribution to world culture, but until now that judgment has been made in a vacuum. Now his first scripts can be read.

Generalizing about Faulkner's career at MGM, Marx said, "I am convinced that those original stories he turned in were part of his desire to give value for value; he was getting paid and he wanted to show that he was a writer. I think he was making these submissions in the hope that we would see in them the same kind of movie that he saw, and get them made. He struck me as being that kind of man." The movies Faulkner saw in these screenplays are well worth attention. The only film actually produced from them—*Today We Live*—for all its merits is not the equal of *Turn About*, nor does it bear serious comparison with some of the films MGM produced while Faulkner was there, such as *Queen Christina*, nor even with Hawks's previous *Scarface*. But the scripts in this volume have much to recommend them. They can enlarge our sense of Faulkner's career; they extend some of the themes of his fiction; they provide examples of screenwriting from the major period of a major studio; they are vital documents in the study of the relations between literature and film; and they are often interesting, moving, and well written. Faulkner may not have recognized how much, indeed, he did give MGM.

NOTES: INTRODUCTION

1. Madison: Univ. of Wisconsin Press, 1980.

2. Joseph Blotner, *Faulkner: A Biography* (New York: Random, 1974), 773.

3. Ibid., note to p. 778.

4. Quotations are from an interview between Marx and myself on 11 July 1980 in Los Angeles.

5. Blotner, *Faulkner: A Biography*, note to p. 774.

6. Quotations are from an interview between Hawks and myself on 24 May 1976 in Palm Springs.

7. New York: Frederick Ungar, 1977.

8. I am indebted to Sam Marx for this information. It should also be noted that "Slim" Hawks told Blotner that she had gone on a genuine dove hunt with Faulkner.

9. Joseph Blotner, *Selected Letters of William Faulkner* (New York: Random, Vintage, 1978), 66.

10. Ibid., 68

11. Ibid., 71.

12. Blotner describes *A Ghost Story* as "a 100-page finished film script" to which Hawks's estate now owns the rights (*Faulkner: A Biography*, note to p. 794). Hawks told me that he and Faulkner had gone to see a ghost picture (which he remembered as *Secrets*). Faulkner had criticized the film, and Hawks had dared him to write a better ghost story if he could. This story has proved impossible to confirm or deny, and there is no record at MGM of who first assigned Faulkner to *War Birds*, nor of whether

Faulkner, Hawks, or MGM decided to graft the *Diary of the Unknown Aviator* onto the ghost story.

Although I have not personally examined *A Ghost Story*, I have had access to Blotner's synopsis and description of that manuscript and feel certain that *A Ghost Story* is not a variant draft. Blotner records that "A GHOST STORY" is typed two lines above "W̶A̶R̶ ̶B̶I̶R̶D̶S̶" on the title page, and that the 100-page script was apparently typed by Faulkner. The strike-out of *War Birds* corresponds with Faulkner's practice in *MLAK* and suggests that it was he rather than Hawks who arrived at the new title. (Faulkner and MGM's payroll cards had used the working title of *War Story*, and Grider's diary had been published as *War Birds*.)

Blotner makes the crucial note that "Camera shots numbered in left-hand margin 1-323, not in WF's hand," then goes on to summarize the script; his synopsis reveals no variations from *War Birds*. The fact that *A Ghost Story* is only 100 pages, while *War Birds* is 143, could be accounted for by differences in format. The fact that *A Ghost Story*, like Faulkner's typescript for *MLAK*, bears no scene numbers and that the Script Department version of *War Birds* is broken into 323 scenes makes it more than likely that *A Ghost Story* is Faulkner's first and perhaps only draft; that he or Hawks preferred to call it *A Ghost Story* but that MGM's title (reimposed for copying by the Script Department) for the property was *War Birds*; and that Hawks or someone else broke the typescript into 323 scenes before sending it on for copying. The only alternative hypothesis—one I find unconvincing—would be that Faulkner wrote a second draft of *War Birds* (*A Ghost Story*), making few substantive changes but shortening the whole, and that Hawks broke it down into exactly the same number of scenes the first draft had had.

13. Blotner, *Faulkner: A Biography*, 802.

14. This telegram was generously provided by Carl Petersen. Reprinted courtesy of MGM.

15. This letter, too, was provided by Carl Petersen. Reprinted courtesy of Jill Faulkner Summers.

16. Blotner, *Selected Letters*, 73. I take "steamed up" to mean that he was working hard, not that he was angry.

17. Ibid., 72. The implication of "downriver" may have been that Faulkner considered himself a slave sold "down the river," but this is only a guess, and the tone seems playful.

18. Ibid., 293.

1

Manservant

Faulkner's treatment for *Manservant* is dated 24 May 1932 and was copied by the Script Department on 25 May. It is presented here in the only surviving studio version, a File Copy of the Script Department mimeograph. Although it commands special interest as the first surviving example of Faulkner's screenwriting (*Night Bird* being more a story outline than a treatment), *Manservant* must also be recognized as a maudlin and overcontrived failure. The file includes no reader's reports, indicating that *Manservant* was never remotely considered for production.

Yet Faulkner seems to have found the story interesting and so cannot be accused of deliberately attempting to pass off inferior work on MGM. The story on which it is based—"Love"—was written in 1921 while he was living in Greenwich Village and working in the book department of Lord and Taylor. When he left MGM, he reworked the story; it was one of the three pieces that convinced him he had "not forgot how to write during my sojourn downriver." Here is Blotner's summary of the first version:

> "Love" was quite clearly apprentice work and very complicated. Set in 1921, it involved two plots linked by a girl named Beth Gorham. In one she courted her father's houseguest, Hugh, a major who had led a French Nieuport squadron composed chiefly of Americans. He had saved from death a young Indochinese soldier called Das, who had become the Major's devoted valet, addressing him reverently as "Tuan." His main task now is to protect the Major from the passionate Italian maid who puts a love potion in the brandy sent up for the Major each night. Das expects her ultimately to substitute poison out of jealousy. Central to the other plot is Bob Jeyfus, Beth's one-time fiancé, now suspected of lying about his war service. Tricked into flying a plane or backing down, he chooses the latter, murmuring only "nerve's gone." The two plots are joined again when the Major verifies Jeyfus' story. Shot down and placed among the dead, Jeyfus was subsequently unable to fly; he then served out the rest of the war in disgrace as a cook. Beth marries him, "to save my self-respect," then sends him away. Throughout, the Major remains a godlike silver-haired figure, sipping tea, standing about immaculate at the Country Club, looking much like the man in Cadillac limousine advertisements. This is in part due to

Das, who not only cares for his impeccable clothes, but insists on sampling his brandy. When it finally contains the poison, he staggers toward the antidote he has prepared. At this point the forty-nine-page typed manuscript breaks off.[1]

Blotner notes that such an "elaborate and melodramatic romantic triangle was quite common both in motion pictures and magazine fiction," so it is possible that Faulkner felt *Manservant* appropriate material for screen production; it may well reflect his apprentice concept of narrative film and thus the reasons he preferred newsreels and cartoons. The story shows the influence of Rudyard Kipling and Joseph Conrad, and the treatment bears this out in its precise use both of Malay and of colonial slang. Although "Tuan" was a general term of address for a white man in Malaya, the "reverent" sense in which Das uses it suggests the specific influence of *Lord Jim*; Conrad's Jim is called "Tuan" (Lord) and earns by his ironic and heroic self-sacrifice the elevation that term is made to imply. In *Manservant*, however, the master is a rather wooden and unexamined figure while Das is the tragic suicide.

The bind in which Das finds himself is structured by Faulkner's concept of servant mentality. When he worked at RKO on *Gunga Din* in 1936, he told Meta Doherty, "The trouble with the script is that these damned fool people don't begin to realize that Gunga Din was a colored man."[2] Although Faulkner had an affectionate regard for his Mammy and created in his fiction many powerful and sympathetic Blacks, he was opposed to forced integration and even wrote in 1958, "Perhaps the Negro is not yet capable of more than second-class citizenship."[3] His remark on *Gunga Din* shows that he thought of Blacks and native colonials in much the same terms. Das (whose name in English hunting slang means "badger") is devoted to his master in "dog-like" fashion; he is unable to read and is continually blocked by his inability to understand the ways of white people. This leads to a situation in which he chooses to risk death rather than to explain to his master what he has discovered. In the end, it is his selflessness that commands sentimental admiration, his taking the role of servant to its logical conclusion.

Blotner calls attention to a fragment of a letter written on the back of one of the draft sheets of *Manservant*: "I am not settled good yet. I have not got used to this work. But I am as well as anyone can be in this bedlam."[4] It is clear that he was attempting to follow Marx's advice to write for the camera, from his cliché use of newspaper stories to indicate the passage of time, to his emphasis on facial expressions. And there are, as the script notes will indicate, some more sophisticated successes. Nevertheless, there are long passages in which he explains what the viewer is supposed to understand— evidently because he did not yet know how to show these things in dialogue and action. He does make effective use of physical props, notably the articles of clothing by which the lovers remember themselves to each other, and also of the windows and doorways through which the characters catch sight of each other (an economical and visual opportunity to show how the observer feels). By the complexity of its plot and the denseness of its narration, *Manservant* shows that Faulkner was not yet adept at telling a story visually; although there is significant action, most of the important motivations and background materials are either explained by the author parenthetically or intended to be conveyed by the characters in long passages of dialogue. Considering the brilliance of the visual imagination evident in such works as *Sanctuary* and *The Sound and the Fury*, this failure must be attributed to Faulkner's not yet having learned how to express himself in screenplay format rather than to his being fundamentally unable to think in terms of images and montage.[5]

NOTES: INTRODUCTION TO *MANSERVANT*

1. Blotner, *Faulkner: A Biography*, 322–23.
2. Meta (Doherty) Carpenter Wilde and Orin Borstin, *A Loving Gentleman: The Love Story of William Faulkner and Meta Carpenter* (New York: Simon and Schuster, 1976), 136.
3. Blotner, *Faulkner: A Biography*, 1686.
4. Ibid., 774.
5. For a discussion of Faulkner's cinematic practice in his fiction, see my article, "The Montage Element in Faulkner's Fiction," in *Faulkner, Modernism, and Film: Faulkner and Yoknapatawpha, 1978*, ed. Evans Harrington and Ann J. Abadie (Jackson: Univ. Press of Mississippi, 1979), 103–26.

NOTES: SCRIPT OF *MANSERVANT*

P. 1 [Blynt], "Das": Indo-Aryan for "man"; *dāsá* means "a non-Aryan, slave." A childlike soldier and "headman" bears this name in "Ad Astra."

P. 1 [Servant], "Ya, Tuan": "Yes, Lord." *Tuan*, a title assigned by modern Malay custom to male Europeans, in both ancient and literary use means "Master," "Liege Lord," or "Sovereign Lady." Faulkner may well have encountered the term in Conrad's *Lord* [Tuan] *Jim*.

P. 1 [Blynt], "tiffin": A light midday meal.

P. 1 [Das], "Mem-petuh": According to the colonial dictionary *Hobson-Jobson*, "Mem-sahib" was "the usual respectful designation of a European married lady in the Bengal presidency"; perhaps this is the complementary term for an unmarried lady. The reference is to Judy.

P. 2 [narrative], "whose reputation is well known": The apparent intent here is to ground Judy's anxiety about her reputation—on which the plot turns—in some real social context.

P. 2 [An Officer], "Just as a wife might. Better —": As in the description of Judy's photograph on the previous page, Faulkner is implying that there is a categorical and even a physically observable difference between wives and mistresses, and emphasizing Judy's devotion to Blynt. While acknowledging the problem of Judy's social unacceptability, then, he is also praising her character—a double-edged convention in this kind of story. Both Judy and Das are presented as selflessly devoted to Blynt.

P. 2 [narrative], "The woman of the photograph": A successful piece of visual storytelling. The audience recognizes Judy without needing to be told who she is.

P. 3 [narrative], "she gave birth to a child which died": In 1931 Faulkner's daughter Alabama had died in infancy. Here and in *The College Widow* the death of a baby is associated with a woman's descent into loose living.

P. 4 [narrative], "He is just packing the slipper and the withered flower": An attempt to tie the story together with a repeated image.

P. 4 [narrative], "We learn that Blynt . . .": The details of this rescue are similar to those in "Love" and show some real understanding of Das's experience. Note "dog-like devotion."

P. 6 [Das], "Ada": Malay for "to be, to be present, to exist." In "Love," however, Das says, "*Ada, Tuan.* It is nothing" (ms. 24). In context, "it is nothing" fits best.

P. 6 [narrative], "The scene waxes": grows in intensity. Note "women of her kind."

P. 7 [narrative], "Her dress is now very sober": This and the newspapers represent a further attempt to indicate visually how Judy feels about herself and Blynt.

P. 7 [narrative], "Bart.": Baronet.

P. 7 [narrative], "Blynt is becoming known as a scientist": No use is made of Blynt's being a scientist; an arbitrary and inefficient choice of detail.

P. 7 [narrative], "His face is not seen": An interesting touch, perhaps suggesting an undercurrent of dark, anonymous, or monolithic power between father and daughter.

P. 9 [narrative], "He is naught": Rather than simply acknowledging Das's culture shock, Faulkner is implying that Das has internalized the imperial attitude toward colonials; there appears to be little or no irony here.

P. 9 [narrative], "the photograph of a young girl": Another attempt to tie the story together through a repeated—though ironically varied—visual detail. Judy's sister Marcia, here a relatively minor character, was—as Beth—the major figure in "Love."

P. 10 [narrative], "As they pass one window . . .": Another successful visual parallel; the maid watches Blynt and Marcia as Das had in Scene 25.

P. 10 [narrative], "She doesn't even see the footman . . .": The footman is taken from Ernie, the butler in "Love." Blotner compares his "realistic-sounding speech" to "the argot of gangsters who would appear in later fiction" (*Faulkner: A Biography*, 323).

P. 11 [narrative], "We learn that it is a love potion": The servant's interference in the maid's love potion–death potion plot may reflect the distant influence of *Tristan and Isolde*.

P. 11 [narrative], "They struggle": There is a similar knife-and-slap fight in *Sanctuary* (New York: Random, Modern Library, 1932), 114.

P. 13 [Blynt], "But I can't offend my host, you know": Note that most of the binds in which the characters find themselves are structured by social conventions.

P. 14 [Blynt], "Have I not told thee . . . Thou knowest . . .": An attempt at anglicizing the familiar form of address (*du* in German, *tu* in French, etc.). Note that Das uses the same mode to Blynt, whereas it would be more common for the servant to address the master formally (*Sie, vous,* etc.).

P. 15 [narrative], "She watches the clock . . .": In her moments of extreme tension and disorientation, Temple Drake focuses on cigarettes and the clock; see *Sanctuary,* 180–89. The mood and point here are of course very different, but what is similar is the treatment of a young woman who is behaving in a drastically new and unconventional manner.

P. 16 [narrative], "He sees the robe beside Blynt's cheek": Although this whole sequence is as contrived as some Restoration comedies, Faulkner is attempting to be more or less cinematic in keying the action and discoveries to a physical prop.

P. 17 [narrative], "CLOSEUP shows . . .": Varying camera-to-subject distance is an important cinematic means of creating emphasis and directing audience attention. Faulkner is beginning to think for the camera.

P. 18 [narrative], "Suddenly he knows that the only person . . .": Note that Das is apparently quite capable of understanding the ways of white people; in fact, the whole plot hangs on his accurate guesses. It is not clear how these thoughts were to be shown on screen, though perhaps Faulkner meant them to be intercut as short scenes, e.g., of "the maid watching Marcia and Blynt together."

P. 19 [narrative], "so he suggests olive oil": Olive oil was sometimes used medicinally in liniments, ointments, and plasters, but it could hardly have been an effective antidote to strong poison. An ironic play on Das's naiveté, becoming pathetic in Scene 60, though a more bitter reflection (on Das's dying because he is unable to function effectively in American culture) was undoubtedly intended. In "Love" (ms. 13), Das had learned French while working as an apothecary's assistant; when Blynt found him wounded, he had compared Das to "a man who had fallen among clumsy but well-meaning barbarians." Later (ms. 15), Blynt explains to Beth that "He is among what he considers barbarians . . . He lets me do our thinking.

5

. . . I'll get him to say it for you sometime. He says, 'In America there is a motto for everything, *Tuan*. I do not know these mottoes. You tell. I do.' You see, he unfortunately learned English from the English. I dont mean language. Language is just the smoke that rolls away from what a man has done." And when Das first shows signs of poisoning, the footman suggests olive oil and egg whites (ms. 32) and Das responds: "'In my country are many herbs,' he said in his own tongue, in a suppressed moaning voice, 'But now what would you, in a climate before which the Creator Himself has obviously turned his face in despair, and where all life is conducted like the nightmare of an idiot child?' swaying from side to side while they watched him. But immediately he ceased and was his inscrutable formal self again and he repeated in his careful English: 'When it get bad, I do.'" It is unclear why Faulkner left this sort of information and character complexity out of *Manservant*; if he had not done so, there would be far less justice in calling the script racist and maudlin. ("Love" is in the Alderman Library of the University of Virginia and has not been published.) It is also worth noting, in the olive-oil prescription as dramatized here, a slight echo of Dewey Dell's encounter with the pharmacist's assistant in *As I Lay Dying* (New York: Random, Vintage, 1964), 233–37.

    P. 19 [narrative], "THE HOUSE FROM THE REAR—As a servant would enter": Another successful use of camera placement to advance the story, in this case allowing the audience to share Das's point of view.

    P. 20 [narrative], "WE FOLLOW HER . . .": A visual echo of Scene 44. Faulkner is using the same camera movement (a boom or crane shot) in a similar situation (the maid's going to Blynt). This shows a definite attempt to create a visual rhythm and to clarify and advance the story through formal repetition, a device whose prose equivalent is basic to his fiction (as in the two jury trials at the end of *Sanctuary*, 349, 373).

    P. 20 [narrative], "Das believes too that if something happened to him . . .": This is the key motivation in Das's self-sacrifice, and it is entirely unclear how Faulkner intended the audience to understand all this.

    P. 21[[narrative], "He leaps to the tray and snatches the glass . . .": Blynt's thoughts are more successfully clarified in action than Das's.

    P. 21 [narrative], "Running through the corridor . . .": It was a convention in many earlier films (some of which Faulkner admired, like *The Birth of a Nation*) to climax with a chase scene.

    P. 21 [narrative], "They are taking Das's ashes . . .": This ironic happy ending both makes it clear that Das is the central figure and accepts his expendability in the service of Blynt's and Judy's relationship.

3691

FORM 112 10M CITIZEN

Date..

No. ....

Please return to Script Dept. 3207

METRO-GOLDWYN-MAYER
STUDIOS

Culver City, Calif.

"MANSERVANT"

Original Story
by
William Faulkner

From
William Faulkner

May 25, 1932

"MANSERVANT"
William Faulkner
May 24, 1932

TITLE:
INDIA, 1921 -
A REMOTE BRITISH ARMY POST -

1.   IN THE QUARTERS OF MAJOR NIGEL BLYNT -

A servant is packing Maj. Blynt's kit, who
is about to depart for Calcutta on leave.
We notice the servant at once. He is a
Malay -- a small, wizened monkey of a man
who moves silently about, handling the
objects which he is packing with the deft-
ness of a monkey.

At the moment, he is taking carefully from
a drawer, a woman's dancing slipper, to which
is attached a dried flower. We learn that
Blynt has carried this in his kit constantly
for some time.

Blynt enters. He is about thirty. He wears
several decorations. He looks at the slipper
which the servant is packing.

                    Blynt
The picture too, Das.

                    Servant
Ya, Tuan.

THE CAMERA FOLLOWS the servant to a chest of
drawers upon which sets a photograph of a
woman. She is about thirty. It is the face
of a high-class demi mondaine and not that of
a wife. Das packs the photograph.

                    Blynt
We will leave directly after tiffin.

                    Das
Ya, Tuan. Mem-petuh will be glad.

2.   THE OFFICERS' MESS -

Officers at the table, finishing the meal.
It is a mild celebration as a send-off for
                                   Continued -

8

2.   CONTINUED (2)

Blynt. We learn that the officers know that
Blynt will spend his leave with the woman of
the photograph, whose reputation is well
known and that he has been doing this for some
time. Their comments are not loud enough for
Blynt to hear.

3.   THE VERANDAH -

At the steps, a vehicle is waiting. Blynt's
baggage is loaded upon it and Das waits beside it. Blynt, in the center of the group
of officers, saying goodbye. He enters the
vehicle, which rolls away. The officers begin to disperse, talking.

                An Officer
She'll meet him at the station. Been doing it now
for two years. Just as a wife might. Better -- a
wife would not always take that trouble!

4.   THE CALCUTTA STATION -

The woman of the photograph, smartly dressed.
A meeting between her and Blynt - of two people who have been lovers for some time and
who must suffer periodical separations.

Das approaches. We learn that between the
woman and Das there is a definite affection.
Das loves her because his master does. She
depends upon Das to take care of the man she
loves.

5.   BLYNT'S HOTEL -

We learn that it has been his custom to stay
here each time he returns from duty. He is
expected and he is told that there is mail
for him, including a cable.

Judy waits for him in the lounge while he
goes up and changes.

In Blynt's room, Das begins to unpack. Blynt
opens his mail, taking the cable first. He
learns that his father has died and that he
has inherited. He goes down to Judy without
                              Continued -

5.   CONTINUED (2)

waiting to change. He tells her the news -
that he will have to leave the army and return to England. She realizes that it means
that they must part. He takes it for granted
that she will go too, but she will not go.
Her reputation is so that she believes that
she will do him harm.

6.   A CLUB VERANDAH -

Some time has elapsed. Two tables - the second
one a little in the background. At the first
table sit Blynt and Judy. At the second table
sit three officers. Their heads are together
and their interest is upon the first table.
We learn that Blynt has resigned his commis-
sion and tomorrow will sail for England. He
is asking Judy again to go with him. Again
she refuses. She believes that for them to
marry and try to live down her past would be
his ruin. They go out.

The focus is now on the three officers at the
second table. We learn that Blynt and Judy
have been lovers for two years - ever since
Blynt came out to India. That Blynt has a
fine war record - that Judy is an American
of good people who came to India ten years
ago on her honeymoon. Her husband wanted to
shoot a tiger. She tried to dissuade him
but in vain. He left her and went on the
hunt but the tiger killed him. Judy went to
pieces, indulging in a course of hysteria and
fast living - though without definitely losing her good name yet. The Consul tried to
persuade her to return home but she refused.
The Consul notified her father, who came out
to get her.

When he arrived, she had gone into the Interior to see her husband's grave, accompanied
by a man who had a very shady reputation about
women.

The father could get no word of her and returned home.

A year after her disappearance, Judy reappeared
in Calcutta, where she gave birth to a child
which died. After that, she no longer made
any attempt to appear respectable, passing
into and out of affairs with civilian and
military men, though never leaving Calcutta.
                              Continued -

6.   CONTINUED (2)

Then, two years ago, she met Blynt. After
that, during his duty periods Inside, her life
was more impeccable than many actual wives.

7.   BLYNT'S HOTEL -

In the background, Das is moving about, packing. He now wears European clothes, looking
more comical than ever. In the foreground,
Blynt and Judy are talking with the idle
anti-climatic talk of two people who have
been a lot to one another and who are now
about to part for good. Judy is watching
Das. He is just packing the slipper and the
withered flower.

We learn that Judy has such love tokens too -
a shaving brush and a pair of sock suspenders.
She tells Das to always take good care of
Blynt. She returns to Blynt and asks him to
tell her about Das, which he has never done.

We learn that Blynt found Das in France in
1915. Das was gathered up out of his native
jungle, for what reason, he did not know,
and with strange European clothes forced upon
him, was sent to France to serve in a labor
battalion.. He suffered from cold. The un-
accustomed food kept him ill all the time.
He did not know who was fighting nor on what
side he was. One day, his company took refuge
in a ruined house from a bombardment and a
shell struck the house. It was here that
Blynt found him, lying in the debris, waiting
to die.

Blynt had him carried to his own quarters and
nursed there. When Das was well, he adopted
Blynt with dog-like devotion. Blynt arranged
for him to be sent back home but Das would not
go. He has been with Blynt ever since.

Exit Judy - after another scene in which Blynt
tries to again persuade her to go with him.
They agree to meet that night.

Exit, Blynt.

Das is now alone. Heretofore, save when addressed, he has paid no attention to them.
Now he makes sure that the room is empty. He
examines the shoe and the dried flower. He
is thinking of something -- of some decision
or plan -- thinking hard. At last he decides.
                              Continued -

7.   CONTINUED (2)

He re-opens one bag and takes from it a pair
of trousers. But he is still not satisfied.
From another bag he takes a dressing gown of
a distinctly oriental pattern. This gown
must register well. Then he is satisfied.

                    Das
One to remember with by day -- and one by night!

He rolls the two garments up and exits with
them, concealed in his blouse.

8.   JUDY'S BUNGALOW -

Judy and Blynt on the verandah. It is Blynt's
last night. Judy reclines in Blynt's arms.
Suddenly Judy hears a noise in the house. She
and Blynt enter and go to her bedroom and
find nothing.

9.   THE SHIP -

Judy is not at the dock. At last, Blynt
gives her up and goes on board. He is at
the rail, looking back, as the ship moves
away.

10.   BLYNT'S CABIN -

Blynt discovers that his dressing gown is
missing. It is a gown which Judy gave him and
he is concerned on this account.

Das is watching him when he makes the discovery. Blynt asks Das if he has looked for it
good.

                    Das
Ya, Tuan. See for yourself.

Blynt looks again. He finds a woman's hat
and nightgown. Then he understands.

                    Blynt
Now I know what it was that Mem-petuh heard in her
bedroom last night!

Das is like a child found in mischief.
                              Continued -

12

10.   CONTINUED (2)

                     Das
Ya, Tuan.

                     Blynt
And now I know where my dressing gown went! Why
did you do this?

                     Das
Ada, Tuan. For little while, from Calcutta to
hills, slipper and shaving brush do. But they'll
fall. I know. Slipper and shaving brush can't
see that far. So I do thus, who am the slave of
Tuan, as Tuan knows.

                     Blynt
Ah, Das.

                     Das
Ada, Tuan, Ada.

11.   JUDY'S BUNGALOW -

          Judy finds the dressing gown and the trousers
          where Das has hidden them.

12.   A RESTAURANT - THAT NIGHT -

          Judy at a table, surrounded by men and two
          other women of her kind. All exhilirated -
          Judy most of all. She dominates the group.
          The men know that Blynt has gone and two or
          three of them are hoping to supplant him.
          The scene waxes. It becomes apparent that
          Judy has tentatively chosen one of the men.

13.   JUDY'S BUNGALOW - A FEW HOURS LATER - LIVINGROOM

          Focus on a clock which says 4:00 A.M. Judy
          is just entering with a man. The man is
          rather drunk. His air is triumphant, eager.
          Judy is still exhilirated. But as soon as
          she enters a change begins to come over her,
          of which the man is unaware. He approaches
          and embraces her. She turns and seems to
          see him - to comprehend what she has been
          about to do - for the first time. She strikes
          him upon the face and drives him from the
          house. She falls to the floor and lies upon
          her face, her head upon her arms, sobbing.

14.   A HOTEL LOUNGE -

Enter Judy. Her dress now is very sober. Her
face, her air is sober, almost demure. She
passes a group of men who look at her and goes
on to purchase a copy of the London Times,
while the men still watch her. She opens the
paper.

THE CAMERA FOLLOWS a list of steamer arrivals,
to the name of....Maj. Sir. Nigel Blynt, Bart.

She goes out, the men watching her. They talk
-- we learn now that ever since the night of
the restaurant party she has lived a life of
almost nun-like seclusion, denying herself to
all who knew her in the old days.

15.   JUDY'S BUNGALOW - LIVING ROOM -

A succession of dated newspapers held in a
woman's hands, the headlines read over her
shoulder. The papers are dated to indicate
the passage of time and they are a chronicle
of Blynt's doings as a wealthy amateur sports-
man, traveller, explorer, and the honors he
has received.

These indicate three years. Blynt is becoming
known as a scientist. He is still unmarried.

16.   JUDY'S BUNGALOW -

Five years have passed. The living room seen
through a door. Judy reclining in a chair,
reading the newspaper. A man's shape fills
the doorway. Judy can still be seen when she
looks up and recognizes her father. He persuades her to return home. His face is not
seen.

17.   AMERICA -

We learn that Judy is now in her father's
house, living a very retired life, going nowhere and seeing no one. The servants do not
even know who she is. We learn that Judy's
father is wealthy and her mother an invalid
and she has a young sister who thinks that
Judy is an eccentric aunt.
Continued -

14

17. CONTINUED (2)

The father comes to see Judy each evening.
We learn that he tried at first to make Judy
come back into the world but it was Judy who
elected to live so and that she and her father
never talk about her life in India. Her father
only knows that something tragic happened to
her.

18. AMERICA -

A succession of newspapers in Judy's hand.
The dates indicate the passage of five years.
The headlines record the doings of Blynt.
He is now a famous scientist. He has received still new honors and he is known as
one of the best marriage catches in the world,
and is much sought after by mothers - as well
as by men of learning. Always, the Malay
servant is mentioned.

19. AMERICA -

We now see the father's face for the first
time. Judy and her father - he tries again
to persuade her to enter the world. He tells
her that he has a very distinguished man coming to visit him. He tells her that it is
Sir Nigel Blynt.

20. ARRIVAL OF BLYNT -

He does not know that Judy is in the house,
nor that this is Judy's father, mother and
sister. Neither does the father know that he
ever knew Judy.

21. DAS -

Helping a footman to carry Blynt's luggage
upstairs. Das now wears a frock coat. He
is more comical than ever. The footman gives
Das directions but Das takes the wrong turn
at a corridor. The footman appears and calls
to him. At that instant, a door opens and
Judy emerges, veiled. She recognizes Das.
Continued -

21.   CONTINUED (2)

                     Judy
                (falling back)
Das!....

                    Das
Mem-petuh!

The footman hurries up. Judy indicates to
Das that he is not to speak about her. She
hurries on. Exit Das.

22.   JUDY -

Has not gone far. The footman has no more
than left when she re-appears. She makes
Das promise to never tell Blynt that she is
there. Exit Judy.

Das is puzzled - troubled - but they are white
people and in a white country. He is naught.
And he has always obeyed white people.

23.   TWO DAYS HAVE ELAPSED -

Indicated by dated newspapers, from which we
learn that Blynt is quite the lion.

24.   PANORAMA OF THE ESTATE - THE HOUSE - THE
GROUNDS - THE TERRACE -

Two figures may be seen on the terrace,
though too far away to be recognized.

25.   AN UPPER WINDOW -

It looks down upon the terrace and the two
people who can now be seen to be a man and
a girl.

In the window, looking down at the two people,
Das stands. Upon his face is an expression
of concern. He crosses the room to a chest
of drawers. On it sets the photograph of a
young girl. It is signed for Blynt but it
is set carelessly there - as though Blynt
                        Continued -

25.   CONTINUED (2)

had accepted it and forgotten it. From this
we begin to learn that Judy's sister is in love
with Blynt, though he does not take it very
seriously because of her age and because he is
a guest in the house. But principally because
he is used to having eighteen year old girls
fall in love with him at sight.

Das stands before the photograph a long time
looking at it. His face is grave. Then he
goes out and down the hall to the service
stairs and begins to descend. However, halfway down, he stops and sits, his arms about
his knees. He is immobile, patient. We know
that he has been doing this each day for more
than one day.

26.   THE TERRACE -

The two people are Blynt and Marcia, the girl
of the photograph and Judy's younger sister.
She is about eighteen, quite pretty, spoiled.
We learn that she is in love with Blynt or
thinks that she is and she is using what
wiles she knows upon him and is both baffled
and fretted by his light, paternal treatment
of her.

They arise and approach the house. As they
pass one window, the curtain is drawn aside
and the face of a maid looks out. She is
watching Blynt. She is young, handsome, in a
sullen, passionate way. When she looks at ,
Blynt her expression is brooding and passionate but when she looks at Marcia it becomes
absolutely ferocious. She, too, is in love
with Blynt and she knows that the girl is
also. The curtain falls.

Blynt and Marcia go on to the entrance. They
enter and stand for a moment, Blynt easy and
quizzical, Marcia becoming angry because she
can make no impression upon him. She turns
and mounts the stairs. Blynt watches her.

Then we see that the Italian maid is also
watching Marcia with that savage malevolence.
Marcia disappears. Then the maid looks at
Blynt and her face softens a little. She
watches Blynt until he disappears. She is
still watching the stairs as though in a
trance. She doesn't even see the footman,
who emerges into the hall behind her as though
he has been watching the three of them. We
see that he has been watching the maid and is
Continued -

26.   CONTINUED (2)

             jealous. He takes her to task. The maid
             defies him and rushes off. The footman follows.

27.   THE SERVICE STAIRS -

             Das sits there. We hear the sound of feet.
             The Italian maid appears, walking swiftly.
             Das doesn't move. She doesn't see him at all.
             She goes on fast, her face sullen, tense.
             Then Das moves and follows her.

28.   THE PANTRY -

             The maid is stooping above an open drawer -
             Das watching her through the door. From the
             drawer the maid takes a phial. Then Das ducks
             back. A moment later, the footman enters.
             The footman knows what the maid has hidden in
             the drawer. We learn that it is a love potion
             and that she has already used up one bottle.
             The footman taunts her with having wasted ten
             dollars. He closes with her. He is coldly
             angry in contrast to her violence.

             CAMERA SHOWS Das again, watching through the
             door. The footman is trying to take the bot-
             tle from the maid. They struggle, the maid's
             hand still in the drawer. She is clutching a
             butcher knife and she strikes full at the foot-
             man's face. He catches her hand and twists
             the knife from it and slaps her on both cheeks
             and lets her go. She falls back, panting.
             She runs past him and out. Again Das' face
             has disappeared. The footman follows. Then
             Das enters. He opens the drawer, takes out the
             phial, removes the stopper and tastes it. He
             is puzzled. He replaces the bottle and returns
             up the stairs.

             We FOLLOW HIM up the stairs to the door of
             Blynt's room.

29.   BLYNT'S ROOM -

             Das enters. He lays out Blynt's dinner clothes
             - then he squats on the floor, his arms about
                                        Continued -

18

29.   CONTINUED (2)

his knees. His face is gray, thoughtful, not
quite alarmed but quite alert.

Blynt enters. He speaks to Das in Malay and
Das rises and goes out to draw the bath.
Blynt removes his coat and vest. He is moving
idly about when his glance happens to fall
upon Marcia's picture upon the chest of drawers.
He pauses suddenly, goes and takes up the picture, as if he suddenly sees something about
it which he had not seen before. A trick of
light, which made the face resemble for an
instant - Judy's! But it is gone. He sets
the picture back and continues to undress.

30.   THE DINNER TABLE -

A large party - the people are all of serious
cast. Blynt dominates. We now see the hostess for the first time. In her face, as in
her husband's, is the indelible, faint trace
of tragedy, sorrow. Blynt remarks how much
older they seem than an eighteen year old
child would indicate.

India is mentioned. By chance Blynt asks the
hostess if she was ever there. The host answers no so abruptly as to cause a moment of
embarrassment. Blynt sees in the hostess' face
an expression of deep emotion - almost terror.
He covers the moment and it passes. The hostess, however, is still distracted. Soon she
gives the signal to arise. The women leave
the room.

31.   JUDY'S LIVING ROOM -

Das and Judy. Das squats on the floor. We
learn that each evening, while the household
is at dinner, Das comes to Judy and that he
has been trying to persuade her to let Blynt
know that she is there, so the three of them
can go away.

Judy refuses for her former reason. We learn
that she still loves Blynt and that she will
not hurt his career. She says that if Das
ever tells Blynt she is there, she will leave
the house. Exit Das.

32.   DAS -

Squatting on the floor. He is worried and
puzzled. But these are white people. He
cannot expect to understand their ways.

33.   THE DINNER TABLE -

The men alone - the host seeks Blynt and
apologizes for his abruptness at dinner. He
tells Blynt that he had an older daughter who
died in India years ago and that his wife has
never recovered from the tragic circumstances
of the death.

Blynt is puzzled, thoughtful. He thinks of the
photograph of the younger daughter as it had
appeared for an instant earlier in the evening.
He has a suspicion, though it never once occurs
to him that Judy is in the house. He asks
what the daughter's name was. The host tells
him it was Judy and asks if Blynt ever knew
her. He asks it with terror, as if he dreaded
the answer. Blynt now has command of himself.
He answers no. Exit host, while Blynt watches
him.

34.-   JUDY'S LIVING ROOM -

Judy is alone. Her father enters. He tells
about the dinner. Judy is too distracted trying to keep her secret hidden from him. The
father tells her of Marcia's interest in
Blynt and how the match would please him, and
that he believes Blynt to be interested in
Marcia. Judy must hide her emotion.

35.   BLYNT -

In a chair - Das squatting at his feet.

                    Blynt
She is late tonight. I wish she would fetch it
along. I want to go to bed.

                    Das
I wish she would not bring it at all.

                    Blyne
So do I. A strange custom. But I can't offend
my host, you know.
                                    Continued -

20

35.   CONTINUED (2)

A knock at the door. Das opens it. It is the
Italian maid with a tray on which sets a single half-filled wine glass. Her face is sullen, demure, inscrutible. Das takes the tray.
But the maid does not retire. She stands
looking at Blynt for so long with a savage,
questioning look that he notices it and asks
her what she wants. She curtsies in some con-
fusion and retires. Das sets the tray on the
table. Blyne takes the glass and sniffs at it.

                    Blynt
It smells worse than usual tonight but I can't
offend my host.
                    (Das is watching Blynt)

                    Das
Tuan, let us go away.

                    Blynt
                (holding the glass)
Go away?

                    Das
Let us leave this house -- this is not a good house.

                    Blynt
Where do you want to go?

                    Das
There is one place which we should never have left
-- There was one there.....

                    Blynt
Stop! -- Have I not told thee never to say that
name -- her name! Thou knowest I have paid, Oh,
Das!....

                    Das
Ya, Tuan, I know. And thou knowest I have not
mentioned it.

Blynt drinks, shudders, wry-faced. Das watches
him soberly.

36.   JUDY -

Is preparing for bed. She is still too distracted to sleep. Her maid is gone. A light
knock at the door. She opens it herself. It
is Das. He enters and squats. Despite her
own emotion, Judy sees that Das is quite
worried. He tells her about the Italian maid
and the nightly drink. We learn that the drink
has been going on ever since Blynt arrived.
                              Continued -

36.   CONTINUED (2)

Judy says it is probably just a love potion and
harmless, but this does not ease Das' mind. He
tells her that if she will just let Blynt know
she is there, he will take her away and they
will be safe. But Judy will not. She doesn't
believe that Blynt cares for her. She thinks
that he is now in love with her sister and
she wants the sister to have him.

Das knows better but Judy is too distracted to
see his fear. Exit Das.

37.   DAS' BEDROOM -

Das, in deep and troubled thought. Blynt will
not let him mention Judy's name and Judy will
not herself tell Blynt that she is in the
house and still loves him.

38.   MARCIA'S BEDROOM -

The Italian maid helping Marcia to undress.
Marcia is angry because Blynt repulses her.
The maid is malevolent, watchful. Marcia
speaks sharply to the maid, asking for her
dressing gown. From the closet, the maid
takes the gown which Judy gave Blynt and which
Das stole and returned to Judy for a keepsake,
ten years ago. We now learn that Marcia
believes that the robe was sent to her by her
dead sister, years ago, with a letter in which
the sister told her that she must keep the robe
and give it to her husband and as long as he
wore it, he would never cease to love her.

At first, Marcia tells the maid sharply to
put it back. Then a thought strikes her. She
takes the robe and dismisses the maid.

Marcia is now determined on something. At the
mirror she fixes her face as though she were
going to a party. She watches the clock,
showing determination and impatience. She
smokes a cigarette, throws it away, goes to
the door, looks out, lights another cigarette,
looks at the clock again - picks it up and
shakes it - watching the hands crawl terrifically to midnight. Then she puts on the gown,
listens for a moment at her door, crosses
swiftly to Blynt's door and slips inside.

22

39.   BLYNT'S BEDROOM - BLYNT

        Is in bed, asleep. Marcia enters. She
        flings off the robe, runs and springs into
        bed beside Blynt.

        Blynt wakes. He makes her get up, threatens
        to spank her. She is quite meek now. He
        is leading her toward the door when he sees
        the robe. He is struck dumb. Then he knows
        the truth, which the photograph almost showed
        him.

        Marcia is surprised at his actions. He asks
        about the robe. She tells him how the robe
        was sent to her from India by her sister to
        bring her luck in love. So she offers the
        robe to him. He accepts it. Exit Marcia.

        Blynt takes the robe back to bed with him,
        resting his cheek upon it.

40.   DAS -

        Has decided - there is one way he can tell
        Blynt that Judy is in the house. He will
        take something which he knows belongs to
        Judy and which Blynt will recognize and leave
        it in Blynt's room. At once he thinks of the
        robe. Exit Das.

41.   JUDY'S ROOM -

        Judy is asleep. Enter Das quietly. He seeks
        the robe which he stole and returned to her.
        He cannot find it. At last he takes a garment
        which bears the scent which Judy has always
        used and goes out.

42.   CORRIDOR -

        Das approaches Blynt's room.

43.   BLYNT'S ROOM -

        Das enters. He sees the robe beside Blynt's
        cheek. He believes that Judy has already been
        there.   Continued -

43.   CONTINUED (2)

                        Das
          Now we can go away!

44.   MORNING -

                     The Italian maid mounting the service stairs
                     with a tea tray. We FOLLOW HER UP the corri-
                     dor to Blynt's door.

45.   BLYNT'S ROOM -

                     Blynt is still asleep - the robe under his
                     cheek. The maid enters and sees the robe.
                     She believes that Marcia was there and blames
                     it on the love potion. Exit maid.

46.   WE FOLLOW THE MAID DOWN THE CORRIDOR -

                     She is walking fast, her face furious. She
                     goes to her room.

47.   MAID'S ROOM -

                     She opens a trunk and takes out a phial.

                     CLOSEUP shows that it is labelled "POISON".
                     She thrusts the phial into her stocking. Her
                     face is furious.

48.   BLYNT'S ROOM -

                     Blynt is awake. He conceals the robe. Das
                     enters. He misses the robe at once. He waits
                     for Blynt to tell him about Judy. Blynt does
                     not know that Das has seen the robe. Das
                     doesn't dare ask about it. He begins to
                     realize that something has gone wrong. He
                     is quite grave again.

24

49.   THE CORRIDOR -

Das is worried. If Judy had been there, he
believes that Blynt would have told him. If
it was not Judy, it must have been someone
who could have owned the robe. Suddenly he
knows that the only person Judy would have
given the robe to would have been her sister.
He thinks of Blynt and Marcia as he has
watched them - Marcia trying to make love to
Blynt. He thinks of the maid watching Marcia
and Blynt together. Then he thinks of the
maid bringing in the early tea and seeing the
robe as he saw it. Now he is more than
puzzled. He is afraid.

50.   JUDY'S ROOM -

Das and Judy - Das learns that Judy gave the
robe to her sister - sent it from India years
ago, about the time she was supposed to have
died, which was just after Blynt left her.
In order to find this out, Das cannot keep
Judy from finding out about the robe being in
Blynt's room that morning. Then Judy knows
that Blynt and Marcia are in love. She says
that Blynt must never know about her and that
Marcia must never know. Because Blynt must
now marry Marcia! She makes Das promise her
that he will never tell. Das goes out.

51.   DAS -

Asks Blynt once more to leave. Blynt wants
a reason. Das can give none. Blynt refuses
to go.

52.   THE PANTRY -

Enter Das stealthily. He opens the drawer
where the maid kept the love potion. It is
gone. In its place is the phial of poison.
Das cannot read. He takes the cork out and
sniffs it and knows what it is.

53.   A DOWN TOWN STREET -

             Das walking along, attracting some little
             attention of an amused nature. But he is
             quite grave, sober - looking at the store
             windows. He comes to a drug store and looks
             at that for a while. Then he enters. He
             has some trouble making the clerk understand
             what he wants. At last the manager comes
             out. At first he thinks that what Das wants
             is poison. Then he understands that Das wants
             an antidote. Das cannot tell him what kind
             of a poison, so he suggests olive oil.

                              Das
                   Is it certain to save?

             The druggist shrugs and says that no one can
             know - that it depends, etc. For a moment,
             Das stands, his face lowered, still. Then he
             makes a gesture - fatalistic, resigned. He
             thanks the man and goes out.

             He now has a train of small boys following him.
             He enters a grocery story and presently
             succeeds in making them understand what he
             wants. With his bottle beneath his arm, he
             emerges and goes on - his train following.

54.   THE TROLLEY -

             Das, with his parcel and the other passengers
             looking at him - laughing.

55.   THE HOUSE FROM THE REAR -

             As a servant would enter. In the distance,
             a gay party on the terrace. Das pauses and
             looks at them. He goes on.

56.   THE TERRACE - NIGHT -

             Blynt and Marcia. Blynt tells Marcia about
             the robe, that it was once his. He tells her
             that he once loved her sister and does still.
             In the talk, Marcia happens to mention her
             eccentric aunt. Blynt believes that the aunt
             is Judy, though the girl doesn't know this.

57.   THE PANTRY -

The maid preparing the evening drink for Blynt.
She puts the poison in it, takes up the tray
and goes out.

WE FOLLOW HER up the stairs and along the
corridor. She pauses at Marcia's door and
makes a gesture toward it -- terrible, triumph-
ant, savage. She goes on to Blynt's door and
knocks.

58.   BLYNT'S ROOM -

Blynt and Das and the poison drink, which Das
knows is poison and Blynt does not. Das knows
that if he were to tell Blynt the drink is
poison, Blynt would not believe him. And he
knows that if he pours it out, the maid will
know that something went wrong and she will
merely fix another one tomorrow and continue
to fix them until the time when Das will not
be there. His only hope is to get Blynt to
leave the house.

He believes that Judy can make Blynt go, but
Judy will not let him tell Blynt that she is
in the house. He asks Blynt again to leave.
Blynt refuses because he knows that Judy is
in the house, though he feels that he cannot
make the first move to see her, after the way
he treated her. He will not leave.

Das believes too that if something happens to
him to show Judy the danger in which Blynt is,
she will show herself and make Blynt leave -
take him away. They will both be together
again, which Das believes they both want.

When Blynt refuses to go, Das offers to take
the drink himself. Blynt agrees, since he
doesn't know it is poison. He merely knows
that Das knows more than he has told him.
And Das knows that Blynt knows more than he
has told. But Das' lips are sealed. All he
knows to do is to take the drink and bring
Judy and Blynt together and get them out of
the house. And then perhaps save himself with
the olive oil, if it is not too late! He
empties the glass. Blynt dismisses him for
the night.

Blynt is puzzled and worried. He is worried
about Das, too. He knows that Das has been
trying to tell him something but he doesn't
know how much Das knows or suspects. As he
walks up and down the room, he looks at the
Continued -

58.   CONTINUED (2)

        glass each time he passes. He is beginning to
        realize that the glass -- the drink tonight --
        has had more significance than heretofore.
        Suddenly a thought strikes him. He leaps to
        the tray and snatches the glass - sniffs it -
        and suspects the truth! He hurls the glass
        down and runs from the room.

59.   BLYNT -

        Running through the corridor to the servants'
        wing. A startled half-dressed footman opens
        the door. He shows Blynt Das' room and
        follows - other servants gathering, half-
        dressed. Blynt hurls himself at the door and
        breaks it in.

60.   DAS' BEDROOM -

        Das is on the floor where he has fallen. He
        is trying to reach the bottle of olive oil on
        a chair. Blynt reaches him and breaks the
        neck from the bottle and tries to help Das
        drink. Das is too weak. He makes Blynt pro-
        mise to take Judy and go away and never leave
        her again. Blynt promises, trying to make
        Das drink the oil. Das dies.

61.   ON SHIP -

        Judy and Blynt - they are married. They are
        taking Das' ashes back to the home which he
        had not seen in fifteen years!

                        THE END

28

2

The College Widow

The College Widow was copied in the Script Department by 26 May 1932; the facsimile is taken from the Vault Copy. Some time earlier, Faulkner had written a 3½-page story outline for which he suggested the title of Night Bird; this may be the piece he intended for Tallulah Bankhead. Both versions bear some resemblance to Sanctuary, especially in their emphasis on the way a teasing virgin becomes fascinated by a dangerous and possessive older man, courts damnation as well as a fall in social status, and becomes indirectly responsible for the deaths or ruin of the men around her. There is even an anticipation of Requiem for a Nun in Mary Lee Blair's attempt to negate her past by marrying a man in whom she does not completely confide. Nevertheless, this is more an original story than a reworking of the perils of Temple Drake.

When Lillian Culver reevaluated The College Widow for the Story Department early in 1945, she suggested that it be retitled Bitch, Triangle, or Femme Fatale. By that time, the femme fatale had become the stock central figure of film noir, and it is especially interesting to observe the industry's turnaround on the advisability of featuring such a destructive and sexually active woman in a movie, since it is clear that Mary Lee's character was one major reason The College Widow was not approved for production in 1932. (Temple Drake was somewhat whitewashed in Paramount's 1933 version of Sanctuary.) The antiheroines of film noir have their origins in the American fiction of the early thirties, notably Dashiell Hammett's The Maltese Falcon (1930) and James M. Cain's The Postman Always Rings Twice (1934). But Sanctuary (1931) is equally important in this tradition, and The College Widow may be the first attempt ever made to transfer this prototype to the American screen. (Overseas, as an updated Lorelei, she had already appeared in The Blue Angel of 1930.)

The Story of Temple Drake, as has already been suggested, was not as censorable as The College Widow, let alone Sanctuary, and from this distance it appears a thoroughly ludicrous attempt at cleaning up a dirty story. It is hardly the story of Faulkner's Temple

Drake and might better have been called *The Bobbsey Twins Go to Hell*. Written by Oliver H. P. Garrett and directed by Stephen Roberts—its only redeeming feature the elegantly pseudo-Expressionist cinematography of Karl Struss—it is the story of two childhood sweethearts, lawyer Stephen Benbow and flirt Temple Drake (played by Miriam Hopkins). When Benbow proposes marriage, Temple refuses because of what she calls her bad side; she finds Benbow, an old friend of her grandfather the judge, too dull. After refusing Benbow, she goes off remorsefully to get drunk with T. D. Gowan, who crashes his car at Lee Goodwin's place. Temple is raped by the gangster Trigger (played by Jack LaRue)—there are corncobs in the scene, but they appear only as iconographic references to *Sanctuary*; Trigger is not impotent and later has some gushy lines about Temple's really caring for him. Trigger takes Temple to Reba's sleazy boarding house (there are no brothel scenes), where they share a room. Benbow is appointed by the court to defend Lee Goodwin (the murder of Tommy and the character of Ruby Goodwin are relatively unchanged from the novel), and he tracks Temple down at Reba's. To keep Trigger from shooting him, Temple tells Benbow she is happy and sends him away. "You came through for me," says Trigger, "stuck up for me against one of your own kind." The truth comes out, however, and Temple shoots him—as, in an emblematic closeup, he stubs out his final cigarette. Back home, Temple asks Benbow not to make her testify, but Benbow—threatened with disbarment by Judge Drake if he involves her in the case—appeals to her family tradition of sacrifice and love for the truth and calls her to the stand. "You're a woman," he says, "but you're still a Drake." Although Benbow then loses his nerve, Temple insists on telling the whole story—that Trigger "attacked" her and that she later killed him. Then she faints and Benbow carries her out of the courtroom; his final line is, "Be proud of her, Judge—I am."

   Although Temple is presented as a flirtatious virgin torn between her good and bad sides, she is basically the clichéd heroine in distress, and the only quality Stephen shares with Faulkner's Horace Benbow is his juridical idealism. The film must have confirmed Faulkner's lowest impressions of movie content and provides a significant background for the attempts he did make to treat adult sexual relationships in his screenplays. The alternately tough and bland, suggestive and sentimental, dark and whitewashed tone of the picture must also have had its effect on his judgment of film aesthetics. (These are guesses; I can find no record of his reaction.) However watered down, *The Story of Temple Drake* did contain a rape, two murders (one in self-defense), a disreputable boarding house, some hints at strong language (mostly Ruby's, and covered by the sounds of a storm), bootlegging, and some highly unattractive males (Goodwin is seedy, Tommy is retarded, and Trigger is so darkly nasty that George Raft is said to have refused the role in fear of "professional suicide"[1]). Partly because of these "tasteless" elements and partly because of the film that it had been feared would have resulted from *Sanctuary*, a censorship problem did arise. In the words of film historian William K. Everson,

> The film, together with Warners' *Convention City*, was literally responsible for bringing about the Production Code censorship crackdown in 1933. Through no fault of its own, the film was pilloried and condemned long before it was completed. Adolph Zukor was advised, in strategically placed advertisements, to burn the negative! All of this was, of course, due to the notoriety of the original novel . . . and a desire to keep such controversial material off the screen.[2]

In this light, it is easy to see why *The College Widow* was not approved for production. Even beyond the question of the heroine's moral character, there was the fear (as a 1934 reader put it) that "Faulkner would obviously develop another SANCTUARY." Ironically, the novel whose success had much to do with his being hired in Hollywood appears to have stood in the way of his working there.

"College Widow" was a slang term for a noncollege woman who goes out with students. Faulkner may have lifted the title from *The College Widow*, a 1904 comedy by George Ade, a midwestern satirist best known for his 1899 *Fables in Slang*. Ade's four-act play told the story of Jane Witherspoon, the daughter of the president of Atwater College; according to a jealous female student, she "wears somebody's pin every year. Why her shirtwaist is so full of holes that it looks like open work." Jane is enticed by some students into dating a promising football player—a fourth-year freshman—so that he will enroll at Atwater and help them win the big game, which he does. Her reputation is treated lightheartedly, though at one point she tearfully reveals that the label "college widow" upsets her and that she is not really a "heartless flirt." Eventually she and the football player leave the college and head happily westward with his father, a railroad millionaire who had been an old friend of her father. Blotner considers it possible that Faulkner had read this play in a collection at Phil Stone's house, and Sam Marx remembers it as having been quite popular. It was even made into a movie called *Freshman Love* by Warner Brothers in 1936. But if Faulkner did draw on this play for anything more than its title, it was from an extremely negative and ironic point of view. To understand fully the quality and tone of the treatment he eventually wrote, it is necessary to examine the first draft of his story outline, keeping Ade's innocent comedy in mind as an example of how these matters might have been treated. College-widowhood was not in itself so darkly damnable.

The following is the complete text of *Night Bird*, which is no longer in the MGM files but which was generously provided by Joseph Blotner. I have italicized those phrases that were crossed out in heavy pencil—changes that deleted the unnamed heroine's pregnancy and miscarriage.

"Night Bird"—suggested title [handwritten].

Daughter of a professor in a small southern college. About eighteen. She is in love with an undergraduate. Her parents do not want her to marry anyone, and when the youth is expelled from college in his senior year for a more or less harmless prank, his name is anathema with the parents. The girl and the youth attempt to elope, and are prevented by parents, who tell the girl that the youth is no good. He goes away to a city. The girl grieves for a while. Her parents make her go out with the college boys, making opportunities for her to become a belle. Gradually she begins to go out with them.

She is of a gay temperament. She begins to enjoy the youths, experimenting with sex. She acquires a lot of technique with the youths, so that after a time, as she grows older, they begin to bore her. She is now about 22 or 23 [handwritten insert]. One day she has an encounter with a stranger in the little town. He is an older man, handsome, of equivocal position. There is something sinister about him which is part of his attraction to her. She knows that her parents would not approve of him. She meets him secretly a few times, trying her college-youth technique on him. But it does not work, and without knowing herself how it had happened, she goes off with him and they spend a weekend together in a city.

When she returns she is frightened. She is both afraid of the man, and that it will be found out. She resolves never to see the man again. But he will not let her alone. He begins to haunt her. She is now physically afraid of him because she realises that there is something wrong with him, though she does not yet know that the man is insane [the last half of the sentence is underlined; "man is insane" is circled]. One afternoon he practically breaks into the house, and that night she slips out of the house and flees to the city where the man with whom she was in love while he was in the college has now become successful. She goes to him and without telling him what has happened, they are married.

She feels that she is safe now. For six months they lead an idyllic married life. *She is with child, and* she has almost forgot the other business. Then one day she discovers that the other man has followed her to the city. Then her terror begins. She feels that he is in hiding somewhere, watching the house. She is afraid to go out, even. Her husband sees that something is wrong, but she will not tell him. When she is with him she tries to be gay. This goes on for about six months longer. Then one night she realises that the man is in the house. She is almost insane herself. She goes to her husband and tells him the whole thing [underlined and bracketed, perhaps for deletion]. He takes a pistol and leaves her in the library and he goes to search the house for the other men [sic].

She waits in the room. It seems to her that she can hear, feel, the man creeping from room to room, hunting for her, drawing nearer all the time. Then she knows that he is just outside the door. She turns the light off. She sees the door open, and a man's body in silhouette in it. The man enters. He approaches her. He touches her and she screams. Her husband runs up the hall and enters and turns on the light and kills the man.

The woman has fainted. She comes to in hospital, days later. The shock *has brought on a miscarriage*. She is ill for some time. In the meantime her husband was cleared of the shooting, and when she is well, he tells her that they are through. He offers her money, but she will not take it. She wires her father for money to come home on. She returns to her old home, where her divorce is carried through.

She is now declassee there, among the better families, the faculty families, also an object of tearful reproach on the part of her mother. She tries to go out again, to resume her old life with the college boys, who are now children to her. At first there is a glamor about her to them, as a woman with a past, a dashing widow. Then they begin to shy off from her, as the faculty disapproves. But she still goes to the college dances, where one of the college boys is enough beglamored to defy the faculty disapproval. At last something happens, something actually innocent but apparently so scandalous that the boy is expelled from the school.

She is now 27 or 28 [handwritten].

Now none of the college boys dare dance or be seen with her, though a few of them try to make[3] her surreptitiously. She will not permit this, so they all drop her. She begins then to consort with young men in the town, men without social position. One evening she brings one of them with her to a college dance. They are asked to leave the ball room. The next morning her father receives a letter from the president of the college, asking for his resignation because of his daughter's reputation. She goes to the president and tells him that if the letter be recalled, she will leave the town and never return.

She goes back to the city, where her ex-husband is now married again, with a son. She is now a night bird. She consorts with equivocal people making one at parties in bachelor hotels and such. There is a wealthy old man who is her friend. One evening in a night club she sees her ex-husband and his wife. They do not see her. She is quite gay that evening, with a party. She raises her glass and drinks "To the mother of my child."

One of Faulkner's great strengths as a writer is his sense of closure, and many of his scripts share with such novels as *Absalom, Absalom!* their manner of building not to a dénouement but to an utterly climactic final sentence. These endings often project—as Walter Slatoff has argued in *Quest for Failure*[4]—the tension of unresolved but fatally juxtaposed contradictory forces. Sometimes—as at the end of *The Sound and the Fury*, where the dialectic is between order and chaos, or rigidity and love—this nonsynthesis finds expression in an ironic or paradoxical line. What is most interesting about *Night Bird* is the heroine's closing toast, whose double appeal to her lost hopes for a family life and to her present outcaste childlessness indicates that Faulkner was applying to this story some of the same imaginative categories and tropes that were basic to him as a novelist. (In the same vein, it should be noted that this is the first script Faulkner set in the South.) That toast is the only line of dialogue in the story outline, and it is modified only slightly in the subsequent treatment, so it was clearly an important key to the story for him, a paradoxical site of coherence.

The heroine of *Night Bird* is in some respects like Judy in *Manservant*. It will be remembered that after the death of her illegitimate child, Judy had ceased to trouble about her reputation, and that many years later she had gone home with the assistance of her father. Both women are presented as having strong contradictory drives to be the good wife and the bad mistress, as if they were trying to live out both sides of the patriarchal double standard for female sexual behavior and had so internalized the gulf between madonna and whore that they became unable to maintain their self-respect. They finally seem able to stabilize themselves only by exaggeratedly playing one or the other role to the extreme: this woman by playing the night bird, and Judy by shutting herself away from human company almost entirely. Neither allows herself to be "centered" (to borrow a term from contemporary psychology). One can only speculate as to Faulkner's reasons for making infant mortality a part of these stories. It is possible that he felt such a loss to be a role crisis for a woman, who might then feel the path of motherhood closed to her—or he may have denied them children as one aspect of a puritanical judgment of his characters. It is interesting that even Temple Drake's youngest child is killed in *Requiem for a Nun*. And it is of course likely that he was still very upset about the death of his own infant daughter in 1931; that was the first occasion on which Estelle Faulkner had ever seen him cry, and he is said to have remained bitterly resentful of the doctors for much of the next year.[5]

The most obvious echoes of *Sanctuary* have to do with the dark stranger, the snake to her bird. During the night at the Old Frenchman Place, Temple spends much of her time listening tensely to the sounds of the prowling men who terrify her. When Temple goes off to Memphis with Popeye, she is passive and at least as unaware of her reasons for this surrender as is the heroine of *Night Bird* when she spends her weekend in the city. These women share a capacity for damnation, though Temple (at least until *Requiem*) is considerably less sympathetic or responsible, having virtually no sense of integrity.

In *Night Bird* and to a lesser extent in *The College Widow*, Mary Lee Blair is developed as a woman with some capacity for strength and honor, notably in her intervention between the college president and her father. She is also presented as sexually self-destructive and as dangerous to others. She is prevented from becoming a happy wife, first by her parents and then by her sexual past, and when she utterly falls, she does so (as the closing scene shows) with a certain flair. This could have been a good and demanding role for a daring actress; there were a number of films that presented sexually active unmarried women during this period (*She Done Him Wrong*, *Queen Christina*, etc.), but such films rarely took a dark view of sexuality. The most objectionable aspect of *The College Widow* was probably not its failure to kill or marry off or otherwise redeem Mary Lee by the end, nor even the powerful way it interrelates sexuality and murder in that scene in the dark house, but the overall bleakness of its point of view.

The College Widow differs from *Night Bird* in a number of striking ways, particularly in regard to Mary Lee's character. She is now much more like Temple Drake in her self-centeredness, her willingness to manipulate others for her own ends, her experience as a flirt, and her frightened vulnerability. She is presented right away as having little interest in marriage and as not having "enough character to stick to" her fiancé when he is in trouble. The minor scandal that resulted in a beau's expulsion near the end of *Night Bird* is moved to the beginning of *College Widow*, and in its former place Mary Lee is made responsible for the youth's suicide. The expulsion scenes focus on male bonding and the themes of sacrifice and honor, none of which Mary Lee is particularly interested in; to a certain extent this anticipates *Absolution*. The dark stranger is a much more active figure, and Mary Lee's ambivalent fascination with him is given an almost hypnotic overtone; her running toward and away from him is very close to Temple's behavior at the Old Frenchman

Place. The note of weariness and fatalism at the end is another new development and one that dominates the close of *Sanctuary*. There is no "harmless prank." The toast remains the only line of dialogue.

When Anne Cunningham wrote a synopsis and evaluation of *The College Widow* on 2 October 1934, she strongly advised against production. "This is told very briefly," she wrote, "but Faulkner would obviously develop another SANCTUARY. It is an evil, slimy thing, absolutely unfit for screen production, in the face of current censorship . . . . . or at any future time." It is apparent from some notes made by Lillian Culver in her much later report that two versions of *The College Widow* were submitted by Faulkner and that the version read by Cunningham was no longer in the files by 1945. In what Culver identified as the earlier version—the evil and slimy one—the differences are as follows: Robert frees Mary Lee of her engagement (this is her doing in the second version); she has "several subsequent trysts" with the stranger after he first seduces her, "until the risk to her reputation makes her try to throw off his spell" (quoting Cunningham); she runs away to Robert because "her wantonness is discovered by her parents"; she is apparently pregnant when Robert marries her, though this is not particularly clear from the synopsis; and there is no killing. Instead, the marriage is dissolved when Mary Lee, frightened by the stranger's reappearance, tells Robert the whole story. Cunningham's reading of the toast, which closes this version too, is that "she thinks of the second wife as the mother of the child she would like to have." There appears to be no explanation in the first version of how Mary Lee miscarries. It seems clear in any case that the basic changes from the relatively sympathetic heroine of *Night Bird* to the more selfish and irresponsibly destructive heroine of the surviving version had already been made in this lost draft of *The College Widow*.

Set in the South, going well beyond studio conventions of good taste, and dealing frankly with extreme and threatening emotions, this sexual horror story reveals Faulkner's concerted attempt to write for MGM one kind of story that interested him seriously as a novelist. It may also reflect some conviction that *Sanctuary*, which had fulfilled his original expectation that it would sell widely, might provide a good model in his attempt to write for the popular medium of film. The fact that *The College Widow* was being evaluated for production as late as 1945 suggests that he was not entirely wrong, and it is intriguing to imagine the film noir that might have been made from this treatment in the era that saw *The Big Sleep*.

NOTES: INTRODUCTION TO *THE COLLEGE WIDOW*

1. Blotner, *Faulkner: A Biography*, 797.
2. Program notes for a Tribute to Karl Struss at the 1980 Telluride Film Festival.
3. Euphemism for seduction and intercourse.
4. Ithaca, N.Y.: Cornell Univ. Press, 1960.
5. Blotner, *Faulkner: A Biography*, 681–83.

NOTES: SCRIPT OF *THE COLLEGE WIDOW*

P. 1 [narrative], "where young men outnumber girls twenty to one": Evidently this was a male college, whereas the one in Ade's play was co-ed. Note the emphasis on her mother's influence.

P. 1 [narrative], "He has a friend, Raymond": Faulkner is setting up a contrast between male-male bonding with its code of honor and sacrifice (important in "Honor," *Turn About, Absolution,* etc.), and male-female bonding. The latter is undermined here—as elsewhere in Faulkner's work—by the woman's selfishness and dishonesty. But Raymond's subsequently allowing Robert to take the blame for the theft shows Raymond unworthy of his friend. Many important codes of honorable behavior are broken in this story, with Robert emerging as an unqualifiedly good person.

P. 1 [narrative], "A figure steals into the office . . .": Although Faulkner did not take the trouble to show how the expositions of Scene 1 were to be managed, here he moves directly into significant action. The knife is an effective prop for visual storytelling.

P. 3 [narrative], "She now sees her chance of getting away . . .": It is interesting that Mary Lee sees marriage as an opportunity for having better affairs. The love for her fiancé that was important in *Night Bird* has been deleted. The father's heavy-handedness and her own vacillation, together with her confused motive for marriage, suggest that Mary Lee particularly wants to get away from her controlling father and that her parents may be responsible for her failure to develop a working sense of autonomy and personal integrity. The lack of "character" revealed here, and her erratic approach-avoidance with the stranger, show that she has not yet learned who she is or what she wants; her dealings with the college president on behalf of her father in Scene 45 show that she has matured and let her appear more sympathetic by the end.

P. 4 [narrative], "He is a stranger—handsome . . .": This figure is better-looking than Popeye, but he still represents what Conrad called the "fascination of the abomination." The snake-bird image introduces the theme of hypnotic or trancelike behavior (i.e., her complicit passivity) as well as one of phallic evil, and partly echoes the symbolic use of birds throughout *Sanctuary*.

P. 4 [narrative], "She at once fears the man and wants to know him": As in *Sanctuary*, Faulkner is investigating or perhaps exploiting the notion that women are drawn to evil, often expressed as promiscuity, and that once freed from social controls—like Temple in the Memphis brothel—they will reveal their wild, destructive, uncivilized perversity. On a less melodramatic level, he is simply observing that a virgin may be frightened of adult sexuality while still desiring it.

P. 4 [narrative], "She knows that her college boy technique will not work here": Ruby tells Temple much the same thing at the Frenchman Place: "Do you think you're meeting kids now? Kids that give a damn whether you like it or not?" See *Sanctuary*, 64–71. Both Mary Lee and Temple are "teases" who get out of their depth, but Mary Lee is more in control (Temple is raped).

P. 5 [narrative], "She is concealing something": It is an unusual and interesting touch that the audience never discovers what happened outside the dance, though it is likely she met the stranger.

P. 5 [narrative], "Mary Lee leans against the door . . .": The door and lock are effective props for visualizing her state of mind.

P. 6 [narrative], "Mrs. Blair is telling the Professor . . .": The stranger is not specifically presented as insane; the likelihood is that the mother recognized the same dark power her daughter did (see Scenes 11 and 33).

P. 6 [narrative], "and Mary Lee gets out, running": Her "distracted" running is similar to Temple's at the Frenchman Place. The subsequent scenes with the stranger are fully visualized.

P. 8 [narrative], "It is the stranger": Here and in Scene 36, the stranger's intrusion into her house is an effective visualization of her sense of how he threatens her—a more or less phallic penetration of her privacy as well as a counterforce to her potential for domesticity.

P. 9 [narrative], "STATION": Here and in Scenes 26, 27, and 47, the emphasis on train travel is similar to that in *Sanctuary*.

P. 9 [narrative], "He tells the stranger where Mary Lee is without knowing why he did so": Evidently the stranger's power goes beyond the sexual.

P. 9 [narrative], "The other is like a bad dream": This may be a cliché, but if taken literally it suggests that Faulkner is symbolically examining the sexual unconscious in his treatment of Mary Lee's attraction to the stranger. It certainly makes sense to read the stranger—especially in Scene 35—as an incarnation of Mary Lee's eruptive unsocialized desires. His intrusion into her married life anticipates that of Red's brother in *Requiem for a Nun*.

P. 11 [narrative], "She tells Robert that now they cannot live together after what she has done, and that she wishes to return to her father": For the first time Mary Lee accepts responsibility for her actions (in the earlier draft, it was Robert who broke off the marriage); it seems appropriate that she accepts her father at the same time. If one pursues a Freudian reading of this script, the killing of the stranger marks the full expression of her repressed eros-thanatos impulses, so that now the superego can assert a stabilizing influence. Her conflicts are not completely resolved, of course, as her subsequent behavior indicates, but without this scene, her behavior with the college president would not have been adequately prepared. In his Introduction to *Mayday* (Notre Dame, Ind.: Univ. of Notre Dame Press, 1980), Carvel Collins argues convincingly that Faulkner was influenced by Freudian theory, notably in *The Sound and the Fury*; see Collins, 32–36.

P. 11 [narrative], "She now has a reputation . . .": Although she was presented as dating students in Scene 1, it is really only here that Mary Lee becomes a "college widow."

P. 12 [narrative], "Mary Lee and her companion are asked to leave": After the death of the stranger, this is the second major climax in the story, and it is well visualized. Her overt and self-destructive defiance of convention is put in a heartless light by the emphasis on the young student's reaction. It is the kind of scene Joan Crawford could have played brilliantly.

P. 12 [narrative], "She is not particularly solicitous": Again, Faulkner is undercutting what might be taken as Mary Lee's potential for honorable self-sacrifice. When she does the right thing, it is as a lost, detached soul—"weary, fatalistic."

P. 13 [narrative], "she is the companion of middle-aged men": The "wealthy old man" who was her particular friend in *Night Bird* has been excised, further contributing to the sense of Mary Lee's alienation. Her lack of fulfillment gives her toast at the "gay party" in the closing scene an especially forlorn resonance.

P. 13 [narrative], "Robert does not see her": Their not speaking together in this scene departs significantly from Hollywood formula and is an effective, unconventional way of showing Mary Lee's isolation.

FORM 112 10M CITIZEN

Date...

No. ....
Please return to Script Dept.

Culver City Calif.

"THE COLLEGE WIDOW"

From William Faulkner
May 26, 1932

"THE COLLEGE WIDOW"

1. A SMALL SOUTHERN COLLEGE TOWN

Mary Lee Blair is the only daughter of
a Professor in the college. She has
grown there, where young men outnumber
girls twenty to one. She has been very
popular since she was about fifteen or
sixteen, pushed onward by her mother.

She is engaged to a student who will
graduate this year, but now she is just a
little bored. The boys are of a type and
she has had a little too much of them. She
does not particularly want to be married,
and she is not particularly in love with
her fiancee, but she is looking forward to
marriage in order to get away -- actually
to meet more men in whom she can find
romance.

Her fiancee, Robert, is a fine young man,
not exactly a school leader, but dependable
and warm natured. He has a friend, Raymond,
to whom he is very much attached. The
friend is a weak sort. He is a good scholar
and will graduate with distinction.

2. THE PROFESSOR'S OFFICE - NIGHT

A figure steals into the office, rummages
hurriedly in the desk, takes out some
papers and turns to go. He is moving
hurriedly and as he turns his watch, dangling
from his pocket, catches on the desk.
Something flips from the end of the chain.
The man is not aware of it. He exits
hurriedly and stealthily.

3. A STUDENT'S ROOM

Raymond is at a table, hurriedly copying
from the stolen papers. He finishes and
discovers that he has lost the knife from
the end of his watch chain. He shows
consternation -- exits hurriedly.

4. INT. PROFESSOR'S OFFICE - NIGHT

Raymond restores the papers, then in the
darkness he hunts for the missing knife
but cannot find it.

5. STUDENT'S ROOM

Raymond hunts for the knife. He is very
worried. Robert enters -- Raymond tries to
conceal his alarm. Robert notices, but
suspects nothing.

6. PROFESSOR'S OFFICE - NEXT MORNING

The Professor finds the knife lodging in
the desk drawer and sees that the papers have
been tampered with. The initials on the
knife are "R.H."

7. STUDENT'S ROOM

Robert sees that Raymond is greatly worried.
He begins to wonder, then he finds the
copied examination questions where Raymond
has hidden them. He takes Raymond to task
about it and Raymond confesses, telling him
about the lost knife. Robert knows that if
the knife is found by the Professor, Raymond
will be expelled and lose the scholarship
which he is sure to win.

The letter from the Dean comes, asking
Raymond to come to his office. Raymond is
now thoroughly terrified. Robert takes the
knife from his chain and puts it on Raymond's
chain.

INT. DEANS' OFFICE

Three other students, whose initials
are also "R.H." are present. The Dean
wants to know what Robert is doing there.
Robert says he took the papers, that he and
Raymond exchanged knives in their Freshman
year. Raymond is the Professor's favorite
student because of his good record. The
Professor believes Robert at once. Raymond
lets Robert take the blame.

The Dean, however, does not believe Robert.
The others are dismissed. The Dean takes
Robert to task. He sticks to his story. The
Dean tells Robert that it means expulsion.

9.   INT. BLAIR HOME

Robert believes that Mary Lee will now
marry him -- that she will believe the truth
-- and they can go away. But Mary Lee will
not marry him. She is angry at him for
getting himself mixed up in the affair.
She now sees her chance of getting away soon
out where she can meet more interesting men
and college boys gone, or at least deferred.

Robert has almost persuaded her to marry
him anyhow when her father enters. Blair
tells Robert that he must never see Mary Lee
again. Mary Lee has not enough character
to stick to Robert. She says that perhaps
later, when people have forgotten it, she
will come to him. She does not know herself
whether she means this nor not. She is too
busy thinking about her disappointment.

Robert leaves the town.

10.   Mary Lee is more bored than ever. She begins
now to see herself imprisoned in the town
for the rest of her life. The college boys
are so easy for her that there is no longer
any fun making them fall in love with her.

11.   DOWNTOWN

Mary Lee getting out of a car -- she sees
a man watching her. He is a stranger --
handsome, striking looking in a bold and
dangerous way. He is completely different
from the college boys. She knows at once
that he is dangerous and fascinating. For
a moment she is like a bird charmed by a
snake, then she recovers herself and hurries
into the store. She is wrought up. She
at once fears the man and wants to know him.

She is thinking of this when she turns
and the man is beside her. He speaks to her.
Instinct tells her to flee, but she does not.
She tells him her name. At once his manner
is possessive. She does not even know how
to get away from him. She knows that her
college boy technique will not work here.

Before she knows it, he is accompanying her
back to the car where her mother is, and
she is telling her mother that she has met
the man before. The mother feels the man's
dangerous quality, too.

When Mary Lee starts the car and drives
away, she is almost running. It is as though
she hurries away before the man gets into
the car.

12.   INT. BLAIR HOME

Mary Lee is excited and afraid and now
relieved. Right now she doesn't even want
to see the man again. That night she goes
out with a college youth. She is calm now
and she begins to compare the college boy
with the stranger. She wants to see the
stranger again; to feel again the thrill of
danger and excitement. They are driving to
a neighboring town to a dance.

Suddenly she knows that a car is following
them. She believes that it is the stranger
and hopes that it is, yet again there is
that feeling of fear. She does not tell
her companion.

13.   THE DANCE

Mary Lee is watching the door. She is quite
excited. She sees the stranger and feels the
terror again. She wants to flee, but she

13.   Continued (2)

can't. She sees the stranger pass
the men who try to stop him and cross
the floor to her and cut in. Again, as
though hypnotized, she tells her companion
that she knows the man well.

14.   DANCE FLOOR - SOME TIME LATER

Her companion is seeking her, but Mary
Lee is not on the dance floor. He is angry.

15.   DANCE FLOOR - STILL LATER

The dance is over. The dancers are departing
and the band musicians are packing up their
instruments . Mary Lee's companion is now
worried. He is inquiring for her.

Suddenly she rushes in. She is disheveled
and panting. She is concealing something.
He wants to know where she has been but she
says nothing -- only to take her home
quickly.

On the way home she crouches beside him,
telling him to hurry. Now and then she
looks back.

When they reach her home she springs out,
runs up the steps and through the door and
bangs it behind her.

16.   INT. BLAIR HALL

Mary Lee leans against the door, turns
the lock tremblingly.

17.   INT. MARY LEE'S BEDROOM - NEXT MORNING

A maid enters and tells Mary Lee she is
wanted on the telephone. Mary Lee knows it
is the man and will not answer it. Again
she is terrified.

18.   INT. BLAIR LIVING ROOM

Mary Lee's parents have realized that
there is something wrong. Mrs. Blair is
telling the Professor about the stranger
and that there is something not right about
him.

19.   INT. LIVING ROOM - PROF. BLAIR AND MARY LEE

Mary Lee is on the defensive. She is concealing what occurred at the dance last night --
at the same time she is still terrified and
she really does not want to see the man again.
She tells her father that she met him sometime ago -- where she doesn't remember --
she hardly remembers him, even. She exits.

20.   INT. MARY LEE'S BEDROOM

She has now lied successfully and now her
terror begins to abate. She begins to think
of the man once more with desire, but she
knows that she must not see him again. She
tells herself that morning that it is not
right.

The maid enters with a note from the man,
saying he is coming to the house. Mary Lee
is terrified. She does not want her father
to see him. She decides that the only thing
to do is to go out and meet the man and
stop him. She puts on her hat and departs
hurriedly.

21.   STREET - DUSK

A car stops at the corner and Mary Lee
gets out, running. She runs into the house
and up to her room, pausing to listen. She
is quite distracted. She packs a bag
swiftly and writes a note saying she is going
to spend the night with a girl friend.

She takes the bag and leaves with that
distracted air, as though she were being
physically drawn forward.

46

22.   STREET

Mary Lee runs toward the car. The door
opens and she springs in. The car moves on.
We see that the stranger is driving.

23.   A CITY STREET - BEFORE HOTEL

The car stops. The man and Mary Lee get
out and enter the hotel.

24.   INT. LOBBY OF HOTEL

The man is at the desk in the background.
Mary Lee is waiting, terrified, fearful
lest she be recognized. The man joins her.
A porter takes their bags. The man almost
has to support Mary Lee to the elevator.

25.   A ROOM DOOR

The porter opens the door and goes in. Mary
Lee holds back, terrified, pleading.

The man is cold, masterful. He leads her
in.

The porter emerges. The door closes behind
him.

26.   RAILWAY STATION - THE NEXT MORNING

Mary Lee enters, buys a ticket hurriedly --
frightened, looking back over her shoulder.
She runs into the **train.** She shows extreme
fear until the train begins to move.

27.   ANOTHER RAILWAY STATION

Mary Lee descends from the train and enters
a cab.

28.

INT. BLAIR HOME

Mary Lee's terror subsides and now she
is safe. She is worried now about how
her people will take the story. She
conceals her agitation while she meets
her mother. She carries off the situation
very well, though her mother is displeased.

However, greatly relieved and believing
she is safe, she goes to her bath and turns
on the shower and stands beneath it for
a long time. When she emerges she is calm.
She will never do this again, since she has
escaped this time. She believes that the man
will never return and that she will never
see him again.

29.

INT. BLAIR LIVING ROOM - THE NEXT DAY

Mary Lee is reading. The maid enters and
says a man wants to see her. She is not
alarmed, merely curious. She tells the maid
to show him in.

It is the stranger. She is terrified.
She has to promise to meet him to get him
out of the house.

30.

INT. MARY LEE'S BEDROOM

Mary Lee is more terrified than ever. She
no longer feels desire for the man, but
only terror of him, lest her people find out
what she has done. She does not know what
to do. She dare not tell her father, lest
they discover the whole thing. She is wild
with remorse, terror and despair. She decides
to flee -- to go away -- but she doesn't
know where to go.

Then she thinks of Robert, who is now in
a neighboring city. She packs her bag and
waits until late at night when her parents
are asleep. She steals from the house and
walks to the station, expecting to find the
stranger hidden behind every tree.

48

31.　　　　　STATION

　　　　　　When the train departs Mary Lee again looks
　　　　　　back terrified.

32.　　　　　ROBERT'S LAW OFFICE - NEIGHBORING CITY

　　　　　　Robert is at his desk. Mary Lee enters.
　　　　　　She says she has come to marry him. She
　　　　　　hides her agitation somewhat, but she is
　　　　　　urgent. They go to the registry and are
　　　　　　married, that noon.

33.　　　　　INT. BLAIR HOME

　　　　　　Mr. and Mrs. Blair seated. The door bell
　　　　　　has just rung and the maid has come to answer
　　　　　　it. She brings back a message from Mary Lee
　　　　　　telling them she is married. They are
　　　　　　relieved. Blair says perhaps Robert isn't
　　　　　　such a bad youth, after all.

　　　　　　There is a commotion at the door. The
　　　　　　stranger almost forces himself in. Mr. and
　　　　　　Mrs. Blair look up in surprise. The stranger
　　　　　　wants to know where Mary Lee is.

　　　　　　Even Professor Blair senses the strange and
　　　　　　ruthless force which the man possesses. He
　　　　　　tells the stranger where Mary Lee is without
　　　　　　knowing why he did so.

　　　　　　The stranger exits.

34.　　　　　MARY LEE'S AND BOB'S HOME - A YEAR LATER

　　　　　　Mary Lee is ideally happy. The other is like
　　　　　　a bad dream. Robert suspects nothing and
　　　　　　she will never tell him. She is pregnant.
　　　　　　She will devote her life now to her husband's
　　　　　　law career and their child.

35.　　　　　CLOSE SHOT MARY LEE

　　　　　　Suddenly she knows that the stranger is some-
　　　　　　where near. She knows that he has found her
　　　　　　somehow and is waiting -- lurking. She
　　　　　　begins to feel that he is hidden, watching
　　　　　　　　　　　　　　　　　　　continued

35.   Continued (2)

the house day and night -- but she cannot
let her husband see her fear, because then
he may find out the truth about her and the
man. All day long she is in terror. She
does not dare go out, and when Robert comes
home she must put on a different face until
he is asleep. Then her terror returns.

Robert notices that something is wrong and
questions her, but she tries to laugh away
his suspicion. She swears that nothing is
wrong. He thinks her behavior is due to her
condition and asks her to be careful.

36.   BEDROOM

Robert is asleep, though Mary Lee is awake.
Suddenly she knows that the man is in the
house. In her terror she wakes Robert and
tells him the whole story, begging him to
protect her. She is crazed with her fear.

Robert realizes that she is telling the truth.
He gets up and gets his pistol. She is
afraid to be left alone. He tries to soothe
her, but cannot. She follows him and he
tells her to go into the living room and
wait there.

37.   INT. LIVING ROOM

Mary Lee is afraid to turn on the light.
She is weak with terror; it seems to her that
she can hear the two men creeping about the
dark house seeking one another. She hears
a sound in the hall. There is enough light
to show the door. A man's figure comes into
the door and enters the room. She tries to
scream, but can't. Only when the man touches
her does she scream and faint.

38.   HALL

Robert hears the scream, runs to the living
room and turns up the light. Mary Lee lies
on the floor, the man bends over her. Robert
shoots him, killing him.

50

39.   HOSPITAL - A WEEK LATER

Mary Lee has suffered a miscarriage.
She is recovering. She tells Robert that
now they cannot live together after what
she has done, and that she wishes to return
to her father.

40.   INT. BLAIR HOME - TWO YEARS LATER

Mary Lee is at home. Her mother is now
dead and Mary Lee believes that the shock
of the notoriety did it. She tries to
become a college belle again. She must do
something to pass the time. She is divorced
and Robert is now married again. She now
has a reputation and as a woman with a past
she attracts the youth more than ever,
although the faculty does not approve.
Already it is beginning to reflect upon her
father.

Presently the college boys begin to pall
upon her. She seeks about in the town itself
for men who can give her a kick of some sort.
She is known to drink and smoke in public.
Her father's home is almost ostracized by
the better people of the town.

There is one student, a boy of about twenty,
who is very much in love with her and wants
to marry her.

41.   BLAIR HOME - ONE YEAR LATER

Professor Blair is breaking fast. She has now
almost lost out with the college boys, save
the youth who pleads with her to marry him.
She is out late at night now with town men
of equivocal character. She is no longer
invited to the college dances.

42.   COLLEGE DANCE

Mary Lee and a man from the town, a rather
tough sort, have crashed the dance. The
youth watches her dancing with the man, his
expression full of despair. Again he pleads
with her. She laughs at him.

                                continued

42.   Continued (2)

Mary Lee and her companion are asked
to leave. They do so defiantly. Mary
Lee stops and drinks from a flask in full
sight. The last thing she sees is the
despairing face of the youth.

That night he commits suicide.

43.   COLLEGE PRESIDENT'S OFFICE

The President and Professor Blair talking.
The President says he is forced to ask
Prof. Blair to resign. Blair is quite
broken.

44.   BLAIR HOME

Mary Lee is not remorseful because of the
dance episode. She is just quite weary
and here is another day to be got through
somehow. Her father enters, broken.

This is the only life he knows.

She asks him what the trouble is. She is
not particularly solicitous. He tells her
he has been asked to resign. Mary Lee
knows why.

She puts on her hat and goes out. Her
air is weary, fatalistic.

45.   PRESIDENT'S OFFICE - MARY LEE AND PRESIDENT

She asks him if he will recall the request
for her father's resignation if she
will leave the town and never return. The
President says he will.

46.   BLAIR HOME

Mary Lee does not tell her father what she
has done. She merely tells him that she is
weary of the town and the college and is
going away. He has received the recall and
is happy over it.

52

47.   AT THE TRAIN

As it leaves the station Mary Lee is
looking back. Her face is still weary.

48.   NEIGHBORING CITY   - ONE YEAR LATER

This is the same city where she and Robert
lived.

Mary Lee has not yet seen Robert. She now
lives in an expensive hotel -- she must get
money to live on somehow, so she is the
companion of middle-aged men at night clubs
and such.

49.   INT. NIGHT CLUB

Mary Lee is in a gay party. Suddenly she
sees Robert and his wife enter. Robert
does not see her. She lifts her glass
and gives a toast:

            Mary Lee
To the mother of my son!

      THE END

3
Absolution

The third of Faulkner's original treatments, *Absolution* was copied in the Script Department by 1 June 1932; this facsimile is taken from the File Copy. Together with *Manservant* and *The College Widow*, it is useful because it indicates some of the themes Faulkner independently considered suitable for film production and his affinities with Hawks, whom he had not yet met. Significantly, it reveals that while he and Hawks had a similar approach to the dynamics of male bonding, they differed markedly in their attitudes toward women. Although *Absolution* does not contain any dialogue or indications of how Faulkner might have preferred it to be shot, and although it appears to have been written hastily if not carelessly, its use of small-town class conflict, the criminal underworld, and the war suggests that Faulkner was trying to imagine a diverse and complex melodrama with an interesting psychological dynamic and a tense if downbeat finish.

If *Absolution* had been produced, it would have been an interesting example of what Molly Haskell, Pauline Kael, and others have called the "buddy film." The buddy film might generally be characterized as a love story involving two heterosexual males[1] who support, enrich, and occasionally destroy each other; often they divert the energy of their relationship into some kind of shared activity (war, adventure, crime, work), and sometimes a woman threatens to come between them. In the typical case of the MGM film *Manhattan Melodrama* (1934), Clark Gable and William Powell play childhood friends who end up on opposite sides of the law and who both love Myrna Loy. Gable kills a man who would have interfered with Powell's chance to be elected governor. Powell, at the prompting of Loy (now his wife), decides to commute Gable's death sentence and resign, but Gable refuses the offer. The usual role of the woman in these pictures is to help sublimate the sexual energy between the men and yet to point out how much the buddies mean to each other; in Hawks's *Red River* (1948), for instance, it is Joanne Dru who stops the climactic fight between John Wayne and Montgomery Clift, first by shooting at them and second by shouting that anyone could see "that you love each other." Calling such direct attention to love is unusual, but the majority of buddy films do deal with male bonding in a positive and heterosexual context. Although women are definitely a minor presence in such contemporary examples as *Butch Cassidy and the Sundance Kid* (1969), *Absolution* goes far beyond thirties or sixties prototypes in its misogyny. It seems that the only way Faulkner could clarify the lifelong bond between Corwin and John was at the expense of Evelyn.

When an MGM reader synopsized this property in 1940, he identified its "theme" as: "A worthless girl destroys a beautiful friendship between two boys. This influences the boys' later life and eventually leads to their death." As in *Turn About*, *The Sound and the Fury*, and *Absalom, Absalom!*, Faulkner seems here to believe that a single childhood incident can be taken as an emblem and even as an active determiner of the rest of a character's life, an approach that encourages a fairly rigid sense of psychological development but that is useful when constructing tragedy.[2] It is interesting to observe in this treatment the raw outline of the influence of a compulsive fixation, which in the context of a finished work like *The Sound and the Fury* can assume both verisimilitude and profundity. Taken on their own, however, the dynamics of *Absolution* appear simplistic and motivated by an embittered, almost hostile sentimentality. The treatment of Evelyn's utter worthlessness—she is destructive, aimless, and, like Mary Lee Blair, selfish and promiscuous—makes even *The College Widow* appear sympathetic and well-rounded in comparison.

It is apparent that Hawks tempered some of Faulkner's misogyny or at least did not encourage him to organize his scripts around it, since *Today We Live* is a buddy film with a strong heroine whose premarital sexual activity—though it complicates the plot and does temporarily estrange Ann and Bogard—is not presented as a mortal sin. Hawks liked strong women and used them in most of his films, even casting Rosalind Russell in *His Girl Friday* (1940) for what had been a male buddy role in *The Front Page*. Many of the scripts Faulkner wrote for Hawks—notably *The Road to Glory* (1936) and *To Have and Have Not* (1944)—present good and sexually active women in the context of a meaningful male-male relationship; in fact, the relatively generous and positive treatment of Eddy (Walter Brennan) in *To Have and Have Not* is one of Faulkner's most significant departures from Hemingway's novel.

In *Absolution*, however, as the title implies, mortal sin is definitely at issue. Essentially a Roman Catholic term, absolution refers to "the formal remission of sin imparted by a priest as part of the sacrament of penance."[3] John's sin is to have valued Evelyn above Corwin, and his penance is suicide. Although at one point John feels that he killed his friend for Evelyn's sake, neither the killing nor this scrambled rationalization can be taken as his crucial transgression since it is clear that he acted in self-defense at the time. When he kills himself, it is not for Evelyn's sake either, but to confirm his bond with Corwin. That final scene is one of the more uncompromising examples of Faulkner's ending his works at moments of maximum tension rather than with dénouements, and it might usefully be compared with the last lines of his shooting script for *To Have and Have Not*, where Frenchy is *about to* go upstairs to kill the Vichy police.[4]

The buddy-suicide nexus turns up in several other Faulkner works. In both *Flags in the Dust* and *War Birds*, John and Bayard Sartoris engage in dogfight duels with each other and with other pilots, using some of the same tactics as in *Absolution*. In *Flags*, Bayard is not content until he has managed to get himself killed in an airplane; in *War Birds*, Bayard works out a more positive reconciliation with the memory of his brother, though the issue of self-destruction still looms as a subtext. *Turn About* is something of a buddy triangle: the focus of the original story ("Turn About") is on the ways Claude and Bogard come to respect each other, and this theme is maintained in the script despite the heterosexual triangle with Ann; the script goes on to develop the lifelong bond between Claude and Ronnie (Ann's brother). So when Claude proposes that he and Ronnie undertake a suicide mission that will leave Bogard and Ann free to marry, he not only sacrifices himself for his lover and for a friend but most significantly unites in death with his buddy and brother, Ronnie. In *The Road to Glory*, it is a father and a son whose suicide mission removes an obstacle from the sexual relationship between the son's comrade and lover. In fact, one of the few instances of a character's *declining* the option of suicide to resolve a relationship occurs at the end of *The Wild Palms*; the despair and rigidity of Quentin Compson are by far the more typical. In *Mayday*, the sexually experienced knight drowns himself partly because nothing else seems worth doing. *Manservant*, though complicated by questions of race and class, is still the story of one man's giving his life for another and facilitating a marriage, and *The College Widow* opens with a relatively long consideration of what a conscientious male might sacrifice for his friend.

One theme that occurs with varying emphasis in all of Faulkner's

MGM scripts, then, is that of male bonding, and it is in relation to this bonding that Faulkner's judgment of his female characters is often determined. Another concern that is clearly drawn in *The College Widow* and *Absolution*, that is a significant presence in *Turn About*, *War Birds*, and *MLAK*, and that turns up repeatedly in the films of Hawks is the definition of a character through his or her attitude toward honor and the moral isolation that goes with cowardice and irresponsibility. It is significant that *Absolution* is primarily the story of John, the character with the most sensitivity to moral and ethical issues, and that he is led by his childhood gallantry into a situation where he can reclaim his honor only at the cost of his life. Like many of Faulkner's works, *Absolution* turns on a tragic sense of order and presents that order as anachronistic yet valid. To a certain extent, John judges Evelyn as Quentin judges Caddy, finding her betrayal of his image of female virtue so destructive to his concept of how the world has and ought to run that he is unable to continue living in that world. John's valorous assumptions are evident in his defending Evelyn against Corwin in the schoolyard, which in the ironic context of this script is the moment of the Fall, and it is a Fall from a presexual playground or garden in which honor could have flourished, friends could have stayed friends, and class differences would not have been articulated. Evelyn's name is, after all, a variant of Eve. The fact that John and Corwin are interested in Evelyn only because she separated them and that they fight because they cannot acknowledge how important they are to each other—a typically Faulknerian conflict-structure—makes *Absolution* the earliest script in which Faulkner skillfully applied his interest in dialectics. And although most of the dialectical energy is focused in the love-hate of John and Corwin, Evelyn must be seen not only as the catalyst of that conflict but also as one pole of a further dialectic. The latter is not just male versus female; in this context it is the fatal interrelatedness of reality and image, idealism and futility, the valuable and the value-less, and it is both regrettable and significant that in this sometimes powerful and sometimes lamentable script, Faulkner apparently considered woman the negative force in each of those conflicts.

NOTES: INTRODUCTION TO *ABSOLUTION*

1. There are female buddy films too, such as Jacques Rivette's *Céline and Julie Go Boating* (1973). For a good discussion of buddy films, see Molly Haskell, *From Reverence to Rape: The Treatment of Women in the*

Movies (Baltimore: Penguin, 1974), 23–26, 134, and 362–65; see 25 for a highly relevant insight into *To Have and Have Not*. Although the term "buddy film" was coined in the early seventies and is usually applied to recent films in which the buddies are all but homosexual (so that we have Newman and Redford where once we had Wayne and O'Hara or Bogart and Bacall), I feel it serves as a good description of earlier films of male friendship.

2. The children's quarrel at the opening of *Turn About* is a miniature of the entire story; Caddy's muddying her drawers in the branch episode of *The Sound and the Fury* focuses many of her brothers' obsessions and was identified by Faulkner on several occasions as the key scene in the genesis of the novel; and Sutpen's "design" begins when he is sent around to the servant's entrance of a big house by a "monkey nigger."

3. *American Heritage Dictionary*. This raises the question of whether John's suicide will undo the Fall from Grace and the influence of Eve.

4. Bruce Kawin, ed., *To Have and Have Not*, 183. Hawks's film has an entirely different ending.

NOTES: SCRIPT OF *ABSOLUTION*

P. 1 [narrative], "JOHN AND CORWIN are 12 years old": It is not clear whether this script was composed or retyped so carelessly, but my experience with MGM Script Department practice suggests the former. In this paragraph "We learned" should read "We learn," and "Neither John nor Corwin are aware" should of course read ". . . is aware," as "neither of them have" should read "neither . . . has." This treatment is divided into numbered plot developments, some of which could have been developed into scenes. Each leading sentence appears to identify the central topic of each paragraph, but there are exceptions. "THE GIRL'S NAME IS EVELYN," for instance, introduces a discussion of Evelyn while advancing what must have appeared to Faulkner a continuous narrative. Apparently this treatment was written hastily and not revised, which might be taken as an indication of Faulkner's relative lack of interest. Note the southern setting and the emphasis on class.

P. 1 [narrative], "THE PLAYGROUND AT SCHOOL": The crucial childhood incident. Here as later, John is the center of ethical consciousness in the story.

P. 1 [narrative], "Both are now interested in the girl because she was the thing which divided them": Note "thing." This is the only significant psychological insight in the script and the key to its emotional dialectic, and Faulkner complicates it considerably in subsequent formulations, but he does not show how it is supposed to be communicated to the audience.

P. 3 [top], "CONTINUED (2)": An indication that a scene begun on the previous page is continuing. If Scene 8 had gone on to the following page, that one would have been headed "CONTINUED (3)," etc.

P. 3 [narrative], "He does not yet understand that it is because of social position": John is determined by social position (until the war, where his natural merit counts) much as Das is determined by racial background.

P. 3 [narrative], "He is in love with her now": An ironic observation and perhaps an effective way to dramatize the sublimation at work. The subsequent statement that "He believes that he hates her and all women" (4) suggests that a complex scene would be called for if John's three-way ambivalence (loving Corwin, loving Evelyn instead, hating Evelyn) were to be clearly developed.

P. 4 [narrative], "He still believes it to be a hopeless love. He never once thinks of touching her": John is a romantic idealist, and like many of Faulkner's other lost idealistic souls, he gets drunk. Much of the emotional conflict in the script seems to focus in these two lines. There is little difference between an elevated concept of Evelyn's virtue and an outright fear of women, and that fear turns quickly into condemnation when it develops that the virgin can be "touched." This double-edged elevation, in which women are caught at their peril, becomes an important aspect of the rivalry between the men, since John is a sexual naif and Faulkner apparently holds a low opinion of Corwin's sexual aggressiveness, as of course he does of Evelyn's availability. It is also possible to read these lines as a joke at the expense of John's naiveté.

P. 5 [narrative], "He enlisted in the French Flying Corps and is now a pilot": There is some similarity here with Faulkner's own attempts to fly in the war via the Canadian RAF (see Introduction).

P. 6 [narrative], "must keep up the moral of the squadron": A typo for "morale"; this shows up again in Scene 24.

P. 7 [narrative], "and they both go for the weapon": Perhaps a typo for "and then." This scene reveals that Corwin has a sense of honor, and their coming confrontation is appropriately modeled less on the showdown than on the duel (the agreement to meet at dawn, the question of choice of weapons, etc.).

P. 7 [narrative], "John does not fire a shot. He outflies Corwin and forces him down": Compare *War Birds*, 83 (Scene 196).

P. 8 [narrative], "She does not particularly want to marry him but she must marry someone and she is afraid that the man who she does marry will learn about Corwin some day": Compare *The College Widow*, Scenes 9 and 35.

P. 8 [narrative], "Now his boyhood social position is forgotten": An overt statement of the war's role in nullifying class distinctions and perhaps an ironic way of implying that only *some* of the unfortunate effects of the Fall can be undone without drastic penance.

P. 9 [narrative], "For the first time he begins to see her as she is": True to tragic form, Faulkner motivates John's suicide with a powerful recognition scene. The run-on sentences here do not appear to have been created by typos ("He asks her if . . . not to betray her" and "John puts her aside . . . will never harm her").

ABSOLUTION

Original Story by

William Faulkner

June 1/32

60

ABSOLUTION

1.   JOHN AND CORWIN are 12 years old.

We learned that John's parents are without social
position in this small Southern town, while Corwin's
family is one of the old families there. Neither
John nor Corwin are aware of this. They are inseparable companions and too young to be conscious
that there is any difference between them. They
are in the same grade in public school. Corwin is
the more brilliant, the flashier; John is stolid
and more dependable. We learn that Corwin's people
are wealthy. John's of plain circumstances. Up to
this time neither of them have attached any importance to this fact.

2.   THE PLAYGROUND AT SCHOOL.

Corwin snatches a hair-ribbon from a girl and the
girl pursues him but in vain. She cries. John
has been watching. At first he is in sympathy with
Corwin, then his mood changes as though he had seen
the girl for the first time. He tells Corwin to
restore the ribbon. Corwin thinks, at first, that
his friend is joking, but John is in deadly earnest.
They fight. John wins and restores the ribbon.

3.   JOHN AND CORWIN are now enemies.

Both are now interested in the girl because she was
the thing which divided them.

4.   THE GIRL'S NAME IS EVELYN.

Her family is like Corwin's, of the same social
position. She is interested in John who championed
her. She is planning to have a party and she wishes
to invite John. Her parents are upset since John
is nobody socially. They agree to let Evelyn ask
him since they are both just children and some day
Evelyn will learn her position.

5.   JOHN'S PARENTS LIVE QUITE PLAINLY.

His mother is pleased over his friendship with
Corwin, the aristocrat. She is not aware that
John and Corwin are now enemies. She is pleased
and proud when John is invited to Evelyn's party.
John is excited. His interest in Evelyn is
because she is the cause of the rupture between
Corwin and himself, though he does not know this.
He thinks that it is Evelyn, herself, in whom he
is interested.

6.   CORWIN IS INTERESTED IN EVELYN FOR THE SAME REASON.

Though he, too, does not know this. Evelyn is
now the bone of contention and the symbol of
victory between John and Corwin.

7.   AT THE PARTY, John and Evelyn both realize now
that there is a difference between them. John
is awkward and ill at ease. Evelyn sees this
lack of grace and compares him with Corwin.
Corwin sees it too. He knows that he has been
in the wrong and he thinks that he hates John
now. He does everything he can to make John
more uncomfortable, though he really cares for
John very much more than he cares for Evelyn.
He taunts John about his parents, speaking of
them in a disrespectful way. He and John fight.
Evelyn's parents separate them. John knows that
he was in the right. He believes that anyone will
see this. He discovers that Evelyn's parents
have taken Corwin's side without even giving
him a chance to explain. He sees that Evelyn is
also against him. He now has not only lost his
friend but has lost everything which separated
them. He leaves the party.

8.   JOHN'S MOTHER IS WAITING UP FOR HIM.

She is pleased and proud that he has gone to
Evelyn's home among the best people. When he
comes in she sees that something is wrong but
John will not tell her what it is, at first.

CONTINUED:

8.   CONTINUED (2)

He is hurt and bewildered. Her sympathy causes
him to break down. He tells her what happened.
He does not yet understand that it is because of
social position. His mother does not tell him
this. She comforts him and tells him to try to
forget all about it. He goes to bed but not to
sleep. He can neither understand, nor forget it.
His mother is worried, though she believes that it
will pass.

9.   TWO MONTHS HAVE PASSED.

We learn that John's parents are worried about him.
His school work has fallen off. He is now either
absent from school or in trouble with the teachers
all the time and he has been reprimanded for
fighting with Corwin. His mother now knows that
something has happened between Corwin and John,
though John will not talk to her at all. He is
cold and sullen and incommunicative. The mother
wants to leave the town. She knows that somehow
Evelyn is at fault in it and that some day John
will be hurt still more by the difference in their
social positions.

10.   THE FATHER HAS A CHANCE TO SELL HIS BUSINESS.

He does so and they leave town. John is still
sullen and unapproachable. His mother cannot
understand him, but she believes that a change will
cure him - a new town and new friends.

11.   TEN YEARS HAVE PASSED.

We learn that the change has not helped John. He
is now on the highroad to becoming a criminal.
His life is dissolute and vicious. He has run
away from home and is now mixed up in a gang. He
has never gotten over losing his friend, and dis-
covering that the girl for whom he had surrendered
a friend can never belong to him. He is in love
with her now. He clips from papers every reference to her. Keeping them in secret.
                                    CONTINUED:

11.   CONTINUED (2)

He believes that he hates her and all women.

12.   HE IS ON A TRAIN ON BUSINESS FOR HIS GANG CHIEF.

He is a little drunk. While passing through a car,
he sees Evelyn. He knows her, though she does not
know him. He retreats and sobers himself up, in
order to be presentable and he talks to her, telling her who he is. He now knows that he is in love
with her, though it actually is an illusion of her
from his childhood. He still believes it to be a
hopeless love. He never once thinks of touching
her. His only thought is that perhaps some day
he might be worthy of her. He does not tell her
this. He watches her leave the train at the town
where he once lived. Then he goes on to the next
station and buys a ticket back.

13.   EVELYN DOES NOT KNOW THIS.

She does not know how deeply he is moved. We now
learn that she and Corwin are lovers. Evelyn's
parents believe that they will marry, though neither
Evelyn nor Corwin believe this themselves.

14.   SOME MONTHS HAVE PASSED.

John is now living in the same city, working in a
factory. He nurses his boyhood illusion of Evelyn,
believing that he is now making himself worthy to
love her. He is saving his money. She has not
yet seen him, though he sees her now and then from
a distance. Corwin does not know that he is in
the same town.

15.   JOHN HAS NOW GAINED HIS GOAL.

Or served the probation which he set himself. He
goes to call upon Evelyn, who does not know that he
is even in town. He finds Corwin there. He does
not once suspect that Evelyn and Corwin are lovers.
CONTINUED:

15.   CONTINUED (2)

He cannot believe anyone capable of having the
temerity to touch her. He thinks that Evelyn and
Corwin are to be married. He realizes again that
his position is hopeless, that he can never sur-
mount the barrier between them. He no longer hates
Corwin, though Corwin remembering the old days when
John had been right and he wrong, sees in John a
potential rival and hates him.

16.   JOHN DOES NOT SEE THIS.

He sees only hopelessness. He sees that he has
wasted his time, that he can and must love Evelyn
but in vain. He leaves the town.

17.   IT IS NOW 1916.

John is in France. He enlisted in the French Flying
Corps and is now a pilot.

18.   THE UNITED STATES HAS DECLARED WAR.

John is transferred to the United States air service
and is given a squadron.

19.   IN AMERICA CORWIN HAS ENLISTED AS AN AIR CADET.

Evelyn's people still believe that they are engaged
to marry.

20.   CORWIN IS COMMISSIONED AND IS TO GO TO FRANCE.

Evelyn meets him in New York and lives with him
until the transport sails.

21.   JOHN A SQUADRON COMMANDER is expecting some new
       pilots to come up. When they arrive Corwin is among
       them. Corwin believes that he still hates John, for
       the reason that he actually loves John and the
       woman for whom he lost John's friendship was not
       worthy of that sacrifice. John learns that Corwin
       hates him. John must teach Corwin combat flying.
       Corwin is always on the verge of insubordination
       at having to take orders and assistance from the
       man whom he once injured. He thinks that he hates
       John because John is his inferior by birth.

22.   CORWIN'S LIFE DEPENDS UPON JOHN, upon what John
       can teach him. Corwin hates this. He drinks
       heavily. One evening while drinking he begins to
       taunt John. John cannot see why Corwin hates him
       since John believes that Corwin who will marry
       Evelyn has everything that he, John, could want.
       Corwin cannot force John to fight. John restrains
       himself and since he is Corwin's superior must keep
       up the moral of the squadron.

23.   CORWIN IS BENT ON FORCING JOHN INTO FIGHTING HIM.

       He cannot do so with taunts. One day he disobeys
       orders and performs a foolhardy action and is saved
       by luck. John reprimands him.

24.   JOHN STILL HAS HIS CLIPPINGS ABOUT EVELYN.

       He believes that he is protecting Corwin for her
       sake. Corwin believes that John would like nothing
       better than to see him killed, in order to get
       Evelyn himself. One evening Corwin is drunk. He
       tells the other officers that Jonn came from nobody
       and that he, Corwin, beat John out of his girl.
       Then he makes a remark about Evelyn's virtue. At
       last he believes that he has made John fight, but
       John remembers his rank and his squadron moral and
       restrains himself. He lets Corwin strike him
       without striking back. They remove Corwin from
       the room.

25.   WHEN JOHN KNOWS THAT CORWIN is sober and alone, he
seeks him out. He tells Corwin that he must
retract what he said about Evelyn. It never occurs
to John that it can be anything but a lie. Corwin
refuses to retract since it was John who asked
him to, though he is already ashamed of what he
said, but pride will not let him retract. John
takes out a pistol and puts it on the table between
them and suggests that they both count three and
they both go for the weapon. Corwin refuses. He
has been wrong all the while. He knows this and
thinks that he does not deserve an equal chance.
He wants John to have what advantage might be. He
knows that he would not beat John to the gun if
he could and that if John killed him, John would
be executed and his war record blackened. He says
that he will meet John only in flight combat.
John tells Corwin that in flight combat he is sure
to kill Corwin because he has had more experience.
Corwin refuses to listen. He says that if John
will not meet him so, he will shoot John down from
behind the first chance he gets. John agrees to
meet Corwin tomorrow at dawn.

26.   THEY MEET ALONE above the clouds where they cannot
be seen from the ground. Corwin attacks John
trying to shoot him. John does not fire a shot.
He outflies Corwin and forces him down. Corwin is
mad with outraged and injured pride at John's for-
bearance. John still believes that he is saving
Corwin for Evelyn. Corwin believes that John is
merely playing with him as a cat does with a mouse.
He tells John to look out for himself that the next
time that he has a chance that he will shoot John
down.

27.   JOHN KNOWS THAT CORWIN is in a desperate state, but
he still does not know why. He does not believe
that Corwin will actually attack him unawares.
Meanwhile, on all the patrols, John watches over
Corwin to protect him. Corwin thinks that John is
watching him so that he cannot get a chance to shoot
John.

28.　　THE PILOTS ARE PREPARING TO GO OUT ON PATROL.

Corwin is absent. While an orderly is looking for
him, a machine passes overhead. John suspects
nothing. He finds one machine missing from the
line and is told that Corwin is already up. He
still suspects nothing, not until Corwin attacks
him suddenly from behind shooting. At first John
merely dodges, thinking that Corwin is temporarily
mad and will regain control of himself, but Corwin
is in deadly earnest, using all the tricks to shoot
John down that John, himself, taught him. At last
John shoots Corwin down in self defense.

29.　　JOHN HAS DONE THE ONLY THING WHICH HE COULD, yet he
has killed the man whom he believes that Evelyn
loves. It is more than the friend whom he loved.
He surrendered that friend to the woman years ago
and now he has slain her happiness, he believes. It
is his duty, as squadron commander, to send home
notification of Corwin's death. He writes Evelyn
telling her of Corwin's heroism, that he was killed
on duty. He encloses one of his own decorations,
saying that the decoration belonged to Corwin and
signing the letter so that she cannot read his name.

30.　　EVELYN HAS KNOWN FOR SOME TIME NOW that Corwin will
never marry her. She does not particularly want
to marry him but she must marry someone and she is
afraid that the man who she does marry will learn
about Corwin some day. She is engaged to be married
when she learns of Corwin's death. She is relieved,
saved. She is married.

31.　　THE WAR IS NOW OVER.

John returns to the town where Evelyn lives. He is
now front page news, an air hero, etc. Now his
boyhood social position is forgotten. He is sought
as a guest by the best people. He puts them off
in order to see Evelyn. He imagines her as grieving
for Corwin. He thinks her more inaccessible than
ever now.

32.   HE FINDS THAT SHE IS MARRIED.

At first he cannot believe it, then he believes
that she was forced into it somehow, that she is
still grieving for Corwin. He goes to call upon
her. For the first time he begins to see her as
she is. He tells her that Corwin was in his
squadron. He sees that she is terribly afraid.
Suddenly he knows the truth. He asks her if what
Corwin said was true and in her fear she believes
that Corwin had already told John that they had
been lovers and that John will tell it in turn,
she admits it and begs him not to betray her. She
abases herself. He has no intention of betraying
her. He is sick. He gave up the friend he loved
for a woman who was not worth it - finally killed
that friend with his own hand for her sake. He
tries to leave but she clings to him. She wants
to know what he intends to do. He tells her that
he is going to Corwin's father and tell that he
killed his son and take the consequences. Evelyn
begs and pleads. She is afraid for herself, that
her husband will learn of her past. She will go
to any length if John will promise not to tell.
John sees that he can have her for the taking.
John puts her aside, telling her not to worry that
he will never harm her. He goes.

33.   HE RETURNS TO FRANCE.

In his hotel room he takes a pistol and puts it
into his pocket. Then he goes to the war cemetery
where Corwin is buried and finds Corwin's grave.
He draws the pistol from his pocket.

THE END.

A two-page spread from Bogart Rogers's "Flying the Mail," *Hearst's International-Cosmopolitan* (1932).

4

Flying the Mail

Flying the Mail was copied in the Script Department by 3 June 1932; this facsimile is taken from the only surviving File Copy, which in the absence of other materials became the Vault Copy. MGM had optioned the property in February of that year, shortly before it began appearing as a series of articles in *Cosmopolitan* magazine (March through June, 1932). Bogart Rogers, who had flown in the war, wrote *Flying the Mail* as a tribute to "his peace-time buddies of the air." The opening of the first article is typical of the tone of the whole; after an epigraph from "Casey Jones," it reads:

> First the pony express rider, then the engineer, and now the mail pilot—successive idols of American boyhood for a century, symbols of courage, of self-disdain, of high, clean adventure.
> Servants of communication, always exalted to humanity's pedestals, since the expiring runner brought the news of Marathon.
> The express rider faced Indian and bandit; the engineer, train robber and avalanche. For the mail pilot there are more insidious foes—low visibility, the failure of intricate machinery . . .
> They chiseled Herodotus' words into the facade of the New York City post office: "Neither snow nor rain nor heat nor gloom of night stays these couriers from the swift completion of their appointed rounds."
> Now, the post office says it in four words: "*The mail must go.*"
> The air-mail pilot, tuning up for a flight under conditions that would daunt even a military ace, translates it today: "Aw, what the hell!"[1]

Rarely deviating from this dime-novel approach, Rogers strung together a history of the air mail service loaded with amusing and heroic anecdotes, such as the story of a pilot who landed in a cornfield and was chased by a bull, or that of the first coast-to-coast flight and the pilot who fought through bad weather only to find that no relief pilot was available and so flew the next several hundred miles through weather that was even worse, in spite of the fact that he was injured and exhausted. An MGM reader felt that "the subject of the air-mail pilot seems to call for screening as an epic. The article here would be valuable for reference. Besides, as history, it is intensely interesting and thrilling."

have seen the bowed, padded figure of a man shuffling slowly through a snow blanket that steadily thinned and every now and then stopping to yell or throw something at a black bird which stood beside his broken path. Late that afternoon Boonstra dragged himself through the door of an upland farmer's cabin.

The next day, with a party of ranchers, Boonstra toiled back up the mountain, rescued his cargo, packed it down to Coalville, Utah, and placed it safely aboard a train. The whole town turned out to pay homage to the pilot who had cracked up on Porcupine Ridge but had saved his mail.

Such is the fiber of the service you buy with a five-cent air-mail stamp. The letter you drop so casually into the box this afternoon may, before tomorrow, become a prop in some drama as tense as that of Harry Boonstra and the carnivorous magpie. There is scarcely a man flying the western divisions of the transcontinental mail who has not at some time found himself in a dire predicament.

Burr Winslow, forced down during a snowstorm in the Sierras, carried the pouches on his back through the drifts to Truckee. His plane was so securely locked in the wilderness that it could not be hauled out till the following spring.

Paul Scott crashed in Saddle Pass, Nevada, dislocating his shoulder. He set out toward civilization, struck a slippery place and rolled down a thousand-foot slope. Picking himself up, he discovered that the tumble had snapped his shoulder back into place again.

Kenneth Ungar made a forced landing in a clearing in the Ruby Mountains between Salt Lake City and Elko. He borrowed a horse and rode off for assistance. On his way back he fell off the horse and broke his ankle. After the mechanics he had brought had repaired his engine, they bound his broken ankle tightly, and he flew the ship on to Elko, working the rudder bar with one foot.

Bob Ellis, flying over White Mountain near Rock Springs, got into a down-draft that deposited his ship, nose pointing uphill, in a twelve-foot mattress of snow that somehow was clinging to the slope of an eighty-percent grade. He was afraid to move in the cockpit, lest he start a snowslide. Fortunately, the accident had been observed from the town. Rescuers came up and hauled him and the mail out with ropes. The post-office wrecking crew had to dismantle the plane to get it off the mountain.

Claire Vance has flown across the Sierras nearly three thousand times. On one occasion, however, he failed to check in at the end of his run. For two days he was missing. Then he appeared at a mining camp with the sacks slung across the backs of a caravan of burros he had hired from prospectors.

Frank Yager had a different sort of experience one sultry summer night when flying over the Nebraska prairies. The weather was menacing—heat lightning all

Harry Stievers bailed out in a smoky fog near Pittsburgh one midnight but saved the mail sack he was carrying.

around the horizon and not a breath of wind. He was passing over the emergency landing field at Chappell, Nebraska, when suddenly the beacon, twenty miles ahead, was blotted out. Prudently, Yager decided to land. Before his wheels touched the ground, a tornado hit him. The next thing he knew he was sitting on the ground near the twisted mass of wreckage that had been his ship.

Of all the mail pilots of the pioneer period, there is none about whom more tales are told than J. D. Hill. "J. D." is dead now. He and Lloyd Bertaud, a brother mail pilot, set out to fly across the Atlantic and were lost at sea. Hill was a marvelous navigator. Several flying instruments used in (Continued on page 190)

83

From "Flying the Mail": "Harry Stievers bailed out in a smoky fog near Pittsburgh one midnight but saved the mail sack he was carrying."

By 26 April 1932, a 63-page treatment of *Flying the Mail* had been completed by Bogart Rogers, Ralph Graves, and John Lynch. Casting decisions had already been made, for the leading males are called Wallace Beery and Bob Montgomery, while Beery's female friend is called Minnie, a part clearly intended for Marie Dressler (who had won the Oscar for her role in MGM's 1930 hit *Min and Bill*, which also starred Beery). Beery was to play a lovable, seedy ruffian of the old school, the type who flies "by the seat of his pants," and Dressler, the middle-aged virgin who helps him out of jams and hopes that someday he will "assault her." Robert Montgomery was to play a young pilot with new ideas; he falls in love with Beery's daughter Jennifer (apparently uncast). Beery had deserted his wife and infant years before; after her mother's death, Jennifer seeks out her father in order to hurt him, and Bob meets her on a train. Eventually, Jennifer warms up to her father and to Bob; just after they become engaged, Bob makes a favorable impression on some businessmen who want to modernize the air mail service (about which he and Beery have been fighting for a long time) while Beery fails an examination, gets drunk, and leaves town. Years later, Beery returns to Bob's modern airfield, meets his grandchildren—for whom he fashions toy airplanes—and flirts again with Minnie. Bob crashes a mail flight, and Beery goes after him, saves Bob, gets the mail through, and dies.

Subsequent treatments adhered to the 26 April model, dramatizing the history of the air mail service in terms of these four characters. On 3 May, Rogers completed a 21-page treatment that more successfully incorporated many of the historical details from his articles. Bob is introduced about halfway through, again as an adult pilot who develops a romantic interest in Beery's daughter, now called Mary. A new scene has Beery's friend Peewee Vernon (later "Pieface" Johnson) crashing his plane in a fog and makes that the occasion for a rupture between Beery and Montgomery. The ending is basically the same, except that Beery's saving Montgomery leads to a happy conclusion, "with Montgomery and the girl marching down the aisle—and Beery, wearing a uniform with lots of brass buttons—pushing the mail through again." By 13 May, Rogers had written a 37-page treatment that supplanted the earlier two versions. Here, Bob is introduced as a youngster who stows away on Beery's plane by hanging onto the wing (as in Faulkner's Scene 2, pp. 2–3). Beery raises the boy; Mary makes her appearance at a party and not via train. At one point Beery, strapped for funds, begins sending bricks through the mail so that he can collect on the extra weight; Bob confronts him with this but controls his anger so as not to embarrass Beery in front of Mary. When Montgomery is made the boss by the businessmen, Beery gets drunk, loses the $2,000 he had realized from the transfer of franchise, has a fight with Bob over Mary, and then goes through the same ending business (only in the 26 April version does he die).

On 17 May, Ralph Graves drafted twelve pages of revisions that recognizably served as the primary model for Faulkner's treatment. Graves opens with the meeting between Beery and the stowaway "kid," then moves directly into a courtroom scene in which Beery is sued for alimony by his "irate wife." Beery trains Bob to be a wing-walker but loses custody of him after "Pieface" Johnson—a stunt man like Beery—is killed in a crash (no fog). The two meet eight years later when they collide in mid-air (as in Faulkner's Scene 16, p. 8). Montgomery talks Beery into securing an air mail franchise with him. Minnie, who had been more or less written out by Rogers, appears here as the keeper of a boarding house and lunchroom at the airfield where they are based: "We perceive between Beery and Minnie a relationship which is quite intimate but not unclean." Bob meets Mary on a train and learns of her plans to "make mince-meat out of a father who has neglected her for years"; she is presented as "a product of hardship and worldliness" and "somewhat of a wanton." When Montgomery finds out that Beery is the father in question, he has a fight with her but refuses to tell Beery the reason; the two men separate, and Beery later loses his franchise and flying license after it is discovered (when he crashes in a fog) that he has been shipping paving bricks to make extra money. Eventually, Montgomery is given Beery's franchise and hires Beery (who had gotten drunk and disappeared, as before) as a mechanic when they meet again. Mary feels that she is the cause of the bad feeling between the men and decides to leave, after asking Minnie for advice (Minnie advises her simply to keep quiet). It turns out that Montgomery pilots the plane Mary leaves on; they crash, and Mary tends Montgomery's wounds. Beery steals a plane and rescues them, finds that they have made up, and hears and dismissses his daughter's confession of "her true status" and previous destructive intentions (long since abandoned). Beery ends up making toy ships for his grandchildren.

On 18 May, Bernard Fineman wrote a 4-page revision of the Graves draft. He suggested introducing "Pieface" Johnson earlier and killing him later, deleting the business with the Welfare Society so that Beery and the kid remain together, and having Bob enlist in the war as a pilot while Beery is turned down. When Bob finds that his wartime letters have not been delivered to Beery, he reads "Nor rain, nor storm . . ." on the post office building and "it thrills him." They collide in an air meet, secure a franchise, and so forth. Bob meets Mary on a train, but she has no nasty plans for her father. Johnson crashes in a fog, and Bob carries the mail through in spite of Mary's protests. The only other change is significant: Bob sees Mary with "some man" who wants her to hurt Beery for some unspecified reason. When Bob confronts her, Mary refuses to explain herself, and that occasions the fight on which Beery intrudes.

At this point, Faulkner was assigned the task of integrating Graves's and Fineman's revisions into the previous treatments. No matter how silly and formulaic much of this material seems today, it should be clear that Faulkner did a very good job of pulling all this together. Despite the names on the title page, there can be no question that Faulkner had access to the entire file on *Flying the Mail*, since some of his scenes came directly from the Rogers treatments as well as the 26 April version. Nor did he collaborate with Graves, as Blotner asserts,[2] though it is possible that the two men conferred on 1 June. His selection of certain scenes and the emphasis he put on more complex emotions indicate his sure creative hand and decidedly improve the property—which nevertheless was not approved for production. The only other manuscript in the file is a 12 September 1932 "Suggested Ending" by a Mr. Cesana that ignores all of Faulkner's changes and is blatantly ridiculous.

Faulkner began by making the relationship between Wally (Beery) and Min more realistic. In the 26 April version it is said that "Minnie's been a virgin since the days when God wore short pants—a fact which she outwardly proclaims as her greatest asset—and inwardly deeply resents"; she is a gossipy nag who spends her nights hoping that "Beery may be coming to assault her." Faulkner dispenses with this nonsense right away, making them longtime sexual companions and having Min simply hope that someday Beery will marry her. When "the girl" (formerly Mary) goes to Min for advice, Min says, "Look at me and Wally, do you think I have told him all I ever done?"—making it clear that Beery is not her first lover, in a line that is drastically candid and would probably not have made it to the screen.

The affection between Wally and Bob is taken for granted in the earlier versions but treated here engagingly and at length. Scene 9 (p. 5) reads very much like a Faulkner story, from the hen-house to the farmers' looks of "slow amazement." It should be no surprise that Faulkner made much of Bob's flying in the war, nor that in Scene 11

(p. 6) the two men fight about aviation because "Each is ashamed to let the other see that he is loved and will be missed." The male bonding theme is here treated without misogyny, and the word "love" appears three times in this paragraph. Only in this version is Beery illiterate, and this not only casts an irony on Bob's frustrated wartime correspondence—and on Beery's choice of profession: flying mail he cannot read—but also motivates a number of scenes in which Beery's affection for Bob is successfully and visually dramatized (Scene 13, pp. 6–7).

But the most significant change is in the treatment of "the girl." She is running away from Al, a man she has lived with; his dark pursuit of her is comparable in many ways to that in *The College Widow*. In this version the girl really does have something to hide, and her confrontations with Bob seem appropriately less contrived than they did before. When she flees to her father and encourages Bob's affections, she does so because she is in trouble and needs protection. (The theme of pilot father and abandoned daughter reappears in *MLAK*.) But Bob's discovery that she is Beery's daughter takes the script on an unexpected and deeply Faulknerian turn (Scene 20, p. 10): "Then you are almost my sister," he says. She asks whether he wants her to be his sister, and he becomes "quite serious" and says, "Say that again."

All this is distinctly related to the Quentin-Caddy relationship in *The Sound and the Fury* and would show up again in the Henry-Judith-Bon sibling triangle in *Absalom, Absalom!* Even in *Flags in the Dust* (where the siblings are Horace and Narcissa Benbow), the sisterless Faulkner seems continually to associate brother-and-sister affection with the roots of mature love. Bob and the girl begin to fall in love partly because they feel like brother and sister. And "say it again" is a key line in this paradigm, appearing most memorably in a scene between Quentin and Caddy in *The Sound and the Fury*:

> do you love him Caddy
> do I what
> she looked at me then everything emptied out of her eyes and they looked like the eyes in the statues blank and unseeing and serene
> put your hand against my throat
> she took my hand and held it flat against her throat
> now say his name
> Dalton Ames
> I felt the first surge of blood there it surged in strong accelerating beats
> say it again

> her face looked off into the trees where the sun slanted and where the bird
>> say it again
>> Dalton Ames
> her blood surged steadily beating and beating against my hand[3]

In this case "say it again" is associated with the intrusion of sexuality (Caddy's affair with Ames) into what Quentin had idealized as an Edenic sibling relationship; the scene threatens to build to a double suicide but does not, and it is in Quentin's mind when he claims to have committed incest. Although incest is the subtext, the blood intercourse that occurs here is more profound than a sexual one. In *Flying the Mail*, the situation is sublimated and reversed so that the presexual couple come together as if they were brother and sister and so could find love. There is a similar scene between a brother and sister in *Today We Live* (not in *Turn About*, however), where Ann and Ronnie affirm their mutual respect and love,[4] and another in *The Road to Glory*, where LaRoche and Monique express their love just after LaRoche has been talking about his sister,[5] always with "say it again."

The crash of Johnson's plane in the fog is augmented in a manner Faulkner admits is symbolic (Scene 22, p. 11). For the first time, this is used as a love scene—though the argument about flying the mail is taken from Fineman—with Al worked in (via letter, appropriately). What is significant is that the lovers find "each other at last, in some place beyond the world and life." This is the absolute and timeless landscape to which Faulkner's romantic imagination often aspires and which for Quentin and Caddy is foregone, an innocence or freedom from history that many of Faulkner's characters find only in death. Although *Flying the Mail* never became the thrilling epic MGM had envisioned,[6] this treatment has survived as a testimony to Faulkner's emerging professionalism as a screenwriter and as an interesting example of the ways he reworked for Hollywood some of the themes that most closely concerned him as a novelist.

NOTES: INTRODUCTION TO *FLYING THE MAIL*

1. *Cosmopolitan*, March 1932, p. 24.
2. Blotner, *Faulkner: A Biography*, 777–78.
3. William Faulkner, *The Sound and the Fury* (New York: Random, Modern Library, 1967), 202–203.
4. Quoted in Kawin, *Faulkner and Film*, 81.

5. Ibid., 91.

6. Not, in any case, as *Flying the Mail*. Though some of Beery's work in *Hell Divers* (1931) and John Ford's in *Air Mail* (1932) is echoed here, the strongest correspondences between *Flying the Mail* and produced films are with Hawks's *Ceiling Zero* (1936) and *Only Angels Have Wings* (1939). *Only Angels Have Wings* was written by Hawks and Furthman and includes an unforgettable scene in which a mail plane crashes in the fog. (Fog also complicates a mail flight in *Ceiling Zero*.) The 1939 film also includes as one of its major symbols a coin with two heads, which is the closing image of Furthman's script for *Honor*. This suggests that Furthman read Faulkner's *Flying the Mail*—or else that Hawks did, referring Furthman to it—and that both that and *Honor* were salvaged by Hawks and Furthman when they came to make *Only Angels Have Wings*. It is interesting to note how long before *To Have and Have Not* and *The Big Sleep* the connections between Faulkner and Furthman were established.

NOTES: SCRIPT OF *FLYING THE MAIL*

P. 1 [narrative], "Wally is a mixture of child and tramp and blackguard": This description indicates that Faulkner had a good grasp of Wallace Beery's typical screen personality and image. The sparring between Wally and Min at the end of the second paragraph is a very successful example of comic screen dialogue, though Min's retort is reminiscent of such tough Faulkner heroines as Miss Jenny (*Flags in the Dust*).

P. 2 [narrative], "Now we see the plane": Faulkner describes this 1910 "pusher" from his own experience. This sort of detail does not appear in the previous treatments.

P. 2 [narrative], "Wally takes off": Although much of the basic action in this scene is taken from Rogers (13 May, pp. 10–11), Faulkner's version is much more tense and funny. Bob has already been presented as a serious boy, "in dead earnest . . . with that fixed stare." All Faulkner's scripts, when they deal with children, take them seriously and honor their emotions and fixations. Here are some excerpts from the Rogers version: "At the end of the wing a hand appears—just a hand, clutching for something to get hold of. It finally fastens, white knuckled, on the leading edge of the lower wing. Then the top of a head appears—a pair of eyes—that stare in terror at Beery. . . . Beery flies very carefully now—a man's life may depend on the steadiness with which he can control his plane. . . . Finally he is on the wing—secure, with his arms and legs wrapped around strut and wires. Then he looks over at Beery and grins with relief. Beery is relieved, too—but not very pleased about the situation."

P. 3 [narrative], "Johnson is leisurely getting on the train": Here Faulkner employs cross-cutting between plane and train in a competent manner.

P. 4 [narrative], "The judge is not surprised at this": This judge, who does not appear in previous versions, is a recognizable Faulkner creation, and his outraged understanding of flyers injects a "Spotted Horses" brand of country humor into the scene.

P. 4 [narrative], "and has the alienist examine him": An alienist is a specialist in diseases of the mind; the term appears in Graves (17 May, p. 1).

P. 5 [narrative], "MIN IS BUYING A TICKET IN A RAILRAOD STATION": Min's chasing Beery does not appear in earlier versions. "Railraod" is a typo.

P. 6 [narrative], "old Betsy": Backwoods and frontier term for a trusty piece of equipment, usually a rifle; also applied to a trusty old car.

P. 7 [Wally], "me and Bob would have made a sucker out of Rickenbacker and Luke and all of them": Eddie Rickenbacker and Frank Luke were the two most distinguished American fighter pilots in World War I.

P. 7 [narrative], "Bob looks at the device for a long moment": Faulkner does not indicate what Bob's reaction is supposed to be, though Fineman showed him as thrilled. Considering the relative complexity of Faulkner's script and the emphasis in this version on people's difficulty in communicating with each other, this long neutral look is a decided improvement. The basic plot function—this is an "inspiration" scene—is not sacrificed.

P. 8 [narrative], "THE WAR IS OVER": The repetition of this lead sentence is not a mistake but an indication that Faulkner is continuing a pattern of cross-cutting throughout the script; this sequence parallels the previous one.

P. 8 [narrative], "He enters his ship at a meet where it is laughed at,": the comma is a typo. The Spad and the Sopwith Camel were single-seater combat planes developed by the Allies in World War I. The collision with Bob appears in several previous treatments—at greater length—but the comparison between Beery and "a plow-horse strayed onto a race track" is Faulkner's.

P. 8 [narrative], "AT WASHINGTON THEY SEE THE FIASCO OF THE FIRST attempt": In 1918, President Wilson participated in ceremonies surrounding the first air mail flight. As Rogers described the outcome, "The northbound ship got lost and cracked up in a cow pasture. The southbound ship made the flight at no greater speed than the fastest trains" (13 May, p. 2). The latter remark may have motivated Faulkner's business about the relative speeds of planes and trains in Scenes 2, 3, and 4 (pp. 2–3), as well as the argument between Wally and Bob at the top of p. 9.

P. 9 [narrative], "He lands on top of a bull": Rogers's first article tells of Tex Marshall, a pilot who regularly landed in an Iowa cornfield to smoke and stretch his legs. One time he landed there and was chased by a bull; a farmer saved him. When Marshall took off, he tried to drop a stone on the bull but hit the farmer instead (*Cosmopolitan*, March 1932, pp. 27, 159–60). Faulkner efficiently uses this incident to get Bob on the train.

P. 9 [narrative], "Bob means no harm, he is merely accustomed now to taking his girls casually": Faulkner has given much emphasis to Bob's successes with women in order to set up this encounter; in previous versions, Bob is assertive with Mary-Jennifer, but she is the only woman he is ever seen with. In Faulkner's version, "the girl" is a much more sympathetic and vulnerable character than Mary-Jennifer.

P. 11[narrative], "Ecstaticas adolescence. . . . She still fleeing, he still pursuing": Ecstatic as (typo); possible typo for "adolescents." There is an

had to hunt awhile before he located the airport.

The field crew filled him up with hot coffee and the ship with gas. Ten minutes later, exhausted, chilled to the marrow, he was clattering off toward the first gray of dawn. He landed at Chicago soon after daybreak.

Jack Webster took the mail on to Cleveland. Ernie Allison climbed the Alleghenies, glided across the New York City sky line and on to Long Island and set it down safely on Hazelhurst Field. Time from San Francisco, thirty-three hours, twenty minutes; average speed, one hundred and three miles an hour.

The success of this flight silenced Congressional

Two of the dials, however, were sending disquieting messages. One was the clock. Its hands pointed to five minutes past five. The other was the gasoline gauge. It told him that his fuel was three-quarters gone.

Almost every moment since he had roared out of Cleveland at one-forty-five with nine hundred pounds of Newark-bound mail, his eyes had been on these instruments. At his start the weather reports were bad. Nasty stuff ahead: rain, fog—snow, maybe, in the mountains. He hadn't given it much thought then. The radio beacon would guide him through. Just as he was leaving the suburbs of Cleveland, he connected his earphones with the socket on the board and tuned in. "Dzt—dzt"—the code signal from Cleveland buzzed assurance. Bellefontaine's "bzzzt—dzt—bzzt," two hundred miles away, came more faintly. He had

ⓒ Marshall was strolling about in the cornfield when he was startled by a sudden noise from behind. He beat the bull to the fence by a stride.

Illustrations by Clayton Knight

critics and focused national attention on the possibilities of the air mail.

1931. Scene: the sky above middle Pennsylvania. A chaos of winter storm clouds. In them, a speck—a United States mail plane. In the plane a mail pilot, John Wolf. A mile below, out of sight most of the time, a rain-soaked December earth.

Driving steadily eastward, Pilot Wolf sat snugly in the cockpit and kept his goggles turned constantly upon the instrument board. Blind flying. The compass said his course was correct—one hundred and ten degrees. The bank-and-turn indicator told him he was flying straight and on an even keel. One disk marked his speed at one hundred and twelve miles an hour; another assured him his engine was running smoothly at sixteen hundred revolutions a minute.

His training made him feel rather than actually see the readings on a dozen pressure and temperature gauges. But had a single needle quivered past a danger line, it would have brought his attention instantly.

but to follow the invisible signboard of the ether, and he couldn't go wrong. Soon Mercer, Brookville and Bellefonte and beyond would be telling him the weather—and whether he should continue aloft or seek safety on the ground.

Wonderful invention, the airplane radio!

Then, halfway to Mercer, the buzz ceased. John Wolf reached forward and jiggled the plug. He twirled dials and fussed with switches. No use—the thing had gone dead as a disconnected telephone.

This was different! Radio silent, and a good four hundred miles yet to go—four hundred miles of storm. And blind flying through it. Wolf stuck his head up out of the cockpit to look. Not so good. Coming into foothills now, and black snow clouds ahead.

He could go back to Cleveland, transfer the bags to a ship with a working radio, and try it again. But first he glanced back over the rudder. The weather had sealed up behind. Six of one and a half-dozen of the other. What the hell—the mail *must* go!

After an hour of compass (Continued on page 156)

27

From "Flying the Mail": "Marshall was strolling about in the cornfield when he was startled by a sudden noise from behind. He beat the bull to the fence by a stride."

echo here of Keats's "Ode on a Grecian Urn," which Faulkner evidently admired and quoted continually in *Flags in the Dust* (misquoted, actually—he keeps writing "quietude"; see 191 of the 1974 Vintage edition, for example), where it is regularly associated with Horace Benbow's feelings about his sister.

P. 12 [narrative], "how she became frightened of her life and of Al": As in *The College Widow*, the pursuing stranger is a sexual force; as in *Sanctuary*, he is violent. There is a further echo of *The College Widow* in the woman's hoping that her marriage with a man in whom she does not confide will protect her from her past if not erase it.

P. 12 [narrative], "A CRISIS COMES IN THE MAIL SERVICE": This coast-to-coast flight is important in all previous treatments, though they differ in making Beery or Montgomery the heroic pilot. The actual flight occurred in 1921, and the pilot who kept flying in spite of a broken nose was Jack Knight.

P. 13 [narrative], "Bob tells her what he thinks of her for having lied to him": Some version of this fight occurs in most previous versions, but this is the only one that makes dramatic sense and is psychologically credible. Scenes 25, 26, and 27 represent a masterful compression and rearrangement of many long and inefficient scenes.

P. 14 [narrative], "He represents to her the sweetheart which she has lost": One of the more interesting aspects of this script is the way the characters are joined by what separates them (as John and Corwin in *Absolution* become interested in Evelyn "because she was the thing which divided them") or relate to presences (here, Wally) in terms of more significant absences (here, Bob). The emphasis on loss that runs through this script is entirely unprecedented in the previous versions: in them, if Beery loses his license or is separated from Bob, that simply advances the plot. This almost Derridean configuration—which in *Flying the Mail* begins with the fog and letter of Scene 22—is reminiscent in some ways of Addie Bundren's view of language as "a shape to fill a lack"; see *As I Lay Dying*, 164–65.

P. 14 [narrative], "when a man flew by shear guts": Sheer (typo). "Respectful contempt" is a typical Faulkner oxymoron. See Kawin in *Faulkner, Modernism, and Film*, 112–14, for a discussion of the montage aspects of the oxymoron.

P. 14 [narrative], "She watches him from hidding": Hiding (typo). At the right margin the partially obscured words are "thing" and "Eastbound." In previous versions she was not the sole passenger.

P. 15 [narrative], "At last Min tells Wally to go out and find Bob": This is the only version in which Min plays a role in the climax, and the only one in which Beery even considers not saving Bob. The partially smudged words at the end of this paragraph are "passed, as Bob was."

P. 16 [narrative], "just a needle on a dial": The quote should be closed after "dial." "Stricking" should read "striking." "Lose living" should read "loose living." This is the only version that has Min and Wally marry. In the next paragraph, the quote should close after Min's "Don't think you can borrow any more money from me," as after Wally's "maybe we might get married."

P. 16 [Wally], "Rickenbackers and Foncks and Richthofen": René Fonck was a French ace pilot in World War I; Baron Manfred von Richthofen, the "Red Baron," shot down eighty planes and was Germany's most accomplished and ruthless pilot in the war.

FORM 112 10M CITIZEN

Date..

No. ....
Please return to Script Dept.

3577

METRO-GOLDWYN-MAYER

Culver City, Calif.

FLYING THE MAIL

by

Ralph Graves and Bernard Fineman

Continuity Treatment
from
William Faulkner

June 3, 1932

COMPLETE

FLYING THE MAIL.

1.   CLEVELAND 1912.

Wally and Min, they are nearing 40. Wally is a
mixture of child and tramp and blackguard. He is
a swaggerer, yet there is a warm and lovable
quality in him. He and Min are not married, yet
Min's attitude toward him is that of a nagging
wife. We learn that this relationship has continued for some time, during which time Min still
hopes that Wally will some day marry her. Wally
is always moving about, though probably without any
intent of leaving her. A great deal of Min's life
consists of trying to keep up with him, in order
to take care of him, or perhaps just to have him
to nag at.

He is now about to depart on another journey. We
see him in a queer costume of gauntlet gloves and
a hunting cap turned rakishly hind part before
trying to get out of the room while Min rails at
him, believing, as she does each time, that he is
trying to escape from her. Wally tries to smooth
her down in a big offhanded way, which is patently
false. Perhaps Wally thinks to himself that he may
escape this time. He tells her that his is a man's
life. There is no place for a woman in it. Min
rejoins that his is the life of a fool and that no
woman wants to be in it.

Johnson enters. He is dressed somewhat like Wally
though perhaps his clothing is a little breezier.
Wally shushes Min down and Johnson tells Wally to
hurry. Min hushes some though not much, nevertheless
Wally now goes out of the room. We see Min watching
the door with a convincing, determined expression.
Then she begins hurriedly to pack some garments into
a carpet bag and puts on her hat.

2   Wally and Johnson are hurrying, talking. We learn
that Wally is an aviator and that he is about to
make a record non-stop flight of 300 miles to Chicago

They reach the fair grounds running but as soon as
they arrive Wally slows, his air changes completely.
With his chest out and with an expression of majestic
condescension on his face, he now stalks through
the gaping crowd. The word precedes him, "Here
comes the aviator." The people look at him as on
some strange beast with awed respect. Little boys
appear from everywhere following him. By the time

                                    CONTINUED:

84

he reaches the plane he is at the head of a parade.
Now we see the plane. It is a vintage of 1910, a
pusher. Flimsy as a box-kite, where the pilot
sits out in front of it on a slat like a fence
rail and flies with a wheel a little larger than
a dollar watch. It, too, is surrounded by people
who gaze at it with that awed respect and at Wally
as though he were a man from Mars or a madman.

We now see that the most interested one there is
Bob. He is about twelve. He swarms about the
people's legs trying to see, working his way in to
where he can almost touch Wally, where he halts and
fixes upon Wally an undeviating stare of complete
worship.

Dialogue between Wally and Johnson:

Johnson is to go on ahead by train and be there when
Wally reaches Chicago. Wally is trying to retain
his majestic dignity and still persuade Johnson to
hurry on and get the train. Johnson, to whom flying is more or less business, thinks that he will
have plenty of time. Wally is outraged at this
aspersion on the speed of his ship, but he dare
not show it lest the crowd hear. He shushes Johnson
down.

Wally prepares to depart. Bob is still watching
him with that fixed and worshiping stare. He asks
for a ride. Wally puts him aside inattentively,
busy about the plane. Bob returns. Wally now sees
that the boy is in dead earnest. He tells Bob to
run on home. We last see Bob watching Wally with
that fixed stare.

Wally takes off. At once he realizes that there is
something wrong with the ship. He has trouble getting one wing up. It requires all his skill to
keep it in the air. He knows that he can never land
it. He is alarmed. He begins to look wildly about
to see what is wrong, when he freezes still. From
the corner of his eye he can see, out at the end of
the wing, two small dirty hands clinging to a bracing
wire like grim death. In consternation and horror
Wally looks a little further and sees two round
fixed eyes watching him. Wally's horror now becomes
rage, but he dare not show this. He must cajole
Bob in from the wing. He beckons the boy in, trying
to keep upon his face an expression of cajoling and
reassurance, smiling. Bob works his way in while
Wally's smile is a fixed smile. Bob's foot goes
completely through the wing fabric. Again Wally
shows helpless rage, hiding it immediately with
the fixed cajoling grin until he can reach out and
catch Bob by the seat of his pants and haul him
into the seat, then Wally shows his rage and fear.
He spanks Bob while the clumsy plane yawls and skids.
Bob does not resist. He does not seem to be aware

                                    CONTINUED:

85

2.   CONTINUED (3)

that Wally is angry or that he is being whipped.
He is looking down with awe and ecstasy. Bob,
"Gee, I'm flying." Wally intends to take him back.
Bob begs to go on. He tells Wally that he has no
people who will miss him. Wally decides to go on
rather than turn back and abort the record breaking
flight. They now sit side by side. Bob looks
about with ecstasy. Now and then he looks at
Wally with worshiping eyes. Wally catches his
glance. Wally swells with importance. He removes
his muffler and cap and gauntlets and makes Bob
put them on. When Bob sees that Wally can fly the
plane without them, his worshiping admiration is
increased tenfold. Wally is now bursting with
swaggering and vain glory.

3.   Johnson is leisurely getting on the train at the
station. There is no hurry about him at all. On
the train he meets Min with her carpet bag. Min
is determined, inwardly seething, Johnson is not
surprised to see her. After a while Johnson looks
out of the window and sees Wally's plane. We see
the train overtake the plane and pass it.

4.   Wally and Bob see the train overtake and pass them.
Bob is a little shaken by this sight, but Wally
explains it by saying that he is flying slowly
on purpose, so as to give Johnson time to reach
Chicago and get the crowd off the field lest
someone be hurt when he lands. Bob's admiration
increases for this god, who is also humane.

5.   Johnson and Min reach Chicago. Johnson is met there
by his wife with a small basket. An affectionate
greeting. We learn that Johnson and his wife are
on the best of terms. Johnson asks if she has the
pie. She produces it from the basket. He eats it
as they go out to the fair grounds. A great crowd
is awaiting Wally's arrival. Suddenly Johnson sees
a woman and a child in the crowd and he ducks down.
Johnson, "My God, his wife." Min, "Whose wife?"
Johnson, "Wally's. A cop is with her." Min, "Well,
Wally might be scared of her but I ain't- I'll tell
her so." Johnson restrains Min, keeping himself
concealed. Wally comes into sight and prepares to
land. Johnson runs out on the field waving Wally

CONTINUED:

5.   CONTINUED (2)

back, shouting at him to go back to Cleveland, to
go anywhere. Wally merely waves grandly back and
comes in for one of his peculiar landings and steps
from the plane with his majestic air. Bob now
imitates him. The crowd comes up. Then, out of
the crowd comes a policeman and a woman and a
sniffling little girl. When Wally sees them he
wilts like a punctured balloon. He is put under
arrest and the plane is attached. The policeman
takes him away. Min and Johnson follow.

6.   IN THE COURT ROOM.

We learn that Wally deserted his wife and child
years ago and is behind in his alimony for the
reason that he never did pay any of it. The
judge is not surprised at this, he says that any
man who would fly, or would want to fly, is crazy
anyway and would do anything. Mrs. Wally agrees
with this, she has had the same belief for years.
She tells how Wally once attempted to fly from the
barn roof with a pair of home-made wings and lit
on his head. The judge thinks that this might
explain Wally and has the alienist examine him.

Min and Johnson are in the background. Johnson
eating pie again. Wally has been too busy to see
that Min is in the room. Min is restive, but
Johnson restrains her. She now listens while the
doctor examines Wally and shows that Wally does
not rate so high above the ears. Min can be restrained no longer. She rushes forward and wants
to know who says Wally is crazy. Mrs. Wally sees
her and gives Min a high-nosed, sneering glare.
Mrs. Wally, "And this is the slut he left me for -
and what a slut." Min attacks Mrs. Wally with her
finger nails. In the uproar of separating them,
Wally and Bob escape.

7.   THEY RETURN TO THE FIELD running, out of breath. A
policeman is guarding the plane. Wally calms himself and cautions Bob. They approach. The policeman is curious about how the plane works. Wally
explains. He starts the engine and he and Bob get
into the seat, showing the policeman how he sits to
run it. The policeman begins to get suspicious,
but Wally talks fast. The plane begins to move.
The policeman holds to the wing, shouting for Wally
to stop. Bob lams out with a spanner and strikes
the policeman's fingers until he lets go. The
plane soars away. Min arrives at the field still
                                   CONTINUED:

7.   CONTINUED (2)

carrying the carpet bag. She is dishevelled. Her
hair is down and her face is scratched. She asks
where the plane went. The policeman says it went
West. Min departs.

8.   MIN IS BUYING A TICKET IN A RAILRAOD STATION.

She is determined, but calm. Min, "Gimme a ticket
West." Agent, "What town?" Min, "I don't care.
You gimme a ticket West, I'll know where to get off.
If that big slob thinks he can run out on me---"

9.   WE SEE WALLY AND BOB LIVING LIKE TWO GODS, flying
from town to town. They have no ties at all now.
They sleep at night in a hammock strung between
the struts of the plane. They take shelter beneath
it from rain. They start cooking fires with gasoline from the carburetor. They steal or beg bail-
ing wire or cloth to patch it with. Perhaps we see
them both at night running from a hen-house with
something hidden in Wally's shirt, while behind
them dogs bark and shot-guns roar and by day they
strut and swagger while about them gawk farmer
families in slow amazement. Bob is now wing walker.
He is a natural flyer. It is Wally who is concerned
for his safety. He makes Bob wear a life-line, at
the end of which Wally plays him like a fish and
hauls him in and removes and hides the line before
they reach the earth.

10.   WE SEE MIN STILL LOOKING FOR WALLY, asking for him
wherever planes fly, describing him as a tramp, a
bum. They ask her why she does not try to write to
him. She says that Wally cannot read.

11.   THE UNITED STATES IS NOW IN THE WAR.

Bob is now grown. He and Wally try to enlist in
the Air Service. Bob is accepted at once, but
Wally is old and soft and illiterate, obviously a
tramp, nevertheless, he remains while Bob is in
training. He is proud of Bob, but he has only

                              CONTINUED:

88

11.   CONTINUED (2)

contempt for new ships. He believes that if he
could only take his old Betsy to France, he could
outfly anything on either side. Bob laughs at him.
Bob now sees that the plane in which he practically grew up as from a cradle is an obsolete man-trap.
They have their first argument about flying. Bob
is ready to go to France. Wally realizes only now
that he is about to lose the boy whom he has raised
and loved as his own. He has never shown active
affection for Bob and now he does not know how to
show the boy how much he loves him. He has taught
Bob to live a hard undemonstrative life and Bob
also does not know how to show the older man his
affection and gratitude. Each is ashamed to let
the other see that he is loved and will be missed.
Each believes that the other will consider him a
sissy. When they part, it is after a bitter argument about aviation.

12.   BOB IS ON THE TRANSPORT.

His companions notice that he is depressed. He
regrets now that he did not throw shame to the winds
and tell Wally that he loves him.

13.   WALLY ALSO MOPES.

He does not fly now, but sits most of the day beside
his plane which was his and Bob's home. He regrets
that he did not make the first move, though he
believes that Bob would not have liked it if he had,
now that Bob is an officer. Wally, "I am just an
old bum, he must be ashamed of me now." He decides
to find Min. He cannot read and write and he has
tried all his life to keep anyone from suspecting
this, hence he is ashamed to ask anyone to write
for him. He takes his plane and hunts until he
finds Min. She is running a boarding house near a
flying field. He moves in on her. His spirit is
now broken. He knows that he is getting old and
now Bob has left him and even flying is outgrowing
him and leaving him behind. In secret he teaches
himself to print and to recognize Bob's name in
the papers. He also learns to recognize the words
'killed' and 'missing', by subterfuge. He examines
all the papers with news from France in them. Now
and then he sees Bob's name. Bob is a natural
combat pilot, one or two of his pictures are in
the papers. By subterfuge Wally gets someone to

CONTINUED:

13.   CONTINUED (2)

read what is said about Bob. He listens with pride.
He tells Min, "I may be a bum and a back number
myself but I taught him to fly, by God and if they
had just let me take old Betsy to France me and
Bob would have made a sucker out of Rickenbacker
and Luke and all of them." But he still believes
that he will never see Bob again. Bob will return
a hero and he, Wally, is just a bum, who has run
out on every chance he ever had. But he can still
fly his plane. He can still get a little notice at
the fairs. Now and then, he lies a little, telling
gap-mouthed farmers that he was sent back home from
France as being too valuable a man to lose, in order
to keep up public interest in aviation. He earns
a little money, which the upkeep of his obsolete
ship drinks up. Meanwhile Min runs the boarding
house and nags and scolds at him. He lives there
perhaps for $6.00 a week and eats $25.00 worth and
never has the $6.00 to pay. He and Johnson meet
now and then. Johnson is now a flyer with a ship
of his own. His wife still waits for him with his
favorite pie.

14.   BOB IN FRANCE.

Now and then he writes to Wally. He is not certain
whether Wally can read or not, since Wally has
always bluffed it out. When he gets no answer, he
believes that Wally is still angry with him, but
perhaps the letters have never reached Wally. Each
time   we see Bob, he has a different girl.

15.   THE WAR IS OVER.

Bob returns to the States. The war, which separated
him from the only father he ever knew, is finished.
Bob is plumped suddenly down in a strange land. His
first thought is of Wally. Perhaps Wally did answer
the letters. Bob goes to the main New York Post
office. There he finds all the letters which he had
written Wally, unclaimed. This is the end. He
leaves the building. Stopping on the street, he
looks up at the device carved in stone across the
front of the building. 'Nor rain, nor storm, nor any
dark of night shall stay these couriers from the
swift completion of their appointed rounds.' Bob
looks at the device for a long moment.

16.   THE WAR IS OVER.

People are now air-conscious. Wally is flying again
in his ancient plane, which no war pilot would dare
to fly. He believes that his kind alone knows how
to fly. He believes that the war pilots are children
who fly by instruments. His own kind alone fly as
birds fly, by skill and will power and daring.

He enters his ship at a meet where it is laughed at.
The other entries are the new types developed in
the war. Wally says that he can make his plane
do anything that a Spad or a Camel can do. He says
that he can spin it and come out. He is laughed at.
They try to ground his plane, but he insists on his
rights. He goes up; however, they make him wear a
parachute. The fast new ships fly all over him. He
is like a plow-horse strayed onto a race track in
the middle of a race; nevertheless, he puts his
ship into a spin. In the spin, which he cannot
control, another ship, a speed job, crashes into
him. He and the other pilot bail out. They are
both raging. While descending they slip their chutes
close together and in the high floating silence they
curse one another bitterly. They land close together and without waiting to remove the chute har-
ness they fight. In the fight their goggles come
off. Wally and Bob recognize one another.

17.   IN A SALOON WALLY AND BOB HAVE A REUNION.

The coldness with which they parted is explained
away. Bob tells about the letters and about the
device on the New York Post Office and he tells of
an idea of his about flying the mail. Wally scoffs
at the idea. He tells Bob that it can never be done
and that he is too late anyway, that the Government
is just about to attempt such a feat between New
York and Washington, a fool idea of some man who
never had his foot off the ground in his life. Bob
says that it was no groundsman who thought of that
first, that a flyer thought of it first, no matter
who gets the credit. Wally says that no one will
ever get any credit for that idea. Nevertheless
they plan to go to Washington and see the attempt.

18.   AT WASHINGTON THEY SEE THE FIASCO OF THE FIRST
attempt. Bob expects Wally to say, "I told you so."
But Wally doesn't. Wally, "They never gave him a
chance." Bob,"Let's you and me show them how to do
it." Then Wally,"It can't be done. Mail goes from
                                        CONTINUED:

18.   CONTINUED (2)

one set place to another set place like a train.
But who in hell wants to fly like a train? Who
can? You can'tfly by a lot of gadgets with needles,
you fly by the seat of your pants." Bob, "Well, I'm
going to try to get in it. Will you come along, or
will you go back to making bicycles?" They go out
arguing about who taught Bob to fly and if Bob
thinks that he now knows more than his teacher just
because he has shot down a Hun or so. Wally, "If
they had just let me go to France with old Betsy, I
would have made Rickenbacker and Luke both---" They
go out talking.

19.   WE NOW FIND WALLY AND BOB in the mail service at
Cheyenne, as alternating pilots on the Eastern leg.
Bob is still hot after girls and usually has one at
hand. We see the crudities of the air mail at this
time, with obsolete war ships and strips of burning
gasoline for field markers and beacons. Johnson is
also on this division, flying west from Laramie. He
still likes his pies. One day Bob takes off with
the mail and crashes in a pasture. He lands on top
of a bull. The two of them are smothered beneath
the parachute. They fight free of it and the bull
chases Bob up a tree, from which the farmer rescues
him. Nevertheless he saves the mail, flags a train
and puts it aboard and boards the return train himself. In the car, he sees a girl. She is attractive
though plainly dressed.   Bob sets out to
make her. She will have none of him at first, but
at last he manages to get in conversation with her.
She might be a stenographer and she is in some kind
of trouble. She is distracted, as if she were fleeing from something. Bob does not see this. He is
doing his best and gradually she thaws. He does
not see that she has a troubled air and is merely
forgetting her trouble by letting him talk to her.

The berths are prepared. She leaves the car for
a while. Bob means no harm, he is merely accustomed
now to taking his girls casually,- believing that all
of them can be taken. He slips into her berth; he
is there when she returns. She dare not scream or
she will be compromised. He does not touch her and
after a time she is intrigued with the situation,
since apparently he intends no harm to her. She
becomes easier, enjoying the indiscreet situation.
He kisses her before she is aware that he intends to.
Then she is hurt. He has spoiled, killed something.
She cries. He is contrite, apologizes, and leaves
her weeping. In his own berth, he cannot sleep at
once. He is not exactly ashamed, but he has been
attracted by the girl more than he knew especially
as since she resisted him, he believes her to be

                              CONTINUED:

92

19.   CONTINUED (2)

impeccable. At last he goes to sleep and oversleeps
so that he gets off the train at Cheyenne just
before it pulls out. He does not know that the
girl also got off there.

20.   The girl is Wally's daughter, whom he hasn't seen
in twelve years. He had forgotten all about her.
In his philosophy, a girl is merely a woman, another
nagger, while a boy can be taught to be an aviator.
And now, he has raised an aviator after his own
heart, a boy in whom he can see his own triumphs,
even if the boy does pay a little too much attention
to instruments to his notion and now a girl, a
daughter. When his life had just gotten settled
down good where he wanted it, with Bob to fly with
and Min to take care of him. He believes that
he will find in the daughter only the nagging wife
whom he finally escaped. Neither does the girl
know what to expect. She knows her father only as
the man who deserted herself and her mother; from
her mother's picture of him, he is a scoundrel and
a bum. But something has happened to her and she
has had to flee her old life. Her mother is now
dead and there is only her father left to flee to.
She comes to him with her mind made up never to
forgive him. When she sees him, he is just what
she thought that she would find. She is reserved,
cold. Wally thinks at once that she will make
trouble between himself and Min when she finds out.
Min, "If we had just gotten married when I first
said so, it would be all right now." Again Wally
puts her off. Wally, "What do we want to get married
for? We're modern, we're above that."

Bob arrives and finds the girl of the train. He is
ashamed and contrite and is very much attracted now.
Then he learns that she is Wally's daughter. Bob;
"Then you are almost my sister." The girl is worried
and desperate. She has seen her father and has
learned the relationship between him and Min. She
feels that she cannot stay here. She knows that Bob
is ashamed and contrite, and that she was attracted
to him at first. She sees in him a possible source
of help. The girl, "Do you want me to be your
sister?" Bob moves suddenly toward her. He is
quite serious. Bob, "Say that again." They are
both moved.

21.   WE NOW SEE THE BEGINNING OF LOVE BETWEEN THEM.

They are both young. She has suffered somewhere
                                        CONTINUED:

93

21.   CONTINUED (2)

and somehow is still afraid of something. Bob was
aware of this once, but now he can see nothing else
except the girl with whom he is in love. His life
has not been so good, but to her he has been made
clean again. They are shy with one another.
Ecstatic as adolescence. Neither dares to speak
out to the other yet. She still fleeing, he still
pursuing. He has never even kissed her since the
night on the train when he hurt her so. This
pleases both Wally and Min. Wally sees his daughter
falling in love with the boy whom he found and
raised and made into a pilot, after what he believes
is his own image.

The girl has also changed toward Wally. Her love
for Bob has opened her eyes to the qualities in
Wally whom Bob loves. Wally's love for Bob has
also opened his eyes toward the girl. He is proud
of her now. Min loves her and Bob both as the
children of Wally which she should have had and will
never have, also, she hopes that with marriage in
the air some of it may fall upon Wally and herself.
She is the only one that has seen that the girl is
worried about something. She hopes that marriage
will cure this. She asks the girl once what it
was, but the girl was at once watchful and defensive
and answered nothing.

22.   A FOG OVER THE FLYING FIELD.

They are all gathered waiting for the Westbound
plane.Johnson flying it. Mrs. Johnson is present
with the inevitable pie. They are all listening
for the sound of the engine, save Bob and the girl.
They are listening to only one another, he is trying
to make her tell him why she holds him off. The
girl is happy, excited, the thing that troubled
her is now like a dream beyond the barrier of her
love for Bob. She is moved more than ever. She
runs from him into the fog and becomes lost. She
knows that he has followed, but she cannot find him.
She is afraid. The fog becomes a symbol of that
which separates them. At last they find one another
in the fog. It is as though they had found each
other at last, in some place beyond the world and
life. For the first time, she tells him she loves
him. He is humble. He tries to tell her that he
is not worthy of her. She stops him, tries to kneel
before him but he will not let her.

Johnson arrives overhead. He cannot find the field
in the fog. They use what crude gasoline flares
they have, but Johnson crashes and burns. The
scorched mail is hauled out - it must go on. Bob
will take it on through the fog. The girl pleads
with him. Nothing matters to her now but him. She
                                        CONTINUED

94

22.   CONTINUED (2)

cannot see his point of view. He loads the mail
into another ship and goes on. In sorting the mail
the girl finds a letter for herself. It is signed
'Al'. "So I have found you at last. Don't think
you can get away from me. You can look for me any
day."   She is terrified. She doesn't know what
to do, where to turn for help, since she has lied
to Bob and Wally. She needs a woman, someone to advise her. She goes to Min.

23.   SHE TELLS MIN HOW SHE LIVED WITH AL ONCE.

How she was out of work and desperate and let herself be persuaded and how she became frightened
of her life and of Al and ran away from him and
came to her father, who was the only person she
know to come to. How she had come there hating
all men until she fell in love with Bob. She
wants to know what to do, to tell Bob or not.
Min tells her not to tell Bob. Min, "You will only
hurt yourself and him. Look at me and Wally, do you
think I have told him all I ever done?" The girl
decides to take Min's advice. When Bob returns she
clings to him passionately. She believes that his
love will save her and she, in turn, will love him
so much that she will be new and clean again. Her
fear that Al will show up begins to abate. The
distance is great and she has Bob to cling to and
his love to shield her from everything.

They plan now to marry.

24.   A CRISIS COMES IN THE MAIL SERVICE.

The Government is about to discontinue it. This
means that Wally and Bob will lose their jobs and
Bob and the girl cannot marry. A coast to coast
flight is planned to show people how swiftly mail
can be carried. Wally is to fly one stretch, a
second pilot will carry the mail from there to
Chicago, where Bob will pick it up and take it on.
Wally injures his wrist. He manages to get to
Laramie where he will be relieved. He turns the
mail over to the second pilot, who crashes taking
off. There is no relief man. For the sake of his
daughter's happiness, Wally, though injured flies
the mail on to Chicago.

25

SOME TIME HAS PASSED.

The Government has sold the air mail privilege
to private companies. Bob and Wally now have a
franchise for their division. The girl is a clerk
operating the new radio, of which Wally is contemptuous. He says that if a man cannot fly and land
a plane by himself, how can another man on the
ground tell him how to do it on the telephone.
He and Bob have violent arguments about this.
Meanwhile they both do superhuman work keeping the
mail going for the sake of their franchise so that
Bob and the girl can be married. Because of their
limited equipment and their desire to excel, Bob
is setting records on his hops. Each flight brings
him closer to his marriage. His name is now known
as a pilot who gets there quickly.

One night at the Eastern terminal, a man accosts him.
The man is tough looking. He tells Bob that he has
heard what a fast flyer he is and asks him if he
goes back to Cheyenne that fast and says that he
would like to go back with him. Instinctively Bob
does not like the man. He tells the man that he
must be in a big hurry to get back to Cheyenne.
The man says it is to see a girl. He says it in a
way which Bob doesn't like. Bob says that there are
not many girls in Cheyenne worth going there for.
The man says there is one who expects him there and
he names Wally's daughter.

Bob learns that the girl once lived with the man.
Bob beats the man too badly to go anywhere. But
he knows that the man has spoken the truth.
Bob returns to Cheyenne and takes the girl to task.
She admits it to be true. Bob tells her what he
thinks of her for having lied to him. Bob, "If you
had told me the truth at first, it would have been
different, but you lied." In his hurt and anger he
speaks bitterly. Wally enters and thinks that Bob
is insulting his daughter. Bob refuses to explain
for the girl's sake. The girl will not xplain.
Bob and Wally say farewell in anger. The girl is
in despair.

26.   TIME PASSES, THE BIG COMPANIES ARE BUYING IN THE
little ones. They hear of Bob occasionally as he
rises in the service of a big syndicate, but Wally
clings to his franchise. It is all he knows. Again,
he has lost the boy he raised and made a pilot of
and has now only a daughter and flying. He tries to
carry on with the mail, but he is not a business
man and his flying ideas are old fashioned. He is
constantly on the verge of losing, not only his
franchise, but his transport ticket as well.
                                    CONTINUED:

96

26.   CONTINUED (2)

To increase his revenues from the Government, he
cheats. He fills mail sacks with bricks and has
them weighed in and then dumps the bricks out
before he lands. One day he is found out in this.
He loses his franchise. He must now sell out. He
has borrowed money from Min to keep going on and he
sells his franchise to a big company, takes all the
money, gets drunk and loses it. He returns home and
confesses to the woman. Min lights into him
bitterly, but it is only on principle. Her affection
for him is quite deep.

27.   WE SEE THAT NEXT THEY ARE RUNNING A RESTAURANT at
an airport. Min remains through a kind of stupid
fidelity of habit. The girl because she has no
where else to go, but she loves Wally. He represents to her the sweetheart which she has lost.
The airport is now a terminal of a modern line. It
has electric field markers and beacons and radio in
tough with the ships at all times. But still Wally,
who has lost his license, whose one remaining ship
has been grounded by the Government inspectors, has
only contempt for the new fangled ideas and the kids
who fly the ships. At every opportunity he tells
them of the old days when a man flew by shear guts
and optimism. While they listen to him with a kind
of respectful contempt.

28.   A REPORT COMES THROUGH THAT THE TRAFFIC MANAGER
will stop there on an inspection tour. The girl
learns that the man is Bob. She dreads to see him
yet she must. She doesn't want him to see her. She
watches him from hidding and sees him enter the
restaurant. Min is glad to see him. She tells him
he has been a fool. He stops her. Will not let
her talk. Wally enters from the kitchen and sees
Bob. He throws the dishes on the floor and refuses
to serve Bob. The girl sees that the feeling between
them is hopeless, that each hates the other and she
is the cause of it. She decides that the only thing
to do is to leave. She decides to take the Eastbound
plane back to Chicago. She slips out the back and
buys a ticket and gets aboard the plane. It is a
two place biplane with a cabin enclosed and the
pilot's cockpit at the rear. She is the only passen
ger. She crouches alone in the cabin while the ship
                                        CONTINUED:

28.   CONTINUED (2)

waits for the pilot to come out. Bob is in the
Operations Office. There he learns that the pilot
who is to take the ship out cannot come. His wife
is sick. Bob says he will take the ship on to
Laramie himself. He goes out to the ship. He sees
that he has a single passenger, but he doesn't
look closely. The girl recognizes Bob and crouches
back and hides her face. They take off. The weather
is bad, a blizzard drives them down and the ship
crashes. In order to save his unknown passenger,
Bob lands the ship so that he alone is injured.
Bob recognizes the girl. She helps him from the
plane and gets the mail out of it, and gets a fire
started so that they can be found. Bob is helpless.
He tries to make her go on and leave him. She
refuses.

29.   BACK AT THE FIELD THEY ARE SEARCHING FOR THE SHIP.

It cannot be found. At last Min tells Wally to go
out and find Bob. Wally refuses. He will let Bob
die first, because he said what he did say to his
daughter. Min then tells Wally that his daughter
was in the ship too. She tells Wally the truth
about the girl and tells him not to be the same
sort of a fellow about what has passed; as Bob was.

Wally steals his condemned plane from the hanger,
goes out and finds the wrecked plane and lands with
food and supplies. He finds that Bob and the girl
have come to an understanding and they have forgiven
one another. By Wally's almost superhuman efforts
they get Bob to safety.

30.   SOME TIME HAS PASSED, we see a huge modern airport
with the planes coming and going like trains. Bob
is the manager of it. We follow him home and find
Wally with his two grandsons. They are playing
with model airplanes which Wally has made, one of
which is his old pusher. Wally is talking. "If
I had just been in Rickenbacker's place and had old
Betsy, do you think they could have stopped me with
any twenty German planes? Why I would have shot
down at least a hundred." Bob,"Now grandpa, it's
time for your hot milk." Wally rises. He is hale
and strong yet. "Milk, why I can still beat hell
out of any whippersnapper who thinks that flying is
                                        CONTINUED:

98

30.   CONTINUED (2)

just a needle on a dial. He and Bob clinch, stricking each other on the back with effection
and pride. Suddenly Bob becomes mock serious.
He takes Wally aside, very serious, he tells Wally
that now that Wally has grandchildren growing up
he thinks that Wally should set them a better
example than his lose living will. That he should
marry Min. At once Wally resists. Prepares to run
away again, but Bob holds him and persuades him.
Bob sends for Min and tells her Wally has something
to say to her. Exit Bob.

Min, "Well what is it now. Don't think you can
borrow any more money from me. Wally hems and haws
but at last he gets it out. Wally, I kind of thought
maybe we might get married. Min, "Marry -- marry
you, a lousy bum like ---". She stops and begins
to cry. It is the first time Wally ever saw her
cry. He tries to comfort her awkwardly. Min,
brokenly,"It's because I never thought, I was afraid
I never thought you would ever ask me." Wally,
masterfully, his composure regained, "Why sure, I
intended to all the time. I just never got around
to it before." Min, clinging to him still crying,
"I know you're lying, you never done anything to me
yet but lie."

31.   THE WEDDING SUPPER.

They have made Wally put on evening clothes. He is
as much at ease as he would be in steel armour,
nevertheless they get him warmed up at last. Bob
asks him to give a toast to the future of aviation.
Wally, "Aviation, it aint got any future. The
future of aviation is all passed. They aint learned
nothing since 1912. Why if I had just had old
Betsy at the front there wouldn't have been any
Rickenbackers and Foncks and Richthofen." He is
laughed down, still talking. Min comes to his side.
Min, "Shut up, if he says he would have done that,
he would have." The guests all cheer. Wally is
puzzled and pleased too. He begins to swell and
swagger.

                    THE END.

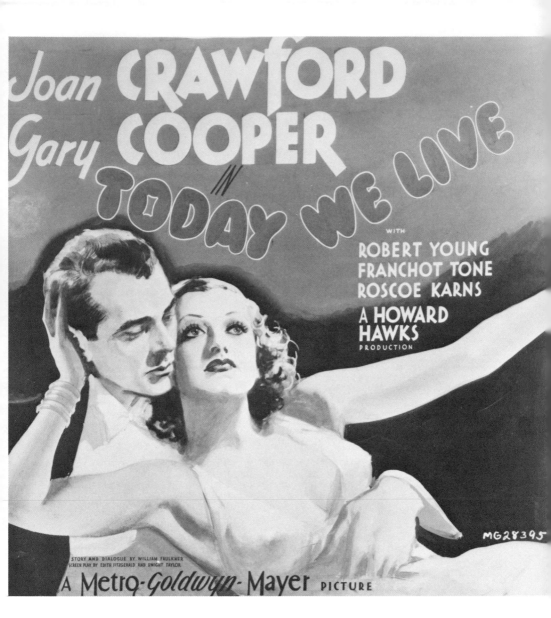

A lobby card for *Today We Live*. (c) MGM. From the collection of Dore Freeman.

Turn About / Today We Live

"Turn About" appeared in the *Saturday Evening Post* on 5 March 1932 and was optioned by Howard Hawks at the suggestion of his brother William. As detailed in the Introduction, Hawks and Faulkner met in July of that year after Faulkner's first MGM contract had expired. In a short five days Faulkner wrote a full-length screenplay that has not survived; Hawks told me that the first draft of *Turn About* was very much like the original story except for a change Hawks had suggested: that Claude be blinded by an exploding shell during the torpedo run with Ronnie and Bogard. Thalberg enthusiastically endorsed this script for production, and Marx put Faulkner back on salary as of 26 July. Within a week, Thalberg told Hawks that Joan Crawford would have to be in the picture, and shortly after that Faulkner received word of his father's death. With Hawks's approval, Faulkner returned to Mississippi and spent the next week completing the second draft of *Turn About*, which is reproduced here. Since this script conforms neither to Faulkner's typing and spelling habits nor to MGM Script Department format, my assumption is that it was copied in Hawks's office; it is typed on tissue-fine paper with the dialogue in red and has several marginal notes in Hawks's handwriting, in pencil. Pages 47–60 were evidently added after a 108-page version had been prepared; then the complete copy was filed at MGM on 24 August.

"Turn About" had been a relatively simple and effective story.[1] Captain Bogard, an American pilot who looks as if he might have been a Rhodes scholar, finds a young English sailor (Claude Hope) blocking traffic on a French street by trying to sleep there. Claude drunkenly explains that his ship is too small to sleep on and is stored under the wharf. Bogard decides to show Claude some combat more dangerous than what he assumes Claude and the boat's commanding midshipman, Ronnie Boyce Smith, encounter in their boat, which he also assumes is some kind of supply or shuttle boat. He and Lieutenant McGinnis take Claude on a bombing mission; Claude takes childlike delight in the adventure and marvels at Bogard's skill in flying and landing with an incompletely released bomb dangling

Joan Crawford and Gary Cooper in *Today We Live*. (c) MGM.

McGinnis, Bogard, and Claude: the "turn about." (c) MGM.

from one of the wings (of which the pilots had of course been unaware). Turnabout being fair play, Claude takes Bogard out on a torpedo run with Ronnie; their boat, it develops, drops a torpedo to the rear and then has to get out of its way. Despite the extreme danger, Claude and Ronnie amuse themselves by playing "beaver," a children's game in which points are made by spotting men with beards, here adapted so that the goal is to spot ships with more or less triangular basket masts. Terrified, seasick, and impressed, Bogard orders a case of Scotch to be delivered to Claude in the street. Later, the boys are killed in action and Bogard conducts a daring raid on enemy headquarters, thinking to himself, "God! God! If they were all there—all the generals, the admirals, the presidents and the kings—theirs, ours—all of them."

When Crawford heard that there had been no plans for a female role in Turn About, she went to Hawks—an old friend—and tearfully apologized. Hawks told her he saw no way for either of them to "get out of this" and suggested they make the best of it. She read the first draft and asked that Faulkner write for her the same clipped British dialogue he had written for Claude and Ronnie so that the picture would be less sentimental than MGM had apparently intended it be.[2] (MGM countered by assigning Adrian to design her a series of ornate gowns and suits; all Hawks could say about these ludicrous outfits was "Jesus Christ!") Faulkner, however, accepted his new instructions without complaint and reworked the story so that Ronnie had a sister, Ann; he made Claude a ward of the Boyce Smith family and had the three of them grow up together, and he developed a romantic triangle among Ann, Claude, and Bogard. In the process he worked in some material from Absolution and something like the branch episode in The Sound and the Fury, without sacrificing the essence of his original story. He also drew on the Kipling story that apparently influenced "Turn About"—"Sea Constables: A Tale of '15"[3]—developing its theme of wartime hostility to "neutrals" in some early scenes between Ann and Bogard.

Faulkner reported back to Hollywood in early October. He wrote several new scenes: a discussion of "damnation" between Claude and Ann; two "say it again" scenes, one with Ronnie and Ann, one with Ronnie and Claude; and one in which Bogard rents the Boyce Smith house (as off-campus housing) and fights with Ann about the sugar ration. Some of these scenes, which considerably intensify the psychological dynamics of the script, are reproduced in the Notes section of this chapter, keyed to the scenes they augment or replace. Evidently at Hawks's suggestion, Marx assigned a young screen-

"Gowns by Adrian . . ." —Ann learns of her father's death. (c) MGM.

writer, Dwight Taylor, to help Faulkner with his revisions. Marx recalls that Taylor was "quite a Faulkner buff," and a publicity blurb Taylor wrote for *Turn About* bears this out.

> "TURNABOUT" [sic] is from a short story by William Faulkner, the famous author of "Sanctuary," "As I Lay Dying," "White Light in August" [sic], etc. It promises to be a picture of unusual distinction. Laid against the colorful background of the Great War, both in England and France, the main characters work out a story of love and sacrifice which has scarcely been equalled for its natural power and sincerity of treatment.
> . . .
> The entire story is written with admirable restraint and with a poignancy which is unusually compelling. The active cooperation of the author himself in the preparation of the script has helped to preserve its fine qualities. Under the distinguished direction of HOWARD HAWKS it can scarcely fail to be one of the most outstanding pictures of the year.[4]

At Taylor's suggestion, Faulkner added a three-part ring worn by Ann, Ronnie, and Claude; it is not clear who decided that the childhood scenes should be presented in flashback, but in any case they were now intercut as reminiscenses during the opening scene, a send-off meal just before the boys are sent to France. This 131-page third draft, marked "from Howard Hawks' office," was copied in the MGM Script Department by 25 October 1932 and represents (except for a few later scenes) Faulkner's final contribution to the project. Because it is not clear how much of it Faulkner wrote on his own (with the exception of a few scenes that exist in independent manuscripts) and because as a piece of writing it is much less interesting than the second draft, it does not appear in this book.

The third draft served as the basic model for later versions; the rewriting became necessary for two reasons. The first was the question of Ann's dialogue. Although Ann is often a formidably incisive speaker in the second draft, Faulkner made her more romantically intense in the third draft, cutting some of her better lines and having her simply cry out "Ronnie! Ronnie!" or the like, even more than she had done in the second draft. Taylor found these outcries "not an adequate substitute for the expression of a thought" and felt that her hysteria was often boring and sometimes ridiculous.[5] Marx assigned Anne Cunningham (who so disliked *The College Widow*) to write a long treatment of the story from the woman's point of view, so that Ann's character might be more fully and intimately developed; what she turned in was extremely sentimental. At that point the script was turned over to Edith Fitzgerald, a sophisticated veteran screen-

Claude and Ann: the send-off meal. (c) MGM.

writer, who wrote Ann a number of very strong scenes (focusing on her activities as a nurse and her friendships with other women) and who had prepared a new script by 28 November. Fitzgerald and Taylor continued to revise this script until it went into production under the new title of *Today We Live*; it is they who received screen credit for the screenplay, while Faulkner was credited with "Story and Dialogue." The second reason for the rewriting was that the children Hawks had hired to play Ann, Claude, and Ronnie in what were now flashback scenes turned out not to be able to learn British accents; Hawks decided to omit the entire opening sequence and to work in dialogue references to these important childhood events as the need arose.

Today We Live was released on 21 April 1933, after several advance showings, one of them in Oxford on 12 April. A few of the changes between it and the second draft deserve mention here. Like the third draft, *Today We Live* includes a humorous subplot—evidently suggested by Hawks—about a large roach named Wellington that Claude pits against a roach named Bonaparte in a barroom equivalent of a cockfight; Wellington gets killed when Claude is grazed during his flight with Bogard. There are of course no childhood scenes: the film opens with Bogard's arrival in England; then the boys leave and Bogard rents the house. Ann and Bogard declare their love for each other in a flat, abrupt, and unconvincing scene (just before she enlists); apparently, Hawks simply threw out Fitzgerald's fuller version and hoped for the best. Most significantly, Bogard's final raid is deleted, along with his powerful curse at the masters of war (which had survived till the shooting script). Ann—her name changed to Diana—was of course played by Crawford. Gary Cooper played Bogard, Roscoe Karns played McGinnis, Franchot Tone (who later married Crawford) played Ronnie, and Robert Young played Claude. The combat sequences are among Hawks's best, and Oliver T. Marsh's cinematography is extremely sharp, rich, and dark (qualities unfortunately missing from the production stills reproduced here).

MGM's publicity department issued a press kit that played up the romantic interest between "Glorious Joan!" and "Ardent Gary!" "CAN ANY WOMAN BE FAITHFUL," they asked, "*in the heart of one man and in the arms of another?*" They called attention to "The only cockroach battle ever filmed," to Franchot Tone's debut, and to the "Romantic William Faulkner Tale of Love 'Behind the Lines.'" One story, addressed to the trade, began:

Ronnie, Ann, Wellington, and Claude. (c) MGM.

MAGIC IN FAULKNER'S NAME

William Faulkner is named as being, with Ernest Hemingway, author of "Farewell to Arms," the greatest literary discovery of the decade.

The former's "Sanctuary" and "Light in August" are still in demand among book shops from which you can expect exploitation cooperation and from librarians who will be glad to help exploit anything which he wrote.

When a 135-minute version was previewed in Pasadena on 16 March, *Variety* found *Today We Live* engrossing, predicted great box-office success, and objected to the monosyllabic dialogue. When the final 110-minute version was shown in New York on 14 April, however, *Variety* panned it: the film was 20 minutes too long, Crawford was unconvincing, Hawks used too much aerial footage from *Hell's Angels*, the "Gowns by Adrian" were extreme and annoying, and the story was superficial. "Treatment of the script will catch attention," they wrote, "in that the effort has been to keep the dialog staccato in the cases of Miss Crawford, Tone and Young to help make them the acme of British repression. It's doubtful if the reaction will be entirely favorable as a worthy intent has been allowed to go overboard via a surplus. Had one character, logically Tone's, been restricted to the one and two-word admonitions of 'Stout fella,' 'Steady,' 'Good girl,' 'Glad,' etc., the effect could have been enlightening. But with all three intermittently in on it the barrage is apt to provoke too many undesired snickers. Hence, for the States it may be that in trying to be smart the writers have outsmarted themselves . . . ."[6] The only career markedly helped by this movie was that of Franchot Tone; in a 1958 interview, Faulkner mentioned "my first picture" and said, "That was Tone's first picture, too—and I still think he owes me a good 5-cent cig-ah."[7]

As a title, one sense of *Today We Live* is that Ann, by giving herself to Claude, has morally "died," and that by sacrificing themselves, Claude and Ronnie make it possible for Ann and Bogard to begin a new life; another sense is existential—that combatants must live in and for the present; there is also an implicit (if not reversed) reference to the script's emphasis on the war's having generated a Waste Land consciousness among its combatants, who were somehow dead regardless of whether they survived (one of the major reasons for Claude's drinking). For the record, it was released in France as *Après nous le déluge* and in Italy as *Rivalità Eroica*. Other MGM releases from that period include *Grand Hotel, Red Dust, Strange Interlude, Men Must Fight, Midnight Mary*, and *What, No Beer?* The film did not make a great deal of money, the opening and closing are fairly weak, and the dialogue is certainly too stiff. But it is by no means a bad film. Compelling, restrained, and satisfyingly long, it certainly merits a revival. If Hawks erred at all, it was during his supervision of the final drafts of the script when he allowed Fitzgerald and Taylor to delete many of Faulkner's more moving passages in exchange for more of the clipped dialogue.

The most significant changes in the plot were worked out between Hawks and Faulkner, judging by those that appear in the third draft; subsequent changes, as indicated above, filled in the details of Ann's wartime service and modified the dialogue. In the third draft, Faulkner sacrificed most of the first fifty pages, deleted the business about Bogard and Ronnie's being classmates at Oxford, had Bogard meet Ann by renting her house (the father's death has left them poor), and had Ann give herself to Claude only when she learns that Bogard has been killed in a plane crash (they meet again in the corridor of a field hospital, when it is too late). He also more fully dramatized the battle scenes but deleted some of the effective montage sequences (p. 46, for example). In retrospect, the absence of some of these plot developments leaves the second draft looking a bit thin. On the other hand, a great deal of what is interesting about the second draft is given such scant attention in the third draft, the shooting script, and the finished film that the second draft appears by far the most effective. The snippets of flashback that Faulkner retained in the third draft (the fight in the brook and the scenes of passing on Ann's care when Ronnie and Claude each leave for school) hardly begin to create the dynamics among these three lifelong friends, and their complete excision from *Today We Live* leaves the film resting on an utterly different balance-point than Faulkner first intended. *Today We Live* is rich where *Turn About* is abbreviated: in the love between Ann and Bogard, which is clearly the focus of the film. The emphasis in *Turn About* is on the deep bonds and shared experience that unite the three children; in that context, Bogard is a catalyst who strains and clarifies the dynamics of the primary, older relationships, rather than the central romantic figure. *Turn About* may be the closest Faulkner ever came to investigating, as Henry James did, the confrontation between American innocence (Bogard's neutrality and the vision of America as a postwar haven) and European complexity, a conflict that focuses—again as in James—in differing attitudes toward candor and sexuality (see p. 89, for example).

The opening scene of *Turn About* is a remarkably interesting reworking both of *Absolution* and of the branch episode in *The*

Sound and the Fury, especially if one goes on to consider Claude's speech on page 62. In that speech, Claude alludes to "the voice that breathed o'er Eden," a line from John Keble's poem "Holy Matrimony," which is itself an homage to "the pure espousal / Of Christian man and maid" and which begins,

> The voice that breathed o'er Eden,
> That earliest wedding-day,
> The primal marriage blessing,
> It hath not passed away.[8]

It is evident that "Holy Matrimony," a popular hymn in Faulkner's circle, was sung at Caddy's wedding. Quentin alludes to it repeatedly, as in this memory of Caddy's running to Benjy after her wedding:

> *That quick, her train caught up over her arm she ran out of the mirror like a cloud, her veil swirling in long glints her heels brittle and fast clutching her dress onto her shoulder with the other hand, running out of the mirror the smells roses roses the voice that breathed o'er Eden.*[9]

Like John in *Absolution*, Quentin has difficulty accepting—as Claude can—the fact that "there's not any Eden anymore," nor any "veils." From the branch episode[10] forward, Quentin resists the evidence that Caddy is an autonomous being capable of taking off her dress and "muddying her drawers," and his suicide is an attempt to deny history, to step out of time into death since he cannot return to the more desirable timelessness of the innocent garden. Both in that novel and in *Absolution*, the blame for the Fall is set on the sexually active woman, and in neither does Faulkner devote significant attention to that woman's thoughts (there is no Caddy section in *The Sound and the Fury*, for instance).

The question arises: what makes *Turn About* so different? The first answer is Ann, who is allowed to be self-reliant and incisive. Despite the fact that Claude and Ronnie feel "girls have no sense" and find it necessary to pass the responsibility of caring for Ann from Ronnie to Claude and from Claude to Bogard, it is clear that Ann is "not a fool," that she is as committed to the war effort as any male, and that she retains her integrity under all circumstances. The second answer, and perhaps the one that explains why Ann is so positively presented, is that in *Turn About* the Quentin figure (Ronnie) has a surrogate self—more or less a brother, since Claude is a ward of their family—who can, without threat of incest, marry his sister. In other words, the incest taboo is sublimated, allowing Ron-

Claude, Ronnie, and Ann: the sibling triangle. (c) MGM.

nie to approve Ann's sexual autonomy because her mate is Claude. This approbation can be transferred to Bogard because the terrors of preadolescent and adolescent sexuality have been passed (as Quentin's never are—he freezes his own development), allowing Ronnie in particular to respond in a flexible and adult manner to changes. This also makes it possible for the story as a whole to celebrate Ann's union with Bogard, who is not even a surrogate sibling: a move away from Eden but not into hell.

All these dynamics are set in motion in the opening scene, then, as the boys fight over the girl who does not (as in *Absolution*) divide them. The fight between Ann and Ronnie is, like that between Caddy and Quentin, provoked by the brother's attempt to control the sister, but it shifts into a free-for-all as Ann defends Ronnie against Claude and the three of them end up sitting in the water. What divides them—or in any case augurs the romantic and military conflicts that will eventually lead to the boys' deaths and Ann's marriage—is the flight of a plane overhead. What replaces the veils is khaki (see p. 62). What creates the sense of doom, of England's being "finished," is the war, and Claude's drinking is similar to that of many of Faulkner's World War I soldiers who are already as if dead in a Waste Land from which the grail has departed or become anachronistic.[11] Because of their sensitivity and toughness, because they support each other while developing self-reliance, Ann and Ronnie and Claude are able to recognize that they "aren't children anymore." Because of his exposure to these Europeans, whom he first loves without understanding, then rejects without understanding, and then finally understands and respects, Bogard is able to become the aviator Ann once planned to marry, in a union that is not that of fixated or idealistic children but that of adults who have learned courage and sacrifice and survival without forgetting how to hope or how to love.

In an early draft of his Nobel Prize acceptance speech Faulkner wrote, "A few years ago I was taken on as a script writer at a Hollywood studio. At once I began to hear the man in charge talking of 'angles,' 'story angles,' and then I realized that they were not even interested in truth, the old universal truths of love and honor and pride and pity and compassion and sacrifice."[12] While it is not certain that he was referring here to his experience at MGM, it is important to observe that *Turn About* does deal with just those old universal truths and in that respect is a key to the intentions and achievements of all the scripts in this volume. Regardless of what might have gone on during story conferences, Faulkner made "love and honor and pride and pity and compassion and sacrifice" the focus and center of every one of these scripts, and the possibility that his unfortunate experiences at Fox and Warner Brothers led him to denigrate the entire film colony and his achievements as a screenwriter should not cut readers off from the satisfactions, the merits, and the humanistic values of his MGM screenplays.

NOTES: INTRODUCTION TO *TURN ABOUT / TODAY WE LIVE*

1. "Turn About" later appeared in *Doctor Martino and Other Stories* (New York: Smith and Haas, 1934) and in Faulkner's *Collected Stories* (New York: Random, Vintage, 1977), 475–509. For the precise genesis of the story, see Blotner, *Faulkner: A Biography*, 732–35.

2. See Harrington and Abadie, eds., *Faulkner, Modernism, and Film*, 168–69, for Hawks's description of his conversations with Crawford.

3. See Blotner, *Faulkner: A Biography*, 118 (note to p. 844, l. 31). "Sea Constables" is available in Rudyard Kipling, *Short Stories: Volume 2*, ed. Andrew Rutherford (New York: Penguin, 1971), 96–113.

4. Dated 21 Oct. 1932.

5. Taylor, "Notes on Final Faulkner Script of 'TURN ABOUT,'" 26 Oct. 1932 (3 pp.). Taylor felt that "the characters remain too much in one key," that the opening scenes between Ann and Bogard were "totally unconvincing and bad," that some of Ann's early scenes were "much too 'literary,'" and that "Mr. Faulkner has used many of the things that I have suggested, but apparently without a clear understanding of the purposes for which they were conceived. As they're used now they are not only meaningless but extraneous. My conception of the ring was exactly opposite from his. My idea was that with the unforeseen possibilities of the war in tearing them apart, the ring was introduced by Ann as a tangible symbol of their always remaining together in spirit no matter what might happen." What he seems most to object to is Ann's giving to Claude her portion of the three-way ring when she decides to sleep with him.

6. *Variety*, 18 April 1933. This review is fairly typical of the film's reception.

7. Howard Thompson, "Through Faulkner's Viewfinder," *New York Times*, 16 March 1958. In that interview Faulkner said, "Well, I made me some money, and I had me some fun. Those were the pictures I enjoyed doing the most, probably my best ones." He was referring to *Today We Live*, *The Road to Glory*, *To Have and Have Not*, *The Big Sleep*, and *Land of the Pharaohs*, all of which were directed by Hawks. (On other occasions he also spoke highly of *The Southerner*, which he did with Jean Renoir.) "Some good pictures come from out there," he went on, "God knows how, but they do. One of my favorites was *Citizen Kane*; and *The Magnificent Ambersons*—and *High Noon*, whatever became of that? Television? You don't say. There's all you need for a good story: a man doin' something he has to do, against himself and against his environment. Not courage, necessarily."

8. *The Home Book of Verse* (New York: Holt, 1922), 1197.
9. Faulkner, *The Sound and the Fury*, 100.
10. Ibid., 19–23.
11. See the "Wasteland" section of Faulkner, *Collected Stories* (407–531), esp. "Ad Astra" and "All the Dead Pilots."
12. Blotner, *Faulkner: A Biography*, 1357.

NOTES: SCRIPT OF *TURN ABOUT* / *TODAY WE LIVE*

P. 1 [margin]: Howard Winchester Hawks signed this copy and penciled marginal notes throughout; the page-number changes (61 onward) were also made in pencil. Most of these are notes on what to show onscreen, how to clarify the action. Beside "TURN ABOUT" he wrote "new title," indicating that he was not satisfied with this one; it seems, however, that *Today We Live* was arrived at only at the last minute, since there are no surviving scripts with that title. Near Ronnie's first speech he wrote "Plant crayfish" (i.e., insert a closeup of the crayfish); near Claude's first speech he wrote "Plant Sister." Toward the bottom he wrote "Name for Claude."

P. 2 [margin]: Near the last narrative paragraph Hawks wrote "look up / make picture of scene—back and forth," calling for shot and reverse-shot crosscutting between the children and the plane.

P. 2 [narrative], "It is a clumsy pusher": An airplane driven by a propeller mounted on the rear end of the engine or propeller shaft, behind the plane's main supporting surfaces.

P. 2 [Ronnie], "You're going to marry Claude": Note Ronnie's continuing attempts to control his sister.

P. 3 [margin]: Near SEPTEMBER Hawks wrote, "Label school tag," calling for an insert shot.

P. 4 [Ronnie], "No. You'll have to stay here and look after Ann": This begins a cycle in which the responsibility of caring for Ann is passed down from one male to another—ultimately to Bogard—despite all the evidence that she can take care of herself.

P. 4 [narrative], "gardner": Gardener (typo).

P. 5 [margin]: Hawks put a question mark opposite Ronnie's calling "Beaver," since there is no mention of a bearded man in this scene.

P. 6 [margin]: Under "Ann and Claude climb up, Claude carrying a letter," Hawks wrote "Hand on rung of ladder shooting down / dialogue give me your hand now careful— / & read address during this." He also inserted "by now" in Claude's first speech, prefacing "The cock of the school?" "Cock" here means chief or foremost figure.

P. 6 [Claude], "We have a good chance at rugger": Rugby football. A "first former" would not be an upperclassman (sixth form is highest), but Faulkner's intention seems to be to show that Claude feels Ronnie has friends in high places.

P. 7 [Claude], "That's private. That's not for girls": Claude is suppressing the line, "Don't forget about taking care of Ann."

P. 7 [margin]: Opposite Claude's third speech Hawks wrote "Plant Claude's going."

P. 8 [Albert], "un": Dialect for "you," at least in this context.

P. 8 [Claude], "And I want you to. eh?": Evidently the period should have been a comma. There are punctuation marks dropped at many points in this script, and only those that might prove confusing have been annotated.

P. 9 [margin]: Before "Claude arrives," Hawks wrote "lapse" (i.e., indicate the passage of time, perhaps with a dissolve). At the bottom right of the page, he wrote "Claude looking everything over."

P. 12 [Ronnie], "I'm his fag": This explains why Ronnie was so nervous and sullen. Fag is a British schoolboys' term for a boy who does menial work for one in a higher form; sometimes such boys were subject to "fagging," or thrashing.

P. 13 [margin]: Above 1914 Hawks wrote "Actors change Here," indicating that from now on Crawford, Tone, and Young were to play Ann, Ronnie, and Claude.

P. 13 [narrative], "Out of the sound of tramping feet and drums scenes dissolve one after the other": This is the earliest and one of the more effective examples of Faulkner's use of the Hollywood montage technique; as opposed to Eisenstein's dialectical montage—of which the first two sections of *The Sound and the Fury* are good examples—the Hollywood montage sequence was usually a series of glimpses of events, often augmented by superimposition, indicating the passage of time or the unfolding of a process. Faulkner's use of sound effects in these transitions is unconventional (most such sequences simply had music tracks) and quite beautiful. See Kawin in *Faulkner, Modernism, and Film*, 103–26, for a discussion of montage theory and its relation to Faulkner's fiction. This particular montage technique reaches its fullest development in *Revolt in the Earth* (1942), Faulkner's unproduced adaptation of *Absalom, Absalom!*

P. 18 [VOICES]: Not a voice-over, but indications for dialogue among the boys in the mess hall. "And his mother dies" should probably read "died." Note that Faulkner's own father had very recently died.

P. 19 [narrative], "hillfrom": Hill from (typo).

P. 20 [narrative], "LIVERPOOL": This is how the third draft and the film begin. Bogard (named Richard in the film, but Harry here; Taylor objected to the original name) goes on from here to a listing agent who directs him to the Boyce Smith home. This is followed in the third draft by a scene between Ann and the local vicar, in which he advises her not to be philosophic but, as a woman, to marry: "If you must be bereaved, be left a mother as well as a widow." "Love? I?" she answers, "Love is as dead as grief, as hope." Speaking of the tenant she has not yet met, Ann says, "Padre, why is he here? Why must he come here from his safe country, to look at us, watch us suffer. 'For study.' Looking at us like an ant hill when you pour the boiling water in." She breaks down, then says, "Perhaps being weak now and then is my way of being strong." At this point they meet Claude and Ronnie, who are on leave; they have five hours before they must report for active duty. On their way home they pass the brook, and there is a dissolve to the crayfish scene; at its conclusion there is a dissolve to the three adults approaching the house. The house dissolves to the house at an earlier time, and the scene of Ronnie's leaving for school is played, with Ronnie taking a cheap ring from his pocket, letting it break into three sections and giving two parts to Claude and Ann ("Ann's is too big"). Over the sound of the horsecart there is a dissolve to the scene of Claude's leaving for school, which in turn dissolves to the three adults passing the gate of their house and discussing what a "neutral looks like." This leads to a long scene between Ann and Applegate, the maid, about the difficulties of running a kitchen in wartime and Ann's careful saving of enough sugar to make the boys a cake. They eat the cake, and at one point Ann asks Ronnie whether she should tell Claude she doesn't love him; Ronnie says to tell him, but she does not. After they leave, Ann receives Bogard (he considers her invitation to tea, in a short note, "Sweet. Like 'Little Women.' Like Louisa Alcott"). At tea, Bogard asks for "just three" spoonfuls of sugar. "*Just* three?" she says, "Are you sure that three will be enough?" "I should think that three would be enough for anybody," he says, as she serves him what he soon realizes is most of her week's ration. When he apologizes, she says, "Why shouldn't you have it, since you have everything else?" and then throws the remaining contents of the sugar bowl at his face. The next time they meet, she calls him a coward. A few days later, Ann and Bogard find each other in a tunnel, taking shelter from an air raid; at Bogard's insistence, they begin singing "Tipperary" to raise the spirits of the others; that night they are shown embracing. Ann writes him a love note and then enlists in the WAAC (Women's Auxiliary Automobile Corps) and is sent to France. Bogard enlists soon after, and the next scene shows Ann reunited with Claude and Ronnie.

The way these scenes are organized in the film—and considerably abbreviated—is as follows. Bogard arrives in London, sees the agent, and meets Diana (formerly Ann) at her house; she has just received word of her father's death in action but says nothing about it. She serves one sugar with his tea, and when he realizes it is rationed he apologizes and says he couldn't drink it now. They look over her father's study, and when he makes himself too comfortable, she becomes upset (but at no point does she lose control, as in the third draft). The servants inform Bogard of the father's death. The next scene is between Diana and the vicar. Claude and Ronnie show up, and the three have their meal (no flashbacks). A week later Bogard and Diana meet on bicycles; he tells her he is going to enlist because he loves her; she says she loves him too, then leaves to join the ambulance corps in France, where she finds Claude and Ronnie.

This brings things up to approximately p. 45 in the second draft.

P. 20 [Porter], "mufti": Plain clothes, as opposed to a uniform.

P. 20 [Bogard], "Yes. I am a Rhodes scholar": In "Turn About" Bogard is described as looking as if he had a Rhodes scholarship (*Collected Stories*, 475). In *Flags in the Dust* (191) Horace Benbow attends Oxford as a Rhodes Scholar.

P. 25 [narrative], "R.F.C. Ground School": The Royal Flying Corps

Bogard and Ann, in a scene deleted from the opening of *Today We Live*.
(c) MGM.

equivalent of ROTC. The "panoramic sequence" was probably supposed to be a Hollywood montage.

P. 30 [Ronnie], "It's only their serpents which are poison": Apparently "their" refers to women in general.

P. 30 [Ronnie], "below the salt": Beneath the amenities. It was often the custom in high British society to set the salt-cellar near the head of the table; those seated "below the salt" (i.e., farthest from the host and distinguished guests) were less prestigious than those above it.

P. 34 [narrative], "He takes her in his arms": This should be followed by a period. Note the way Faulkner continually works in the sounds of warfare, letting them clarify the characters' thoughts.

P. 34 [Clerk], "YOU've": You've (typo).

P. 35 [narrative], "The hill top": An effective repetition and integration of the scenes on 2 and 19, with Claude introducing the theme of maturation. It returns on 36.

P. 36 [narrative], "NAVAL DEPOT AT BLANK": Blank (and later, Dash) are perhaps meant to stand in for the actual locations. See *Collected Stories*, 509.

P. 40 [Claude], "O you putt": Variant of "put," a rascal or dolt. From here on, "Beaver" is called when a ship with basket masts is sighted.

P. 40 [narrative], "Bogard taking flying instruction—his solo": Late in November 1932, Hawks's office sent a scene to MGM (author unknown) in which Bogard does some flashy and reckless practice flying. An officer says, "Did you ever see anyone that wanted to get to France as badly as that chap?" Then Bogard collides with another plane. The subsequent report that Bogard has been killed in this accident motivates Diana's decision to have sex with Claude, both in later drafts and in the film.

P. 41 [narrative], "THE TARMAC": A paved area around a hangar.

P. 41 [Albert], "them bleeding hengines": The engines of such small planes were often unreliable; Albert is suggesting an excuse for lateness.

P. 42 [narrative], "P.O.": Petty officer.

P. 45 [margin]: Hawks crossed out this scene and wrote "Omit."

P. 45 [narrative], "As he does so his tunic becomes American": The dissolve that changes Bogard's wings from British to American is the only one of Faulkner's arty transitions that Hawks used in the film; the snapshot, however, was deleted.

P. 46 [narrative], "M.P.": Military police.

P. 52 [Ann], "Kiss me goodnight, Ronnie": In the third draft, this important scene is longer and clearer. It begins with Claude's rushing in with his new find, the cockroach Wellington. When he runs out to get a bottle to christen it with, Ann tells Ronnie that she loves Bogard, that "He's real" and that Ronnie would have liked him (in this version, of course, Bogard has not met Ronnie or Claude yet). Ronnie suggests that Claude will get over it, but she prefers to remain "Steady" and holds up her ringed hand, saying, "When I took this? When it means the three of us, when divided it isn't even a ring? Never! Never!" "Stout fellow," he responds, and she says, "There! That's what I wanted you to say! Say it again, Ronnie! Say it again!" Ronnie then kisses her, for the first time in their lives, and she reacts in surprise. Then Claude returns and they drink to Wellington. A few days later she gets a letter from Applegate about Bogard's enlisting and trying to find her. The next scene shows her reading the news of Bogard's death, in Claude's presence.

P. 53 [Ronnie], "funk": To smoke or stink from fear.

P. 55 [narrative], "Ann takes bottle from him, pours two huge drinks": An anonymous and undated scene, evidently by Faulkner and pinned to another version of the scene on 60, supplies what had been deleted from the third draft but does appear in the second: an exposition of Ann's decision to sleep with Claude. She finds him drunk on the steps and brings him in so that they can get drunk together. He promises not to break his promise (not to drink) again, but she says, "Don't promise anything—I don't ask you to. We're all damned anyway. What difference does it make what route we take to damnation, Claude—?" He watches her; "she is about to break after the long strain." Then he says, "My love for you is not damnation, Ann. Unless—but even then it's not damnation. I'd still be glad." "Unless what, Claude?" "Unless you wanted to call 'mistake,' I meant." (They have an understanding that when Claude finally proposes, Ann will say "right" or "mistake.") Trying to laugh, Ann says, "Who said I wanted to call 'mistake'?" "I've—I've thought—you haven't seemed the same." "But I am the same, Claude!" she says "bravely," "I am—you silly boy." "Are you, Ann—are you? They've haunted me—your eyes. There's been something in them—something I couldn't—" Ann replies "hysterically," "Damnation, Claude—only damnation—" "I know what you mean," he replies mistakenly (since much of what bothers her is Bogard and the difficulty of being with Claude), "—all this death and dying—the fear of it touching us. Is that it, Ann?" She says "Yes—yes. Hold me, Claude—hold me—" and Claude "lays his head on her breast as she stands above him . . . agony in her face for Richard—as she lifts her head." Bogard was called Richard after the third draft; evidently Faulkner was still supplying Hawks with new scenes. In the film, the scene is calm and moving, with Diana reassuring Claude of her affection and taking him inside.

P. 59 [Ann], "You've kissed me twice now": In the third draft this kiss is saved for an evening scene after Claude has told Ronnie about sleeping with Ann; in the film he kisses her just after Claude's speech. In each instance, the kiss has the same meaning of rare, intimate acceptance, a gesture that in this context is totally unprecedented in Faulkner's work.

P. 60 [narrative], "Boat drifting in toward wharf": In the revision of this scene (see note to 55) Faulkner deleted the excellent business about lying and had the whole encounter take place in an evening fog (perhaps to the same end as the brother-sister fog scene in Flying the Mail). Ronnie kisses Ann after saying "I know," and she says, "Twice you've kissed me, Ronnie." See Kawin, Faulkner and Film, 81.

P. 62 [margin]: Hawks wrote "out" next to Claude's first speech.

P. 63 [narrative], "NIGHT—A NARROW STREET": This is the point at which the story "Turn About" begins. Much of the dialogue is unchanged in this scene (see Collected Stories, 476–80).

P. 67 [McGinnis], "Archie": Fire from an anti-aircraft battery.

121

Claude and Ann: "Who said I wanted to call 'mistake'?" (c) MGM.

P. 67 [Bogard], "herein": Here in (typo).

P. 67 [narrative], "Handley-Page": A British bomber with a crew of five, two Rolls-Royce engines, five machine guns, and a maximum speed of 98 mph.

P. 67 [margin]: Hawks called for a "New scene of start from aerdome."

P. 68 [Bogard], "But he did fire that gun": In the third draft, Faulkner restored a scene from the original story in which Claude displays his prowess with the plane's machine gun, as well as a scene of McGinnis's instructing Claude how to deal with airsickness. See *Collected Stories*, 486–92.

P. 69 [narrative], "Bogard fires the Very signal": A Very pistol was a flare gun; sometimes red, white, and green stars were fired in a special code. At the end of this sentence "follows" should read "follow," and in the next "withon" is a typo for "with on." Claude is manning a machine gun.

P. 70 [McGinnis], "aileron": A movable control surface on the trailing edge of the wing.

P. 70 [Bogard], "Iguess": I guess (typo).

P. 71 [margin]: Hawks made a note to "Show part of fight."

P. 72 [McGinnis], "tracer": A tracer bullet burns in flight.

P. 73 [Bogard], "So you didn't wait for me": In the third draft, Bogard and Ann meet in the corridor of a field hospital and have a beautiful but overwritten reunion. "Darling, you're dead," Ann begins, moving toward him slowly and smiling peacefully, "serene." She goes on, "I'm dead then. I didn't even know it." She almost touches him, then pulls back: "You see, I'm not used to being dead yet. I'm still afraid." They break down into a page of "Harry!" and "Ann!" until Bogard says, "I refused to die. I refused to. Not even when that ship spun and my controls were gone and I was waiting for it to hit. And when I was in the hospital, listening to them saying that I was dead and I was just waiting until the time came for me to say I wasn't dead—" Clinging to him, Ann says, "Yes! I knew! It was one night and I wasn't asleep and I turned and I found that I had turned and I was saying 'You are Harry' before I—before I—" (i.e., before she realized the man beside her was Claude). She struggles away and after another hysterical page says, "You are dead and I am dead. But you died one way and I died another. That's why I'm laughing. Don't you see?" McGinnis intervenes and eventually leads Bogard off. A few pages later, Ronnie finds Claude drinking "to damnation," partly because Bogard is alive and Ann obviously cares for him. This is followed by the scene of Claude's sleeping in the street.

P. 75 [Bogard], "You and your borther": Brother (typo).

P. 75 [narrative], "THE WHARF": At this point "Turn About" resumes. See *Collected Stories*, 493–508. Note the movie images on 503–504. For a description of the Coastal Motor Boats, about which Faulkner learned from a World War I veteran (R. A. Lovett, a model for Bogard), see Blotner, *Faulkner: A Biography*, 732–33.

P. 77 [narrative], "mole": A large stone barrier enclosing a harbor.

P. 83 [Claude], "O damn you!": Claude is being ironic, since he has just gained two points.

Bogard and Ann in the hospital corridor. (c) MGM.

P. 85 [Ronnie], "Nous sommes des touristes Americains riches": We are rich American tourists.

P. 86 [Ann], "That you are anybody": Or (typo).

P. 88 [Ann], "Claude and I are not married": In the third draft, Bogard finds this out when he brings the drunken Claude home from his sleep on the street. The emphasis in this version on lying and candor is considerably more dramatic.

P. 99 [Admiral], "theorder": The order (typo).

P. 101 [Claude], "Takecare of Ann": Take care (typo). Conclusion of the business of passing Ann's care from one male to another. In the third draft, this scene is augmented in a significant way, allowing the love between Ronnie and Claude to be directly expressed and linking them as Ann and Ronnie are linked, in an intense sibling triangle that has room for adult emotion. Claude: "I'm blind—finished! When war's over, will be chap tapping about with stick in everybody's way. And England finished when this over. House gone already. But America, though—far away, out of it; not hurt. Soon people living there get over hurt, forget: children, such. Know what I mean, Ronnie?" Ronnie: "Yes, know one thing—love—you." Claude: "No, not love, just habit. War, maybe. You remember? How we talked as children? Not children now. [Ronnie approaches, stands before Claude] Grown up, now—" Ronnie: "Look at me." Claude: "Eh? What?" Ronnie: "Look at me. [Claude turns toward voice] Say it again." Claude: "What?" Ronnie: "Not love." Claude: "Not love." Ronnie: "You're lying." Claude: "No." Ronnie: "You're lying." Claude [hand gropes out]: "Ronnie. [Touches Ronnie's arm, grasps it] What else, Ronnie?" Ronnie: "Quite [they face one another]." Soon Ronnie starts to leave, intending to take on the suicide mission so that Bogard and Ann can marry, but Claude stops him, pointing out that he need not see to pull the lever. Then they go in to look at the sleeping Ann. In this case, the third draft clearly improves on the second; one interesting change is that the idea to replace Bogard comes from Claude in the earlier version, but the brother in the later one.

P. 106 [Major], "youget": You get (typo).

P. 109 [narrative], "quiltily": Guiltily (typo). Note that they are "like two small boys" in this last scene with Ann, an ironic restoration of the innocent triangle at the instant of adult disaster.

P. 116 [McGinnis], "Areyou crazy?": Are you (typo).

P. 117 [narrative], "Lewis drums": Magazines of ammunition for a Lewis machine gun.

P. 117 [McGinnis], "his Bristol": Evidently the plane Bogard took on 116. In McGinnis's final speech on this page, the partially obscured word is "Right."

P. 119 [narrative], "It has pole masts": Ronnie is generously allowing Claude to catch up at last; this ship would not qualify for a "Beaver." In the third draft (and the film), this scene is longer and more detailed: the torpedo fails to drop twice, and Ronnie tells Claude to take a life belt and jump overboard, but Claude refuses and they die together. Much of this was suggested by Hawks, as the next note shows.

Bogard's view of Ann at Claude's Door. (c) MGM.

P. 119 [margin]: Hawks wrote: "Show torpedo stick on first try—Claude blind—Ronnie has to steer—boat dives straight into enemy ship."

P. 120 [narrative], "A BULLETIN": As in the story, Faulkner completes his tale of turnabout and of parallel heroism by offering two parallel memos. In the third draft, he decided (or was instructed by Hawks, which seems more likely) to show Bogard's raid on the enemy headquarters before dissolving to a final and very short scene between Ann and Bogard in the church (same text as 122, but that is all there is). See *Collected Stories*, 508–509.

P. 121 [Bogard], "That's why I should have been there": Though this has some resemblance to Bayard Sartoris's distress at surviving the conflict that killed his brother, this functions primarily as the close of the theme of Bogard's neutrality and involvement; he no longer wants anyone to do his fighting. But as his great last lines—and Ann's response—show, he has certainly not become a warmonger. Hawks reduced this entire closing scene to a short silent sequence of the couple in the church, with Ann wearing on her thumb all three parts of the ring—an extremely unfortunate substitution, but one in line with his own politics.

B1927

1927

METRO-GOLDWYN-MAYER
STUDIOS

Culver City, Calif.

TURN ABOUT

By

Howard Hawks and Wm. Faulkner

VAULT COPY

August 24, 1932

128

A.W.Hawks *(signature)*

"TURN ABOUT" *(new title)*

ENGLAND - SUMMER, 1910

Three children, wet and muddy, catching crayfish in a brook.
They are Ronnie - 12, Claude - 11, and Ronnie's sister, Ann -
10. Claude is lively, talkative, vivacious; Ronnie is sober,
almost dour. He and Claude are quite busy when Ann comes up.

> RONNIE
> (Turns upon Ann)
> Why do you have to tag along after me all
> the time?

Plant crayfish

> ANN
> I'm not tagging after you. I have just as
> much right here as you have.

> CLAUDE
> We're busy. We can't be bothered with girls.
> Go away.

Plant Sister

> ANN
> I won't.

> RONNIE
> (Approaching)
> Oh, won't you?
> (He is intent and purposeful. Ann
> watches his approach with some alarm)

> CLAUDE
> Oh, she won't hurt anything. I suppose. Let
> her stay, so long as she doesn't muddy the
> water.

Name for Claude

> RONNIE
> (Walks purposefully toward Ann)
> I told you not to.

Claude volatile, is suddenly grave. He follows Ronnie. Ann
holds her ground for a moment, then she falls back. It is
apparent that she knows from experience that she will receive
little mercy from Ronnie.

-1-

129

                         CLAUDE
          Oh, I say now, Ronnie.

                         Ronnie
                (Pays no attention to Claude.
                Suddenly he shoves Ann into
                the brook.
          Didn't I tell you, eh? Didn't I now?

At that moment Claude springs upon Ronnie. They fall to the
ground, wrestling and pummeling one another.

                         ANN
                (Gets up, soaking wet. Rushes out
                and begins to belabor Claude)
          You stop hurting Ronnie! You stop it, now!

 They pay no attention to her; soon the three of them are
inextricable, rolling and surging, drawing nearer and nearer
to the brook, until at last all three roll into the water and
sit up. Claude whooping with laughter. Ronnie is unruffled,
unmoved. He is getting deliberately up when Ann, a damp
thin fury, hurls herself down upon him. Ronnie is about to
hurl her methodically down again, when they all pause.

                         RONNIE
          Listen ----there's the aeroplane.

As one they scramble out of the brook and rush out into an opening, looking up. The aeroplane passes overhead. It is a clumsy
pusher, flying low. Yet to the children it is a thing of magic.

                         ANN
          When I am grown, I'm going to marry
          an aviator.

                         RONNIE
          You're not any such thing.

                         ANN
          Yes I am.

                         RONNIE
          You're going to marry Claude.

                         ANN
                (Looks at Claude)
          Are you going to be an aviator?

                         -2-

130

                    CLAUDE
          Yes.
                    (Looks at Ronnie, who is staring
                    into the sky with a preoccupied
                    air.)

                    ANN
                    (Also looks at Ronnie)
          Are you going to be one too, Ronnie?

                    RONNIE
          What?

                    ANN
          Are you going to be an aviator too?
          Claude says he is.

                    RONNIE
          No. I'm going into the Navy, like I
          always was.

                    CLAUDE
          So am I. I'm going into the Navy too.

                    ANN
          You're scared, both of you.

Ronnie and Claude gaze into the sky with preoccupied airs.

SEPTEMBER

Ronnie preparing to go away to enter school. He is very serious
very much the man. He and Claude are alone. Claude is bustling
about, trying to do things, doing the wrong thing.

                    RONNIE
                    (Annoyed)
          Let be, can't you? What's the matter
          with you?

                    CLAUDE
          You'll have a topping time.

                    RONNIE
          I dare say.

                    -3-

                                                    131

                    CLAUDE
          I wish I were going too.

                    RONNIE
          You aren't old enough. You'll come
          up next year.

                    CLAUDE
          I could work hard.

                    RONNIE
          No. You'll have to stay here and look
          after Ann.

                    CLAUDE
          Yes. But she'll get along.

Ronnie moves to the window. Looking down, he can see a gardner
with a beard, working.

                    CLAUDE (Cont'd)
          I say, Ronnie. Why not?

                    RONNIE
          Beaver.

                    CLAUDE
              (Rushes to window)
          O damn!

                    RONNIE
          I told you, no swearing

                    CLAUDE
          I forgot. That puts you ten up. O da -----O
          dunder.

                    RONNIE
          Remember - no swearing. And look after Ann.
          Girls don't seem to have any sense.

                    CLAUDE
          I will. But I say. I'd work ha -----

                    RONNIE
          Stow it, now.

                    CLAUDE
          Right.

                         -4-

PORTICO OF HOUSE

Ronnie departs for school. His baggage loaded on a dogcart.
His parents, who are Claude's guardians, Ann, Claude present.
Ronnie is still very much the man, quite grave. He tells
them all goodbye. He says goodbye to Ann in a very cavalier
way.

                    RONNIE
                (He comes to Claude)
            Remember, now, look aut for her. She
            hasn't got any sense, you know.

                    CLAUDE
            I will.

                    RONNIE
            And no babying. You'll be coming up
            next year.

                    CLAUDE

            Right.

Ronnie descends and gets into the dogcart and waves. The
cart moves.

                    RONNIE
            Wait.
                (Cart stops.Ronnie descends. He
                comes up to Claude, very grave.
                They all watch him in surprise.
                He looks at Claude)
            Beaver
                (Adds, before Claude can speak)
            No swearing!

                    CLAUDE
            O dunder. O blitzen. Now you are eleven
            up.

Ronnie returns to cart and gets in. Cart drives away.

                    ANN
            You swore.

                    CLAUDE
            I didn't.

                    ANN
            Anyway, you're crying.

                    -5-

                                                    133

                        CLAUDE
        I'm not.

A HAYMOW

Ann and Claude climb up, Claude carrying a letter.

                        ANN
        Hurry. Open it. Perhaps he is in
        trouble.

                        CLAUDE
                (He is exasperatingly deliberate)
        Ronnie? In trouble? The cock of the
        school?

                        ANN
        How do you know he's cock of the school?

                        CLAUDE
        Don't be silly. Do you think he would be
        anywhere without being cock of the school?

                        ANN
        No....open it.

                        CLAUDE
                (Opens the letter, reads)
        "It is quite a bore, waiting for the
        Christmas vacation. We have a good
        chance at rugger. We have that to
        look forward to. Wyatt (He is a first
        former)" ----- What did I tell you?
        Listen: "--Wyatt and I both think we
        have a good chance." Didn't I tell
        you? A first former.

                        ANN
        Yes - yes - go on.

                        CLAUDE
                (Reading letter)
        "---at rugger. Don't forget about taking
        care ......
                (Ceases)

                        ANN
                (Leans forward)
        Taking care of what?
                (Tries to see letter. Claude
                 prevents her.)

                        -6-

134

                    CLAUDE
        That's private. That's not for girls.

                    ANN
        Please.

                    CLAUDE
        No.

                    ANN
        Read the rest, then.

                    CLAUDE
               (Reading)
        "Aylesford, M.A., who teaches Latin, has
        a beard. Beaver. Now I am eleven up."
        O damn!

                    ANN
        Ah, swearing! You told Ronnie you
        wouldn't.

                    CLAUDE
        But eleven up! I don't care. I'm going
        to say it. O damn. There. Shall you tell?
        I shan't marry you if you tell. Are you?

                    ANN
        No. Read the rest of it.

                    CLAUDE
        Didn't I tell you he would be cock of the
        school? He and a first former thinking
        they will have a good chance at rugger.
        Didn't I tell you?

        The beginning of the easter term. Claude preparing to go up to
        Ronnie's school. His baggage is in the dogcart, his foster
        parents and Ann on the portico saying goodbye.

                    CLAUDE
               (Nervous)
        Just a moment. Something I forgot.
               (He rushes out and around to the
                stable, where a stable boy is
                cleaning a harness. Claude
                approaches, Breathless.)
        Albert, I say.

                        -7-

                                                    135

                    ALBERT
        Yes, Master Claude.

                    CLAUDE
        I say. I'm going away to school.

                    ALBERT
        Yes, Master Claude. I'm sure we all
        wishes un a pleasant journey.

                    CLAUDE
        I say. I'll be away you know. And
        there's Ann.

                    ALBERT
        So it is, Master Claude.

                    CLAUDE
        And girls have no sense. You know.
        And I want you to. eh?

                    ALBERT
        Wants un to what, Master?

                    CLAUDE
        Look after her. I promised Ronnie.
        Look after her, eh? Girls have no
        sense. Do you see?

                    ALBERT
        I'll do my best, Master Claude.

                    CLAUDE
        Good. and I say, Albert. I'll fetch you
        something. What?
                (Offers his hand. He and Albert
                shake)
        I'll tell Ronnie. It will make him easier.
                (He turns and rushes back to dogcart)

    Ann is watching him from the steps.

                    GROOM
                (Watching Claude)
        Ain't un going to say goodbye to Miss
        Ann?

                    -8-

    136

                    CLAUDE
            (Pauses, looks back)
    O damn. I daresay I must.
            (Jumps down, rushes to Ann - halts)
    Well?

                    ANN
    Well?

                    CLAUDE
    No mischief, mind, while I'm gone. I've
    told Albert to watch you. But he's work
    to do. Can't tag about after silly girl
    all the time. Try not to be a fool, eh?

                    ANN
    I'm not a fool. I never am.

                    CLAUDE
    Well, don't be. Well...

They look at one another.

                    ANN
    Well?

                    CLAUDE
    I suppose you'll want me to kiss
    you goodbye now.

                    ANN
    You don't have to.

                    CLAUDE
    Might as well. Silly business,
    though.
            (They kiss. They look at
            one another again)
    Well?

                    ANN
    Well?

                    GROOM
            (Dryly)
    Best finish telling un goodbye in a
    letter, young master. T' train munna
    wait.

                    8-A

                    CLAUDE
          Quite. Gad, yes.
                  (Rushes down and into dogcart)

Ann watches it drive away. Claude turns and waves with
a lordly air.

THE STATION

The train comes in. The groom puts Claude into the
compartment.
                    GROOM
          Take care of unself, young master.

                         8-B

138

                    CLAUDE
          I? O gad! I? With Ronnie cock of the
          school? Why, I'll be second cock as
          soon as I arrive. Take care of myself?
          O gad!

Claude is confident and eager. Guard comes through the
train, looks in at Claude.

                    CLAUDE
          O yes. I'm going up to school.

                    GUARD
          After the vacations, eh?

                    CLAUDE
          Well, not exactly. I haven't been
          yet.

                    GUARD
          Oh. Are you going alone?

                    CLAUDE
          Oh, no. Ronnie's there already. He's
          cock of the school. He's the same as
          my brother. I'm going to marry his
          sister, that is.

                    GUARD
          I see. You'll be all right, then.

                    CLAUDE
          O, quite. He's cock of the school.

Claude arrives, Ronnie meets him. Ronnie's air is strained, a
little distracted. Claude is bubbling with eager excitement -
talkative. He does not see that Ronnie is more than usually
sober, almost morose, watchful.

                    CLAUDE
          She'll be all right. I asked Albert to
          look after her. I told him girls don't
          have any sense. He said he would.

                    RONNIE
          Come along; come along.

                         -9-

                                                        139

They reach the dormitory.

                    CLAUDE
              (Looking at all the cots)
         O gad! You have them all here where you
         can watch them all the time.

                    RONNIE
              (More nervous than ever)
         I must cut along for a moment. You
         wait here.

                    CLAUDE
         I'll come with you.

                    RONNIE
         No - you wait here.

                    CLAUDE
         I shan't mind coming. I've nothing to
         do
              (He is happy, eager.)

                    RONNIE
              (Looks at Claude with a kind of
               helpless distraction)
         Damn!

                    CLAUDE
         Oh, damn! You're swearing too.

Ronnie doesn't answer. He goes out, Claude following, still
talking. They cross the quad and approach another building.

                    RONNIE
              (Stops)
         Look here.

                    CLAUDE
         Yes. You have some   з of them here too?
         No wonder you are so   usy.

                    RONNIE
         Damn!

They mount to a door and Ronnie knocks.

                    CLAUDE
         O Gad! Is this the head master?

                    -10-

140

Ronnie does not answer.

> VOICE
> (Beyond door)
> Come.

They enter. Ronnie is quite diffident. Claude apes him. The room is occupied by three seniors, boys not so very much larger than Claude.

> FIRST
> Where the devil have you been?

> RONNIE
> (Sullenly)
> I've been busy.

> FIRST
> Busy what?

Claude listens and watches with growing astonishment.

> RONNIE
> Busy, sir.

> FIRST
> Who is that with you?

> RONNIE
> New boy, sir.

> FIRST
> Why did you bring him here?

Ronnie says nothing, sullenly. Claude is astonished, too astonished to be anything else yet.

> FIRST (Cont'd.)
> You have not cleaned my boots, and we have been waiting twenty minutes for tea. What do you mean, Smith?

> CLAUDE
> (Whispering)
> Clean his boots?
> (Aloud)
> Look here.

The three seniors look at Claude; as he speaks they look at him with horrified astonishment.

-11-

141

                    CLAUDE (Cont'd.)
          You can't talk to Ronnie that way.

                         FIRST
          Can't _what_?

                         RONNIE
                    (Hissing)
          Shut up, you ass!

Claude advances into the room.

                         RONNIE
                    (Tries to catch Claude)
          I'm his fag! That's the way we do
          here!

Claude is not listening.

                         CLAUDE
                    (Advances upon the senior, who
                    rises.)
          Take that back and apologise.

                         RONNIE
          O damn! I told him not to come!

                         FIRST
          Get this boy out of here, you, Smith.

                         CLAUDE
          Boy, eh? I'll show you about talking
          that way to Ronnie.

He springs at the senior and hits him. A melee. Ronnie looks
on for a moment.

                         RONNIE
          Now you've done it.

He leaps in to help Claude; soon all five of them are fighting
The senior and Claude are on the floor, the other three trampling
back and forth; suddenly the three of them spring back and become rigid. The two on the floor have not heard the door open
nor seen the bearded master who enters. He jerks the senior to
his feet. Claude still lies on the floor.

                         -12-

142

MASTER
What's this? What the devil's this?

CLAUDE
(He is still shadow boxing, lying
on his back on the floor. He sees
the bearded master and stops.)

Beaver, Ronnie! Beaver! Beaver! Now
I'm just ten down.

(Actors Change Here)

1914

War begins. Flags, drums, marching troops throughout England.
Out of the sound of tramping feet and drums scenes dissolve
one after the other

Ronnie and Claude at school, reading war news in papers. Ronnie
is grave - Claude eager.

The tramping feet become the sound of a train. Ronnie and
Claude going home. They are met at the station by Ann in an
officer's fatigue cap, very military. When Claude tries to
embrace her she repulses him, stands to attention, salutes.
Leads the way to the dogcart, very military, officerlike, gestures them in. The tramping feet and the drums blend with the
sound of the horse's hoofs.

The tramping feet continue. The library. Ronnie's and Ann's
father saying goodbye to the tenants and servants as they file
into the room. He is a colonel. All the while Ann tramps up
and down the room with a sword improvised from a poker. Ronnie
is still grave, Claude grave and eager.

The sound of the tramping feet continue. The portico - the
colonel saying goodbye to his family; military car waiting.
His wife clings to him. Ann still marching up and down. Colonel
turns and puts his hand on Ronnie's shoulder. They look at one
another. Then colonel enters car and drives away. Ronnie and
his mother and Claude look after the car. Ann comes up to
Ronnie and Claude and draws poker with flourish. Only Claude
turns and salutes her. Ronnie and his mother looking after car.
Sound of tramping dies away.

1915

Ronnie and Claude back at school. The mess hall. A vacant place
at the table.

-13-

143

                    VOICES
               (In the background)
        Cardon. His brother was killed last
        week. He's gone home for a week.

Ronnie looks at the vacant place, very grave.

                    CLAUDE
               (Is Grave - then volatile he
                changes.)
        O gad, I know it will be over before we
        get there.

                    RONNIE
        I wish we'd hear from father.

Ronnie's room. He and Claude with a letter from Ann.

        "Mother is not well. I'm bothered
        about her. If we would only hear
        from father. I hate this old war.
        I don't care who knows it."

CHAPEL

                    HEADMASTER
               (Behind him are three young
                officers)
        ......Do our bit with any school in England.
        It has been said that England's battles are
        won on her cricket and rugby fields. Where
        can England find three better soldiers than
        these lads who are about to go out to France
        to command English troops. Wyatt, Richardson,
        Amberley.
               (The three officers rise, diffident,
                young)
        Only the new boys to whom their names will
        be unfamiliar

They cheer, the students, orderly yet wild too, the three young
officers grave among the pandemonium.

                    -14-

                    CLAUDE
          O gad! I know we will be too late.

                    RONNIE
          It won't be long. We'll be eighteen
          soon.

                    CLAUDE
          You'll be eighteen before I shall, though.
          Will you wait for me?

Ronnie hesitates.

                    CLAUDE
          Swear you'll wait for me, Ronnie. It'll
          only be five months.

Ronnie is looking out the window. Claude watches his
back anxiously.

                    RONNIE
          Why wait? Only five months, then you can
          come. Be plenty left for you.

                    CLAUDE
          But you'll be so far ahead of me. Never
          catch you up, then.

                    RONNIE
          How catch me up?

                    CLAUDE
          In sinking German ships.

                    RONNIE
          You couldn't catch me up in German ships
          if you started first. You can't even
          catch me up at Beaver.

                    CLAUDE
          But I am. I was twelve down once, and
          now I'm only nine.

                    RONNIE
          Ah. That's it. You'd be no good in the
          Navy. Aim the gun, then instead of shoot-
          ing a Hun with it, you'd turn and call a
          Beaver on the ship commander's beard.

                    CLAUDE
          I swear I wouldn't.

                        -15-

                                                         145

                    RONNIE
               (Looking out the window)
          Can't trust you. Navy couldn't. You
          might even get the ship sunk playing
          Beaver.

                    CLAUDE
          I swear I shan't.

                    RONNIE
          Swear what?

     Claude looks at the back of Ronnie's head.

                    RONNIE
          Swear you'll never say beaver again?

                    CLAUDE
          Will you wait for me, if I swear?

                    RONNIE
          Swear.

                    CLAUDE
          Damn! All right. I swear.

                    RONNIE
          All right, Beaver.

                         -16-

146

                    CLAUDE
              (Jerking his head up)
         What?

                    RONNIE
              (Without turning)
         Beaver. Down there in the quad. Now
         you're ten down again.

                    CLAUDE
         O damn! O you putt!
              (Runs to window and looks out.
              Ronnie pushes him back)

                    RONNIE
         I saw it first.

                    CLAUDE
         That wasn't fair. Just when you --- O
         damn you!

                    RONNIE
         Ah, swearing.

They begin to scuffle.

                    CLAUDE
         I don't care!

They scuffle. A knock at the door. They cease, dishevelled.

                    RONNIE
         Yes?
              (He goes to the door and opens
               it. It is the ancient messenger.)
         For me?

                    MESSENGER
              (Extends wire)
         For Mr. Boyce Smith, sir.

                    RONNIE
              (Takes message)
         I'm Boyce Smith, thanks.

Messenger goes.

                    -17-

                    CLAUDE
               (Watching Ronnie)
          What is it?

                    RONNIE
          I don't know. Haven't opened it yet.
          Daresay that's why he brought it to me:
          so I should find out.
               (Opens message. Then he stands
               looking at it, quite still)

                    CLAUDE
          What is it?
               (Ronnie does not answer, does not
                stir)
          Ronnie!
               (Goes to Ronnie. Ronnie looks up)
          Why, Ronnie.
               (He reads message)
          O gad, Ronnie! O gad, Ronnie!
               (He puts his arm over Ronnie's
                shoulder, but it is Claude
                who breaks down)
          Ogad - they were so good to me! so
          damn good to me!

The drums begin. They are not swift marching now; It is the
slow beat of the Dead March from 'Saul'.

The march continues. The mess hall - Ronnie's and Claude's
seats vacant.

                    VOICES
          Boyce Smith's father was killed. He and
          Hope have gone home. And his mother dies
          too. She was sick, and when the message
          came about Smith's father, it killed her
          too.

The march continues. A lane. It is raining. The funeral
procession. First is the Colonel, beneath the flag, with
file of soldiers, then his wife. Behind walk Ronnie, Ann
and Claude, the sergeants following. Horse with empty saddle
and crossed stirrups.

                         -18-

148

Churchyard. The graves are filled, the volley fired. The people begin to disperse save Ronnie, Ann and Claude. Suddenly Ann turns, weeping. It is to Claude that she turns, into his arms.

The dogcart before the house. Servants putting baggage into it. Ann, Ronnie and Claude emerge and get into the cart. Ann turns back to look at the house. Ronnie touches her arm. She turns and gets into the cart; Ronnie and Claude follow. The cart goes on. It reaches the top of a hillfrom which the house can be seen. Claude looks back.

> CLAUDE
> I say. You know. To look at it. Things ought not to happen in a place like that, eh? You know. It ought to just go on and on. Things ought not to happen. There are so many places where they might happen, eh?

> ANN
> Go on! Go on! Hurry!
> (She is crying)

The cart goes on.

A hilltop. Ronnie, Ann and Claude with locked arms. Behind them the life of the school goes on: shouts from the playing field, etc. Beneath this a faint mutter of gunfire, as though heard from France. They are looking toward the sound, as though waiting. The three faces are quite grave.

> CLAUDE
> You and Ann will be going up to Oxford next term, and you will forget about me. They will persuade you to go on without me. Swear you will wait.

> RONNIE
> I'll wait for you. I promise.

> ANN
> And then kill them! Kill them!

-19-

Ann is between them. The three of them gaze eastward, toward
the remote mutter of the guns.

LIVERPOOL

A camouflaged liner comes in. Bustle and excitement; sirens,
tugs. The gangplank. porters, passengers descending. Bogard
comes down the gangplank, looking about him, grave and curious.
He is about twenty-five. A porter with Bogard's bags. Bogard
behind him as he is taking them up. They move on down the
shed.

                         PORTER
              American, Sir?

                         BOGRRD
              Yes.

                         PORTER
              Ay. I don't 'ave no <u>Henglish</u> young gentle-
              men as 'ale and 'earty as yerself in mufti
              these days.

                         BOGARD
              No.

                         PORTER
              Of course, yer own country aint in it yet.
              more luck to them and to yerself. No
              offense, sir.

                         BOGARD
              No.

They reach the barrier. An official and an army officer. The
officer examines Bogard's papers)

                         OFFICER
              For Oxford. College, eh?

                         BOGARD
              Yes. I am a Rhodes scholar.

                         PORTER
              I was just telling him, sir, there's better
              wear these days than mufti for a young
              gentleman 'ale and strong, sir.

                         -20-

150

                    OFFICER
          And I daresay you've better use for
          your strength than wasting it with
          your tongue, too.

                    PORTER
          Ay, sir. Very good, sir. No Offense,
          sir.

                    BOGARD
               (Gives Porter a coin)
          No offense.

Porter departs.

                    OFFICER
          Oxford, eh? I was Cambridge, myself.
          One term.

                    BOGARD
          Perhaps you'll go back when this is
          over.

                    OFFICER
          Can't say. Not much incentive to a man to
          go to school after a year or so of that
               (Jerks his hand toward the east)
          Out you go. And good luck. Though you
          already have that.

Bogard goes on.

THE TRAIN

Bogard sees signs of war; soldiers in the stations, etc.
The train goes on. A station. A porter enters, with a
basket.

                    PORTER
          Tea, sir.

                    BOGARD
          What?

                    PORTER
          Tea, sir. Special military. Like officers
          in the trenches.

                              -21-

                                                        151

                         BOGARD
          Military?

                         PORTER
          No sugar, sir.

                         BOGARD
          What shall I do with it?

                         PORTER
          Why, it's tea, sir.

                         BOGARD
          Am I to deliver it to someone in
          Oxford, or what?

                         PORTER
          You're a wag, sir.

Exit porter. The train goes on. Bogard looking out with sober
interest.

ANOTHER STATION

A porter opens the compartment and enters with baggage and stows
it in the rack. Bogard watches him, then he hears voices and
sees three people just outside the train. They are Ronnie, Ann
and Claude. Bogard leans and looks at them.

                         CLAUDE
          O gad! And you will wait for me? It
          will be only five months now, and I
          shall be eighteen too. Make him wait,
          for me, Ann.

                         ANN
          He'll wait. Come along Ronnie.
               (She turns to Claude. He takes her
               in his arms and they kiss)

Bogard sees that there is no passion particularly in it. He
sees Ronnie and Claude shake hands; he sits back as Ann and
Ronnie enter the compartment. Ronnie has a cold pipe in his
teeth. Ann pauses momentarily, and gives him a single fierce

                         -22-

152

brooding glance, then goes on. Ronnie pauses to, nods; he
and Ann sit opposite. Ann gives Bogard another of those
fierce looks, meeting his eyes full for a moment. The train
moves. Ronnie is searching through his pockets. Bogard
produces a match.

                          BOGARD
                This what you want?

                          RONNIE
                Thanks
                     (Lights his pipe)
                You're an American.

                          BOGARD
                Yes.

                          RONNIE
                Thought so. Having a look at us, eh?
                Write it up for the papers, eh?

                          BOGARD
                No. I'm going to Oxford. The university.

                          RONNIE
                Really? That's nice.

                          ANN
                     (Looking at Bogard, fiercely)
                You're lucky, aren't you?

                          Bogard
                Lucky?

                          RONNIE
                Ann.

Ann continues to look at Bogard with that fierce look.

                          BOGARD
                Yes. I guess all Americans are lucky
                now. Is that why you look at me like
                that?

                          ANN
                It's because you look so small.

                          RONNIE
                Ann.

                          -23-

                                                    153

                    BOGARD
Small?

                    ANN
I suppose it's seeing a man your age
who's not in khaki.

                    RONNIE
Ann. Shut up
     (To Bogard)
'Pologise. Girls have no sense, you
know.

                    BOGARD
It's all right, I'm sorry I look small
to her.

                    ANN
That can be easily remedied. Or maybe
they won't let you?

                    RONNIE
You beast, will you shut up?

                    ANN
Give me my book .

Ronnie takes book from his pocket and gives it to her. She
reads. Bogard cannot see her face for the book. Ronnie
sucks at the pipe; it is out again.

                    RONNIE
So you're going to Oxford, eh?

Without answering and without taking his eyes from the book,
Bogard produces another match and hands it to Ronnie.

                    RONNIE
Oh, thanks.
     (Lights the pipe)

Ann looks up, over the top of the book, her glance fierce, belligerent; meets Bogard's eyes and looks quickly down again. The
train goes on.

                    -24-

THE STATION AT OXFORD

Bogard descends and stands while Ronnie and Ann get out. He
is watching Ann. She passes him without a look even. He
looks after her. Ronnie pauses.

                    RONNIE
          Thanks for the matches.

Without looking at him, Bogard produces another match and gives
it to him.

                    RONNIE
          Oh, thanks.

Ann has gone on.

OXFORD

A military air: R.F.C.Ground School: Cadets in white cap bands.
Panoramic sequence of Bogard entering and getting settled.

CHAPEL

Bogard sees Ronnie. Bogard is with a companion.

                    BOGARD
               (Indicates Ronnie)
          Who is that?

                    OTHER
          That's Boyce Smith.

                    BOGARD
          He has a sister, hasn't he?

                    OTHER
          Yes. They're orphans. Father was killed
          last year, and when the mother received
          the news, she died too. Buried on the
          same day. Boyce Smith and his sister live
          in the town somewhere. Sister's a regular
          fire-eater. Wants to kill all Germans out
          of hand.

                         -25-

                                                          155

                    BOGARD
          Oh, I see, so that was why ---

                    OTHER
          Why what?

                    BOGARD
          Nothing. Shall we go?

COLLEGE QUAD

Bogard sees Ronnie in the distance, follows him. Follows Ronnie
to his lodgings, stands looking at the windows. Has to stand
aside to let a company of air cadets pass. Looks after them,
then up at the windows again.

THE QUAD

Bogard emerges from a door and meets Ronnie and Ann face to
face.

                    RONNIE
          Ah, the match one.

Ann gives him another single hard look and goes on without a
word.

                    RONNIE
          Ann.

She doesn't pause.

                    RONNIE
          I say, Ann.

Ann goes on.

                    BOGARD
          I guess she'll never forgive me for having
          been born on the other side of the Atlantic.

                         -26-

156

                    RONNIE
Nonsense. Silly girl. Child yet. I
say. I have intended to call on you.
But you know how it is. What?

                    BOGARD
Will you come up now and have a whiskey?

                    RONNIE
Right you are. Always did want to know
an American. See what makes them tick.
eh?

                    BOGARD
What about her? Your sister?

                    RONNIE
Oh, she'll be all right, I daresay. Knows
the way home.

**Ann, looking back, sees Ronnie and Bogard enter the door. Her
face is hard, almost contemptuous. Turns and walks fast. Returns home, sits at desk and writes furiously to Claude:**

          "....sickening, Beasts filthy strong and
          hale, going to school, with fathers safe
          in New York, getting richer and richer
          because of the war. Why don't you hurry
          and be eighteen so you and Ronnie can go
          out there and kill them and kill them..."

BOGARD'S ROOMS

He and Ronnie with drinks.

                    BOGARD
I know now why she hates me so.

                    RONNIE
Not hate. Awful infant. Frightful.
But how know?

                    BOGARD
I know about -
          (Ceases. They look at one another.
          Then Ronnie looks down; he is quite
          still)
I know about your father and mother.

                    -27-

                                                       157

                    RONNIE
Oh, that. Everybody's father, brother,
someone, these days. and if you don't
mind......

                    BOGARD
Yes. I'm sorry. I just wanted to tell
you how I know now why she ----

                    RONNIE
        (Looks up - looks at Bogard)
I say. You like her.

                    BOGARD
Yes.

                    RONNIE
Come for tea some afternoon, eh?

                    BOGARD
What will she think?

                    RONNIE
Throw teapot at you, daresay. Think
she likes you too. Talks about you
too much. Curses you too much. Will
you come?

                    BOGARD
Yes.

                    RONNIE
        (Raises his glass)
Done.
        (They touch glasses, drink)
Like you myself. Not bad for
American.

Ronnie has departed. Bogard sitting in his chair. The window
is open. The sound of a drum begins, and men marching. It
grows louder. Bogard goes to window, looks out and sees party
of cadets marching past in the street. He closes the window
suddenly.

Ronnie and Bogard approaching Ronnie's lodgings.

                    BOGARD
        (Stopping at the door)
I'm afraid.

                    -28-

158

                    RONNIE
              (Looks at Bogard intently)
         Actually?

                    BOGARD
         Yes. I am.

                    RONNIE
         You do like her, don't you?

                    BOGARD
              (Soberly)
         Yes.

                    RONNIE
         Come along.

They enter and mount the stairs. Their feet are loud, the sound
carrying over to

THE SITTING ROOM

Ann hearing the approaching feet. She springs up and is watching
the door when it opens and Ronnie and Bogard enter.

                    RONNIE
         I say. Friends. Don't shoot. Here's the
         match chap. Tell him he is welcome.

Ann says nothing. She and Bogard look at one another.

                    RONNIE
         Come on. Come up within range. Ann is no
         good save at point blank.

Bogard approaches. Ann gives the effect of being at bay against
a table.

                    RONNIE
         Say How do you do, can't you?

                    ANN
         How do you do.

                      -29-

                    RONNIE
          You can touch them too. It's only
          their serpents which are poison.

Ann offers her hand. Bogard takes it for a moment.

                    RONNIE
          Ah, tea.
               (Looks about and sees table.
               Goes to it and turns.)

Ann is still looking at Bogard, hard, belligerent.

                    RONNIE
          Well. Am I to pour it too? Gad, am
          I to play dowager duchess too?

Ann comes to the table. Bogard follows. Ann pours tea,
gives Bogard a cup without a word, then Ronnie.

                    RONNIE
          Talk, say something.

                    ANN
          Say what?

                    RONNIE
          Ask him something. Ask him how he likes
          Oxford.

                    ANN
               (Without looking at Bogard, without
               inflection, like a parrot)
          How do you like Oxford?

                    BOGARD
          I don't know. I haven't --- I like it very
          much. I----

                    RONNIE
          You see? He doesn't like it.

                    ANN
          Perhaps the sound of the drums and the
          soldiers marching annoys him.

                    RONNIE
          As you were. He's not below the salt,
          remember.

                        -30-

    160

ANN

Or perhaps, being an American, he's
beyond being annoyed by soldiers.

RONNIE

I say. Don't you ever get tired?

ANN
(Looks at Ronnie)
Tired? Tired? When I think --- when I
can't help but ----when I am always
thinking -----

A knock. Ann ceases. They look at the door.

RONNIE

Come in.

LANDLADY
(Enters)
Them stairs. I'm that tuckered.

RONNIE

Have a spot of tea; buck you up. Give
you steam to get back down.

LANDLADY

Thank you, I've ad my tea. It's a
message.

RONNIE

Right. Let's have it.

LANDLADY

It's at the postoffice.

RONNIE

Why didn't they send it?

LANDLADY

I don't know, I'm sure. Shall I tell
them to send it?

RONNIE

Damn! Tell them to keep it.

ANN

You go and get it. It may be important.

RONNIE

I daresay I'd better.
(Rises)
I'll not be long.

-31-

                        ANN
            You don't need to hurry. It will be
            a pleasant stroll. Mr. Bogard can
            keep you company.

Bogard has risen.

                      RONNIE
                    (Pauses)
            Mr. Bogard can wait here.
                    (Looks at Bogard)
            Will you wait here?

                      BOGARD
                    (Looks at Ann's hard face)
            Perhaps I'd better go.

                      RONNIE
            What? Is this American courage? Are
            you afraid to stop alone with a seventeen
            year old girl?

Bogard looks at Ann. She looks at him, but she makes no
move.

                      RONNIE

            Good. I'll leave you to beard the
            British she-lion.
                    (Returns to table and takes
                    up bread knife)
            Best take this along, though.
                    (To Ann)
            You still have the poker, you know.
                    (He exits)

Bogard looks at Ann. Her hand crumbles bread, fast, hard, she
watching it. Glances up and sees Bogard watching her sobefly.
She springs up, panting.

                      BOGARD
                    (Rising)
            Do you want me to go?

                        ANN
            Why did you come? Why didn't you stay in
            America and let us alone?

                      -32-

162

                         BOGARD
          Who knows why I came? Maybe it was the
          same thing brought me to England that
          brought me to this house.

Ann is panting. He goes toward her, stops. She looks at
him.

                         BOGARD
          I know why you hate me. I didn't at
          first. But I do now.

                         ANN
          Know what?

                         BOGARD
          About your mother and fa......

                         ANN
          Stop. Don't you dare!
               (She is breathing hard)
          You're so safe, you Americans. It can't
          touch you. And we ---- I ---- Ronnie
          and me -----
               (She begins to cry. hard not hiding
               her face, her fists clenched at her
               sides. Bogard goes to her; suddenly
               she is in his arms, crying hard.)
          He was so damn fine! I liked him! I liked
          him! Things ought not to happen! They
          ought not to! God ought not to let them!
               (She is crying uncontrollably, on the
               verge of hysteria. Bogard holds her.
               Her hands wander about him, Clutching
               him)

                         BOGARD
          Now. Now. I'll get you out of it. Away
          from it. We'll go back to America, where---

                         ANN
               (She springs free, looking at him)
          What?

                         BOGARD
          We'll go back to America. I have been to
          school, enough

                         ANN
               (She slaps him hard, taut, furious)
          You coward.
               (She breathes hard.)

                         -33-

                                                        163

                    BOGARD
               (Falls back, looking at her)
          Coward, am I?
               (He moves slowly toward her. She
               holds her ground, defiant, glaring
               at him. He takes her in his arms
               She resists. He kisses her by force.
               For a moment longer she resists.
               Then she succumbs, crying again. He
               holds her quietly now. From outside
               the window the tramp of soldiers begins
               and passes and dies away. He listens
               to the sound, turning his head as it
               passes.)

A street, a recruiting office, ROYAL FLYING CORPS. Bogard
enters.

The postoffice. Ronnie receives the wire, opens it:

          "O Gad arriving today beaver. Claude"

                    RONNIE
               (At window)
          What time does the down train come in?

                    CLERK
          It arrives at ten after four. YOU've
          just time to reach the station.

                    RONNIE
          Damn!
               (Rushes out, hails cab and enters)

THE STATION

Ronnie waiting. The train comes in and Claude springs down,
waving his arms. Porter behind him, shouting at him. Claude
turns and rushes back and begins to hurl his bags down. One
Bursts open; he and porter cram clothing back into it, Claude
waving socks and shirts at Ronnie. At last he reaches the
barrier. He has in his hand a calendar, with a huge black
circle about a date. He waves this in Ronnie's face.

                    -34-

164

                    CLAUDE
Oh, Gad. Do you see? Do you see?
O gad!

                    RONNIE
I can't see anything until you hold it
still, you ass.

                    CLAUDE
              (Holds the calendar before
               Ronnie's face)
Regard, Admiral!

                    RONNIE
Regard what? The twenty-first. What
about that?

                    CLAUDE
It's today, ass.

                    RONNIE
Not really. I say, now. Think of it. And
then what? What do you mean, cutting away
from school ------

                    CLAUDE
I'm eighteen today! I'm eighteen!

                    RONNIE
What?

Claude hurls the calendar away, steps back and salutes. Then
he hits Ronnie on the back. Ronnie hits Claude on back.
They gravely and intently exchange hard, smacking, flathanded
blows while porters and passers look on.

The hill top, the school in the background. Again Ronnie,
Ann and Claude stand arm in arm, looking eastward toward the
faint muttering of far guns. An aeroplane passes overhead.
Claude looks up at it.

                    CLAUDE
              (Soberly)
Do you remember when you said you would
marry only an aviator? Gad, people know
so little. What we didn't know then. and
what we know now. I'm glad we didn't know
then. Aren't you?

                          -35-

Ann and Ronnie don't answer. The three of them look eastward
toward the guns.

NAVAL DEPOT AT BLANK

Background of ships, cadets, enlistments. Ronnie and Claude
in mufti march into office to take oath. Claude is eager,
excited, looking this way and that, talking.

> CLAUDE
> O gad, Ronnie! O I say!

> PETTY OFFICER
> You, there! Silence in ranks.

Claude looks about, ceases yet he is still ill contained as the
line files into the office. Behind a table sit three officers,
the chief one bearded. The line files before the table and
halts, Claude still looking about, eager, bright, excited. He
turns and sees the bearded captain.

> CLAUDE
> Beaver, Ronnie! Beaver! Beaver!
> Now I'm just eight down!

Another hill, this time above the sea. The guns in the distance.
Ronnie, Ann and Claude arm in arm as before, though now Ronnie
and Claude wear the uniform of naval cadets, Ann that of the
W.A.A.C. they gaze out over the sea, toward the guns. They are
quite sober.

THE STREET
R.F.C. RECRUITING STATION

Bogard emerges in new ill fitting private's uniform and with the
white cap band of a cadet and with swagger stick. He goes to
Ann's lodgings. He is eager, running up the stairs. Knocks
at door. No answer. Knocks again. No answer. He hears footsteps
on the stairs. It is the landlady.

> BOGARD
> Miss Smith, Miss Boyce Smith -------

> LANDLADY
> They have gone.

-86-

166

                    BOGARD
Yes - I didn't get any answer
          (Looks at Landlady)
Gone?

                    LANDLADY
Yes, sir. It was quite sudden. They
left last night, the three of them.

                    BOGARD
You mean, they have left Oxford?
For good?

                    LANDLADY
Yes, sir. The two young gentlemen went
for the Navy. It was quite sudden.

                    BOGARD
The two of them?

                    LANDLADY
Mr. Boyce Smith, and the other young
gentleman. A very talkative young one,
sir. It fair done my 'eart good to
see 'im and Miss Boyce Smith 'ugging
and kissing.

                    BOGARD
Oh, I see. Gone. He ----the other one
-----They are to be married, I suppose?

                    LANDLADY
You wouldn't 'ave to suppose, sir, if
you had seed them.

                    BOGARD
Oh, yes. Well, thanks
          (He moves)

                    LANDLADY
          (Watches Bogard)
This way out, sir.

                    BOGARD
Oh, yes, thanks.
          (He descends the stairs and enters the
          street. He stands for a moment in
          deep thought. He raises his swagger
          stick as though about to break it,
          then he desists and goes on down the
          street, walking fast. At the corner
          he passes an officer without seeing him,
          without saluting. The officer turns and
          looks after him.)

                    -37

                                                            167

THE ORDERLY ROOM

A corporal at the desk. Enter Bogard. He goes to the desk.
After a while the Corporal looks up.

                    CORPORAL
          Yes? Wot might you want?

                    BOGARD
          I want to know where they enlist in the
          Navy. The cadet school.

                    CORPORAL
               (Looks him up and down)
          So the flying corps don't suit yer, eh?

                    BOGARD
          No. I have a friend who has just enlisted
          in the Navy. I want to find where he is.

                    CORPORAL
          There's a cadet depot at Blank. Yer
          might write to 'im there.

                    BOGARD
          Thanks.
               (Turns toward door)

                    CORPORAL
               (Looks after him)
          Cadet

Bogard turns

                    CORPORAL (Cont'd.)
          Don't come in ere agayn unless yer
          sent for. Do you 'ear?

Bogard goes out.

THE STREET

The Sergeant-Major going on. Bogard overtakes him, stands to
attention.

                    BOGARD
          Sir, I want two days leave

                    SERGEANT-MAJOR
               (Looks at Bogard)
          You do, eh? And what for?

                         -38-

168

                    BOGARD
I must go down to Blank. To see
a friend.

                SERGEANT-MAJOR
E must go down to Blank. 'Ow long
'ave you been in.

                    BOGARD
I enlisted yesterday.

                SERGEANT-MAJOR
E enlisted yesterday, and already 'e
must 'urry away.
          (Suddenly fierce)
You're the Hamerican, aynt yer?

                    BOGARD
Yes.

                SERGEANT-MAJOR
Yes what?

                    BOGARD
Yes, sir.

                SERGEANT-MAJOR
And now yer've got a belly full.
Want to quit, eh?

                    BOGARD
No. No. I don't want to quit.

                SERGEANT-MAJOR
Still 'ave to go down to Blank?

                    BOGARD
No.

                SERGEANT-MAJOR
Carry on, then.

The drums and the tramping feet sound through a sequence of scenes;
Bogard as a cadet corporal, then a sergeant, very grave, very
determined. The ground school examination. A number of names
posted on bulletin board. Bogard's leading.

                        -39-

                                                            169

The feet and the drums are drowned by the sound of gunfire.
Ann, in uniform, beside her halted car, standing on the headland,
looking out to sea. Her face is cold, grave.

The guns continue. Ronnie and Claude are midshipmen on a cruiser
which is engaged with a German cruiser. The german is sinking,
the Englishman steaming down upon it. Ronnie and Claude watching, Claude tense, eager. Ronnie grave, contained. Suddenly
they rush toward a binocular hanging beside the port and scuffle
for it. Ronnie gets it and fending Claude off with one hand,
he looks at the sinking German. Focus on basket mast.

                         RONNIE
              Beaver.

                         CLAUDE
              O damn! O you putt. Now I'm ten down
              again!

The gunfire becomes the drone of aeroplanes, which continues
through a sequence of scenes.

Bogard taking flying instruction - his solo.

THE ORDERLY ROOM

Bogard and six other cadets and a sergeant. They are at ease.
The inner door opens - the Adjutant appears.

                         ADJUTANT
              All right, Sergeant.

                         SERGEANT
              SHUN!

The seven men fall into attention.

                         SERGEANT (Cont'd.)
              Right dress! Smartly there!

They dress right

                         SERGEANT (Cont'd.)
                      (Watches fiercely)
              Right turn! Forward, march!

They file into the inner office.

The seven men lined up, facing the table behind which the Commanding Officer sits. The Commanding Officer finishes giving the
last one his rank.

                          -40-

170

                    COMMANDING OFFICER
          Sergeant, show these gentlemen out.

They turn, the Sergeant is at the door, holding it open, standing
at salute as they pass and salute him in turn.

THE STREET
                         FIRST
          Let's go to town and celebrate.

                        SECOND
          Right. Gad, I've ten thousand salutes
          to recover.

                         THIRD
          I shan't even go to town. I shall go
          out and parade the Sergeant-Major.

                         FIRST
          I'm for town. Come along, Bogard --
          Why, where are you going?

                        BOGARD
                   (Already walking off)
          See you later. Got an engagement.

THE TARMAC

A machine stands on it, warming. Bogard approaches, fastening
his helmet.

                        MECHANIC
                   (Salutes)
          Never gave a salute with more
          pleasure, Sir.

                        BOGARD
          Thanks, Albert. If they ask where
          I have gone, you can tell them I am
          getting in a little more time.

                        ALBERT
          Right, sir. And if you 'ave to land
                   (Winks)
          There's always them bleeding hengines,
          you know.

Bogard takes off.

                         -41-

                                                         171

<u>BLANK</u>

Bogard comes down. He goes to the Naval Base Office. A
P. O. on duty.

                     BOGARD
          I'm looking for a friend. He'll be a
          midshipman by now. Mr. Boyce Smith.

                     P. O.
          Boyce Smith? No one of that name here
          now, sir.

                     BOGARD
          Could you find where he went to when
          he left here?

                     P. O.
          I'll see
              (He **exits** - He **returns**)
          He left here on May 7 for Dash, Sir.

                     BOGARD
          Thanks.
              (**Turns away**)

                     P. O.
           He'll be there, unless they have assigned
          him to the Fleet, Sir.

                     BOGARD
          Right. I'll find him
              (**Exits**)

He returns to his machine and takes off again. The drone of
the engine continues into the scene.

<u>THE ORDERLY ROOM AT DASH</u>

Another P. O.

                     P. O.
          Yes, Sir. He was assigned to the Suffolk
          last week.

                     BOGARD
          Where is the Suffolk?

-42-

172

                    P. O.
          Under sealed orders, Sir. I
          doubt if even Mr. Boyce Smith
          knows just where he is now.

                    BOGARD
          But he lived in town here. Likely
          his sis -- he still holds his
          lodgings.

                    P. O.
          I can't say, Sir. I can give you
          the address, though.
               (Goes out and returns with
               address)

                    BOGARD
          Thanks.

Bogard goes out. He takes cab to the address. He is about to
enter when he sees in the window a placard: APARTMENT TO LET.
He stands looking at the placard. He tosses the address
away and is about to go himself. Then he turns and rings the
bell. The Landlady comes to the door.

                    BOGARD
          You have an apartment to let.
          The one Mr. Boyce Smith had?

                    LANDLADY
          You knew them? She was as sweet
          a young lady as ever lived. Come
          In.

Bogard enters. She leads the way up stairs talking.

                    LANDLADY
          A jewel she were. The man as gets
          her will be a fortunate gentleman,
          I'm thinking.

                    BOGARD
          He was here too, was he?

                    LANDLADY
          Bless you, sir; they was like one
          family. You couldn't hardly have
          knowed which were the brother and
          which the fiancey. And you knowed them?

                    -43-

                         BOGARD
              Yes, slightly.

Landlady unlocks the door. Bogard enters. She is still
talking but Bogard does not listen. He moves quietly about,
touching the chairs, curtains, etc. He opens the door and
looks in at the bedroom.

                         BOGARD
              Which bedroom is this?

                         LANDLADY
              That was hers. Many's the morning I
              have come in with the tea and she would
              be ----

                         BOGARD
                    (Closes the door quickly)
              Yes. I believe you.

                         LANDLADY
                    (Looks at Bogard, taken a
                    little aback. She begins to
                    talk again)
              Come this way and I will show you --

She goes on through another door, her voice is still talking.
Bogard has paused; he is looking at an etagere. He takes
from the top of it a small square of paper and turns it over.
It is a snapshot of Ann. He looks at it. The Landlady's voice
can still be heard from the other room. In this room she is
tugging a folding bed down, still talking.

                         LANDLADY
              This here is where the gentlemen slept. Mr.
              Boyce Smith often congratulated me on how
              convenient it is. He said it always got
              him up, the same as an alarm clock. He al-
              ways had to have his little joke ----
                    (She turns and looks behind her; shows
                    astonishment)
              Why -----
                    (She returns hurriedly to the other
                    room - It is empty. As she stands in
                    outraged astonishment, the sound of an
                    aeroplane begins).

                         -44-

    174

Dissolve through sound of engine to Bogard taking off. As
his ship diminishes in flight, it dissolves to a bomber. The
sound of the engines carries through a sequence of scenes.

A BOMBER SQUADRON AT THE FRONT

Bogard a Junior Officer - a co-pilot.

Four ships go out - three return.

New pilots come up from Pool; a ship preparing to go out.
Bogard now pilot - one of the new men his co-pilot. The
engines continue. Bogard looking at the snapshot of Ann. It
is beginning to be dog-eared. Enter another pilot, sees
snapshot before Bogard can hide it.

                    PILOT
          Why so formal?

                              Omit.

                         BOGARD
          Formal?

                    PILOT
          All the clothes. Here's how I photograph
          my girls
                    (Shows Bogard snapshot of girl in
                    underclothes)

                         BOGARD
          You have a different kind of girl from
          this one.

                    PILOT
          Go on. They're all that sort of girl.

Bogard knocks him down.

Dissolve through engines to newspaper headline: AMERICA
DECLARES WAR.

Bogard looking at snapshot. As he does so his tunic becomes
American - his pips the twin bars of a captain - his wings
U. S. wings. The photograph is quite dog-eared now; he
handles it with extreme care.

The flight going out. Bogard now in command. The engines
continue.

                         -45-

                                              175

DISSOLVE THROUGH

Panoramic scene of Boulogne harbor; engines continuing.
Torpedo boat going out.

DISSOLVE THROUGH

Engines to a german ship at sea, firing. Torpedo boat rushing down upon ship with shells bursting over boat.

DISSOLVE THROUGH

Sound of engines. In dissolve the sound of torpedo exploding
Sound of engines dies slowly in

DISSOLVE TO

Claude in a cafe, drinking. He is flushed and lively, though
not yet in bad shape.

With drunken sounds in background, focus on clock face, with
hands moving to midnight.

DISSOLVE THROUGH

Clock to Ronnie entering a cafe where officers are drinking.

                    RONNIE
                 (Approaching)
          Has Hope been here?

                    MAN
          Who?

                    RONNIE
          Claude Hope.

                    MAN
          He was here. But he left. About two hours
          ago. Have you looked in all the gutters
          yet?

Ronnie goes out.

DISSOLVE TO

Claude in another cafe, asleep on a table among spilled drinks
and overturned glasses. A British M.P. trying to rouse him.
Focus on clockface at four o'clock, M.P.'s voice in background.

                    -46-

176

                    M. P.
                 (In background)
          Mr. Hope. Mr. Hope. Nah then, Sir.
          Come.

                    CLAUDE
          Go 'way. Want sleep. Got tight so
          can sleep. Go 'way.

                    M. P.
          Nah, Mr. Hope. Come along, Sir. Let's
          go 'ome, where you can sleep comfortable.

DISSOLVE TO

THE SITTING ROOM

Ann in chair beside window, watching the door as Ronnie
enters.

                    ANN
          You didn't......?

                    RONNIE
          Couldn't find him. Looked everywhere.

                    ANN
          Oh, Ronnie.

                    RONNIE
          Be all right. Wilfred will find him
          somewhere and fetch him home.

                    ANN
          Can't you get transferred back into a
          ship? Where he won't drink so much?

                    RONNIE
          Won't hurt him. Always sober enough to
          go out.

                    ANN
          But it doesn't make you get tight and
          lie in the street.

                    -47-

                    RONNIE
Older than Claude. Not highstrung, either.
No fun, even to me, dashing out at battle-
ship in Wapping Stairs ferry.
        (He goes to window and looks out)
Annoying, though.

                    ANN
Yes. I'm so afraid that some time in the
boat.......Thank God you don't have to go
out tomorrow.

                    RONNIE
Do have to. That's why annoyed.

                    ANN
But you just went out yesterday!

                    RONNIE
Yes. Orders, though. Admiral.

                    ANN
Oh, Ronnie!

                    RONNIE
        (His back to her, looking out the
        window)
I say. Why not marry?

                    ANN
Marry?

                    RONNIE
You and Claude. Might straighten him up.
Keep him out of gutters, anyway.

                    ANN
Do you think it would? Ought I?

                    RONNIE
Don't know. You always talked about it,
both of you. Thought you wanted to. Don't,
if you don't want to, though.

                    ANN
But not yet, Ronnie. Not right now. Let me
wait until I.....until I can....until I can
stop.......?

                    -48-

178

"She holds his hand, leaning her head against it" (*Turn About*, p. 49).
(c) MGM.

                              RONNIE
          Stop what?
                    (Looks at her)

          Ann looks at him with desperate beseeching.

                              RONNIE
                    (He comes and pats her head,
                    as he might the head of a dog.)
          All right. Shan't try to make you.

                              ANN
          I do want to. I've never thought of
          anything else. I won't think of any-
          thing else. But not right now, Ronnie.
                    (She holds his hand, leaning her
                    head against it.)

                              RONNIE
                    (Looks down at her, sober,
                    thoughtful)
          Right. Do as you like, of course.
                    (He looks at the clock. It is
                    half past four.)
          Been out all night, now. Must keep
          him in, today. Not let him barge
          about again this evening.

                              ANN
          I will. I'll make him stay at home
          this evening.

                              RONNIE
          Best so. Don't know what this is. Will
          see Admiral first thing today. Better
          get to bed.

                              ANN
                    (Doesn't move. She sits with
                    her head against Ronnie's arm)
          Is this......something special?

                              RONNIE
          Yes. Secret mission. Means they have
          invented something with Sweepstake odds.

                              ANN
          Oh, Ronnie.

                              -49-

          180

                    RONNIE
          Steady. No funking, now.

                    ANN
          No. No funking.

A blundering sound from without. Ann and Ronnie look
toward the door.

                    ANN
          There they are.
               (Rises, draws her robe together.)

Ronnie opens door. M. P. enters supporting Claude.

                    RONNIE
          Hullo, Wilfred. Found him, eh?

                    M. P.
          Yes, sir.

                    RONNIE
               (Supporting Claude)
          Thanks. Sorry to trouble you.

                    M. P.
          No trouble, Sir. Mr. Hope never gives
          no trouble, Sir. All 'e wants now is
          bed.

                    CLAUDE
          Not bed. Must take care of Ann

M. P. exits. Ronnie leads Claude toward bedroom. Ann moves
ahead. They enter the room where a corner of the bed can
be seen. Sounds of stumbling.

                    RONNIE
               (Off-stage)
          Now. In you go.

                    CLAUDE
               (Off-stage)
          No. Must take Ann home.

                    -50-

                    RONNIE
                 (Off-stage)
         Right. Get away. I'll undress him,

                    ANN
                 (Off-stage)
         No. You get on to bed yourself. I'll
         undress him.

                    RONNIE
                 (Off-stage)
         Well. You should know how by this time.
         Done it enough.
                 (He enters room and makes himself
                 a drink at table.)

                    CLAUDE
                 (Off-stage)
         Abshlutely. Must take care Ann. Good
         girl. Going marry her when war over. But
         war not ever over. So can't marry Ann.

                    ANN
                 (Off-stage)
         Yes. Now. There. You can go to sleep
         now.

                    CLAUDE
                 (Off-stage)
         O gad yes. Must get tight so can sleep.
         Then war be over and can go to England.
         No war then. Quiet, then.

                    ANN
                 (Off-stage)
         Yes. Go to sleep, now.

                    CLAUDE
                 (Off-stage)
         O gad, I'm tired! Ann! Where's Ann?

                    ANN
                 (Off-stage)
         Hush. Here I am. Go to sleep, now.
                 (She enters room.

                    RONNIE
                 (Is drinking. Looks at her)
         All right?

                    -51-

182

                    ANN
Yes.

                    RONNIE
Must go to Admiral first thing today.
You won't let him go out, mind.

                    ANN
Yes. I'll keep him here. Oh, Ronnie!
I'm afraid!

                    RONNIE
Steady.
         (He looks at her - she is
         trembling)
Right?

                    ANN
         (Controls herself)
Right.

                    RONNIE
Good. Get on to bed with you.

                    ANN
Kiss me goodnight, Ronnie.

                    RONNIE
O gad, what for? I never kissed you
in my life.

                    ANN
Yes.
         (She comes to him; he leans and
         kisses her. She clings to him)
Ronnie!

                    RONNIE
Steady, now.

                    ANN
         (Controls herself)
Yes, I will.

                    RONNIE
Good girl. Get on to bed, now.

DISSOLVE TO:

                    -52-

Morning. Ann and Ronnie in same positions. Ronnie about
to depart. Ann still in robe.

                    RONNIE
          Mind, now. Don't let him go out. I
          may be late with Admiral. You keep
          him here, eh?

                    ANN
          Yes. I will.
               (She looks at him)

                    RONNIE
          Steady.

                    ANN
          Yes. I will. Is this one going to be
          very bad, Ronnie?

                    RONNIE
          Can't say. Always get back, though.
          Our names not in pot yet. Know that,
          don't you?

                    ANN
          But this time. A secret one. Ronnie,
          Ronnie!

                    RONNIE
          Steady. Come here.

Ann approaches, watching his face, her face strained,
anxious. Ronnie takes her hand and leads her to mantel.
Focus on photograph of their father in uniform.

                    RONNIE
          He didn't funk it. Did he?

                    ANN
          No.

                    RONNIE
          Course not. Steady now?

                    ANN
          Yes.

                    RONNIE
          Swear.

                    -53-

184

                    ANN
        I swear.

                    RONNIE
        Stout fellow. Back when I can.
        (He goes out.)

Ann watches door, rigid with control.

DISSOLVE TO

Clock - half past nine. Hands move to half past five.

DISSOLVE TO

LIVING ROOM
Ann and Claude facing one another. Ann still in the robe,
Claude dishevelled though sober.

                    CLAUDE
        So going out again tomorrow. Knew they
        would think of it in time, Wish they
        would give us big boat, with lots of
        torpedoes. Cruiser. Then go out and sink
        the whole Hun fleet at one time. Then
        would have to let us go home. Stay home.
        Get married then, you and I. What?

Ann watches him. He looks past her and sees the bottle on
the table. Goes to it.

                    ANN
                (Watching)
        Don't, Claude.

He turns - bottle in hand.

                    ANN
        Please.

                    CLAUDE
        Why not? Going out again tomorrow; must
        teetotal all day.

                    ANN
                (Goes to him, puts her hand on the
                bottle.)
        Please.

                    -54-

                                                    185

```
                    CLAUDE
              (Looks at her, astonished)
         O good gad.  Not turning temperance?

                     ANN
         No.
              (Changes her anxious expression)
         We'll both drink.

                    CLAUDE
         What?

Ann takes bottle from him, purs two huge drinks.

                    CLAUDE
         Good gad.  Can't drink all that.

                     ANN
         I can.  Can't you drink as much as a girl?

                    CLAUDE
              (Watching her as she tries to con-
              trol her face, keeping upon it the
              bright, reckless expression)
         Right.

They touch glasses.  Claude drinks.  Ann pours her drink
out.  Claude sees her do it, but he does not let on.  Ann
pretends to drink.

                     ANN
         There.  Isn't it nicer, drinking at home?

                    CLAUDE
         Quite.

                     ANN
         Now I'll get you some breakfast.

                    CLAUDE
         Quite.

Ann goes out.  Claude watches her.  Then he returns to bedroom.
Through the door he can be seen putting on collar and tie.
He re-enters buttoning his coat, his cap in his hand.  At
once Ann emerges from other door.  Claude puts down the cap
before she sees it.  Apparently she has been waiting just
inside the door, watching.

                     ANN
         You're dressed.


                    -55-
```

                    CLAUDE
        Quite. Feeling quite fit now.

                    ANN
                (Comes into the room. When Claude
                looks away she glances swiftly about,
                sees his cap.
        Shall we have another drink.
                (She goes to the table and takes
                up the bottle)

                    CLAUDE
        Quite.

Ann fills two more drinks. They raise the glasses. Claude
makes to drink, pauses, catches Ann in the act of pouring
out her drink. She recovers, lifts her glass, her face
bright, tense, strained.

                    ANN
        To tomorrow.
                (Her expression changes)

                    CLAUDE
                (Sets his glass down and takes
                hers from her hand, gently)
        No use.

Ann watches him, wide eyed.

                    CLAUDE
        Saw you before.

He sets his glass down and turns. Ann watching him with
despair. He goes and takes up his cap.

                    CLAUDE
        Must go see about the boat.

                    ANN
        Ronnie has done that.

                    CLAUDE
        No. Not Ronnie's job. My job.

                    -56-

                                                    187

Ann comforts the despairing Claude; note the ring on her thumb. (c) MGM.

                    ANN
Will you come straight back home?

                    CLAUDE
          (Looks down at his cap, turns
          it in his hand, Looks up at
          Ann, quizzical)
Can't lie to you, can I? Never could.
Never could make tongue say the words.
          (He goes toward the door)

                    ANN
          (Watches him, then she runs forward
          and intercepts him)
Claude.

                    CLAUDE
Must, old chap. No good otherwise.
Might let Ronnie down someday.

                    ANN
          (Grips his arms)
Claude. Claude.

                    CLAUDE
Mess, isn't it? Used to think it be
over, Someday. Live sanely again. But
never be over. Say it's over, England
be dead. Perhaps best for England to
live and us die. Gad, I'm just nineteen,
too. Should be in school. Oxford.
Ronnie and I coming home for holidays.
Ann there. Talking about marrying Ann in
quiet where things can't get in and hurt
you. Holding Ann's hand in conservatory,
talking about marrying. But that's
finished. Whole world drunk now; must
stay tight to live in it.
          (He takes her hands to put her aside)

                    ANN
          (She clings)
Claude. Stay here. Claude.

                    CLAUDE
          (Smiling, gentle, slowly breaking her
          grip)
No.
          (Frees himself and takes up cap and
          goes toward door.)

                    -57-

                              ANN
                          (Watches him)
                    Claude.

Claude turns and looks at her. She looks at him, then
suddenly she puts her hands to her face and begins to
cry.

                              CLAUDE
                    Ann! Why, Ann!
                          (He drops his cap and goes to her
                          and puts his arms around her)
                    Crying.

                              ANN
                          (Raises her head)
                    I'm not crying.
                          (She stands easily in his arms;
                          she is suddenly soft, though
                          her face is quite grave)
                    It's not love, though, Claude.

                              CLAUDE
                    Not.....What do you mean?

She looks at him. Her face, her expression now melting.

                              CLAUDE
                    Ann!
                          (He kisses her, at first tenatively
                          then as a lover)
                    Ann! Do you mean......?

                              ANN
                    But not love, Claude!

                              CLAUDE
                    Gad, no. Love dead now. Maybe come back to
                    life someday.

With his arms about her, they move toward Claude's door as
scene dissolves. They enter door and it closes behind
them as scene fades.

                              ANN
                          (Voice, comes out of dissolve)
                    But not love, Claude! Not love!

                              -58-

190

The clock face at eleven O'clock. Ronnie enters. He halts,
looking about room. He sees Claude's cap on floor, picks
it up and goes to Claude's room. The door is closed; He
is about to open it, then he pauses, tiptoes away, and goes
to Ann's door. He knocks. There is no answer. He opens
the door quietly and looks in. The bed is empty. Ronnie
is puzzled. He is about to withdraw, when he pauses. He
goes to the bed and looks down. Upon the bed lie Ann's
stockings and underthings, as though discarded hurriedly.
Ronnie looks at themquietly, touching them. He returns
to the living room. His face is quite grave. He looks
soberly at Claude's cap. Then he puts it on the table
beside the bottle.

Dissolve to

Sound of engines begin and carry through to morning.
Ronnie and Claude dressed to take the boat out. Ann in
the robe. Ann facing Ronnie. They look at one another.

                    RONNIE

        Steady.

                    ANN
        Yes.

Ronnie moves; he comes to Ann, puts his hands on her shoulders,
stoops and kisses her. She is quite still, yet her fingers
are white with gripping Ronnie's arms.

                    ANN
            You've kissed me twice now.

                    RONNIE
        Yes.   Steady, now.

                    ANN
        Yes.

Ronnie and Claude go out. The engines continue through

DISSOLVE TO

                        -59-

The boat leaving the wharf. Beginning to go fast. The
engines louder. Dissolve interspersed with bursting
shells and the sound of the torpedo. the engines sink.

DISSOLVE TO

Boat drifting in toward wharf. Ann waiting on wharf.
Ronnie and Claude in the boat, their faces tired, greasy.
Claude looking up at Ann. But they make no sound, no
movement as the boat is warped in and they mount the
ladder.

                         ANN
                    (Looks at them)
            You're back!

                         RONNIE
            Quite.

                         ANN
                    (Looking at Claude)
            Did you make a hit? Did you?

                         RONNIE
            Quite.

                         ANN
                    (Moves. She goes to Claude,
                    grips his arms)
            You did it. It's all right, now.

Ronnie watches them.

                         ANN
            I was afraid. I was afraid. But you
            had to go. You have to kill them.
                    (She clings to Claude with
                    her hands, hard. She looks
                    back at Ronnie.)
            Go on for a minute, Ronnie, do you
            mind?

                         -60-

192

                    RONNIE
Right.
          (He goes on)

                    ANN
We must tell him.

                    CLAUDE
Yes. We must tell him.

                    ANN
Because we don't lie. Ronnie and
I don't lie.

                    CLAUDE
Yes. I'll tell him now.
          (Tries to free himself.)

                    ANN
          (Suddenly clings to Claude)
Now? Are you going to tell him now?

                    CLAUDE
Why not now?

                    ANN
Suppose he hates it,

                    CLAUDE
All right - suppose. We have already
lied to him. Let's don't lie any
more.

                    ANN
I'm afraid. Let me tell him.

                    CLAUDE
No. It's my do.
          (He looks at her)
I say. We'll be married as soon as
it's over. If it ever is.

                    ANN
Yes. If that matters. But weddings are
as dead as peace.
          **(She releases him; he moves toward
          Ronnie.)**
Claude.
          (He pauses, looks back)
You won't lie, now?

                    CLAUDE
Lie?

                    ~~-47-~~
                    -61-

                    ANN
Are you going to tell him we are
in love?

                    CLAUDE
What? Love? O good gad.

                    ANN
Don't lie to him any more, Claude

                    CLAUDE
No. But aren't we?

                    ANN
Are we?

                    CLAUDE
Right. You know. I don't. Are you?

                    ANN
I don't know either.

                    CLAUDE
Right. I shan't lie.
        (He goes on. Ann watches him. He
        approaches Ronnie. Ronnie looks
at him quietly)
Ronnie, when we were tykes, messing
about in the brook and all she said
she would marry me. You remember. How
she always said it; all three of us
said it. And when we were bigger we
talked about how it would be in the
chapel, with Mr. Thorndyke and veils
and wreathes and the voice that
breathed O'er Eden? You remember?
Still children, you know. Well, we
aren't children anymore, She's not
and I'm not. And, gad, that chapel
and Mr. Thorndyke seem a million miles
away, and there's not any Eden anymore,
and the wear is khaki and not veils.
        (He is serious, intent, watching
        Ronnie, who watches him in turn
        quietly)
We didn't wait, Ronnie.

                    -48-
                    - 62 -

194

                              RONNIE
                    (Looks at Claude gravely for
                    a long moment - then quietly)
          I know it.

NIGHT - A NARROW STREET

Choked with a long line of halted trucks. Neither end of the
line can be seen, from each truck the driver leans angrily out,
looking ahead, shouting.

An American M.P. running beside the line. He is angry. The
line is apparently endless, blocking the intersections. The
M.P. grows angrier and angrier; pedestrians halt and look back.
At last the M. P. Comes in sight of the head of the line. In
the street before it is a group of people: the drivers, French
soldiers and civilians with gesticulant arms waving loaves of
bread and bottles. The M.P. runs up, raging. Then, between the
legs he sees a foot. It is swinging idly, the invisible owner
apparently lying on his back in the street, one leg crossed over
the other knee. The M.P. thrusts himself into the group and sees
Claude lying on his back in the street, one leg swinging idly
across the other knee, his hands behind his head and his head
pillowed on an empty bed.

                              CLAUDE
                    Good day, Corporal. Perhaps you can
                    persuade these chaps to not drive
                    through my bedroom.

Bogard and McGinnis walking along the street. They come in sight
of the group before the halted trucks.

                              McGINNIS
                    It's a fight. Come along.

The line of trucks is now moving past. Bogard and McGinnis facing
the M.P. and Claude. The M.P. is holding Claude on his feet.

                              BOGARD
                    What's this, Corporal?

Claude is quite drunk. The M.P. is having trouble holding him up.

                                -49-
                                -63-

                                McGINNIS
                    It's just another of those Navy eggs.
                    The ones that dash about the harbor
                    in those little boats. They pick
                    them out of the gutters here all night
                    long. But I didn't know our M.P.'s
                    had to nurse them too.

Claude is quite drunk, swaying - the M.P. holds him up.

                                M. P.
                    Stand up! These are officers!

                                CLAUDE
                        (Focuses his eyes on Bogard,
                        swaying. His arms about the
                        M.P.'s neck.
                    Cheer-o, Sir! Name's not Beatty, I hope.

                                BOGARD
                    No.

                                CLAUDE
                    Ah. Hoped not. My mistake. No offense
                    what?

                                BOGARD
                    You'd better take him to his boat,
                    hadn't you?

                                M. P.
                    I thought of that before the Captain did.
                    He says he can't go aboard his ship after
                    dark because they put the ship away at
                    sundown.

                                BOGARD
                    Puts it away?

Claude sways; the M.P. jerks him savagely up.

                                M. P.
                    Stand up, you! Maybe the Captain can make
                    sense out of it. Damned if I can. He
                    says they keep the boat under the wharf.
                    Run it under the wharf at night, and they
                    can't get it out again until the tide falls
                    tomorrow.

                                -50-
                                - 64 -

                    BOGARD
              (Looks at McGinnis)
What's this?

                    McGINNIS
You know. You've seen them. Those
little boats, launches. Camouflaged and
all. Dashing up and down the harbor.
they do that all day and sleep in the
gutters here all night. Gutters full,
and their M.P.'s carting them away like
nursemaids in a park.

                    BOGARD
Oh.
              (Looks at Claude)
Well, you can't leave him here in
that shape.

                    CLAUDE
          (Glassily, his voice pleasant,
          cheerful, courteous.)
Quite all right - 'sure you. Used to it.
Confounded rough pave though. Should
force French do something about it. Visting
lads jolly well deserve decent field to
play on, what?

                    M. P.
And he was jolly well using all of it too.
Had them trucks stopped for three blocks,
blocking the cross street too, and him done
gone to bed in the middle of the street.
Laying there and arguing with them whether
he ought to get up and move or not. He
said the trucks ought to turn back and go
around by another street because he couldn't
use any other street to sleep in because
this street was his.

                    BOGARD
His?

                    CLAUDE
          (Pleasant, cheerful)
Billet, you see. Must have order, even in
war emergency. Billet by lot. This street
mine; no poaching, eh? Next street Jamie
Wutherspoon's.But lorries can go that street
because Jamie not using it yet.Not in bed
yet. Insomnia. Knew so. Told them.Lorries
go that way. See now?

                    ~~51~~
                    - 65-

                                                      197

                    BOGARD
          Was that it, Corporal?

                    M. P.
          He told the captain. He wouldn't get up.
          He just laid there, arguing with them.
          telling somebody to go and get one of
          their books, their -----

                    BOGARD
          King's regulations?

                    M. P.
          Yes, sir. To see if the book said if he
          had the right of way, or the trucks. and
          then I got him up and then the Captain
          came along. What shall I do with him?

**Bogard looks at Claude. Claude yawns, terrifically. Bogard
looks across the street, toward a cafe.**

                    BOGARD
          I'll take him. Will you go across there
          and ask for my driver? Captain Bogard.
          I'll take care of him.

**The M. P. salutes and departs. Bogard supports Claude. Again
Claude yawns.**

                    McGINNIS
          What are you going to do with him?

                    BOGARD
          I don't know. Take him out to the aerodrome and
          put him to bed. I can't leave him here in
          this shape.

                    McGINNIS
          Won't that be getting him awful close to the
          war? You might scare him to death. But
          then I guess he wouldn't know what it was.

                    BOGARD
          Nonsense. They must do more than just ride
          around the harbor in those launches. It
          must be more than that.

                    -58-
                    - 66 -

198

                    McGINNIS
Maybe they give them the boats to keep
them out of the street during the day.
Look here. Why not take him along in the
morning? Show him some war. It would
be a shame for him to spend the war
in France and never see a gun shot at
him.

                    BOGARD
No.

                    McGINNIS
Oh, come on. Give him something to
get tight for.

                    BOGARD
I guess not.

                    McGINNIS
Oh, come on. Think of coming out of
a drunken stupor in a necklace of Archie
a thousand feet over Mannheim. You'll
never have such a chance again. Give
the guy a break.

                    BOGARD
We'll see.

Claude sways, yawns.

                    BOGARD
Steady. The car will be herein a minute.

The car comes up; they help Claude into it. It goes on, the
sound of the engine carries over and becomes the sound of
the Handley-Page in flight.

New scene of start from aerdrome

Darkness, save for the instrument panel light; clock says
ten past two. Bogard and McGinnis in the office; forward
in the gunner's pit in the nose Claude's head can be seen.
He is looking constantly about, like a curious countryman
come to town.

                    ~~-53-~~
                    -67-

                    BOGARD
        I shouldn't have brought him. But he did
        fire that gun, though. He even put the
        drum on himself, didn't he?

                    McGINNIS
        Yes. If he just doesn't forget what it is
        for. Or let it flop around and shoot
        back this way. If he wants to shoot
        himself in the leg with it, that's all
        right. But ---

                    BOGARD
        He seems to know how to shoot it. Don't
        you remember what he was telling tonight?
        Something about shooting out a channel
        marker light at seven hundred yards?

                    MCGINNIS
        Good Lord. Do they let them have bullets
        in those boats?

                    BOGARD
        Maybe I shouldn't have brought him.

They look forward, where Claude is looking ceaselessly this way
and that.

                    BOGARD
        We'll get there and unload and haul air
        for home. Maybe in the dark they won't
        find us.

                    McGINNIS
        Don't you kid yourself. There's not a
        Hun squadron between Wipers and the coast that
        don't know we have passed and that we
        will have to come back. They're probably
        already drawing lots for us. In about
        three hours he's going to see something
        he never saw before.

                    BOGARD
        Damn it, it would be a shame, like you said,
        for his country to be in this mess for four
        years and him not even to see a gun pointed
        at him.

                        -54-
                       -68-

200

                    McGINNIS
          He'll see more than one this morning if
          he don't keep his head in,

They approach the objective. McGinnis climbs down to the bomb
toggles. Searchlights begin to probe, and shrapnel. Bogard fires
the Very signal and dives, the three other machines follows. In
a searchlight beam he sees Claude, leaning far overside, looking
down, withon his face an expression of rapt and childlike interest.
But he is firing the Lewis gun. Bogard signals with his hand and
zooms, the bombs whistle down. Archie again; he dodges through
it, dodging the lights, Another beam catches them; in it he
sees Claude hanging out the cockpit, looking back toward the lower
right wing.

They fly out of the lights and the shells. McGinnis returns and
fires the Very, standing up and looking back. Three other
Very lights show behind them; McGinnis sits down.

                         McGINNIS
              All right. I counted all of them
                   (Looks forward. The forward
                   cockpit is now empty)
              Where's the King's own? You didn't
              dump him out, did you?

Bogard also looks at the empty gun pit.

                         McGINNIS
              No; there he is: see? Hanging out the
              side. Damn it, I told him not to spew
              it overside. There he comes back.

Claude's head comes into sight; at once he sinks from view
again.

                         BOGARD
              He's coming back here. Stop him. Tell
              him to stay out there, that we'll have every
              Hun in their channel group on us in a half
              hour, and we'll need that gun.

McGinnis climbs down and goes to the entrance to the passage forward. He stoops; Claude is on his hands and knees in the
passage, almost out.

                         -55-
                         - 69-

                                                    201

                    McGINNIS
Get back!

                    CLAUDE
Bomb!

They shriek above the noise of the engines.

                    McGINNIS
Yes! They were bombs! We gave them hell!
Get back, I tell you! Have every hun in
France on us in twenty minutes! Get back
to your gun!

                    CLAUDE
Bomb! All right?

                    McGINNIS
Yes! Yes! All right. Back to your
gun, damn you!

Claude goes back into passage. McGinnis returns to the office.

                    McGinnis
He went back. Want me to take her
awhile?

                    BOGARD
All right.

McGinnis takes the wheel.

                    BOGARD
Ease her back some. I'd just as soon
it were daylight when they come down on
us.

                    McGINNIS
Right.
          (He eases back the throttle.
           Suddenly he moves the wheel)
What's the matter with that right
wing? Watch it ...... See? I'm
flying on the aileron and a little
rudder. Feel it?

                    BOGARD
          (Taking the wheel)
I didn't notice that; maybe because she
was wide open. Wire, I guess. I didn't
think that Archie was that close. Watch
her, now.

                    -56-
                    - 70 -

202

                    McGINNIS
                 (Takes the wheel again)
Right. So you're going with him
on his boat.

                    BOGARD
Yes. I want to see what they do.
There must be more to them than
we know about.

                    McGINNIS
Why don't you take Collier along,
with his mandolin? Then you could
sail around and sing.

                    BOGARD
Get that wing up.

                    McGINNIS
Right.

The ship goes on. It begins to be dawn. Then the Germans
appear, squadron after squadron of scouts.

                    McGINNIS
Well, here they come.
Look at them. They look like
mosquitoes in September. I hope
he doesn't get worked up and think
he's playing that beaver game with
his pal he kept on talking about
If he does, he'll be just two down,
provided the devil has a beard ..
Want the wheel? *Show part of fight —*

DAYLIGHT

The sun is up. The ship landing on the beach. Bogard and
McGinnis are strained, tired. Claude is hanging over the cockpit,
looking back at the right wing with that rapt and childlike
interest.

                    McGINNIS
What do you suppose he is looking at now?

                    BOGARD
Maybe at bullet holes.
                 (He blasts the starboard engine)
Must have the riggers go over this
ship right away.

                    -57-
                    -71-

                                                              203

                    McGINNIS
        He could see some closer than that. I'll
        swear I saw tracer going into his back at
        one time. Or maybe it's the ocean he's
        looking at. But he must have seen that
        when he came over from England.

The maching levels off and lands. Yet still Claude hangs far
overside. Looking backward and downward at something beneath
the right wing. The Machine stops. He ducks down. Bogard
cuts the engines; they can hear Claude in the passage. He
emerges just as Bogard and McGinnis climb down from the office.
Claude's face is bright, eager, his voice high, excited.

                    CLAUDE
        O, I say! O good gad! What a chap! What a
        judge of distance! If Ronnie could only have
        seen! O good gad! Or maybe they aren't
        like ours? Don't load themselves as soon as
        the air strikes them?

Bogard and McGinnis look at him.

                    McGINNIS
        What don't what?

                    CLAUDE
        The bomb. It was magnificent; I say,
        I shan't forget it. Oh, I say, you know!
        It was splendid!

Bogard and McGinnis look at him.

                    McGINNIS
                 (In a faint voice)
        The bomb?

McGinnis and Bogard glare at one another.

                 BOGARD & McGINNIS
        That right wing!

They spring to the trap and hurl themselves through it, Claude
following and run around the ship and look under the right wing.
A bomb hanging by its tail, the tip just touching the sand. Beside the print of the tire is the delicate line where the tip
has dragged.

                    -58-
                    -72-

    204

                    CLAUDE
               (Bright, eager, excited)
          Frightened, myself. Tried to tell
          you. But realized you knew your business
          better than I. Skill. Marvelous! Oh
          I say, I shan't forget it.

A STREET

Bogard and Claude walking along.

                    CLAUDE
          Marvelous. Absolutely. Gad, when
          I tell her.

                    BOGARD
          Who is this we are going to call on?

                    CLAUDE
          Not call. It's home. We'll stop
          in for a moment. Ronnie may be there.

                    BOGARD
               (Stops)
          Ronnie? Home? Is your wife's name Ann?

                    CLAUDE
               (Looks at Bogard)
          Her name is Ann. Do you know her?

LIVING ROOM

Bogard and Ann. They are standing.

                    BOGARD
          So you didn't wait for me.

                    ANN
          Wait for you?

They look at one another.

                    ANN
          Was there any reason why I should have?

                    -59-
                    -73-

                                                        205

                    BOGARD
          No.
                  (He looks about; his expression
                  is quizzical.)
                    ANN
                  (Watches Bogard)
          What do you mean?

                    BOGARD
          Nothing. It just struck me as amusing.
          When I saw you in England you seemed so
          bloodthirsty. Wanted to kill all the
          Germans. And now I find you married to
          a toy sailor.

Ann watches him, grave, still.

                    BOGARD
          But It's not him I am laughing at.
          I'm laughing at myself. As you are
          doing.

Ann watches him, grave, still.

                    BOGARD
          You knew I was going to enlist.
          I didn't lie to you.

She doesn't answer - watches him.

                    BOGARD
          And that wasn't all you knew that after-
          noon in Oxford.

She doesn't answer.

                    BOGARD
          Was it?

                    ANN
          No.

He moves toward her. She doesn't stir. He stops.

                    BOGARD
          You needn't be afraid. I burned this
          all out of me two years ago, looking
          for you.

                    ANN
          I'm not afraid.

                    -60- -74-

     206

                    BOGARD
          No. You and your borther and your hus-
          band have all escaped into that little
          boat.
                    (He looks at her, quizzical)
          Well. I looked for you for two years.
          At least I have found out that I will
          never find you. That's something, isn't
          it? But I'm not laughing at your husband.
          It's myself I'm laughing at.

The door opens; Bogard turns. Ronnie and Claude enter.

                    CLAUDE
          There he is. He said he knew you
          and Ann. A lark that he should be the
          one who took me, eh?

The sound of the engine begins and carries over to

THE WHARF

The boat beside it, the engine running. Two seamen in the boat.
Bogard, Ronnie and Claude come up.

                    CLAUDE
          Careful, now. Frightful ladder.

Ronnie descends. Bogard is about to follow, when he pauses;
he and Claude look back down the wharf. A mechanic from the
aerodrome, accompanied by a British sentry with a bayoneted
rifle, comes up. The mechanic carries a bundle.

                    MECHANIC
          From Lieutenant McGinnis, sir.

                    BOGARD
                    (Takes bundle)
          Thanks.

Mechanic salutes and he and sentry retreat. Claude looks brightly
at bundle.

                    CLAUDE
          I say. It's large enough to be serious,
          isn't it?

                    BOGARD
                    (Opens bundle)
          Yes.

                    -61-
                    -75-

                                                    207

Claude watches. The bundle contains a sofa cushion, a Japanese
parasol, a comb and a few sheets of toilet paper and a note.
Bogard looks at the objects; Claude with interest.

                         CLAUDE
              I say. You shan't need that!

                         BOGARD
              No
                    (He opens note)

              "Couldn't find a camera, and Collier
              wouldn't let me have his mandolin.
              But maybe one of them can play on the
              comb. Mac"

Bogard looks at the note.

                         CLAUDE
                    (Watching Bogard)
              No bad news, I hope.

                         BOGARD
              Not for me. No.

                         CLAUDE
              Shall we go aboard, then? Mind that
              ladder. Frightful
                    (He ceases, looks up grips
                    Bogard's arm)
              There! See?

                         BOGARD
              What? See what?

                         CLAUDE
                    (Pointing across basin)
              The Ergenstrasse'. That I told about last
              might.

Focus on rusting trap, with mass of cables about the mast.

                         CLAUDE
                    (Voice goes on)
              You know. The one that doesn't count any-
              more, and the one who calls her by mistake
              loses two beavers. Gad, if Ronnie were only
              to call her I'd be only one down.

                         =68=
                         - 76 -

208

The sound of the engine increases and carries over.

The boat leaving the harbor.

                    BOGARD
              (Looking about in a kind of
               sober alarm.)
         Are we going outside?

                    CLAUDE
         Quite.

                    BOGARD
              (Looks about at the machine gun
               and the torpedo tube)
         Look here. What's this?
              (Touches the tube)
         What's in here?

                    CLAUDE
         It's the torpedo.

                    BOGARD
         Torpedo?

                    CLAUDE
         I thought you knew.

                    BOGARD
         You mean that you ---- that we -----
         where are we going?

                    CLAUDE
         Zeebrugge.

                    BOGARD
         Zeebrugge?

                    CLAUDE
         Quite. Lark, eh?

The sound of the engine carries through

ZEEBRUGGE HARBOR ENTRANCE
The boat going fast. Bogard crouching, terrified. Machine guns
fire at them from the mole. They enter the harbor. Ahead a
crusier begins to fire at them. Bogard glares about at Claude
at the torpedo release, at Ronnie steering straight toward
freighter. The cruiser fires again. Ronnie turns his head
slightly.

                    ~68~
                    - 77-

                         RONNIE
           Beaver!

                         CLAUDE
                    (Jerks up, looks at Cruiser's
                    basket masts)
           O damn! O you putt! Now I'm three down
           again!
                    (He stoops again)

Bogard crouches, glaring wildly. Ronnie heads straight for the
freighter, which now also fires at them. Shot of the freighter
as it appears to the terrified Bogard, as if the boat were about
to ram it.

                         BOGARD
              Man! Man!

Ronnie signals. Shot of Claude's hand pulling lever. Under
water shot of hull, showing how torpedo drops only part of
the way out and then hangs.

The boat turns. Bogard crouches looking back at the cruiser which
is still firing at them. It stops; Bogard looks forward again
and sees that they are rushing down on the freighter again. He is
terrified, the boat shoots past close under the freighter's side.
Bogard looks back at Claude in terror.

                         CLAUDE
                    (Speaking to Bogard)
           Under Ronnie's seat there. A bit of a
           crank. If you'll just hand it to me ---

Bogard finds the crank and passes it back. Claude fits it into
socket on tube. Bogard watching. The boat rushes in a close
circle about the freighter. Claude glances up and sees Bogard's
wild face.

                         CLAUDE
                    (Cheerfully)
           Didn't go that time.

                         BOGARD
           Go? It didn't --- the torpedo ----

                         -78-

                    CLAUDE
            (He and one seaman drawing the
            torpedo back into tube)
No. Clumsy. Always happening. Should
think clever chaps like engineers ---
Happens, though. Draw her in and try
her again.

                    BOGARD
But the nose! The cap! It's still
in the tube?

                    CLAUDE
Absolutely. But it's working now,
loaded. Screw's started. Get it back
and drop it clear. If we should slow up
or stop, it would overtake us. Drive
back into tube. Bingo! As Mac says,
What?

                    BOGARD
            (Rises. Leans toward seaman,
            reaches his hand.
Letme have that winch!

                    CLAUDE
Steady. Mustn't draw her back too fast.
Jam her into head of tube ourselves. Same
bingo. Best let us. Every cobbler to
his last, what?

                    BOGARD
Quite. Oh Quite. Oh absolutely.
            (Leans on tube)

The seaman turns the winch slowly while Claude taps on tube
with spanner, delicately, listening to the sound, following
the torpedo up the tube. A long thread of saliva drips
from Bogard's mouth. He wipes it away.

                    CLAUDE
            (Rises)
Right, Ronnie!

                    ~~65~~
                    -79-

                                                        211

The boat straightens out, draws off and heads for the freighter
again. Again the two ships begin to fire at it. Bogard watches
the freighter in quiet horror. A shell bursts right over the boat.
Bogard looks back and sees Claude down. Bogard springs to the
lever before the seaman can move.

                         BOGARD
          I'll pull it!
                    (He grasps the lever and looks
                    forward at Ronnie's lifted hand,
                    his face gray, sick looking. Ronnie
                    signals and Bogard pulls lever.)

Underwater shot shows torpedo leaving tube.

The boat shoots aside, the torpedo goes on and strikes the
freighter. Bogard becomes sick, vomits. The sound of the
engine carries through.

The boat approaching Boulogne. Bogard and one seaman stooping
over Claude. Claude is conscious again. Bogard putting a
bandage on his head.

                         CLAUDE
          Frightfully stupid of me.

                         BOGARD
          How do you feel now?

                         CLAUDE
          All right, thanks, not hurt. Frightful
          headache; that's all. Daresay they'll
          patch it up all right again. Where are
          we Hubert?

                         SEAMAN
          Almost back 'ome, sir.

Claude sits up and looks about. Closeup shows him blinking; a
puzzled look comes into his face. Blinks again, draws hand
across his eyes. He is suddenly quite grave.

                         BOGARD
          Eyes hurt, too ?

                         CLAUDE
          Oh no. I feel quite fit.
                    (Looks at Ronnie's back)
                    (Lowers his voice)
          I say. He didn't notice, did he?

                    BOGARD
Notice what?

                    CLAUDE
The Ergenstrasse. That they had
shifted her.

                    BOGARD
Oh.

                    CLAUDE
He didn't notice at all. O Gad! O
Jove!

The boat now inside harbor.

                    BOGARD
          (Touches the tube)
Does this often happen. Failing to
go out?

                    CLAUDE
Oh yes. Why they put on the windlass.
Made first boat; no windlass; Whole
thing blew up one day. So put on
windlass.

                    BOGARD
But it happens sometimes, even now? They
blow up sometimes, even with the windlass?

                    CLAUDE
Well, can't say, of course. Boats go out.
Not come back. No way of knowing what
happened. Not heard of one ever being
captured yet. Possible. Not to us, though.
Not yet.

                    BOGARD
No. No.
          (Looks gravely and soberly about)
Look here. May I call/your wife again?

                    CLAUDE
O gad, yes. Knew her before; old friend
Call anytime.

                    BOGARD
Thank you. I have something -- there is
something I want to ---

                    -61-
                    -81-

                                        213

                    CLAUDE
O quite. Must see more of one another.
Ronnie likes you too. Not talk much, but
I can tell.
          (He is looking forward; there
          is an expression sober, strained
          tense about his eyes; again he
          draws his hand across them.)

                    BOGARD
          (Watches him)
You'd better go straight to the hospital.

                    CLAUDE
Oh no. I'm all right. Headache gone by
morning. Daresay good stiff drink will
do it. But still a little groggy; eyes
woozy a bit.
          (He lowers his voice)
Listen. Is Ergenstrasse still there?

                    BOGARD
Yes. She's in plain sight now.
          (He is looking at Claude)

                    CLAUDE
Watch, now!
          (Raises his voice)
Ronnie. That Argentine ship. How
do you suppose it got past us here? Might
have put in here as well; French would
have bought the wheat. I say. How long
has it been since we had a strange ship
in here. Been months, hasn't it?

Ronnie doesn't move, doesn't answer. Claude sits tense, his
face strained.

                    RONNIE
          (Suddenly points)
Beaver!

                    CLAUDE
          (Whispering)
Is it the Ergenstrasse he's pointing at?

                    BOGARD
          (Watching Claude)
Yes. Look here -----

214

                    CLAUDE
          O damn you! O you putt! It's the
          Ergenstrasse! O confound you!
          Now I'm just two down!

                    BOGARD
          Look here. I'm going to take you
          to the hospital.

The boat drifts into the wharf. The seamen make fast.
Bogard stands up, looking down at Claude.

                    BOGARD
          You come along now.

                    CLAUDE
          I'm all right. I shall see to it. Right
          away. Soon as we put the boat away ship-
          shape.

                    BOGARD
          I'll wait and go along.

                    CLAUDE
          Absolutely not. You go along. Ronnie
          and I will see to it.
               (He looks past Bogard at Ronnie)

Ronnie pauses.

                    BOGARD
               (Looks from one to the other of them)
          You see to it, Boyce Smith. Let them
          look at his head right away.

                    RONNIE
          Right.

Bogard mounts the ladder, looks back. Ronnie and Claude look
at him.

                    BOGARD
          Well, cheereo. And thanks. I'll see
          you soon. I'm going to use the permission
          you gave me, Hope.

                    CLAUDE
          O quite. O absolutely.

Bogard goes on. Ronnie looks at Claude.

                         RONNIE
                  What's the matter?

Claude indicates the seamen with his head.

                         RONNIE
                     (Looks at them.)
                  Go topside a moment, will you?

The seamen mount to the wharf.

                         RONNIE
                     (Looks at Claude)
                  What is it?

                         CLAUDE
                  I can't see.

                         RONNIE
                  Gad, what did you do that for?

                         CLAUDE
                  Gad, its a mess, isn't it? O good gad.

NIGHT - A STREET
HOUSE OF FRENCH CIVILIAN DOCTOR

Ronnie and Claude get out of a cab. They wear civilian clothes.
Ronnie gets out first, looks both ways along the street, turns
back to cab.

                         RONNIE
                  All right.
                       (He steadies Claude out.)

Claude cannot see. They stand side by side so that Claude's
elbow just touches Ronnie's.

                         RONNIE
                  All right?

                         CLAUDE
                  Right.

They cross the pavement so Claude able now to walk as if he
could see. They ring the bell, the sound of the bell carries
through to.

RECEPTION ROOM

The doctor is oldish man.

                         ~P4~

                    DOCTOR
          Messieurs.

                    RONNIE
          Monsieur le docteur. Nous sommes des
          touristes Americains riches. No, not
          rich. Tourists. Americans. Not
          soldiers.

                    DOCTOR
          You are fortunate, monsieur.
                    (He speaks in a dray tone; he
                    knows that they are concealing
                    something)

                    RONNIE
          Yes, Monsieur. Not soldiers. My
          friend here has suffered an accident
          to his head.

                    DOCTOR
          So I see. And not being solide s, you
          cannot take him to the army base.

                    RONNIE
          Yes. Will you examine it?

                    DOCTOR
          Why not? Come this way.
                    (He turns toward door)

Claude moves before Ronnie does and so loses contact with
Ronnie's elbow. The doctor watching sharply.

                    DOCTOR
          Ah.

Ronnie tries to recover, but Claude has already given himself
away.

                    DOCTOR
          Your friend has suffered more than an
          injury to the back of his head, eh? Now
          he could not be a soldier even if he
          wanted to, eh?

                    RONNIE
          Yes.

                    DOCTOR
          Your friend undoubtedly stumbled and
          fell on the stairs, eh?

                         -95-

                                             217

                    RONNIE
        Undoubtedly, Monsieur the Doctor.

                    DOCTOR
            (Takes Claude's arm quite gently)
        Come. Will you wait here, Monsieur who
        is not a soldier?

                    RONNIE
        Undoubtedly, Monsieur the Doctor.

Exit Doctor and Claude. Ronnie goes to the window and stands
looking out.

THE SITTING ROOM

Bogard and Ann. They are standing.

                    BOGARD
        I have come back to apologize.

                    ANN
        Oh, I see.

                    BOGARD
        Did you think I had another reason
        for coming back?

Ann doesn't answer, watches him gravely.

                    BOGARD
        I went with them today in the boat.

                    ANN
        Oh, to apologize.

                    BOGARD
        For what I said -- thought.

                    ANN
        Did you think that you are anybody
        could hurt me about Claude and Ronnie?

                    BOGARD
        No. It wasn't you or Claude or Ronnie I
        was trying to hurt. But that's over now.
        So shall we stop pretending and say good-
        bye and good luck?

                    ~~73~~
                    -86-

218

                    ANN
Pretending?

                    BOGARD
You knew I was going to enlist that
afternoon. You knew why. You knew
that when I was holding you in my
arms. You knew what I was thinking.
Do you want me to say it, or had you
still rather pretend?

                    ANN
No.

                    BOGARD
You knew I loved you, And that I
thought you would love me. Didn't you?

                    ANN
Yes.

                    BOGARD
And then I came back, in uniform, a
foreign uniform, and you had not even
left a message. You didn't even say,
well done, like the sergeants and the
corporals did. And then when I find you
again, you are married. You lied to me.

                    ANN
Yes. I have lied.

                    BOGARD
But you can always say you had to. I will
believe you. I can understand how Ronnie
should have thrown his weight for Hope.
And you young too, with no people except him.
That was it, wasn't it?

                    ANN
No.

                    BOGARD
            (Takes cigarette, crushes it slowly.
            Looks down at his hand)
Well. I can understand that too. I know
now that Hope is a better man at eighteen
than I was, and he will be a better one
at twenty-five than I am. Well --
            (He throws away the ruined cigarette
            and approaches, his hand extended.)

                    -87-

                                        219

                    ANN
          (Lifts her hand, falls back.
          Faintly)
      No. No.

                    BOGARD
          (Moves quickly)
          No? No? Ann! What does that mean?
    She looks at him, her hand raised, palm out.

                    BOGARD
          (He moves, he is about to take
          her in his arms, then he pauses)
      I can't now. Not after today. I
      would have before. Before I went with
      them, with him. I can do that, at least;
      at least there won't be any more lying
      in it. Will you say goodbye?

                    ANN
          (She does not take his hand)
      Yes. No more lying. No more anything
      now. Not after I tell you.

                    BOGARD
      Tell me what?

                    ANN
          (Looks at him)
      Claude and I are not married.

                    BOGARD
          (Moves toward her)
      Ann!
          (He pauses, looks at her)
      But he said ..... I don't
          (He looks at her)
      Oh. I see. You just didn't
      wait for the parson.

                    ANN
      Yes. I was lying about that. And
      you didn't lie to me. So I'm not
      lying to you, either, now.

                    BOGARD
      No. No. Very honorable. Very. It's
      Ronnie you're lying to, eh?

                    ANN
      No. He knows.

                    -88-

                    BOGARD
          Oh. I see. A family affair of not lying.
          I see. God, you are a filthy lot, aren't
          you?

                    ANN
          Filthy?
                    (She looks at him. They look
                    at one another. Then she goes
                    to the door and holds it open)

                    BOGARD
          Forgive me.- for saying that. I'm not
          cringing, understand. I just ask pardon
          for saying what I should not have said
          even to a streetwalker.

Ann doesn't answer. She stands holding the door open. For a
moment longer they look at one another. Then Bogard goes out.
Ann closes the door, stands beside it. Suddenly she begins
to cry, quietly.

THE DOCTOR'S RECEPTION
ROOM

Ronnie looking out the window. The Doctor enters. Ronnie
turns.

                    DOCTOR
                    (Puts his hand on Ronnie's
                    shoulder.)
          Report your friend to the basem my friend.

                    RONNIE
          Sorry.

                    DOCTOR
          He cannot hide the fact that he cannot see.

                    RONNIE
          Perhaps have a boat. Don't need to see in
          boat. Do the seeing myself. Claude only
          pulls gadget, anyway. Won't need to see.
          You mean, he won't see again?

                    DOCTOR
          He can see a little. But he will be completely
          blind in a month.

                    RONNIE
          Fix him. Doctors should know how.

                         -78-
                         -79-

                                                      221

                    DOCTOR
          I can operate; yes.

                    RONNIE
          Good. Then he'll be all right, eh?

                    DOCTOR
          Who knows? It will do one of two things;
          It will restore his sight, or send him
          completely blind at once.

                    RONNIE
          Oh. And if you don't operate, he will
          go blind anyway? That it?

                    DOCTOR
          Yes.

                    RONNIE
          Oh. I see. Well. Will have to think
          about it.

THE STREET

Ronnie and Claude emerge. Ronnie looks both ways along the
street, then he and Claude take positions, Claude's elbow just
touching Ronnie's.

                    RONNIE
          All right?

                    CLAUDE
          Right.
               (They cross toward the waiting cab)
          Now we'll have to tell, Ann. Gad, it's
          a mess, isn't it?

                    RONNIE
          Don't know. Can't tell yet. We'll see.

They enter cab and drive away.

THE LIVING ROOM

                    ANN
               (Hears their feet, dabs at her
               eyes. She is watching the door
               when Ronnie leads Claude in. She
               runs to them.
          What is it?

                    -76-
                    -90-

222

                    CLAUDE
          Nothing - absolutely.

Ann runs to him, clings to him; she has not seen that he
cannot see. She begins to cry.

                    CLAUDE
          Why, what is it?

                    ANN
          Nothing'. Nothing!
               (She pulls herself together)
          You're hurt. How badly are you hurt?

                    CLAUDE
          Just a scratch. Be patched up good as
          new in a few days. But I say. What is
          it? What's happened to you? You're
          crying.
               (Touches her wet face)
          You've not cried since that day back
          home.

                    ANN
          Nothing, I tell you. How badly is
          he hurt, Ronnie?

                    RONNIE
          Not much. Just can't see.

                    ANN
               (Holds back, looks at Claude)
          Can't see? You can't see?

                    CLAUDE
          Mess, isn't it? But be fixed up right
          away. Doctor says so. Came to tell
          you.

She looks from Claude to Ronnie.

                    RONNIE
          Ask you.

                    ANN
          Ask me?

                    RONNIE
          French sawbones. Seems to know. Can't
          tell Navy office, you see. Sawbones
          says operate, may see, may not. If not
          operate, go blind anyway. What do you
          think?

Ann looks at him, wildly.

                    RONNIE
          Buck up, now. Steady.

                    ANN
          Yes. Yes. I will be.

                    RONNIE
          See nothing else. Claude says right, too.
          What?

                    CLAUDE
          Right.

                    RONNIE
          Right here, too.
                    (He looks at Ann)
          Steady now. Will do what you say.
          Must decide now, though. Boat won't
          wait.

                    ANN
                    (Strives for control)
          Right.

                    RONNIE
          Stout fellow. Knew you would.

                    ANN
          When must it be?

                    RONNIE
          Tomorrow.

                    ANN
                    (Clings to Claude again)
          Not tomorrow!

                    RONNIE
          Silly to wait. Best get it done with.

                    CLAUDE
          O quite. Absolutely.

                         ~~76~~
                         -92-

224

                        ANN
                  (Clings to Claude)
            Claude! Claude!

                        CLAUDE
            Now, now. Never saw you in such a state
            before. What is it? What has happened?

                        ANN
                  (Wildly)
            Nothing! Nothing! I have you and
            Ronnie. I don't want anything else.
            I don't ! I don't!

DOCTOR'S ANTEROOM

Ronnie and Ann.

                        RONNIE
            So it's this American.

                        ANN
            Yes.

                        RONNIE
            Thought so. Thought something back
            at Oxford there. Knew you didn't
            hate him like you said; you savaged
            him to much. Suspected something.

                        ANN
            But it's all right now. I told him
            about Claude and me, and he hates
            me now.

                        RONNIE
            H'm. Shall you tell Claude?

                        ANN
            No! No! Never. Not now. Not ever now.
            I tell you, it's all finished.

                        RONNIE
            You mean, you and Claude will go on like
            this?

                        ANN
            Yes. Don't you see, I can't let him down
            now?

                        -93-

                                                            225

                    RONNIE
        I know you wouldn't.

Ann walks up and down, beating her fists together.

                    RONNIE
        But suppose Claude sees again. Is all
        right again.

                    ANN
                (Pauses - looks at Ronnie.
                Whispers)
        If he should see ...... No! No! It's
        all finished, I tell you! He said I
        was filthy, and so I knew it was
        finished, ended. I just want you and
        Claude. You and Claude.

                    RONNIE
                (Grips Ann's shoulder)
        But if Claude sees again. No lying
        now.

                    ANN
        Ronnie! Ronnie! He wouldn't have
        me now! What have I done! What have
        I done!

                    RONNIE
                (Holding her)
        But you'd try. You'd want to. No lying,
        now.

                    ANN
        Yes. I can't help it. I can't help it.
        If he only sees! It's not love. We've
        never pretended that. You know that.

                    RONNIE
        I daresay.

                    ANN
        If he only sees! If he only sees!

The door opens; they turn. The Doctor enters. Ann starts
forward.

                    ANN
        Can he .... will he.....?

                    DOCTOR
        Courage, Madam. Though no English or
        French lady has to be reminded of courage
        these days ......

                    -94-

226

                              RONNIE
                    No go, eh?

Ann watches him, lips parted.

                              DOCTOR
                    He has looked his last on fighting
                    and on anything else.

                              ANN
                         (Turns quietly to Ronnie)
                    That answers that, Ronnie.
                         (To Doctor)
                    May we see him now?

Doctor bows, indicates door. Ann and Ronnie pass through it.

Claude in bed, his face bandaged. Ann approaches, fearfully,
essays twice to touch Claude's hand before she does so.

                              ANN
                    Claude.

                              CLAUDE
                    Hullo. That you, eh?

                              ANN
                    Claude! Claude!
                         (She is trembling, slowly she
                         begins to kneel, touching
                         Claude's face with her hands.
                         Suddenly she sprawls beside the
                         bed, her head on the bed beside
                         him.)
                    Harry! Harry! Harry!

                              CLAUDE
                         (His hand fumbles out and touches
                         her, patting her shoulder)
                    O gad. O I say, now. Crying again!

Ann Continues to sob.

                              CLAUDE
                         (His face is quite grave. He
                         pats her shoulder)
                    Now, then. Now then.

                              ⌁
                              -95-

THE LIVING ROOM

Claude in a chair. He is blind. He holds a stick. Ann sits
on the floor beside him, her face hidden in his lap. Claude's
hand rests on her head, moving faintly and lightly.

                    CLAUDE
          You called his name, you see. Harry
          three times.

                    ANN
          Did I?

                    CLAUDE
          Yes. Tell me. What?

                    ANN
          There's nothing to tell. When I saw him
          in Oxford, I thought that I hated him. But
          it was his clothes - mufti. And father
          killed, and you and Ronnie waiting to go.
          And he so safe. So I thought I hated him.
          And then when I saw that he didn't hate me.
          And I thought how it would be to get him
          into it, when he thought he was so safe.
          Because I thought I hated him.

                    CLAUDE
          But you don't.

                    ANN
          It doesn't matter. It's over now. It
          was over that day when they told Ronnie
          and me that you were ----would never ---

                    CLAUDE
          How do you know it's all over now?

Ann doesn't answer.

                    CLAUDE
          Look at me.

Ann doesn't move.

                    CLAUDE
          (Fumbles and turns her face up with
          his other hand he touches her face as
          if he were trying to read it with his
          fingers.)

For a moment Ann suffers him. Then she begins to pant.

228

                    ANN
Oh! Oh!
          (She rises stoops over him, putting
          her hands on him)
Claude! Claude!
          (His hand touches her, fumbles; she
          sinks beside him again, holding him;
          he holds her face up.)
I love you! I don't love anybody but you!

               CLAUDE
Hold hard, now. No lying, remember.

                    ANN
Lying?

               CLAUDE
About love. Not love, remember. We agreed
on that, you know.

                    ANN
Yes.

               CLAUDE
Quite. Can't love blind chap, just as
blind chap has no time to love. Go to
him.

                    ANN
Never! Never!

               CLAUDE
Go to him. Go to America with him. War
be over some day, but England will be
finished. Nothing there. Go to him.

                    ANN
Do you want me to?

               CLAUDE
Quite. Girls need husbands. But don't
need wife myself. Got no use for one.

               ANN
          (Clutching him)
No! You're lying! Now you're lying!

                                        229

MARINE OFFICE

Officers with plans, maps. British Admiral, generals, American
wing commander. Ronnie present. A pilot is reporting.

                    ADMIRAL
          And the cruiser is trained on the mole?

                    PILOT
          Yes, sir. Lying about a mile away. The
          mole and the whole harbor entrance are under
          her guns.

                    ADMIRAL
               (Turns to Ronnie)
          Is that right, Boyce Smith? You've
          been in there.

                    RONNIE
          Quite right, Sir. Seen it myself.

                    ADMIRAL
          That means we'll have to eliminate the
          cruiser first.
               (Turns to American Wing Commander)
          What's your opinion, Colonel?

                    COLONEL
          I think I can do it, Sir.

                    ADMIRAL
          Thinking is not enough, Colonel. The
          lives of a whole brigade may depend on
          whether that cruiser is put out of action
          or not.

                    COLONEL
          If it can be done, sir, my men can do it.
          Of course, it will cost a machine. The
          pilot can get enough height and get in
          there before he is stopped, but he will
          never get out again.

                    ADMIRAL
               (Looks at pilot)
          What's your opinion about that, Mister?

                    -94-
                    -98-

230

                    PILOT
          The Colonel is right, sir. A ship could
          get in there all right. And a cruiser is
          big enough to hit. But he'll never get
          out.

                    ADMIRAL
               (Muses. - They watch him. He
               looks at Colonel)
          Well, Colonel?

                    COLONEL
          I'll send Bogard, sir. If it can be done,
          he will do it.

                    ADMIRAL
          Good. Theorder will go through tomorrow.
               (Rises)

They all rise, salute.

THE SITTING ROOM

Claude in his chair; he is watching the door as Ronnie enters.

                    RONNIE
          Where's Ann?

                    CLAUDE
          In there. Better see.
               (He sits motionless as Ronnie goes
               to the door, opens it, looks in,
               closes it again, and returns,)

                    RONNIE
          Did she tell you?

                    CLAUDE
          Yes.

                    RONNIE
          Said she wouldn't. Wasn't going to.

                    CLAUDE
          Yes. It was too late, though. After the
          other day, when she came in and called his
          name. And this afternoon she told me. She's
          in love with him, Ronnie.

                    RONNIE
          Yes. Silly mess
               (He sits down)
          Been with Admiral

                    _AM_ _99_

                    CLAUDE
Is it on?

                    RONNIE
Yes. They're sending him.

                    CLAUDE
Him? Not ------?

                    RONNIE
Yes - Bogard.

                    CLAUDE
O I say. O good gad.

                    RONNIE
Yes.

                    CLAUDE
O gad, Ronnie.

                    RONNIE
What to do? I'm not admiral.

                    CLAUDE
Ronnie.
          (His face is lifted toward the
          light. Ronnie muses, sucking at
          his cold pipe)
I'm blind, and England finished. Or
will be, when this is over. America
though. Far away out of it where she
can forget about it; children and such.

                    RONNIE
Not mawkish, now.

                    CLAUDE
No. He'll never get back, Ronnie.
Flown myself. Know.

                    RONNIE
Yes. What his wing commander said. Not
get back.

                    CLAUDE
Gad, Ronnie. What will she do, with me
finished and England done for.

                    RONNIE
Would she marry him? Would he have her?

                    -94-
                    -100-

232

Claude and Ronnie: "We know the harbor." (c) MGM.

CLAUDE

Yes, I know he would. Daresay eating his
heart out, like she is. Send him a message;
say, Takecare of Ann. Don't you know he
would?

RONNIE

Yes.

CLAUDE

Ronnie?
        (His hand fumbles out. Ronnie
        does not move. After a moment
        Claude's hand touches Ronnie's)
Ronnie? We know the harbor. Know
cruiser too. Can get in before they
know we are there. Done it before.....
Ronnie?

RONNIE

Right.
        (Gets up and goes out.)

ANN
    (Enters)
Where has Ronnie gone?

CLAUDE

Gone to see Admiral.

ANN

Didn't he just come back?

CLAUDE

Yes. Forgot something, though.

ANN
    (Comes and rests her hand on
    Claude's shoulder)
You're out of it. I wish Ronnie were out
of it, too. Are they going to send him out
again?

CLAUDE

Not without me. They won't send him
without me.

-87-
-101-

234

                          ANN
            Oh ...... would you like tea now?

                        CLAUDE
            Right.

AT THE ADMIRAL'S

                        RONNIE
                (At attention before desk)
            I can get in, sir with the boat. Be in
            before they know it. But aeroplane
            different. No chance; all Hun squadrons
            be watching for aeroplane.

                        ADMIRAL
            What makes you think you can do it?

                        RONNIE
            Know harbor. Know cruiser. Been before.
            Aeroplane chap never saw place before.

                        ADMIRAL
            You may be right. If you can get in, you'll
            have a better chance of sinking it than they
            would with bombs. Don't trust aeroplanes
            myself. But the chances are you won't get
            out, yourself.

                        RONNIE
            Much chance as aeroplane, Sir.

                        ADMIRAL
            And you wish to volunteer for it? Why?

                        RONNIE
            Don't know, Sir. Hadn't thought.
            Lark, perhaps. Might let me try. If
            no go, then send aeroplane.

The Admiral looks at Ronnie. They look at one another.

                        ADMIRAL
                (Presses buzzer: orderly enters)
            Tell Mr. Morse to rescind that order to
            Colonel Watman at Blank squadron.

                          -88-
                          -102-

Orderly salutes and goes out. Admiral rises, offers hand
Ronnie shakes it.

                    ADMIRAL
          Very good, Boyce Smith. You will go out
          tomorrow. And good luck.

Ronnie salutes, exits.

THE HANGAR

Mechanics going over Bogard's bomber. Bogard watching.
Watts and Harper, his two gunners. Harper is frightened,
trembling, on the edge of funk.

                    WATTS
               (Goes to Harper)
          You yellow son.

                    HARPER
          I won't go. They can't make me. I'm
          engaged to be married.

                    WATTS
          I've got a wife and kid. What do you
          think of that?

                    HARPER
          Then she was a fool to marry a man that
          will let them send him out to commit
          suicide. Let Bogard go by himself.
          I'm not going.
               (Harper grasps him by the throat;
               they glare at one another. Then
               they struggle. The gunnery sergeant
               comes up.)

                    SERGEANT
          What the hell is this?

                    Harper
               (Is about to speak; he sees Watts
               glaring at him. Sullenly his hand
               to his throat)
          Nothing.

                    SERGEANT
          It better be nothing. Captain Bogard
          wants you.

They follow him to Bogard beside the machine.

                        -89-
                        -103-

    236

```
                    BOGARD
            I suppose you both know where we are
            going tomorrow.

                    WATTS
            Yes, sir.

                    BOGARD
            One of you has a wife and child.  Which
            one is it?

They don't answer for a moment.  Suddenly Harper moves forward.
His face is wild,  his voice wild.

                    HARPER
            I ain't going.  By God,  you can't....

Watts turns, fiercely.  Bogard watches.  Harper ceases, cowering.

                    BOGARD
            Are you the one with the family, Harper?

Harper doesn't answer.  Bogard looks at Watts.

                    BOGARD
            It's you, is it?

                    WATTS
            Yes, sir.

                    BOGARD
            Do you want me to ask the major for
            a volunteer substitute?

                    WATTS
            No, sir.

                    BOGARD
            Sure?

                    WATTS
            I guess I can go where the captain goes.

                    BOGARD
            Right.  If you men have any letters to
            write, you'd better attend to it tonight.
                (Turns and goes out.)

                    HARPER
                (Again moves suddenly)
            I wont go!  I won't!  You can't make me, you son...


                    -90-
                    -104-
```

237

Watts turns upon him, grasps him. Harper cowers, then he suddenly strikes at Watts. Watts knocks him down. Harper lies on
the floor, glaring up at Watts. Watts lifts Harper up and
draws his fist back again. Harper collapses. Watts drops him;
he lies on the floor, his face in his hands. Watts stands over
him. Bogard returning toward the mess. He passes another pilot.

                    PILOT
          You're it, eh?

                    BOGARD
          Yes.

                    PILOT
          Have you got a spare tank in your crate
          yet?

                    BOGARD
          A spare tank?

                    PILOT
          To pour Mac into
               (Jerks his head toward the mess:
               from which comes a drunken voice
               singing.)
          By morning you'll have to take him up
          with a blotter.

                    BOGARD
          Oh.
               (Goes on)

                    PILOT
          Well, good luck. You're going to need it.

Bogard goes on and enters mess.

                    McGINNIS
               (Is drunk - singing. He sees
               Bogard and stops. He is unsteady
               on his feet.)
          Hullo, teacher. Have drink.

                    BOGARD
          No.

                    -911-
                    -105-

238

                    McGINNIS
              (Approaches, drapes arm across
              Bogard's shoulder)
         Oh, come on.

                    BOGARD
         You'd better drink water for a while.

                    McGINNIS
         Water? Water? Have you forgotten
         the Johnstown flood?
              (He speaks in maudlin, breaking
              voice)

                    BOGARD
         Here. Pull yourself together.

                    McGINNIS
              (Straightens up a little)
         Don't worry about me, skipper. I
         wouldn't miss it for worlds. I've
         never been shot at by a battleship.
         Lark, eh? Beaver, what? And a
         couple of loons - that's you and me.
              (He raises his glass to drink.
              The glass is empty. He looks
              at it in drunken astonishment)
         Who in hell drank my drink?
              (He turns and weaves back toward
              the table)
         Jackson! You, Jackson!

    Mess orderly enters with fresh bottle. Bogard goes on.

    SQUADRON OFFICE

    Bogard and the Major. Map on the table.

                    BOGARD
         I will get in high and start back here
         and dive in. I should get down before
         they stop me.

                    MAJOR
         Yes. And how will youget out?

                    BOGARD
         I don't know. Swim, I guess.

                    -93-
                    -106-

                                            239

                    MAJOR
        Yes. Damn them, I wish they had to
        do one of their dirty jobs themselves,
        once.

                    BOGARD
        Yes. I'd like to see that, myself.
        Well ------
            (He rises)

                    MAJOR
        Will you have a drink?

                    BOGARD
        No, thanks. I have some letters to
        write.

                    MAJOR
        I'll see you in the morning then.

                    BOGARD
        Yes, Sure. Goodnight.
            (He goes out)

BOGARD'S HUT

He is writing at a table. On the table sits an envelope sealed
and addressed to his mother. He writes, pauses, reads what he
has written, scratches out, writes again. Facing him on the
desk lies the dogeared snapshot of Ann. He reads what he has
written, starts to write again. Then he puts down the pen and
takes up the letter and the picture and tears them slowly and
drops the pieces onto the floor. Then he stoops and gathers
them carefully up and burns them, watching the flame. Then he
goes to the window and stands there, looking out into darkness.

RONNIE'S ROOM

It is dawn; he and Claude are in uniform. When they move, it
is quietly, not to wake Ann. Claude has a bottle of whiskey
and he is dabbing it about himself as if it were perfume.

                    CLAUDE
            (Whispers)
        There. How do I smell now? Like a
        binge?

                    -95-
                    -107-

240

```
                         RONNIE
               Yes.  Are you all ready?

                         CLAUDE
               Yes.

They are dressed as when they take the boat out.

                         RONNIE
                    (Takes Claude's arm)
               Quiet, now.

                         CLAUDE
               O gad. O absolutely!

They enter the sitting room, quietly.

                         CLAUDE
                    (Turns his face toward
                    Ann's door.)
               Let's look at her, Ronnie

                         RONNIE
               Might wake her.

                         CLAUDE
               We'll be quiet.  I'll be careful.
               I shan't try to move without you.

                         RONNIE
               Well.  But careful, now.
                    (He leads Claude to the door
                    and opens it quietly, inch by
                    inch.

Ann is asleep.  They stand in the door.

                         CLAUDE
                    (Whispers)
               Ronnie.

                         RONNIE
               Hush.  Come out.  Careful, now.
                    (He leads Claude out and closes
                    the door.  They cross the floor.)
```

                    CLAUDE
               (Blunders into a chair)
          Damn!

                    RONNIE
          Now you've done it. Quick now,
          before .....
               (He ceases)

They pause and look back at the door as it opens and Ann
looks out.

                    ANN
          What is ....Ronnie! Claude!

                    CLAUDE
          O damn!

                    ANN
               (Enters looking at them, brushing
               her hair back. Her eyes are wide,
               but she is not yet alarmed.)
          Why, you're dressed to .....
               (She moves swifter, her eyes
               wide.)
          What does this mean? You're not....

They look at her quiltily like two small boys.

                    ANN
               (She runs forward and grasps
               Claude)
          Ronnie. What are you doing? Are you...?

                    RONNIE
          Job to do.

                    ANN
          But Claude! Blind! He can't......
          You must not! You must not!

                    CLAUDE
          Oh, I say. Don't need eyes to pull
          gadget.

                    ANN
               (Wildly, clinging to Claude)
          But you can't! You can't! Ronnie, don't
          let him! Don't let him, Ronnie!

                    -85-
                    -109-

     242

                    CLAUDE
Now, then. Now, then.
          (He holds her, she looking at
           him, wild and strained)
Can't let blindness lick me. Don't
you see I can't? Should be miserable
sitting here day after day. But in
boat all right. Living - not dead.
Like sitting here. Don't you see I
can't sit here and do nothing? I'm
a sailor. Been a sailor all my life.
Don't you know that?

                    ANN
Yes.

                    CLAUDE
          (He releases her; she stands
           before him)
Understand now? You see I can't sit
here and do nothing? Save that for
when I am old. Be blind long time,
but not young long. See now?

                    ANN
          (Whispers)
Yes.

                    CLAUDE
Good girl. Knew you would.
          (He takes her face between his
           hands and kisses her. She does
           not move)
Stout fellow. Know waiting's hard. But
you have waited before. And Ronnie can
see for both. All right now, eh?

                    ANN
          (Whispers)
Yes.

                    CLAUDE
Good. Where are you, Ronnie?

Ronnie takes his arm and they go out.

                              ANN
                    (Watches them with that sleep-
                    walker's expression, until the
                    door closes. Then she runs to it.)
              Ronnie! Claude!

There is no answer. After a moment the sound of a car comes.
Ann brushes her hair back, both hands to her face, panting,
striving for control. The sound of the car carries over.

THE WHARF

The sound of the boat's engines in background. A group of
officers waiting on wharf. Ronnie and Claude approaching,
walking so that Claude's elbow just touches Ronnies.

                              RONNIE
                    There they are. Steady now.

                              CLAUDE
                    Right. Can you still smell the
                    whiskey?

                              RONNIE
                    Yes.

                              CLAUDE
                    Gad, Maybe I should have put on
                    more.

They reach the officers. With his elbow Ronnie signals Claude
when to halt and salute.

                              ADMIRAL
                    All ready, are you?

                              RONNIE
                    Yes, sir.

                              ADMIRAL
                    Good. You know your orders. That cruiser
                    must be eliminated. At whatever cost.
                    Do you understand?

                              RONNIE
                    Yes, sir.

                              ADMIRAL
                    At whatever.......
                         (He ceases. He looks at Claude, he
                          sniffs)
                    So this is the way you come on duty, Hope.

                              -M-
                              -///-

                    CLAUDE
Sorry, sir.

                    ADMIRAL
Captain Cook said there was something
strange about your gait when you came
up.

                    CLAUDE
Be all right, sir, soon as I get on
the water.

                    ADMIRAL
It's disgraceful. I don't think you
can even see. If you had not volunteered
for a dangerous mission, and there was
anyway of replacing you for it, I would
have you paraded.

                    CLAUDE
Yes, sir.

                    ADMIRAL
Is he competent this morning, Boyce
Smith?

                    RONNIE
Quite, sir. Be all right once we put
out. Done it before.

                    ADMIRAL
I don't doubt it. Well.....
        (Looks from one to the other
        of them)
Let him excuse it by his conduct today,
        (Offers his hand)
Goodbye and good luck.

Ronnie takes his hand. He offers it to Claude. Ronnie nudges
Claude. Claude's hand fumbles out, misses the Admiral's, who
draws his hand sharply back.

                    ADMIRAL
Into your vessel. Perhaps some sea air
will sober you up.

Ronnie and Claude salute. The officers retreat. Ronnie and
Claude go on toward the boat.

                    -98-
                    -112-

                    CLAUDE
          Gad, Ronnie. That was touch and go,
          eh?

                    RONNIE
          All right now, though.

They reach the boat. The two seaman come to attention. Ronnie
steadies Claude to the ladder.

                    RONNIE
          You, Reeves, give Mr. Hope a hand here.
          He drank his breakfast this morning.

                    REEVES
          Ay, sir!

The seaman helps Claude into the boat. The engine is running.
The seamen take their stations.

                    CLAUDE
          Cast off forward, Burt.

The seaman casts off the headline. Reeves waits to cast off
the stern line.

                    CLAUDE
          Come aft, Burt.

Burt comes aft.

                    CLAUDE
          Hold her against the ladder while
          Reeves casts off.

                    BURT
          Sir?

                    CLAUDE
          Hold her by hand and let Reeves cast off
          that sternline.

Reeves does so; they watch Claude in surprise; Ronnie is also
looking back.

                    RONNIE
          What's that?

                    CLAUDE
          Do it ourselves, Ronnie.

                         -99-
                        -113-

246

                    RONNIE
Ourselves?

                    CLAUDE
We two enough.

                    RONNIE
Oh, yes.
          (Turns to Seamen)
Go ashore.

                    SEAMEN
Sir?

                    RONNIE
Go topside

The seamen mount to the wharf and look down into the boat,
puzzled. The boat moves, surges away from the wharf.

                    REEVES
Mr. Boyce Smith! I say, Sir!

Ronnie jerks his hand back at them. The seamen begin to run
along the wharf as the boat gains speed. It distances them.
They stop and look after it. The engine is quite loud as the
boat begins to gain speed.

THE AERODROME

The Handley-Page on the line, ready. Bogard, McGinnis, Harper
and Watts in flying clothes. Bogard is grave, Watts sober.
McGinnis is sober now. Harper looks sick.

                    BOGARD
All ready, Sergeant?

                    SERGEANT
All ready, sir.

                    BOGARD
          (Gestures at Watts and Harper)
In you go.

Watts and Harper are moving toward the trap when someone shouts.
Bogard and McGinnis turn. An orderly comes up.

                    -300-
                    -114-

                         ORDERLY
Adjutant, Sir.

                         ADJUTANT
                  (Comes up)
God, you're lucky.

                         BOGARD
Lucky?

                         ADJUTANT
It's countermanded. It's off.

                         BOGARD
Off?

                         ADJUTANT
Admiral's orders. They are sending a
torpedo boat instead. And her 's a
note for you that came out with the
order.
                  (Gives Bogard envelope)

Watts and Harper are looking on, stupefied.

                         BOGARD
                  (Opens note)
"Dear Bogard. Take care of Ann. I
know you will though. I know I don't
need to ask.   Hope"

A boat? They sent a boat?

                         ADJUTANT
Yes. I don't.......

Bogard runs. They look after him. Then they follow. Watts
and Harper have listened. Harper looks at Watts.

                         HARPER
                  (Shrieking)
I told you I wasn't going!
                  (He hurls himself at Watts before
                  Watts has time to guard himself.
                  They go down. Harper on top, beating
                  Watts' head while the Sergeant tries
                  to pull him off.)
I told you I wasn't! I told you they
couldn't make me!

The sound of an engine. The squadron Commander's two seater
on the line. Bogard runs and scrambles into it, the Adjutant
and McGinnis following. The engine is missing, cold; it has
just been cranked. McGinnis and Adjutant rush up as Bogard
settles down.

                    McGINNIS
          Where are you going?

                    BOGARD
          Boulogne! Get away!
               (He guns, the ship begins to move.)

                    McGINNIS
               (Holds onto cockpit)
          You can't take off with that cold engine!
          Are you crazy?

                    BOGARD
          Get away. Let go.

The ship moves, mechanics scramble aside. McGinnis tries to
hold on, running. Bogard tears his hands free; the ship
rushes on.

                    McGINNIS
          The fool! The fool! He didn't even
          wait to warm it!

The ship diminishes rapidly.

THE HARBOR

Bogard lands the ship on the twenty-five foot mole beside which
Ronnie's and Claude's boat lay. Two sentries rush up with
rifles in consternation.

                    BOGARD
          That boat! Mr. Boyce Smith's boat!

                    SENTRY
          It's out, Sir. They left at dawn!

Bogard glares at him, then he guns the ship, it begins to move.

                    SENTRY
          Sir! You can't do that! It's not allowed!

                    -108-
                    -116-

                                                        249

                    BOGARD
          Get out of the way!

The sentry retreats; the ship rushes toward him. He falls
flat on his face as it passes over him and takes off. Again
it fades rapidly away, the sound of the engine carrying over

THE AERODROME

Bogard lands, springs from the ship and runs toward the hangar.
He passes a mechanic.
                    BOGARD
          Get Mr. McGinnis! Quick!
               (He rushes on and into the hangar
               The sergeant is there)
          Get my ship ready.

                    SERGEANT
          Why, the Adjutant said ....

                    BOGARD
          Get my ship ready, I tell you!

The sergeant turns away, Bogard is gathering up Lewis drums
when McGinnis enters.

                    McGINNIS
          What the hell? I thought you were in
          Boulogne. The Major is raising hell
          about his Bristol.

                    BOGARD
          Get your helmet. We're going out.

                    McGINNIS
          Going out?

                    BOGARD
               (Turns upon him a wild, distracted
               face)
          Will you get your helmet and goggles?

                    McGINNIS
          Sure. Right.

Exit McGinnis. Bogard loading Lewis drums furiously into ship.
The engines begin to turn over. the sound mounting through
dissolve and continuing. The sound of exploding bombs enter
and cease, but the sound of the engines continue into and
through

                    -103-
                    -117-

250

Ronnie and Claude at sea, approaching Zeebrugge. The boat is
going fast. A line of battleships approaches. Ronnie sees
them and changes course to draw near.

                         CLAUDE
              You changed course. I felt it.

                         RONNIE
              No. Just cross swell

He steers toward the ships, the smoke of which blows low upon
the sea.

                         CLAUDE
              She'll be all right now, Ronnie.

                         RONNIE
                    (Steers toward ships)
              Yes.

                         CLAUDE
              He can take her to America. No war
              there. Quiet. Can know that tomorrow
              it will be quiet too. Not like old
              dead countries where things can come in
              and happen to you,

                         RONNIE
              Yes.

The boat passes into the smoke of the first ship. It has basket
masts.

                         CLAUDE
              And then after a while she can remember, it
              it will be quiet too then. She can be glad
              again. Like when we were all three.....
                    (He ceases. His head is raised He
                    sniffs.)
              Ronnie! I smell smoke! Beaver, Ronnie!
              Beaver!

                         RONNIE
              Right.

                    CLAUDE
          O gad! Now I'm just one down! Gad,
          Ronnie!
                    (He leans forward, his face lifted,
                    tense, bright, eager)

The boat passes into the smoke of the second ship. It has
pole masts.

                    CLAUDE
                    (Smells the smoke)
          I smell smoke! Beaver, Ronnie!

                    RONNIE
          Right.

                    CLAUDE
          O gad! We're even now! I've caught
          you! O gad! Ronnie! We're even now!

                    RONNIE
          Right.

The boat travels fast. Diminishing swiftly in

DISSOLVE

The sound of engines grows quite loud and in

DISSOLVE

Are again interspersed with the sound of bombs, then the sound
dies slowly away.

THE WESTMINISTER GAZETTE

          "FOR VALOR. MIDSHIPMEN R. BOYCE SMITH AND
          L. C. W. HOPE, R.N.R.

          By entering Zeebrugge harbor on a hazardous
          special mission and sinking an enemy cruiser
          which commanded the mole, these two officers
          gave their lives to facilitate the landing
          of troops on the mole."

DISSOLVE TO

[handwritten marginal note:] Show torpedo stuck on first try – Claude blind – Ronnie has to steer – boat dives straight into enemy ship.

                              -105-
                              -119-

252

<u>A BULLETIN, AMERICAN HEADQUARTERS</u>

"For extraordinary valor over and above
the routine of duty. Captain H. C. Bogard
with his crew composed of Second Lieutenant
Darrel McGinnis and Aviation Gunners Watts
and Harper, on a volunteer daylight raid
and without scout protection. Having arrived
too late at Zeebrugge to assist in clearing
the mole, these men proceeded to and
successfully bombed an ammunition depot
and the enemy's corps headquarters at Blank.
On the way home, although beset by enemy
aircraft, Captain Bogard succeeded in bringing his crippled machine back into our lines
before it crashed, injuring the pilot. The
rest of the crew escaped injury."

DISSOLVE TO

<u>HOSPITAL</u>

Bogard in bed, bandaged. Ann kneeling beside bed, her head
bowed and Bogard's hand lying upon it.

DISSOLVE TO

Bogard with stick and arm in sling. Ann beside him.

DISSOLVE TO

Motor car, ship, train

DISSOLVE TO

Bogard and Ann being married in chapel in England where Ann and
Ronnie and Claude grew up.

DISSOLVE TO

Bogard and Ann, his arm about her, looking up at a window in the
chapel. Workmen just finishing it.

-105-
-120-

"To the memory of Ronald Boyce Smith
Liam Claude William Hope, Midshipmen,
Royal Naval Reserve. Killed at
Zeebrugge, October, 1918."

                    BOGARD
That's where I should have been. I
should have been in that boat instead
of him.

                    ANN
No! No! Not you too. Never!
          (She clings to him. Suddenly
          she turns, crying)·
He was blind, blind! He couldn't
even see it when it came. Ronnie
could see it, but he couldn't.
He couldn't even see it when it
came to kill him. He couldn't even
say, now I've got one second more!

                    BOGARD
Hush. Hush, now. It's all right.
He's all right now.

Ann grows quiet, clinging to him.

                    BOGARD
Don't you know he's all right, when he
knows now that nothing can ever hurt
us again?

                    ANN
Yes.

                    BOGARD
Not ever, now. That's why I should
have been there.

                    ANN
But you did. You went. When you flew
down at that chateau and knew that you
wouldn't get home again.

                    -107-
                    -121-

254

                    BOGARD
Yes. God, God. If they had only all
been there: generals, the admirals
the presidents, and the kings -- theirs,
ours, all of them!

                    ANN
Hush.
        (Draws his head down to her
        breast, holding it there)
Hush - hush.

A page from *War Birds* in *Liberty* magazine (21 August 1926).

War Birds / A Ghost Story

War Birds was written in Oxford between late November 1932 and early January 1933; this facsimile is taken from a File Copy later stored as a Vault Copy, produced by the Script Department on or before 12 January 1933. Faulkner's 100-page typescript, called *A Ghost Story*, is in the possession of Hawks's estate, but as detailed in the Introduction (see note 12) it seems likely that it and *War Birds* are identical, though *A Ghost Story* may well have been the title Hawks and Faulkner preferred.

In 1926, *Liberty* magazine published serially *The Diary of the Unknown Aviator* under the title of *War Birds*. This anonymous diary, which broke off at the point of the author's death, was largely authentic. It had been written by John McGavock Grider, a young southerner whose grandfather had served as a captain in the Confederate Army and later become a banker. Major Elliot White Springs, who had served with Grider, rewrote the diary and sold it to *Liberty*, to a publishing house, and to MGM.[1] There is some evidence that Faulkner read the diary when it appeared in *Liberty*.[2] An MGM reader said of it:

> Honestly, this is the best account of a man's part in the war that I have read, it is the most thrilling. It is almost a work of unconscious art. Who touches it touches a man! The air battles are positively unequaled in war literature. I make no bones about detailing a few [i.e., in his synopsis] as he writes them; it was the only way to do the MS justice. What this boy writes makes me, who had such a comparatively feeble part in the war, feel simply toadish—it is epical, romantic, oh, incomparably romantic, on a heroic scale! A picture, with those 3 incomparable young Americans, I should say so![3]

This reader was responding to the diary, however, and not to a treatment by Springs and Merlin Taylor (May 1926) that had been bought by MGM along with the screen rights—a treatment, focused on a ludicrous love triangle, whose only relation to the Faulkner script was some business about pursuing a German aviator who had shot down one of the heroes and who turned out, on his deathbed, to be a relatively sympathetic figure; it had little or no relation to the original diary.(It is, however, quite possible that this treatment gave Faulkner the idea of linking *War Birds* with the story of John Sartoris's death, via the figure of Dorn.) It appears that no other treatments were written until Faulkner submitted a (lost) outline, "Faulkner Story No. 2," which apparently interested Hawks and led to Faulkner's being put back on the MGM payroll despite the fact that he had returned to Oxford after completing the third draft of *Turn About*.

There are many aspects of the diary that might have interested Faulkner and prompted his revision, in *War Birds*, of the story of John and Bayard Sartoris. Grider had left Memphis to join the Royal Flying Corps, had been trained in England, and had fought in France—a course of action similar to that which Faulkner had attempted. Grider's grandfather shared professions with "old Bayard" Sartoris (a banker) and had served in the same war as Colonel John Sartoris (who was modeled on Faulkner's great-grandfather, Colonel William Clark Falkner). Grider began as an enthusiastic romantic, attracted to the war partly because "it's the North and South over again"[4]—his point being that the Germans had better equipment but that the cause of the Allies was just. By 1918, he was capable of writing:

> I have never been serious about anything in my life and now I know I'll never be otherwise again. But my seriousness will be a burlesque for no one will recognize it. Here I am, twenty-four years old, I look forty and I feel ninety. I've lost all interest in life beyond the next patrol. . . . Oh, for a parachute! The Huns are using them now. I haven't a chance, I know, and it's this eternal waiting around that's killing me. I've even lost my taste for likker. It doesn't seem to do me any good now. I guess I'm stale. Last week I actually got frightened in the air and lost my head. Then I found ten Huns and took them all on and I got one of them down out of control. I got my nerve back by that time and came back home and slept like a baby for the first time in two months. What a blessing sleep is! I know now why men go out and take such long chances and pull off such wild stunts. No discipline in the world could make them do what they do of their own accord. I know now what a brave man is. I know now how men laugh at death and welcome it. I know now why Ball went over and sat above a Hun airdrome and dared them to come up and fight with him. It takes a brave man to even experience real fear. A coward couldn't last long enough at the job to get to that stage.[5]

Much of this is similar to Faulkner's treatment, in many of his works, of the questions of fear and courage and is implicit in the reckless exploits of his overstressed pilots, especially John Sartoris. In the final, undated entry, Grider wrote of the futility of the war effort in terms that not only are politically astute—in fact prophetic—but also return to the question of the legacy of the Civil War.

> War is a horrible thing, a grotesque comedy. And it is so useless. This war won't prove anything. All we'll do when we win is to substitute one sort of Dictator for another. In the meantime we have destroyed our best resources. Human life, the most precious thing in the world has become the cheapest. After we've won this war by drowning the Hun in our own blood, in five years time the sentimental fools at home will be taking up a collection for these same Huns that are killing us now and our fool politicians will be cooking up another good war. Why shouldn't they? They have to keep the public stirred up to keep their jobs. . . . The worst thing about this war is that it takes the best. . . . Even those that live thru it will never be fit for anything else. Look at what the Civil War did for the South. It wasn't the defeat that wrecked us. It was the loss of half our manhood and the demoralization of the other half. . . . My grandfather was a Captain in the Confederate Army and served thruout the war. He became a banker, a merchant, a farmer and a good citizen, but he was always a little different from other men and now I know where the difference lay. At the age of seventy he still hadn't gotten over those four years of misery and spiritual damnation. My father used to explain to me that he wasn't himself. But he was himself, that was just the trouble with him. The rest were just out of step.[6]

A few pages later, Grider indirectly suggested what would become one of the major tropes of Faulkner's wartime and postwar ghost story:

> I saw a man in Boulogne the other day that I had dreamed I saw killed and I thought I was seeing a ghost. I can't realize that any of them are gone. Surely human life is not a candle to be snuffed out. The English have all turned spiritualistic since the war. I used to think that was sort of far fetched but now it's hard for me to believe that a man ever becomes even a ghost. I have sort of a feeling that he stays just as he is and simply jumps behind a cloud or steps thru a mirror.[7]

Whether or not Faulkner read this diary in 1926, drew on it for some of the details of air combat in *Flags in the Dust* and *Absolution*, or deliberately echoed some of its sentiments in the closing lines of *Turn About*, it is certain that he made use of it while writing *War Birds*, and more than likely that he respected it.

The task he set himself in *War Birds* was to adapt this diary while also revising and incorporating the story of the doomed twins, John and Bayard Sartoris. He accomplished this by having Caroline Sartoris (here married not to Bayard but to John, and allowed to survive) explain to her son the circumstances of his father's death by reading to him from the wartime diary she had asked John to keep, and by having some of its passages echo Grider's. The changes he wrought in the Sartoris saga were far more intriguing and amount to an important shift in ethical perspective, one that first appeared in his fiction only in the final chapter of *The Unvanquished*, "An Odor of Verbena," in 1938 (written in 1937).

Flags in the Dust (1926–27), like the abbreviated *Sartoris* (1929), tells how the heritage of glorious recklessness begun by John and Bayard Sartoris during the Civil War is ironically fulfilled in the self-destructive exploits of their namesakes during and after World War I. John jumps to his death after his Camel has been mercilessly barraged, before Bayard's eyes, by a German pilot with a "skull and bones" on his plane. Bayard returns to Jefferson overwhelmed by the guilt of having survived. Bayard's wife Caroline has died the year before, and eventually he marries Narcissa Benbow. When he causes the death of old Bayard in an automobile accident, Bayard runs away and finally gets himself killed while testing a plane he has been warned is unsafe. Narcissa refuses to carry on the namesake tradition and gives her and Bayard's son the name Benbow Sartoris, as if hopeful that that would bring an end to the related tradition of glamorous disaster.

In two subsequent stories, Faulkner explored further aspects of the complex of self-destructiveness and doom that pursued the Sartoris brothers and their wartime generation. "Ad Astra" (1930), set the night after Armistice (11 November 1918), shows time stopping—at least for Bayard—on 12 November, as he and his friends get drunk and come to terms with the possibility that they are all as good as dead and have simply not realized it. With them is a German pilot who is determined not to inherit his family title, partly because he does not want to be an aristocrat and partly because that way of life is both ethically and politically finished; Monaghan, who captured him, jokes about taking him home to America. No longer soldiers but exhausted beyond the point of returning to civilian innocence, watching their commitments dissolve into anachronisms and illusions (the last image is of one man's crying over his imaginary wife), the men discover that they are in limbo. "This life is nothing," says the German who will not become a baron; Bayard, who will not survive to extend the more positive aspects of the Sartoris tradition, insists that time has stopped; and a subadar who, like the German, is prepared for a life of exile and will renounce his own title in India, sums it up by saying that "All this generation which fought in the war are dead tonight. But we do not yet know it."[8]

"All the Dead Pilots" (1931) fills in the story of John Sartoris's death and his rivalry with Captain Spoomer for the favors of a French woman, Antoinette. John makes a bitter game out of releasing Spoomer's dog—who will track Spoomer to Amiens and Antoinette, or else simply grub in the refuse from the enlisted men's mess hall should Spoomer not be in Amiens. Finally John finds his rival with Antoinette, steals his clothes (putting them on an unconscious ambulance driver), and sees Spoomer disgraced when he shows up at the base in the dress of a peasant woman; in revenge, Spoomer has John transferred to a night-flying Camel squadron, indirectly causing his death. A third story, "With Caution and Dispatch," begun just before *War Birds*, details John's uncautious and interrupted attempts to fly a Camel across the English Channel to join his outfit.[9]

In "An Odor of Verbena," Bayard (the old Bayard in *Flags in the Dust*, grandfather of the twins, John and Bayard, who figure in *War Birds*) finds that his father, Colonel John Sartoris, does not intend to defend himself against his former partner, Ben Redmond, although Redmond intends to kill him. The colonel speaks of "men who have killed too much, who have killed so much that never again as long as they live will they ever be alone. . . . Yes, I have accomplished my aim, and now I shall do a little moral house-cleaning. I am tired of killing men, no matter what the necessity nor the end. Tomorrow, when I go to town and meet Ben Redmond, I shall be unarmed."[10] This is much like what happened to Colonel Falkner, but his son was simply persuaded not to continue the feud and to renounce vengeance.[11] In Faulkner's story, however, Bayard is pressured to shoot the man who shot his father; what he does instead is to let Redmond fire at him, thus not simply abandoning the feud but rising above it in a demonstration of charity and moral courage. And although this story concerns not young but old Bayard, it is clearly related to the same tangle of moral issues and fatality that the earlier Sartoris stories had presented in a more hopeless light. "An Odor of Verbena" is a story of man's ability to rise above the compulsive fixations and destructive inheritance that so regularly (at least in Faulkner's work) force him into tragic repetitions and hopeless quests for oblivion; it is a story of how to find peace, in fact, how to create it. And it is in *War Birds* that this level of hope, of ethics, is first approached.

War Birds has many problems as a piece of writing. The story line is sometimes inefficient, the dialogue often hysterical and melodramatic. Antoinette is a ludicrous caricature of female sacrifice and sex-guilt. On many occasions, characters who can speak only French deliver long English paragraphs. Much of the story Caroline relates from John's diary takes place after John's death. And there are other, minor irritations, most of which—like the script's excessive length —might well have been taken care of if there had been a second draft. But *War Birds* is also one of the better *ideas* for a script that Faulkner ever had, and it is evident that he put a great deal of imagination and emotion into realizing it. For rather than have Bayard return from the war destroyed by guilt and looking only for a way to atone for surviving his brother, rather than leaving him—as in "Ad Astra"—vomiting on the streets of the Waste Land with a metaphysically stopped watch, Faulkner here makes Bayard a strong figure and lets him discover a way to keep John alive (in memory, much like the ending of *The Wild Palms* [1939]) and to bring his family into a renewed future, even retaining some of the old Sartorian splendor as he jumps his horse at the finish and releases the ghost of his brother into a serene and satisfying peace. In *War Birds* there is no need to name the latest offspring Benbow: he can be Johnny and can learn, like the adults around him, to forgive and endure.

Some of these changes resulted from the need to work in the diary, some from Faulkner's evidently taking a new look at the ironic and negative elements of the earlier fictions. It is unlikely, however—judging from the dark resolutions of *The College Widow* and *Absolution*—that Faulkner felt any pressure to rework his story in the interest of a conventional "happy ending," though it is always possible that Hawks urged him to close on a relatively uplifting note (much as in *Turn About* and *The Road to Glory*, where mortal sacrifice makes some kind of future possible). Even so, the logical twist that makes Johnny understand the makeup of the extended family Bayard has created is peculiarly Faulkner's and is far more involuted than anything in Hawks's work.

In "All the Dead Pilots," John is described as having a vocabulary of perhaps two hundred words, and a letter he sends home bears this out. As the author of the diary in *War Birds*, he is necessarily more articulate and thoughtful (see Scenes 214–16, p. 95). So that it would be John's son rather than nephew who would have to deal with the question of hating or forgiving Dorn (the German pilot) and Antoinette, Bayard is childless while Caroline is married to John. These changes also make the diary a more natural focal point for the unfolding of John's story, as a document Caroline had initially hoped would strengthen the sense of closeness between herself and John and which comes at last to clarify and validate the bonds among the surviving family unit, however unconventionally constituted that family first appears. So that the twins John and Bayard can accumulate to one good man (see Scene 197, p. 85) rather than one dead man, Bayard is made more articulate, effective, and concerned than he is in *Flags* or "Ad Astra," and he is led from concerns of revenge on Spoomer and Dorn to an experience of forgiveness—a shift in which Faulkner reinforces the insight of the German in "Ad Astra" that love is superior to force and brotherhood to the barbaric, immoral hierarchy of any "fatherland."[12] Monaghan's jest about taking the German home with him is reworked in *War Birds* into Bayard's bizarre but elevated gesture of ethical renewal, as he brings home to Caroline the woman who loved John and the man who killed him. When reading over a synopsis of *War Birds* to decide how much of it was new and how much supported Faulkner's demand to be paid for the rights to "Ad Astra" and "All the Dead Pilots" (see Introduction), M. E. Greenwood wrote that "There is nothing unusual in this thought because the majority of Americans going overseas were promising to bring back Germans as presents to their friends, etc."[13] But the reasons behind Bayard's action are quite obviously "unusual," and one could argue that financial motives led Greenwood to miss the point.

In terms of the previous fictions, then, Faulkner substantially revised the outcome of *Flags in the Dust* while retaining the theme of the Sartoris tradition, and he incorporated most of "All the Dead Pilots" while augmenting or reversing many of the elements from "Ad Astra." The only use he made of "With Caution and Dispatch" was to emphasize John's difficulty in piloting Camels. He rose to the challenge posed by these works as well as by Grider ("Even those that live thru it will never be fit for anything else") and proposed a way to leave the Waste Land and to allow history to assume a new, positive course—a way of looking both backward and forward, a paradoxical optimism that would inform the conclusions of *The Unvanquished* and *The Wild Palms* some six years later. *War Birds* is a conclusive example of Faulkner's having used screenwriting as a trial ground for later fiction and of his having attempted to integrate many of the concerns and even the characters explored in his two careers as screenwriter and novelist.

It should be borne in mind that *War Birds* is only a first draft, especially when one encounters the hysterical Antoinette and the unnecessary repetitions in John's early conflicts with Spoomer. Much of the script is out of control; the characters' stresses are too much on the surface. But there are many points in *War Birds* where

Faulkner makes great strides forward as a professional screenwriter. It is uncommon for a script to bear such explicit directions for cutting and camera movement, and these suggest that Faulkner was working as hard as he could to write a *movie* as well as that Hawks—who would have discouraged most of this—was not a significant presence in the day-to-day composition of the script. In many ways (see notes to p. 141) *War Birds* has the most complex and experimental narrative structure of any Faulkner screenplay. Faulkner's use here of double exposure (superimposition) and special effects is unique (the only other script in which he goes into such visually complex detail is *Revolt in the Earth*, a luckless adaptation of *Absalom, Absalom!*[14]) and reveals some indebtedness to silent German cinema, particularly in the shadow-play with Spoomer and his dog (Scene 19, p. 17) and the visualization of Johnny's thoughts about Dorn (Scene 5, p. 6). The use of double exposure to convey the ghostly presence of John's plane (e.g., Scene 323, p. 143) is more conventional but still effective, and the diary is made a significant icon both of John's thinking and of Caroline's narration, even when its pages are blank. But the most powerful special effect (Scene 297, pp. 131–32) has the transformative power of a major visual metaphor, as Bayard's renounced pistol is thrown through a window and leaves the glass in the shape of "a star," a star that begins to glow with a light that is brightest at the instant that all around it has dissolved into darkness, before it too begins to fade.

NOTES: INTRODUCTION TO *WAR BIRDS* / *A GHOST STORY*

1. Blotner, *Faulkner: A Biography*, p. 113 (note to p. 792, l. 35).
2. Ibid., 648.
3. R.B. Wills, 30 Sept. 1926.
4. *Diary of the Unknown Aviator*, MGM typescript (Vault Copy), 25.
5. Ibid., 293–95. In *Flags* and *War Birds*, John jumps to his death without a parachute.
6. Ibid., 295–97.
7. Ibid., 299. A note indicates that shortly after writing this, Grider was killed in action.
8. Faulkner, *Collected Stories*, 421. "Subadar" was a term for a viceroy or provincial governor in colonial India, and for a native regimental commander.
9. *Uncollected Stories of William Faulkner*, ed. Joseph Blotner (New York: Random, 1979), 642–64, 711.
10. William Faulkner, *The Unvanquished* (New York: New American Library, Signet Classics, 1960), 175.

11. Blotner, *Faulkner: A Biography*, 44–51.
12. Faulkner, *Collected Stories*, 417.
13. Memo from Greenwood to Rapf, 16 Jan. 1933.
14. See Kawin, *Faulkner and Film*, 126–36, for a discussion of *Revolt in the Earth*; an excerpt appears on 133.

NOTES: SCRIPT OF *WAR BIRDS / A GHOST STORY*

P. 1 [narrative], "Two boys, about fourteen, fighting": Like *Absolution* and *Turn About*, *War Birds* begins with a fight between children, a fight that introduces the basic preoccupations of the script; here, the issue is the makeup of the Sartoris household and extended family.

P. 2 [Dorn], "He too is brave, but in a different way from your father": Essentially, Bayard has the courage to live, John to die.

P. 3 [Dorn], "Ja, prinz": Yes, prince.

P. 3 [narrative], "as the sound of Johnny's feet die away": Dies (typo). Many of the transitions in this script involve sounds that die away, perhaps to prepare the effective closure of Scene 323 (p. 143) and to suggest the central theme of understanding and releasing the past.

P. 3 [narrative], "CLOCK TO": This is not a conventional camera direction; in this script it indicates that the camera should move from one object of attention to another—whether by panning, tilting, dollying, or the use of a crane is unspecified.

P. 5 [Antoinette], "Zut": An expletive corresponding to "Hmph!" or "Bother!"

P. 6 [narrative], "FOCUS on coat, DOUBLE EXPOSURE DISSOLVE to Dorn standing in coat": It is conventional to capitalize camera and sound directions in a script. By "DOUBLE EXPOSURE DISSOLVE," Faulkner evidently meant to call for the superimposition of two images, one of which fades in over the other. Since any dissolve is created by the superimposed fade-out of one image and fade-in of another, he probably meant that in this case both images should remain visible until the image of Dorn fades out.

P. 8 [narrative], "her hand on the know": Knob (typo).

P. 9 [narrative], "R.F.C.": Royal Flying Corps. The subsequent direction, "Caroline's Voice," indicates that the camera should hold on the diary while Caroline is heard voice-over or simply off-camera.

P. 10 [John in diary], "At sea. Well, here I am, approaching what the Y.M.C.A. guys call the Great Adventure": Grider's diary begins in a similar manner. The first entry, dated 20 Sept. 1917 (six weeks later than John's), includes the lines, "Well, here I am aboard ship and three days out of New York, waiting for a convoy at Halifax. This seems to be a fitting place to start a diary. I am leaving my continent as well as my country and am going forth in search of adventure . . . ."

P. 12 [narrative], "RESOLVE TO": Fade in on, come out of the dissolve to.

P. 13 [narrative], "13xy1": Equivalent to 13A, as 13xy2 would be to 13B, indicating that this scene has been inserted between 13 and 14, i.e., written at some later date than those around it.

P. 14 [John in diary], "God knows, I do enough things that I wonder the next minute why in the world I ever did it. . . . And if I must die, I am going to try to die well": Early in his diary (ms. 4) Grider writes, "I never have done anything constantly except the wrong thing, but I want a few recollections jotted down in case I don't get killed. . . . I haven't lived very well but I am determined to die well."

P. 15 [Bayard], "Thanks. No more tonight": I can think of no example in Faulkner's fiction where Bayard refuses a drink; this change is in line with others that make him more effective, responsible, and articulate than he was in *Flags in the Dust*, etc., while retaining his cold intensity and his deep care for John.

P. 15 [First]: The partially obscured word is "stay."

P. 15 [John in diary], "Here we are in England. . . . We are to go through the regular Royal Flying Corps course": On 3 October, Grider wrote (ms. 17), "So this is England. We landed yesterday morning and took a train right at the dock for Oxford. We aren't going to Italy after all. We've got to go to Ground School all over again."

P. 16 [narrative], "As it writes, there falls upon the page the silhouette of a girl's head": Like the later silhouettes of Spoomer and the dog (Scene 19, p. 17), this use of superimposition—which may owe something to Expressionist silent film—makes John's diary a more cinematic (rather than purely verbal) narrative device and visually clarifies his thinking.

P. 16 [John in diary], "Then I told him about Shiela": In "All the Dead Pilots" John has a girlfriend in London, and she becomes involved with Spoomer; John dresses his sparring partner in a captain's tunic and woman's garter, jokes about the decoration ("Dishtinguish Sheries Thighs"), and boxes with him. See *Collected Stories*, 514–15. Bayard is not involved.

P. 17 [John in diary], "They tell a story about the dog": See *Collected Stories*, 515–28. Most of the story of Spoomer, the dog, and Antoinette is the same here as in "All the Dead Pilots," including much of the dialogue.

P. 17 [narrative], "A girl bohind it. . . . she becomes nervour": The struckover word is "behind"; the typo, "nervous."

P. 18 [Girl]: The d's in "you'd" and "dog" are partially obscured. In her first direction, the mistyped word is probably "nervous." For "20XY1," see note to p. 13.

P. 19 [narrative], "DOUBLE EXPOSURE DISSOLVE TO": As on p. 6, it is not clear whether Faulkner meant for both shots (26 and 27) to be *held* onscreen simultaneously before the first faded out or was simply calling for a dissolve. The former might have been an interesting way to portray drunkenness.

P. 20 [narrative], "He is a little drunk savage": There should be a comma between "drunk" and "savage."

P. 20A [narrative]: The partially obscured word that begins the final sentence is "Man." It is not clear whether "20A" reflects this page's having been written after 20 and 21, or a typist's attempt to rectify a numbering error.

P. 21 [John], "Not": Probably "No."

P. 22 [John in diary], "the symbol of my conscience and the mentor of my behavior is a dog": This explanation is not offered in "All the Dead Pilots."

P. 23 [John], "Couldn't you get them to delay you for one posting?": This is similar to Claude's asking Ronnie to wait for him so that they can serve together, early in *Turn About*.

P. 26 [John in diary]: The partially obscured word is "mucky."

P. 27 [Waiter], "Monsieur, fait peut-etre bein dur et sec, n'est-ce pas?": Apparently referring to the saucers (as a way of prompting John to order more soft, wet drinks), or perhaps to John's ability to pay, the waiter says something like, "A bit hard and dry, no?" "Bein" should be "bien."

P. 27 [Antoinette], "Quel dommage, alors? Ne sais tu que monsieur est officier Americain? Allez! Vite!": What a pity then. Don't you know this man's an American officer? Go! Quick!

P. 27 [John], "Wee, wee, wee. Angcore": John responds to Antoinette's "No, no, no" with his version of "Oui, encore" (Yes, again).

P. 27 [Antoinette], "Quel heure? Il faut partir": What time is it? We must leave.

P. 28 [Antoinette], "queek": Her version of "quick." In the direction above, "tryingto" should read "trying to." From here on, only those typos that might prove confusing will be noted.

P. 28 [Antoinette], "Tante": Aunt.

P. 28 [Waiter], "L'addition!": The bill!

P. 28 [Antoinette], "A demain?": Till tomorrow?

P. 29 [narrative], "ESTAMINET": Tavern.

P. 30 [John], "Bong jour": His version of "bonjour" (good day).

P. 30 [Old Woman], "Vous voulez?": What would you like?

P. 30 [narrative], "His face . . . becomes chocked": Hardens or fixes, as if wedged. This might be a typo for "shocked," but see Scene 219, p. 96. Other possibilities are "checked" and "choked."

P. 31 [Old Woman], "Monsieur voulait?": The gentleman desires—?

Pp. 31–32 [narrative], "John . . . finds Old Woman watching him, and and the French people covertly, looking away from his gaze": This should probably read, "John . . . finds Old Woman watching him, and the French people covertly looking away from his gaze."

P. 32 [John], "Orderly sets bottle": This is a direction but has been placed as if it were dialogue.

P. 35 [narrative], "The dog is bribbing in the barbage can": The dog is grubbing in the garbage can (typo).

P. 38 [Old Woman], "Pas d'ici": Not here.

P. 38 [John], "Soldat Anglais. Ici—": English soldier. Here—.

P. 38A [narrative], "John blares at Peasant": Glares (typo). Later in the paragraph, as elsewhere in several screenplays, Faulkner writes "off stage" for "off-screen" or "off-camera."

P. 39 [John in diary], "all those frogs": Derogatory term for the French.

P. 41 [narrative], "TARMAC": The paved area around a hangar.

P. 42 [narrative], "the dog tropping on toward gate": Probably a typo for "trotting."

P. 43 [John], "Ou est-elle Toinette?": Where is Toinette?

P. 44 [Woman's Voice], "Maman?": Antoinette calls "Mamma?" but means her aunt.

P. 44 [narrative], "as she shrings before him": Shrinks (typo). The obscured word at the end of this line is "to."

P. 46 [A Voice], "Que faites-vous en haut?": What are you doing up there?

P. 46 [Corporal], "Descendez donc": Come down, then.

P. 47 [THE PAPER], "L 19.10": John's uniform cost 19 pounds, 10 shillings.

P. 53 [Hobbs], "Gor": Cockney expletive for "God!"

P. 54 [Woman], "Par ici. Arretez": Over here. Stop.

P. 56 [Bayard], "If anything happens to him because of those rotten machines you have sent him to fly": This concludes the adaptation of "All the Dead Pilots" (in which Bayard did not figure) and marks the shift to material loosely adapted from "Ad Astra" and *Flags in the Dust*, involving Bayard in the fight with Spoomer.

P. 57 [Bayard], "He's always been white to me": A racist remark; to "be white" means to behave as Caucasians ought to behave with each other, as opposed to the less desirable or honorable behavior of other races.

P. 57 [Bayard], "I'll go to Pershing with it": General John J. Pershing was commander in chief of the American Expeditionary Forces in World War I.

P. 58 [John], "You mean go A.W.L.": Absent without leave.

P. 61 [Bayard], "Je suis Sartoris. Vous desiriez, madame?": I am Sartoris. What do you want, madam?

P. 61 [Antoinette], "Vous parlez! Jean m'en dirait!": You speak French! John told me that! (It is not clear whether the rest of their dialogue is understood to be conducted in French.)

P. 62 [narrative], "with her fi fist": With her fist (typo).

P. 62 [Antoinette], "He struck me too! Ah, you're not cold! Oh, thank you!": In what are probably her worst lines, Antoinette is glad to find this evidence of kinship between John and Bayard. Her becoming "serene" at this moment, however perverse, is meant to indicate that she has now found a role or outlet for her guilt and self-sacrifice. None of this is suggested by "All the Dead Pilots."

P. 64 [Antoinette], "We are brothers now": Having become like "a man" and "a soldier" on the previous page, Antoinette now makes herself an equal in relation to the bond between John and Bayard; it is significant that she does not say "friends."

P. 64 [John in diary], "R.E. and Fee guys": The RE-8 was a British light bomber; the FE-2 was a British light bomber and reconnaisance plane used only occasionally as a fighter.

P. 64 [John in diary], "You have to land a Camel by setting the air valve and flying it into the ground": See *Collected Stories*, 528, where this joke first appears. An "ace" is a pilot who has destroyed five or more enemy aircraft.

P. 66 [narrative], "Beside bunk a kit bag": "kit" is obscured.

P. 67 [Patrol Leader], "one of those popguns": Camels. Throughout

Flags in the Dust (e.g., 44), Bayard insists that he "tried to keep him from going up there on that goddam little popgun."

P. 68 [narrative], "Ther he desists": Then (typo).

P. 68 [John], "Argent": Silver, cash.

P. 69 [Antoinette], "C'est rien": It's nothing.

P. 70 [Patrol Leader]: The obscured word is "paraded," i.e., assembled for a formal review.

P. 70 [Antoinette], "Dieu! Sauvez! . . . Mère de Dieu, pleine de grâce": God! Save [him]! Mother of God, full of grace . . .

P. 70 [narrative], "Batman": Enlisted servant of a British army officer.

P. 70 [Antoinette], "Du lieutenant Sartoris, n'est-ce pas?": From Lt. Sartoris, isn't it?

P. 70 [Antoinette], "Venez": Come.

P. 71 [narrative], "as Baran enters": Batman (typo).

P. 71 [Antoinette], "Dites-lui, Monsieur": Tell him, sir.

P. 71 [Proprietor], "Alors—Regardez": O.K., look.

P. 72 [Antoinette], "L'argent de monsieur le lieutenant. Il y en a. Dites-lui revenir et lui y donner": The lieutenant's money. He has it. Tell him to go back and give it to him.

P. 72 [Proprietor], "Alors, Monsieur le brave": In that case, brave sir.

P. 73 [narrative], "Pilots cone up": Come (typo).

P. 73 [narrative], "Spoomer gets oh hun": On (strikeover).

P. 75 [REPORT]: "E.A.": Enemy aircraft.

P. 76 [John in diary], "not going to keep me from being an ace": Each of the five or more downed enemy aircraft had to be confirmed before a pilot could be recognized as an ace. In collaborative kills, fractions were authorized.

P. 79 [Kaye], "I know he's a rotter": A highly objectionable person.

P. 80 [narrative], "Sergeant cuts switch": "Cuts" is obscured. The failure of this engine is an authorial contrivance to pit John and Bayard against each other in an air battle. (On. pp. 97–98 they "fight" again, with Bayard firing.) In *Flags in the Dust* (46) John knowingly shoots at Bayard, who is trying to keep him from fatal combat, and Faulkner evidently felt that some such battle between the brothers (i.e., with John the aggressor) was still necessary.

P. 83 [narrative], "He is flying south, to tachometer": "To" indicates a camera movement from the compass to the other instruments.

P. 83 [narrative], "watches it zoom and Immelman again": Named after the World War I German aviator Max Immelmann, the Immelmann turn was a half a loop followed by half a roll, resulting in a gain in altitude and change of direction. The description of Bayard's outmaneuvering John without firing is similar to that in *Absolution*.

P. 84 [Bayard], "any S.E.": The SE-5 was a single-bay British fighter plane capable of flying 122 mph, with a 22,000 ft. ceiling and a 210 h.p. engine.

P. 87 [Proprietor], "Bon": Good.

P. 88 [Antoinette], "Cochon": Pig.

P. 88 [Bayard], "Y a t-il Mademoiselle Gaussart?": Is Mlle. Gaussart here?

P. 88 [Proprietor], "Vraiment, mon general. Montez au premier": Truly, my general. Go up to the first floor.

P. 89 [Bayard], "Merci": Thanks.

P. 89 [Antoinette], "Zut!": This French expletive makes it difficult to tell whether the conversation is supposed to be taking place in English or French. Faulkner is oddly careless about this except on p. 127, where a dissolve clearly indicates that Dorn and Bayard's French conversation is being translated for the sake of the audience. In any case, this scene entirely exceeds Antoinette's English vocabulary.

P. 92 [Bayard], "You've ground him": Probably a typo for "grounded."

P. 95 [John in diary], "Washout": I.e., he hasn't encountered Spoomer, let alone shot down a German. These entries are some of the best writing in the script.

P. 98 [narrative], "229–233": At some earlier point this might have been broken into five scenes, though it is also possible that four scenes have been omitted. For the description of John's death as Faulkner first conceived it, see *Flags in the Dust*, 44–47 and 280–81. In *Flags* the German pilot, Ploeckner, bears a "skull and bones" on his plane and is a ruthless "pupil of Richthofen's." The humanistic and unnamed pilot in "Ad Astra" had not shot down any Sartoris; the skull and pipe insignia is one sign of the difference between Ploeckner and Dorn. Bayard's search for the pilot who shot John down is referred to in "Ad Astra"; see *Collected Stories*, 414. By uniting the vicious Ploeckner and the sympathetic German of "Ad Astra" in the figure of Dorn, Faulkner efficiently integrated the previous Sartoris stories into *War Birds* and credibly motivated the resolution of Bayard's—and his generation's—conflicts.

P. 100 [narrative], "men grasp-at it wildly": The hyphen is a typo.

P. 100 [General], "Your medicine is ... to continue to kill": An extremely effective foil to what will emerge as the script's dominant insight (that one must accept, forgive, endure)—even if the general's ultimate sentiment is antiwar.

P. 102 [narrative], "Increase to tag": I.e., pull the camera back from a closeup to a view of the entire tableau.

P. 103 [Batman], "Bokoo'uns": His version of "beaucoup (many) huns."

P. 103 [narrative], "Lewis drums and Vickers belts": Machine-gun ammunition.

P. 104 [Bayard]: The obscured word in his direction is "grim."

P. 106 [narrative], "A TREE IN SUMMER FOLIAGE": See Scene 251, p. 107.

P. 106 [narrative], "As he reaches cloud, ghost of John's ship resolves as though waiting him": Waiting for, or awaiting (possible typo). It should be remembered that the alternate title of *War Birds* was *A Ghost Story*. There are many ghosts in *Flags in the Dust*: some dead, some symbols of the past, and some obsessed mortals who have lost touch with contemporary life; often Faulkner's living characters simply turn into "ghosts," as other characters feel haunted by their unresolved presence (see the opening pages of *Absalom, Absalom!*). In *War Birds*, John's ghost is a uniquely friendly and determined emblem of the deathless but positive continuity between the brothers. For Bayard's guilt at John's death, the imagery of ghosts and haunting, and the fearful quality of the latent rendezvous between the brothers in Faulkner's earlier version of the story, see *Flags in the Dust*, 94, 330, 359, 369, etc.

P. 107 [narrative], "glasspicks up": Glass picks up (typo).

P. 108 [narrative], "kaleidoscopic double exposure": Hollywood montage, in this case with the emphasis on superimposition as well as succession of images. Faulkner heightens this with a sound montage and describes the camera movements for the final shot in detail, beginning with a resolve (fade in, as if the image emerged from the dissolve) on a closeup, an increase (dolly back) to a long shot, a clock (pan or lateral dolly) to Bayard's empty place, and a shift in focus (or a deliberate pause in camera motion, perhaps a short dolly forward) before both sound and image dissolve (fade out as the next scene fades in, with overlap) to the sound and image of Bayard flying alone. It should be remembered that sound film was still young in 1932 and that such creative uses of sound were well in advance of contemporary practice; Faulkner seems to have "heard" as well as "seen" his way through this sequence of nine (252 to 260) scenes.

P. 108 [narrative], "prie-dieu": Praying stool.

P. 109 [Old Woman], "Allors! Vite! Ton aviateur à toi. Tu peux lui donner l'embrassade de gloire et de victoire. Allez!": Hey! Quick! [Take] your flyer to you. You can give him the embrace of glory and victory. Go! ("Allors" should read "Alors"—a typo.)

P. 110 [Brown], "I'll tell 'Aig": Field Marshal Sir Douglas Haig.

P. 111 [Antoinette], "Pitié": Compassion, pity.

P. 111 [Sergeant], "Vous ne parlez pas anglais, eh?": So, you don't speak English? (Apparently, the rest of the conversation takes place in French.)

P. 111 [Antoinette], "that God Himself had said: Good. You have tried . . . into his aeroplane and depart, as if I had heard the engine": Some of these words are obscured.

P. 113 [narrative], "Mechanics and sergeant are busy": "Sergeant" is obscured. Note the correspondence ("gaunt as bronze") between the direction and the sergeant's dialogue at the bottom of p. 111 ("a bronze man just out of the furnace").

P. 113 [The voices], "Armistice!" A Joycean hallucination, like John's ship. Armistice was declared at 5 A.M. on 11 Nov. 1918 but became effective at 11 A.M.

P. 114 [narrative], "FOLLOW him look to": Camera tilts up to follow his (typo) gaze.

P. 115 [narrative], "A CHURCH": There is a similar insert in *The Road to Glory*, as the Catholic heroine prays for the soldiers, though in the later film we hear her moving, almost ironic prayer ("Let them believe that they will live"—paraphrase). The effectiveness of this scene depends instead on the sound montage.

P. 116 [narrative], "He raises his head, also flings binocular overside": Bayard repeats John's gesture when sighting Spoomer (Scene 225, p. 97). As in *Turn About*, Faulkner leaves out a big action scene (the dogfight with Dorn), preferring that the audience imagine it for themselves—a device that is of course unconventional but can, as here, be very effective. From here to the end of the page, the dissolving sound effects carry the story and the metaphors.

P. 116 [narrative], "John looking down, bright, peaceful": A sign that Bayard has found peace, and a cleverly false resolution; only in the final scene (p. 143) is this release truly achieved.

P. 117 [narrative], "God Save the Kinf": King (typo). This begins the adaptation and revision of "Ad Astra."

P. 117 [Bayard], "Garçon!": Waiter (literally, boy). The obscured words in this scene are "Stow it," "Right," and "FOLLOW." "Messieurs?" translates as "Gentlemen?"

P. 118 [Second], "lorry": A motor truck.

P. 118 [Voice], "signing . . . beacause": Singing . . . because (typos).

P. 119 [Marley], "Nich wahr?": Drunken rendering of "Nicht wahr?" (Isn't that true?). In "Ad Astra" this man was named Monaghan, the central character in "Honor."

P. 119 [Dorn], "Ja, Herr Leutnant": Yes, Lieutenant.

P. 119 [Marley], "breeks": Trousers, britches.

P. 120 [Bayard], "Parlez-vous francais?": Do you speak French? (Dorn answers "Yes" first in German and then in French; apparently, they continue their discussion in French.)

P. 121 [narrative], "DORN—looking into camera, facing pistol": Subjective camera, Bayard's point of view.

P. 122 [Patronne], "Voila, mon commandant! Boche! Un boche chez la maison Charlet! Une outrage affreuse a la France!": There, Commander! Hun! A Hun in the Charlet establishment! A frightful outrage to France!

P. 122 [Voices], "Allemand, mon colonel!": A German, Colonel!

P. 122 [Spoomer], "Faites se charger cette prisonnier": Take charge of this prisoner.

P. 122 [Bayard], "Arretez": Halt.

P. 123 [Bayard], "Ne bougez. Rien de personne": Don't move. Nobody.

P. 125 [Patronne], "Boche! Broken!": "Boche" is a derogatory term for German. For this outburst, which appears at a similar point in "Ad Astra," see *Collected Stories*, 422.

P. 125 [narrative], "First swings chair at light as Bayone falls": In "Ad Astra" it is Bayard who "swung a chair at the single light" (*Collected Stories*, 424); Spoomer is of course not involved in that story. "Bayone" is probably a typo for "bayonet," though it could refer to Bayard.

P. 125 [Dorn], "I haf voundt": His version of "I have a wound."

P. 126 [First], "Comment ca va?": How are things? (If the bayonet had Dorn's "name on it," he would have been killed.)

P. 126 [Dorn], "Ca va": O.K.

P. 126 [First], "in the darkness someone": "Someone" is obscured.

P. 126 [First], "M.P. patrol": Military police.

P. 127 [Dorn], "Je parle francais plus": I speak French more (easily). (The dissolve indicates that Dorn continues to speak in French, though the audience hears him and Bayard in English.)

P. 128 [Dorn], "My people are little barons in Prussia": See *Collected Stories*, 417–20.

P. 130 [Dorn], "But unfortunately the circumstances in which that man became the slayer of your brother and the object of your vengeance have passed away, ceased": "Circumstances" and "ceased" are obscured; Dorn's point is that the war is over. Dorn's freeing Bayard's hand (reminding him of how John died, to negate any gratitude concerning the deflected bayonet) is a remarkably powerful gesture and the first real sign of the ethical complexity—the twists of Faulkner's poetic logic—in this script.

P. 131 [narrative], "The fractured glass is in the shape of a star": A symbol of grace and ethical renewal, and the climax of the script.

P. 132 [narrative], "A PAGE OF THE DIARY / Caroline's hand holding it open, one of Johnny's hands beside it": Since the events since John's death could not have been recorded in the diary, one must assume that the previous narration has been largely Caroline's, with occasional intrusions and examples offered from the diary. Her turning to the blank page and stopping, however, makes it seem as if everything has been from the diary and is confusing. The hands indicate that the diary has at last brought the family together.

P. 132 [Caroline's voice], "And then Uncle Bayard came home, bringing them with him": See *Collected Stories*, 412, and *Flags in the Dust*, 32 (where a joke is made about Horace Benbow's bringing home "some war-orphan's mamma").

P. 134 [Caroline's Voice], "But I knew that they were somewhere near": "Somewhere" is obscured.

P. 134 [narrative], "DORN AND ANTOINETTE WAITING": "WAITING" is obscured.

P. 135 [narrative], "Johnny looking back reluctant": "Back" is obscured.

P. 138 [narrative], "Bayard down't answer": Doesn't (typo).

P. 138 [Bayard], "When we can't keep the dead out of our lives, how can you hope to keep the living?": Such an insight is unprecedented in fictional treatments of Bayard, who otherwise tends to fixate on the dead to the exclusion of the living. The obscured word in the next sentence is "them."

P. 139 [Caroline], "Bayard says that in us he is not dead": Compare the ending of *The Wild Palms* (New York: Random, Vintage, 1964), 324.

P. 139 [narrative], "Dorn comes foward": Forward (typo). At the end of this scene, the obscured direction is "DISSOLVE TO."

P. 140 [Caroline], "Say his name": Compare Scene 148, p. 64, where Antoinette helps Bayard find a similar emotional release.

P. 140 [Caroline], "I left like you do at first": Felt (typo).

P. 140 [Caroline], "that I began t cry": To (typo).

P. 140 [Caroline], "and the earth in which he is buried, all in one. And now your Uncle Bayard": The quotes should close after "one."

P. 141 [narrative], "Dorn's overcoat on rack": Compare Scene 5, p. 6.

There is a graceful and nearly exact symmetry between the opening and closing scenes, so that the long bedroom scene between Caroline and Johnny stands at the center of the structure (with John and Bayard at the center of her narrative). Now Faulkner moves out from the hatrack, to a scene between Johnny and Dorn, to Bayard's jumping the fence; the script opened with a scene between Johnny and Dorn, Bayard's jumping the fence, and Johnny's striking the hatrack. The effect of these repetitions-in-reverse is to suggest a transformative insight, an unrolling in which the earlier expositions and conflicts can be seen in a more deeply accurate way; the mirror structure, besides being beautiful in its own right, puts the story of the twins at the hinge-point of a diptych. This intensifies and compresses the inner wartime narrative (as conflicts are often augmented or pressurized in Faulkner's fiction) by putting it at the center of a non-linear narrative structure; it also makes of the structure of *War Birds*—as a mirrored narrative line—an emblem of the relationship between the different but fundamentally inseparable twins. Without being at all difficult to follow, this is the most complex structure Faulkner attempted in any of the MGM scripts. It is also significant that *War Birds* contains the most elaborate and experimental use of mindscreens (cinematic analogues to first-person narration) in *any* of Faulkner's scripts. For the larger significance of such narrative devices, see Kawin, *Mindscreen* (Princeton, N.J.: Princeton Univ. Press, 1978).

P. 141 [narrative], "Antoinette and Dorn standing beside lane, also waiting": "Beside" is obscured. This scene indicates that Bayard is the central figure in the extended family—i.e., that he has survived the war to renew the Sartoris tradition, has accepted his patrimony (a crucial change from "Ad Astra" and *Flags in the Dust*)—though he has not played a visible part in the narrative present. This is comparable to the absent centrality of Sutpen in *Absalom, Absalom!* and Kane in *Citizen Kane*, all of whom are presented largely in the stories told about them by figures in the narrative present. See Kawin, *Mindscreen*, 23–44.

P. 142 [Antoinette]: The obscured word in her direction is "yearning."

P. 143 [narrative], "Johnny does not more": Move (typo).

P. 143 [narrative], "They go on toward land": Lane (typo).

WAR BIRDS

1st dialogue script
~~from~~
William Faulkner

Copied in MGM Script
Dept. Jan. 12/33

WAR BIRDS

1 ·   A STREET BEFORE A SCHOOLHOUSE.

Two boys, about fourteen, fighting, silently
and intently, rolling on the ground, other
boys watching. Suddenly Dorn appears. He is
about forty, a German. He pulls the boys
apart, hauls them to their feet.

                    Dorn
Johnny! What does this mean?

The boys glare at one another, panting,
dishevelled.

                    Johnny
You take that back!

                    Other Boy
Yaah. Make me.

Johnny tries to spring at the boy; Dorn holds
them apart.

                    Dorn
Stop it! At once! You, boy. Go away.
          (The two boys glare at one another.)
Go. At once.

                    Johnny
Let me go, Uncle Lothar! He can't say what he
said!

Johnny struggles; Dorn holds him.

                    Dorn
                 (to other boy)
Go.

The other boy retreats. Johnny struggles,
ceases. Dorn watches him.

                    Dorn
Come. Let us go home.

They turn and walk on along the street,
Johnny straightening his clothes, Dorn
watching him.

                    Dorn
What was it he said to you?

                    Johnny
Nothing.

                    Dorn
Come. What was it?

                                        CONTINUED:

276

1   CONTINUED (2)

> Johnny doesn't answer. Dorn stops, puts his
> hands on Johnny's shoulders, turns him, Johnny
> looking down, stubbornly.

                    Dorn
Come. What was it he said?

                    Johnny
He said....that I had lots of fathers and mothers
at my house....

                    Dorn
Ah. So.

> He looks at Johnny. Suddenly Johnny looks
> up at him.

                    Johnny
What is there about our family that's different
from other families? What is there about you and
Aunt Toinette and my father?

                    Dorn
Your father was a brave man. Perhaps that is what
is different.

                    Johnny
He was killed in the war. I know that. And I
know that you and Aunt Toinette are not my real
aunt and uncle. I know that you are a German and
she is a French woman. But that's all you will
tell me. And now I'm fourteen. I'm big enough to
know now.

                    Dorn
I have thought so for some time. I have said so
too...
             (He looks at Johnny)
Ask your Uncle Bayard.
             (He is quite grave; they look at one
              another, then Johnny looks down.)
So. You will not ask your Uncle Bayard. Are you
afraid to ask him?

                    Johnny
I'm not afraid.

                    Dorn
I know you are not.
             (Puts his hand again on Johnny's shoulder)
I know. It is that your Uncle Bayard is not a man
to ask idle questions of. He too is brave, but in
a different way from your father.

> Johnny is watching Dorn, wide-eyed, still,
> with a kind of dawning comprehension.

                                   CONTINUED:

1   CONTINUED (3)

                 Johnny

You are a German. You came back from the war with
Uncle Bayard, and you knew my father. You were a
soldier too. And dad and Uncle Bayard were aviators, and so you were an aviator too.
               (He looks at Dorn; he is about to learn
                 something which he wishes to flee from.
                 His gaze is wide, still; before him Dorn
                 gradually becomes stiff at attention)
They won't tell me, but I know. You were a German
aviator. It was you that killed my father.

                 Dorn
             (stiff at attention, as though it were
             his Crown Prince whom he faced)
Ja. Ja, prinz.

Johnny looks at Dorn with a kind of horror.

                 Johnny
You did? You did?
             (Dorn stands stiffly before him)
Oh, damn you! Damn you!

       Johnny turns and runs. Dorn stands stiff,
       frozen-faced as the sound of Johnny's feet
       die away.

                       DISSOLVE TO:

2   PANORAMA OF A HOUSE

       A manor house, Southern Colonial, with gardens,
       stables. A saddled horse at the back porch,
       held by a negro boy, two or three other
       negroes nearby. CLOCK TO:

       Back door. Bayard emerges. He is not forty,
       yet his hair is white, his face cold, almost
       grim, lined by tragedy. As he approaches the
       horse the negroes rise with alacrity, with al-
       most fearful deference, holding the horse while
       he mounts.

                 A Negro Man
             (to the negro boy)
Run open dat gate! Don't you see Mr. Bayard's ready
to start?

       The negro boy scuttles toward gate. Bayard
       does not wait for him. He spurs the horse,
       lifts it into a run, passes the boy and jumps
       the gate and gallops on, the negroes looking
       after him. CLOCK up facade of house to a win-
       dow.

                     DISSOLVE THROUGH WINDOW TO:

3   A ROOM, FEMININE.

        Caroline sits beside a window, sewing. She is
        about thirty-five. Antoinette stands at win-
        dow, looking out, watching Bayard jump the
        gate and gallop away. She is about thirty-
        five also.

                  Antoinette
He departs. See? Like a bird he sails over the
gate. But stiff as iron, himself. Like a bayonet.
An iron bird. And as dangerous as a bayonet.

                  Caroline
Dangerous to whom? Not to me. And I don't think
to you, either.

                  Antoinette
Ah.

                  Caroline
              (looks at Antoinette's back)
I will never understand why you and Bayard have not
married. I have been expecting it ever since that
day when he brought you here.

                  Antoinette
              (turns, looks at Caroline. Antoinette is
              French, about the same age as Caroline,
              yet there is a world of difference in
              their faces. Caroline seems almost a
              child compared with Antoinette)
Me? Bayard and me?

                  Caroline
Why not? We settled it years ago that I am not
jealous of you and John. I knew John before I
married him.

                  Antoinette
Then why do you not marry Bayard?

                  Caroline
That's different. I was John's wife. I have his
child. While you...

        She ceases, looks at Antoinette with a resur-
        gence of antagonism, looks down while Antoin-
        ette watches her, cold, speculative.

                  Antoinette
While I am neither. Is that it?

                  Caroline
You would take him. Wouldn't you?

                  Antoinette
No.

                              CONTINUED:

                    Caroline
What? Nonsense. You know you would.

                    Antoinette
My poor child. How little you American women understand your men.

                    Caroline
Perhaps that's because we didn't have the chance to
practice on them that French women did in 1917 and
1918. You can't tell me. That my husband should
have left me a month after our marriage, with an un-
born child, and taken a mistress before that child
was even born. But understand: I'm not jealous any
more. I was at one time. I was bitter at one time.
At one time I believed there was a kind of justice
in the fact that he was killed before he ever knew
that he had a son. But I do think it's carrying
things a little far when his own twin brother should
bring back to me the woman with whom he betrayed me
and the man that killed him, bringing them into my
house and more or less flinging them at my feet, as
if to say, 'There. That should satisfy you.' But
I'm not bitter any more now. You know that. I like
you and I admire Lothar, if only for his affection
for Johnny. But with Bayard going around like he
had a poker down his back, so that you don't dare
speak to him hardly.

                    Antoinette
Ah. I say that you do not understand your men.
Don't you know that his heart is broken?

                    Caroline
What about my heart? John was his twin, but he was
my lover and husband. What about my heart?

                    Antoinette
Zut. No woman with a son ever had a broken heart.

                    Caroline
Oh, of course you know more about men and broken
hearts too, I dare say, than I do...What time is it?
Johnny should be getting home from school.

                    Antoinette
Here he comes now. Up the drive. I have been watching him. He is in trouble.

                    Caroline
             (rising quickly, going to window)
In trouble?....Nonsense. He's only been fighting
again.

                    Antoinette
It is his heart too that is in trouble. I can see
that, though I am not his mother.

        CLOCK to Johnny coming up drive, slowly. He
        disappears beyond window.
                                        CUT TO:

4   JOHNNY MOUNTING THE PORCH

Slowly, very grave. He enters house.

CUT TO:

5   HALL

A hatrack, coats and hats upon it. Johnny
facing hatrack, looking at a coat. FOCUS on
coat, DOUBLE EXPOSURE DISSOLVE to Dorn standing in coat, stiff, erect. Johnny grasps a
riding crop from the hatrack and strikes Dorn,
hard.

                  Johnny
               (whispering)
Murderer! Murderer!

He continues to strike as the figure fades and
it is the empty coat which he is striking. He
ceases, looks at the crop in despair, flings
it down, runs up the stairs. His feet die
away in

DISSOLVE TO:

6   A BEDROOM

The room which Bayard and John used as boys.
Their photographs at various ages on the walls,
guns, etc. The windows are closed, to indicate
that the room is never opened. CLOCK to bed.
Johnny lying face down on the bed.

DISSOLVE TO:

7   CAROLINE'S ROOM

She and Antoinette as before. Caroline's sewing now lies in her lap; she is listening.

              Caroline
Didn't you hear him come up the stairs?

              Antoinette
Yes.

They look toward the door.

              Caroline
He's gone to the bathroom, I suppose, to bathe his
face so that I won't find out he has been fighting.

CONTINUED:

7 CONTINUED (2)

        Antoinette
Do you think so?

        Caroline
    (looks at Antoinette sharply)
You know quite a lot about John's children never to
have had one of them.

        Antoinette
Perhaps that is why.
    (They look at one another.)
Will you go and see what hurts him, or will you per-
mit me to?

        Caroline
    (rising)
I think I am still competent and cognizant of a
mother's duties.

        Antoinette
    (bows her head)
I ask your pardon, madame.

        Caroline
    (pauses, returns, touches Antoinette's
    arm)
Forgive me, too. I know that you also loved him and
lost him.

    Antoinette takes Caroline's hand, touches her
    lips to it. Caroline snatches her hand self-
    consciously back, goes out.

        CUT TO:

8 CORRIDOR

Caroline going on, enters another door.

        CUT TO:

9 JOHNNY'S BEDROOM

It is empty. Caroline looks about, a little
surprised.

        Caroline
Johnny.
    (No answer)
Johnny.

Exit Caroline.

        CUT TO:

10   CORRIDOR

            Caroline puzzled, looks at various doors,
            suddenly approaches one, pauses, her hand on
            the know, seems to draw herself together,
            opens door and enters.

                                        CUT TO:

11   JOHN'S ROOM

            Johnny lying face down on the bed, Caroline
            standing beside the bed.

                    Caroline
Johnny. Son.

            Johnny turns, looks up at her.

                    Caroline
What is it? You've been fighting again.

            Johnny sits up; she stands beside him, her
            hand on his shoulder; suddenly he puts his
            arms around her waist.

                    Johnny
Mamma. Mamma.

                    Caroline
                (holding him)
Why, what is it, son?

                    Johnny
                (releases her, sits on side of bed, look-
                ing straight ahead)
Uncle Lothar killed my father. Didn't he?

            Caroline looks at him. Her face blanches,
            fills with surprise and dread; her hand
            rises to her mouth. Johnny looks straight
            ahead, his voice quiet.

                    Johnny
I know. You don't have to lie to me about it any
more. Who is Aunt 'Toinette, mamma?

                    Caroline
                (her hand to her mouth, her face blanched,
                her eyes wide with dread; whispers)
No. No. No.

                    Johnny
I'm fourteen. I'm old enough to know now. If it
was my own father, I ought to know.

                                        CONTINUED:

                    Caroline
                  (whispering)
Yes. Bayard said that some day....But not yet,
Johnny!
                  (She clutches him, fiercely)
Not yet, Johnny!

                    Johnny
Yes. Now. Everybody knows except me. Even the
other boys at school know there is something about
you and Uncle Lothar and Aunt 'Toinette and me that
I don't know. Tell me.

                    Caroline
                  (turns up his face, looks at him; she has
                    got control of herself)
Do you want to know now?

                    Johnny
Yes. Now. You just said that Uncle Bayard said
that you would have to tell me some day.
                  (He looks at her; she stands, her hands
                    on his shoulders, her face lowered)
Mamma.

                    Caroline
                  (suddenly, quietly)
Yes. All right.

                She crosses the room, he watching her, to a
                chest of drawers. It is dusty, she disturbs
                dust when she moves. She takes a key hidden
                behind the chest, unlocks a drawer, takes out
                a book and stands, the book in her hands and
                her head lowered, an expression almost of
                anguish on her face; recovers control, moves
                to a chair beside window and sits down.

                    Caroline
Come here.

                Johnny comes to her, quiet, eager, sits on arm
                of chair, looks down at book. FOCUS on book,
                with hand printed lettering on back beneath
                the word DIARY:

                  Lt. JOHN SARTORIS
                  --th Squadron, R.F.C.

                    Caroline's Voice
I gave this to him the day he sailed. He was already
a soldier then, going to England, he and Bayard, to
learn to fly. We had been married only a week, and
we went to New York on our honeymoon to wait for the
ship to go. And I gave him this. I thought that he
could write in this what he did while we were separated, and that he could bring it back to me and we
would read it together and it would be like we had
not lost so much of each other. This is what he
wrote in it.
                            CONTINUED:

11   CONTINUED (3)

Caroline's hand turns the page. The writing
fades, her hand becomes a man's hand, writing.

Aug. 5th, 1917. At sea. Well, here I am,
approaching what the Y.M.C.A. guys call
the Great Adventure. I don't know what I
am approaching, but I know what I am leaving. For the first time in my life I am
afraid of something I have done. I am
afraid of what I have done to Caroline.
My God, a man who will marry a girl, knowing that he is going away to war right
after, is a criminal. But it's done now.
If I have got a child, that is done now
too. If I have been a scoundrel, I can't
help it. But I can try to help being a
coward, if I am a coward at heart too. My
wife and my child may hate me, but God
willing they will not despise me. Well,
I'm not worried about the fighting. The
only trouble I ever had with fighting was
trying to keep Bayard from helping me out
whether I needed help or not. Bayard's a
better man than I am. I wish for Caroline's sake that she could be his wife
until this is over. Funny we should be
twins and still be so different.

The hand stops writing, withdraws, CLOCK to
John sitting in stateroom, reading what he
has written. He looks up, closes book quickly
as door opens and Bayard enters. They are
both in uniform.

                John
Well?

                Bayard
I'm going to the bar. Coming?

                John
All right.

Puts book away, almost concealing it while
Bayard watches. They exit.

                    CUT TO:

12   THE BAR

Many officers, Bayard and John drinking. A
drunken major in background, talking loud.

                    CONTINUED:

12   CONTINUED (2)

                    John
                  (quietly)
God, I shouldn't have done it. She's just a child.

                    Bayard
You should have thought of that before you married
her. I tried to get you to wait.

                    John
I know.
          (The drunk major shoves toward them.)
I know you are a better man than I ---

                    Major
Well, well, well. Here's the bird himself. Come
on, War Eagle. Show us a little flying.

          John looks around at him, ceasing. The Major
          is drunk, but not belligerent; he is trying to
          kid John rather than pick a fight with him.
          John turns back to Bayard.

                    John
I'd almost cut off an arm if I could undo it.
Going away like this, leaving her after only a
week. I may not even come back.

                    Major
Come on, War Eagle. Stop being a bar fly and be a
humming bird for the soldiers.

                    John
                  (turning)
Are you talking to me?

                    Major
Sure, War Eagle. War bird. War--

          He makes sound known as the bird. John hits
          him, not hard, yet the Major falls backward
          over his own feet.

                    John
How's that for a humming bird K.O.?

          The Major is helped to his feet, looking at
          John in a puzzled way; he springs forward.
          Bayard grasps John's arm, who struggles. Bayard
          jerks him back and steps in between in time to
          be hit by the Major's wild swing. Bayard
          knocks the Major down; others surge forward as
          Bayard faces them, holding John behind him
          with one arm. Tableau for a moment, then a
          whistle blows, a voice shouts.

                    Voice
Submarine!........Stations!

                              CONTINUED:

12   CONTINUED (3)

They all turn, running out. The lights go out.
An interval of darkness, running feet, then
the sound of a gun begins, firing rapidly into

                                        RESOLVE TO:

13   DECK

Boat deck, the men gathered at the boats. The
gun ceases.

                    Voice
All clear.

                    Another Voice
All right, men. Return to your quarters. No
lights and no smoking.

The men disperse, leaving two standing at the
rail.

                    John's Voice
Well, we got by again.

                    Bayard's Voice
Yes.

                    John's Voice
Maybe that would be the best thing that could happen.
To me, I mean. It would be hell for you to have to
go, too.

                    Bayard's Voice
What do you mean?

                    John's Voice
God, she gave me a diary. To write in. A little
book, to put down in what I do while I am away
from her, so she won't have to lose so much of my
life. That's what she said.

                    Bayard's Voice
Well, do it, then.

                    John's Voice
That's the trouble. That's the hell of it.

                    Bayard's Voice
What do you mean?
          (John doesn't answer leaning on the rail)
Oh. I see. You mean, you are going to do things in
Europe you don't want her to know about. Is that
it?

                                        CONTINUED:

                        John's Voice
I'm a man, and a soldier. I may die any day. If
I've got just a few more days or months to live,
I'm not going to live them like a monk.

                        Bayard's Voice
You have just been accusing yourself of being a
scoundrel for marrying her a week before you went
to the war. So now you're going to go on and be a
scoundrel and prove your own point. Is that it?

                        John's Voice
I guess so. Yes. But I am what I am. She knew
that when she married me. It's not that I don't
love her. I do. That's why I'm so sick over it
when I think that I --

                        Bayard's Voice
Ah, come on to bed. You got along fine for twenty-
five years without any conscience, and yet here you
haven't been married a month and you sound like an
old woman. You've been chasing girls ever since you
put on long pants; who in hell expects you to stop
now?

                        John's Voice
I guess you're right.
                (Brightens up)
Sure. You're right. Drink and be merry, for
tomorrow we'll be dead---maybe. So come on and
let's begin the drinking, huh?

                Exit.

                                        CUT TO:

13xy1   PASSAGEWAY

                Bayard and John approaching their door. Bayard
                pauses; John about to go on. Bayard grasps his
                arm.

                        Bayard
No, you don't.

                        John
Ah, just one more.

                        Bayard
                (opens door, thrusts John in)
No. Since you've got your mind made up to go com-
fortably to hell, you can wait until in the morning to start.

                                        CONTINUED:

13xyl   CONTINUED (2)

                         John
          Where are you going?

                         Bayard
          That's all right where I'm going. You get on to
          bed, now.

                    Bayard goes on down corridor. John looks
                    after him, then enters room and shuts door.

                                             CUT TO:

14   THE ROOM

                    John writing in diary. FOCUS on his hand
                    writing on the page:

                              11 P.M.---Another fight, Bayard horning
                              in as usual. It's funny how he thinks I
                              can't take care of myself. Well, maybe I
                              can't. God knows, I do enough things
                              that I wonder the next minute why in the
                              world I ever did   it. Maybe his exam-
                              ple will be something to me. I wish I
                              were as good a man as he is. But I'm not.
                              I guess there's no use in worrying about
                              it. But I swear I'm going to try to stay
                              clear of women until I get back to Caro-
                              line. I can try to do that much for her.
                              And if I must die, I am going to try to
                              die well. I can do that much.

                                             DISSOLVE TO:

15   THE SALOON

                    The Major and his companions at a table. The
                    Major is sober now. They look up as Bayard
                    enters, looks about, sees them, approaches.
                    They sit alertly, watching him, the Major
                    about to rise. Bayard stops at table, cold,
                    calm.

                         Bayard
          I have come to apologize.

                         A Man
          Apologize?

                         Bayard
          Yes. For my brother.

                                             CONTINUED:

15   CONTINUED (2)

                         The Man
            What about yourself?
                    (Bayard says nothing, looking at the
                    Major)
            Yóu're not included, eh?

                         Bayard
            I'll give the major any satisfaction he wants.

                         Major
            It's all right. My fault. Had a little too much
            to drink.

                         Bayard
            Of course, if you'd ----

                         Major
            No, no. Call it quits all around. Shake, will you?
                    (Offers hand; he and Bayard shake)
            Sit down and have a drink.

                         Bayard
            Thanks. No more tonight, if you'll excuse me.
            Well, see you tomorrow.

                 Turns and exits, they watching him.

                         A Man
            There's a cold, unpleasant devil for you.

                         Second
            I knew them in school, he and his brother. They
            were always like that; the other one getting in
            trouble, usually about women, and this one getting
            him out and sending him home like a kid. This one
            acts a damn sight more like the other one's mother
            than his twin brother. They say it just about
            broke this one's heart when John got married.
            Jealous, like a woman.

                         First
            Well, he sure ought to stay happy when the other one
            gets to France, with all those semi-detached women
            there.

                                        DISSOLVE TO:

16   JOHN'S HAND WRITING IN THE DIARY:

                    Aug 30----Here we are in England. It
                    seems that we are to be British aviators
                    after all. We are to go through the regu-
                    lar Royal Flying Corps course, just like
                    Englishmen. I came over here to fight a

                                        CONTINUED:

290

16   CONTINUED (2)

> foreign country, but I didn't think I was
> going to serve in the army of one. The
> English seem as foreign to me as the Ger-
> mans, even though we do spell our language
> the same way.

                    DISSOLVE THROUGH:

17   HAND STILL WRITING.

As it writes, there falls upon the page the
silhouette of a girl's head.

> Sept 12---Not so foreign. Or maybe all
> women just speak one language and the
> words they use don't matter. Poor Caro-
> line. God help her, and let Him punish
> me if He sees fit to. I almost wrote,
> God help Caroline because I can't. But
> I haven't got that low, at least. I
> won't start lying to myself. I guess I
> can help it, but I know I am not. I'm
> young, and maybe I'm going to die in this
> war. And I believe that even Caroline had
> rather have me a brave blackguard than a
> chaste coward.

                    DISSOLVE THROUGH:

18   HAND STILL WRITING

The girl's head still lying upon the page:

> Sept 19---Bayard has gone on to Scot-
> land. He volunteered, telling them that
> he can fly and making it stick. I could
> have done the same thing, but I didn't.
> Bayard and I had it out. He said I was
> yellow. Then I told him about Sheila.
> Then he said I am worse than yellow.
> Maybe I am. Anyway I am just what I am.
> I didn't make myself. This is the first
> time in our lives that Bayard and I ever
> parted in anger.

                                        291

19   DISSOLVE THROUGH WRITING HAND

The girl's shadow is now gone, in its place
the silhouette of a man's head, and the head
of a dog.

Sept. 27 ---. Another fight, and Bayard
not here to horn in. His name is Spoomer.
He is a captain, with a dog almost as big
as a calf. They tell a story about the
dog, about how every time it gets loose
it goes and digs in the garbage can behind
enlisted mens' messes, and Spoomer gets
all in a flutter over the dog eating common mens' grub. Only he wouldn't fight.
And I won't say what it was about. I'm
ashamed of that part of it. I like fighting and I respect it. But you'll lose
your luck with fighting when you once
start fighting over things that are lower
than your self respect. I'm going to see
Sheila one more time tonight and then I
am through, I swear it. I'm going to tell
her why, too. And it's not going to be
for the reason she will think.

The hand withdraws, as if John were reading
what he has written. The man's head begins
to laugh in pantomime, and the dog to bark,
making no sound.

                        DISSOLVE TO:

20   A CANTEEN - EVENING

John enters, goes to counter. A girl behind
it. When the girl sees John, she becomes nervour, in a flutter, watchful.

                Girl
Hullo, Yank.

                John
Hello.
        (he looks about. Girl continues, swiftly,
        too swiftly, so that John watches her cold,
        steadily)
Sheila was awfully sorry she couldn't wait. She
said she would telephone. . . .

                John
        (watching girl)
Couldn't wait, eh?

                Girl
It was her mother again. Another of her headaches
. . . Sheila had to run. She was frightfully cut
up about it. She said she would telephone to you
tomorrow. For me to tell you that she would telephone. . . .
                        CONTINUED:

                    John
Hah. Her mother should take a pill or something.
                 (turns, retreats, girl watching him,
                 alarmed)

                    Girl
Oh, I say. Aren't you going to stay? Do stop a
while, won't you?

                    John
Sure. I may give your mother a headache too.

          he goes out, Girl watching him anxiously, with
          increasing alarm. She turns and runs.
                                            CUT TO:

20XY1   TELEPHONE GIRL GETTING A NUMBER HURRIEDLY.

                    Girl
Are you there? Hello. Hello. . . Miss Atkinson.
She's there. She must be. . . Yes. . . . I'll hold
the line.
                 (waits nervous, fidgeting; makes swoop-
                 ing movement upon phone, almost whisper-
                 ing)
Sheila. . . He's just left here. . . I tried, but
I couldn't make him stay. . . Yes. He must know
something. Yes. . . Left just this moment. . . .
Yes. Perhaps you'd better. . .If you could just
make him leave that dog behind. It's as unmistak-
able as a hangar. . . . Yes. Right.
                 (she hangs up, exits.)
                                            CUT TO:

21   A TAVERN

          A cab drives up and John gets out just as a
          car dashes out from the rear, containing
          Spoomer and Sheila. In the rumble seat a
          huge dog. It dashes past, the girl with her
          head down. The dog barks at John, who looks
          after the car in outraged anger. He runs
          back to cab, gets in, indicates flying car.
          The cab takes up pursuit.
                                            CUT TO:

22   A ROAD SEEN FROM THE CAB.

          John leaning forward. Far ahead the car dis-
          appears.
                                            DISSOLVE TO:

                                            293

23   CAB STOPPING BEFORE A RESTAURANT.   19.

John gets out, enters, cab waits.

                        CUT TO:

24   INTERIOR.

John in doorway, looking around, a waiter at
his elbow. He thrusts waiter aside, goes on
to bar.

                        CUT TO:

25   BAR.

John has a drink, hurriedly, exits.

                        CUT TO:

26   THE STREET.

John entering cab. It goes on.

              DOUBLE EXPOSURE DISSOLVE TO:

27   CAB STOPPING AT ANOTHER RESTAURANT.

John gets out and enters.

28   INTERIOR.

John looking about, waiter at his elbow.
Puts waiter aside, goes on to bar.

                        CUT TO:

29   BAR.

John has two swift drinks, exits.

                        CUT TO:

30   CAB-WAITING IN STREET.

John enters, cab moves on.

              DOUBLE EXPOSURE DISSOLVE TO:

31   CAB STOPPING AT THIRD RESTAURANT.

John gets out and enters.

32   INTERIOR.

John looking about, waiter at elbow. Puts
waiter aside and goes on to bar.
                           CUT TO:

33   BAR.

John has three swift drinks, exits.
                           CUT TO:

34   THE STREET.

John enters cab, it moves on.
               DOUBLE EXPOSURE DISSOLVE TO:

35   CAB STOPPING AT FOURTH RESTAURANT.

John gets out, enters.
                           CUT TO:

36   INTERIOR.

John looking about, waiter at his elbow. He
is a little drunk savage. He sees Spoomer and
Sheila at table, intimate, leaning toward one
another, Spoomer's hand on her knee. John
turns, almost knocking waiter down, exits,
passes couple, bumps into man, who looks angrily after him.
                           CUT TO:

37   THE STREET.

John enters cab, it moves away, swiftly.
               DOUBLE EXPOSURE DISSOLVE TO:

38   CAB STOPPING BEFORE GATE TO FLYING FIELD.

John gets out, pays cabman. Cab moves away.
John enters gate, passing sentry's salute
without replying. Hurries on.
               DOUBLE EXPOSURE DISSOLVE TO:

39   A CORRIDOR.

John examining doors as he goes swiftly on.
Enters a door.
                         CUT TO:

40   A ROOM.   29 A

             A captain's equipment about. John looks about,
             sees bottle on the table, drinks from it,
             sways a little, goes to closet and begins to
             hurl garments out onto floor until he finds a
             tunic. Examines captain's pips, wads tunic
             under his arm and goes toward door, sees
             bottle, pauses, drinks again, exits.
                                                 CUT TO:

41   THE CORRIDOR.

             John walking a little unsteadily now. Enters
             another door.
                                                 CUT TO:

42   JOHN'S ROOM.

             Lays tunic on bed, goes to chest and opens
             drawer, delves, pauses, takes out bottle,
             drinks, sets bottle down, delves and takes
             out a woman's garter. Goes to bed, finds pin
             and pins folded garter to tunic, like a decora-
             tion ribbon, takes another drink from bottle,
             takes up tunic, exits.
                                                 CUT TO:

43   CORRIDOR.

             John hurrying down it.
                                                 CUT TO:

44   ENTRANCE.

             John emerges, hurries across aerodrome toward
             mechanics' barracks, enters.
                                                 CUT TO:

45   DORMITORY ROOM.

             John enters, blunders among cots to a cot,
             shakes sleeper. Man awakes, sits up in long
             drawers.
                                 Mechanic
             Yes, sir?

                                 John
             Get up.
                                                 CONTINUED:

                        Mechanic
             Sir? Is that you, Mr. Sartoris?

                        John
             Yes. Get up.

                        Mechanic
             Very good, sir.
                        (gets up; feels for clothes)

                        John
             Here. I've got some clothes for you. Put this on.

                 Mechanic takes tunic, looks at it.

                        Mechanic
             This, sir?

                        John
             Yes. Hurry up.
                        (Mechanic puts on tunic over under-cloth-
                        es while John waits impatiently)
             Now. Come on.
                        (he goes on, Mechanic following)
                                                    CUT TO;

46   THE FIELD.

                 The Mechanic, following John to a hangar.
                 They enter. John turns.

                        John
             Not. Put up your hands.

                        Mechanic
             My hands, sir?

                        John
             Yes.
                        (taps Mechanic on chest)
             Name's Spoomer, see? Captain Spoomer.
                        (touches garter)
             Ribbon. Distinguished Series of Thighs, see?
             Put up your hands.

                        Mechanic
             Very good, sir. Shall I get the gloves?

                        John
             No. Put 'em up. Give you ten bob.
                        (Mechanic does so; they begin to swing at
                        one another, hard, panting.)
                                                    DISSOLVE TO;

47 JOHN'S HAND WRITING IN DIARY:

Oct, 15 - - -. That's over. Maybe I am
luckier than I know. And if that's so, I
know that I am luckier than I deserve.
Only it makes me feel pretty low in the
self respect to know that the symbol of
my conscience and the mentor of my behavior is a dog. Or maybe that's as it
should be too. But thank God I'll never
see that dog again. I'm posted for
Scotland tomorrow. I'll see Bayard. I'm
going to try to work like hell and keep
up with him from now on. He's like snow,
like a hard, stiff wind blowing over
snow; not all hot and mucked up like I
always get my life when I am away from
him. And I'll never have to see that
dog again.

48 THE DIARY DISSOLVES BENEATH THE HAND,

to a telegraph form, the hand writing:

Lt. Bayard Sartoris,
S. of A.F., R. F. C.,
Ayr, Scotland

Posted at last. Leaving tomorrow.
John.

Hand withdraws, the telegraph form
DISSOLVES TO:

49 A SECOND ONE:

Lt. John Sartoris, R. F. C.,
London Colney, Herts.

So am I.
Bayard.

DISSOLVE with sound of train in motion, TO:

50 JOHN IN TRAIN -

looking out as train draws into station. He
gets down swiftly as soon as door is open,
looks about platform, sees Bayard. Bayard
dressed to depart, his luggage and orderly
beside him. John approaches; they look at one
another, Bayard very grave, cold. They don't
shake hands.
CONTINUED:

                         Bayard
Well?

                         John
Hello.

                         Bayard
What is it this time?

                         John
Nothing. It's finished.
          (Bayard looks at him)
I swear it is. I'm through. I'm going to behave
better. Damn it, I'm not a hopeless rotter.

                         Bayard
What happened?

                         John
 You think I'm no good, don't you? That I have to
be forced to behave.
          (Bayard watches him, cold, intent)
So you're leaving. You're through.

                         Bayard
Yes. I'm posted for the Front.

                         John
Damn.

                         Bayard
You had the same chance I did. You know that.

                         John
I know. God, I was a fool. Look. Couldn't you
get them to delay you one posting? I'd work hard.
I'd work like hell.

                         Bayard
I don't know. But I'm not going to try it. I
came over here to learn to be a pursuit pilot and
to get out to the Front.

                         John
- - Meaning that sooner or later I'll be in another
jam, fumbling around under another skirt?
          (Bayard looks at him)
Well, I don't guess I ever gave you any reason to
believe different. But I'm through, now. I swear
it.

                         Bayard
Show me.

                         John
Show you?
          (eagerly. His face fades)
You won't wait?

                                        CONTINUED:

                                                    299

                              Bayard
I waited for you once.

                              John
Yes. Yes .....Come on. Let's get a drink. How
much time have you got?

                              Bayard
                       (looks at his watch)
Train's due in thirty minutes.

                              John
Come on. There's a canteen in the station, isn't
there?

          They turn and walk down platform.
                             DOUBLE EXPOSURE DISSOLVE
                             TO:

51.   JOHN AND BAYARD

                entering canteen. They go to the bar, a
                barmaid serves them, they look at one another
                gravely, drink.

                              John
You were right. I can't even turn good by myself.
I have to be forced into it. And this time it was
by a
                     (John laughs, briefly, sardonic,
                      mirthless)
dog.

                            Bayard
A dog?

                              John
Yes. A dog. Pretty appropriate, isn't it? The
man's name is Spoomer. He's a captain. Or was.
He's a major now,. and they have given him a
squadron. He was to go out the day I left, him
and the dog. I guess the dog will be a flight
commander. Damn him.
                     (Bayard watches John, cold, grave. John
                     looks down at his empty glass)
Damn it, I hate to be made to do something right
that I had already made up my mind to do. And it
wasn't easy, too. She was a sweet thing.....Here,
miss.
                     (Extends his glass toward barmaid, moves
                     Bayard's toward her)

                            Bayard
No. I don't want another.

                                      Continued:

51. CONTINUED (2)

                         John
          Ah, come on. You're going to the front, and I've
          got to dogfight Camels.

                         Bayard
          No.

                         John
          Then I won't, either.
                    (To barmaid)
          Never mind. We're on the wagon for the next ten
          minutes.

               Noise of train without.

                         Bayard
          There's my train, anyway.
                    (Faces John)
          Well?

                         John
          Come on. I'll go out with you.

               They leave canteen.
                              DOUBLE EXPOSURE DISSOLVE TO:

52.   JOHN AND BAYARD

               walking along platform beside train, guard
               waiting to close compartment. Bayard halts,
               they look at one another.

                         John
          I know you think I am lying again, or weak. But I
          mean it. No more women until leave England.

                         Bayard
          And then what?

                         John
          I'll let France take care of itself. No; I don't
          mean that. I'm all right now. It was that dog,
          that damn dog, that set me wild. Thank God I'll
          never have to see it again. I'm through. I mean
          it.
                    (They look at one another. The guard
                     blows his whistle)

                         Bayard
          I must go. I'm taking you at your word.

                         John
          Right.
                                        Continued:

52.   CONTINUED (2)
                         Bayard
          Well, so long. See you in France.
                    (He goes on. John watching him)
                         John
          Bayard.
                    (Bayard pauses, turns, John approaches,
                     his hand extended)
          Good luck.
                    (For a moment they look at one another,
                     then they shake hands)
          Don't worry about me.

                         Bayard
          Right.
                    (He goes on, enters train without looking
                     back, John watching. The train moves
                     away. John watches it out of sight. Then
                     he turns, his face grave, quiet. SOUND
                     of aeroplane begins, whining in dive,
                              IN DISSOLVE TO:

53.   SHIP DIVING at ground target, firing, zooms on.
                              CUT TO:

54.   GROUND TARGET. It is a dummy in Captain's
             uniform, the folded garter pinned to the breast.
             Again sound of diving ship, a rake of bullets
             strikes the dummy, the shadow of the ship
             sweeps past as engine whines into zoom and dies
             away.

54XY1   JOHN'S HAND writing in diary:
             Mar. 2----. Goodbye England. Maybe goodbye
             everything I ever knew. I am going to France
             tomorrow, to Bayard's squadron. Then he will
             see, if he will only believe. My life has been
             short and there hasn't been much in it, and
             what there has been, has been pretty mucky,
             due to nobody's fault but mine. But now I can
             make up for it, and I am going to. I'm going
             to be an ace and I'm going home, if I go home
             with ribbons on my uniform. And I'm going to
             be able to say to any man or woman, This is
             one thing I haven't ever stained. Thank God I
             will never have to see that dog again.
                              DISSOLVE TO:
55.   An aerodrome, France. A car stops at the squad-
             ron office and replacement pilots get out, John
             among them. He is looking about for Bayard,
             eagerly. Suddenly he stops, an expression of
             shock and outrage comes over his face. The door
             opens, a sergeant comes out with a list, and
             behind him Spoomer's huge dog emerges, strolls
             out and trots away.   SLOW DISSOLVE WITH:
56.   SOUND OF ENGINES, shots of ships landing and
             taking off, of combat, etc. to show that John
             is settled in the squadron and some time has
             passed.   DISSOLVE TO:

DISSOLVE through it to:

58   A SECLUDED CORNER.

The legs of a waiter in an apron.
CLOCK past to a pair of boots and a pair of
girl's legs, in attitude to show that owners
are kissing.
CLOCK to John and Antoinette, kissing, the
waiter looking on with a weary air, wiping
table top with napkin. On the table two
fairly tall stacks of saucers. Waiter rattles
saucers. John looks up without haste.

                    John
What do you want?

                    Waiter
Monsieur, fait peut-etre bein dur et sec,
n'est-ce pas?

                    John
What?

                    Antoinette
Quel dommage, alors? Ne sais tu que monsieur est
officier Americain? Allez! Vite!

                    John
Sure. Vite. Beat it. Rat off. This is a duet,
not a chorus.

          Waiter shrugs, exits. John prepares to
          take Antoinette again in his arms. She draws
          back.

                    Antoinette
Non, non, non.

                    John
Wee, wee, wee. Angcore.

          He tries to take her in his arms. She holds
          him off, tugging at his wrist. He pauses,
          watching her, puzzled.

                    John
What? What do you want?

                    Antoinette
Quel heure? Il faut partir.

                    John
Her what? What her?

                              Continued

58   CONTINUED (2)

>   Antoinette
>   (tugging his sleeve up; he realizes
>   that she is tryingto see his watch, turns
>   his wrist; she looks at watch. She
>   shrieks)
I mus' depart, queek.

>   John
Aw, no. Come on, now

>   Antoinette
>   (rises as he holds to her)
Oui, oui! Tante she wait, she lock.
>   (goes through pantomine of a woman,
>   anxious and angry, looking for her)

>   John
Tante? Oh. The old dame. Aw, come
>   (He holds her, she leans and kisses him
>   swiftly, breaks free, runs toward door,
>   turns and throws him a kiss, exits.
>   John springs up and is running out when
>   Waiter enters hurriedly, waving his
>   hands)

>   Waiter
Monsiuer! L'addition!

>   John pauses, reaches in his pocket, flings
>   money back and runs out.
>   CUT TO:

59   THE STREET

>   Antoinette hurrying along, John following.

>   John
'Toinette!

>   Antoinette turns, shakes her head, waves him
>   back, hurries on. John overtakes her. She
>   turns, her face is anxious.

>   Antoinette
Non non non! Please! Please, Jean!

>   John
Well, All right. But what's your aunt got against
me? She don't even know me.

>   Antoinette
Non, non non!
>   (Grips his arm)
A demain? Tomorrow?
>   Continued

304

59 CONTINUED (2)

29

                              John
      Right.
                  (Reveals watch, points to an hour. Antoinette
                  nods, glances about, leans to him and kisses
                  him swiftly, turns and runs on. John looks
                  after her. He beings to frown, puzzled.
                  Suddenly he moves on after her, slowly.
                                              CUT TO:

60   A DINGY DOORWAY, A DINGY SIGN:

                ESTAMINET. VINS. TABAC

            Antoinette enters hurriedly.
                                              CUT TO:

61   INTERIOR

            French soldiers and civilians, an old woman
            behind the bar, locks up as Antoinette enters
            hurriedly, avoiding the old woman's eye. She
            goes around behind the bar, the old woman
            watching her.

                          Old Woman
      Where have you been?

                          Antoinette
      Shopping. Walking. I stay in here so much that I..

                          Old Woman
      Don't lie to me. You have been with that American.

                          Antoinette
      I haven't.
                  (The old woman looks at her. Antoinette's
                  gaze falls; she looks up again, defensive)

                          Old Woman
      Hah. I have warned you. But little you care. Will
      he buy you clothes? Will he put bread in our mouths,
      eh?
                          Antoinette
      No! I wouldn't let him! I wouldn't ask him to! I..
                  (She ceases, panting, fearful. The old
                  woman watches her coldly)

                          Old Woman
      Go upstairs.

                          Antoinette
                  (an expression of despair comes into
                  her face)
      Is he....
                                              CONTINUED

305

61   CONTINUED (2)

                    Old Woman
          Go upstairs.

               Antoinette looks at her a moment, bows her
               head and exits slowly by door behind bar.
               The old woman watches the door until it closes,
               then she looks around, pauses, becomes still
               as John enters and approaches bar, looking
               about.

                    John
          Bong jour, madame.

                    Old Woman
          Monsieur. Vous voulez?

                    John
          Cognac.

               The old woman serves him, stands behind bar,
               her hands in her apron, cold, still, as John
               drinks. He looks at her, she stares at him.
               He pays, turns toward door, looks back, finds
               her still watching him, goes on to door and
               opens it. His face is thoughtful; as he opens
               the door it changes, becomes chocked as he
               looks down at something.CLOCK to floor as
               Spoomer's dog enters and passes John, who
               looks at it in baffled and groping astonishment.
               He finds the old woman watching him, recovers,
               exits.
                              CUT TO:

62   THE STREET

               John standing, puzzled, astonished.

                    John
          Not that again. Good God, not that again.
               Suddenly he turns, reenters estaminet hurriedly,
               with determined air.
                              CUT TO:

63   INTERIOR

               John enters, the old woman watching him, still,
               alert, inscrutable, as he approaches.

                    John
          That dog.
               (Raises his voice)
          Dog!
               (He glares at the old woman, who watches
               him)
                              CONTINUED:

                    Old Woman
          Monsieur voulait?

                    John
          Dog! Dog!
                    (Glares about, baffled)
          Spoomer! Major! Major!
                    (Tries to indicate major's insigne on his
                    own shoulders. The old woman watches
                    him., shrugs. John glares about.
          CLOCK tc

          A British soldier rises from a group in a
          corner, where he has been concealed, approaches.
          John glares at him as he comes up, salutes.

                    John
          You, Hobbs? What are you doing here?

                    Hobbs
          I 'ope you wcn.'t be mentioning it at the haerodrome,
          sir, I was just-

                    John
          Is that dog with you?

                    Hobbs
          Yes, sir. Major Spoomer told me to toike 'im out
          for a bit of a airing, sir, and I just came on tc
          town, meaning no 'arm, sir.

          John glares at Hobbs, wanting to believe.

                    John
          Where's Major Spoomer?

                    Hobbs
          At the haerodrcme, sir.

                    John
          Don't lie to me. He's not in town here?

                    Hobbs
          S'elp me, sir.

          John glares at him, looks about; the French
          people and the old woman are all watching
          him. He gives Hobbs a coin.

                    John
          Here. Have yourself a drink.

                    Hobbs
          Right, sir. Thank you sir.

          John moves toward door, looks back once again,
          puzzled, finds Old Woman watching him, and
                                        CONTINUED:

63   CONTINUED (3)

          and the French people covertly, looking
          away from his gaze. Exit John.
                                        CUT TO:

64   AERODROME

          Motorcycle side car stops at office. John
          gets out and enters, still puzzled, worried.
                                        CUT TO:

65   THE OFFICE

          Adjutant behind desk, looks up as John
          enters.

                         John
          Where's Spoomer?

                         Adjutant
          He went down to Wing. Not back yet.

                         John
          You'r lying.

                         Adjutant
          What?
                    (Rises slowly)
          What's that?

                         John
          I'm sorry. I didn't mean that. Don't you know
          where he is?

                         Adjutant
          I told you. Confound you, Sartoris, what's the
          matter with you?

                         John
          Nothing. I know that's where he told you he was
          going. Sorry.
                    (Turns swiftly and exits, Adjutant
                     looking after him)
                                        CUT TO:

66   THE MESS, JOHN AT BAR.

                         John
          Smythe!
               Orderly appears. John jerks his hand at shelves
          Orderly sets bottle and glass on bar, John drinks
          hurriedly, fills glass again.
                                        CONTINUED

                    John
Send word down to have my bus on the line.

                    Orderly
Very good, sir.
                    (Exit Orderly. John drinks. DISSOLVE
                    with sound of spluttering and warming
                    engine TO:

67   SHIP ON THE LINE

                    Mechanics warming it. Enter John, in flying
                    clothes. Sergeant gets out of cockpit.

                    Sergeant
All right, sir! I put on that new magneto today!

                    John
Right!

                    Gets in and takes off, mechanics watch him
                    out of sight. Engine dies   DISSOLVE:

68   THE ESTAMINET

                    The old woman behind bar, serving customers.
                    Door behind bar opens and Spoomer enters.
                    The French people look at him, covertly. The
                    Old Woman looks around, Spoomer beckons her.
                    She approaches, watchful, cold. They speak
                    in low tones.

                    Spoomer
Well?

                    Old Woman
Well, then?
                    Spoomer
I won't have it. What am I paying you for?

                    Old Woman
Have no fear, monsieur the commandant. Am I not
here? I promise you.

                    Spoomer
You promised me before. Yet I come today, as you
were informed, and what do I find?

                    Old Woman
An accident, I assure you.

                    Spoomer
An accident that happens too often.
                                        CONTINUED

　　　　　　　CONTINUED (2)　　　　　　　　　

　　　　　　　　　　　Old Woman
I do what I can. But I am not an officer; I cannot
command your soldiers. I will watch my niece; let
you watch your young men as well.

　　　　　　　　　　　Spoomer
I will do that. See that she does not go out alone
again. Or I shall..
　　　　　(looks at her, hard, cold, makes gesture)
You understand?

　　　　　　　　　　　Old Woman
Good. It is understood. Have no alarm.

　　　　Exit Spoomer, followed by the dog, and Hobbs,
　　　　the French people watch him covertly. The Old
　　　　Woman watches him out, then she turns and
　　　　passes out door at back.
　　　　　　　　　　　　　　　　CUT TO:

69　　　　　　　A NARROW STAIR

　　　　The Old Woman mounts to a door, opens it and
　　　　enters.
　　　　　　　　　　　　　　　　CUT TO:

70　　　　　　　A LIVING ROOM

　　　　A table in the center, another door beyond.
　　　　The Old Woman goes on, passes through this
　　　　door.
　　　　　　　　　　　　　　　　CUT TO:

71　　　　　　　A BEDROOM

　　　　The Old Woman approaches the bed. CLOCK to
　　　　bed. Antoinette lying on it, half dressed,
　　　　face down, crying. The Old Woman stands be-
　　　　side the bed, looking down at her, cold, still.
　　　　　　　　　　DISSOLVE with sound of engines
　　　　　　　　　　　　　　　　　　　TO:

72　　　　　　　THE AERODROME

　　　　The patrol coming in.
　　　　　　　　　　　　　　　　CUT TO:

73   JOHN BANKING OVER FIELD, PASSES OVER MECHANICS'
      MESS.

      The dog is bribbing in the barbage can behind
      it. As John watches, Spoomer appears and drags
      the dog away, the dog straining backward.
      John's face is savage.
                                         CUT TO:

74   THE SHIPS LANDING, TAXI-ING UP TO HANGERS.

      John and Bayard get out as Spoomer appears,
      dragging dog across field. John watches,
      savage, Bayard watching John as Spoomer drags
      the dog on to the squadron office, thrusts it
      in and shuts door and goes on toward mess.

                     John
                (in cold, savage, low voice)
      Don't you know you mustn't eat that muck? That's
      for soldiers.

                     Bayard
                (watching John)
      What in hell's the matter with you?

                     John
      Nothing
                (John goes on, Bayard watching him.
                                         CUT TO:

75   JOHN'S HAND WRITING IN DIARY:

      Mar 15....Bayard is right. I guess I am
      pretty rotten. But this is different.
      She is different from any woman I ever
      knew. I know she is not a virgin,
      probably by several different occasions,
      but there is something about her that
      makes me feel that she is a better woman
      than I am a man. And now he's in it
      again. There is a fatality about him and
      me. . And I mean fatal too. I know that
      one of us is not coming out of this war.
      And when I think of that, I get a little
      afraid, not of what might happen to me,
      but of what I might do if the fates have it
      that he is the one who will not get through
      and not I.

      The hand ceases, the book shuts suddenly. . CLOCK
      to John looking up as Bayard enters. It is
      their hut. Bayard in flying clothes, John
      dressed.
                                         CONTINUED:

                                                         311

                              Bayard
          Going to town again?

                              John
          What's that to you? Town's free, yet.

                              Bayard
          Are you going to paw at women's skirts for the rest
          of your life, John?

                              John
          I hope so. But this is different. But I don't
          expect you to understand, though.

                              Bayard
          How different? There's a woman back home that you
          went through a wedding ceremony with. I hope it's
          different from that.

                              John
          I don't know whether it is or not.

                              Bayard
          You what?

                              John
          I don't think I will ever see Caroline again,
          Bayard.

                              Bayard
          Nonsense. What the hell kind of mawkish drivel
          are you talking now?

                              John
          I don't mean that. I've got just as good a chance
          to live as anybody has.

                              Bayard
                    (looks at him; suddenly comprehends)
          You mean, when this is over you're not even going
          back home? That you are going to throw Caroline
          over for a --------for...Stand up.

                              John
          What?

                              Bayard
          Get on your legs.

                              John
          No. I won't fight you. Go on and hit me. I'm in
          the wrong. I know it. But I'm not going to try
          to help it. Go on and hit me. But I won't fight
          you.

                                             CONTINUED:

CONTINUED (3)

        For a moment longer Bayard glares at him, then
        he turns and exits. John is very grave, watch-
        ing the door. Then he opens diary again.
        CLOCK to his hand writing:

            So this is the end between Bayard and me.
            I guess I knew it was coming, sometime.
            That same day a woman would separate us
            for good and all. Poor Caroline. What
            an insult to her that she couldn't even
            do it by marrying me, that it remained
            for a

        The hand ceases

                                              DISSOLVE TO:

JOHN ENTERS MESS

        Looks about, sees Orderly, beckons.
        Orderly approaches.

                        John
        Get me a sidecar.

            Orderly turns away. Adjutant turns from bar.

                        Adjutant
        Oh, I say. Sartoris. I was looking for you.

                        John
        What is it?

                        Adjutant
        Manning has been relieved of Officer of the Day.
        You are to carry on with it.

                        John
        What?

                        Adjutant
        Sorry. Major's orders.

                        John
        Hell. I'm going to town.

                        Adjutant
        Against orders?
                (John glares at him, baffled, furious)
        Shall have to report you, of course.

                        John
        Report and be damned.
                (Turns; Bayard approaches)

                        Bayard
        John

                                            CONTINUED:

                                              313

76   CONTINUED (2)

John moves fast toward door; Bayard moves
forward and grasps his shoulder. John whirls,
knocks Bayard's hand down, exits, Bayard
locking after him.
                           CUT TO:

77   THE OFFICE

John approaches fast, jerks door open and
looks in for the dog. The dog is gone.
             DISSOLVE with motorcycle engine
                               TO:

78 ·   MOTORCYCLE RUSHING AWAY FROM MESS.

DOUBLE EXPOSURE DISSOLVE TO:

79   MOTORCYCLE STOPPING AT ESTAMINET.

John gets out, enters swiftly.
                           CUT TO:

80   INTERIOR

French people all ceasing to watch John. The
Old Woman behind the bar, watching him, her
face watchful, hard.

                 John
'Toinette.

                 Old Woman
Pas d'ici.

                 John
           (restrained, a little wild, groping)
Je veux-------Je------'Toinette.
            (looks wildly about, baffled, glares at
            Old Woman, who faces him steadily. He
            looks about, at the French people all
            watching him. John moves among them,
            hurling them aside as if he were seeking
            someone. They move, sullenly, watching
            him as he looks among them, wild,
            baffled, glaring)
Soldat! Soldat Anglais. Ici--ici---Christ, Christ!
Yesterday! English soldier here yesterday!
            (Gripping a peasant by his shoulder, shout-
            ing at him, gesturing with his other hand)
English soldier! Here yesterday with dog! Big dog!
                         CONTINUED:

80   CONTINUED (2)

                    PEASANT
                  (cringing away)
        Non, monsieur! Non, monsieur!

            John blares at Peasant, flings him aside and
            starts back toward bar when he stops. Off
            stage a dog begins to bark. John locks up-
            ward toward sound, on his face an expression
            of raging and despairing comprehension. Runs
            toward bar and behind it, the Old Woman watch-
            ing. She realizes what he is about and springs
            forward before the door, her hands in her
            apron, staring at John, who glares at her
            raging, baffled. The dog continues to bark.
            DISSOLVE with sound of engines TO:

81   BULLETIN BOARD, ADJUTANT STICKING UP ORDERS:

82   INSERT
        Mar. 16 ----Officer of the Day: Sartoris, J.
                                        DISSOLVE TO:

83   AERODROME. JOHN making inspection tour with
        sergeant and orderly. In distance a car before
        Squadron Office. SPOOMER emerges, gets into
        car, drives away, John watching.

                        John
                  (turns to sergeant)
        That'll do. Carry on.

        Sergeant salutes. John goes on to office, opens
        door. The dog emerges, looks about for a
        moment, trots off. John follows, watches dog
        turn up road toward town.
                                        DISSOLVE TO:

84   A HANGAR, John and a mechanic taking off their
        tunics and shirts, an Orderly nearby with two
        pairs of gloves. He puts the gloves on John
        and mechanic; they square off and begin to box.
        Soon they are slugging at one another, hard,
        John's face grim, cold.
                                        DISSOLVE TO:

85   BULLETIN, Adjutant's hand posting orders:
        Mar. 17---Officer of the Day: Sartoris, J.
                                        DISSOLVE TO:

86   JOHN'S HAND-WRITING IN DIARY:
        Mar. 18-----Officer of the Day: Sartoris, J.
        Ha ha.
                                        DISSOLVE TO:

87   HAND WRITING IN DIARY:
        Mar. 19----Officer of the Day, Sartoris, J.
        Four days in succession. Ha ha ha. I'm well
        out of it. It's not her. If she wants him
        more than she does me, that's all right with me.
        It's not knowing. I know he is there, because
        when he has really gone to Wing, the dog will
        go straight to the garbage can. But when the
        dog strikes straight for town, I know where he
        is. But I have no proof. That's it. And I go
        in there, and all those frogs laughing at me
        and I can't do anything about it because they
        know that if I break in that door and go up
        there, whether I find him there or not, they
        will have me court martialed for infringing
        the articles of alliance by invading property

316

87 CONTINUED (2)
of an allied nation without warrant. That's it.
To have those frogs laughing at me. I've held
in so far, but if it happens one more time I'm
going to blow. I'm sick to think of the dis-
grace to Bayard, but I can't help it. They're
expecting too much of me. It's not her any
longer. I swear that. It's having him and
those frogs laughing at me.

DISSOLVE TO:

88 BULLETIN BOARD, John standing before it. Bayard
comes up. John looks at him, then back to order,
raises his hand to it. Bayard puts out his hand,
John looks at him, slowly tears paper from
board, tears it slowly up, watching Bayard.

              Bayard
You can't do that. John.

              John
I've done it, though. Didn't you just see me?

              Bayard
John.

              John
Let be, now. This is not your trouble. I'll
promise it won't reflect on you.

              Bayard
To hell with that. John, listen. It won't be
much longer. I saw the colonel at Wing yesterday
and he's going to put you in for transfer, so this--
this--- he can't ride you-----

              John
Me? Transfer? I won't take it.

              Bayard
What?

              John
I won't take it. And to hell with you for meddling.

              Bayard
John.
              (Raises his hand again as if to touch
              John. They look at one another. Bayard
              lowers his hand)
              John
That's right. Just let me alone. I'm all right.
              (Lets the scraps of the order fall to
              the floor, exits, Bayard looking after
              him, grave, troubled. Orderly appears
              behind Bayard with his flying suit and
              goggles. After a moment the orderly
              coughs. Bayard turns)

88   CONTINUED (2)

                     Bayard
          What? Oh. Thanks.
                     (Takes suit, Orderly exits. Bayard
                     looks again after John, then begins
                     to put on suit. With engine,

                                        DISSOLVE TO:

89   PATROL TAKING OFF.

            John watching from door of hangar until machines
            vanish, the sound becoming that of a motor car
            stopping before squadron office. John looks, sees
            Spoomer emerge, get in car, drive away. John
            watches car from sight. Then he moves toward
            Squadron office, enters.
                                        CUT TO:

90   THE OFFICE.

            John looking about for the dog. It is not there.
            He exits, shuts door behind him.
                                        CUT TO::

91   TARMAC.

            John standing in deep thought, alert, grave. He
            moves toward hangar, enters.
                                        CUT TO:

92   INTERIOR.

            John looking about for the dog. It is not there.
            He exits.
                                        CUT TO:

93   TARMAC.
            John walking toward next hangar,
                                        CUT TO:

94   INTERIOR.
            At the rear a pile of empty packing cases. John
            looks about, sees packing cases, stares at them,
            approaches and begins to haul them down. Turns
            one over, dog emerges, sidles past him. He
            follows it to door.
                                        CUT TO:

95   THE TARMAC, the dog tropping on toward gate,
John follows.

                                  CUT TO:

96   THE GATE. The dog turns up road toward town,
beginning to lope. John turns back, walking
back to hangar.

                                  CUT TO:

97   HANGAR, mechanics working over a ship. John
enters; they look up.

                       John
Get my bus on the line.

                     Sergeant
But, Mr. Sartoris, sir-----

                       John
Will you get my bus out?

                     Sergeant
Very good, sir.

           John turns, exits. Mechanics roll ship out
and crank engine. DISSOLVE with sound of
engine to:

98   THE MESS. John drinking, takes two or three
in succession, hurried, grim, savage, thrusts
bottle in his pocket, exits,

                                 CUT TO

99   THE SHIP warming on Tarmac. John enters,
without helmet or goggles, gets in, takes off
savagely, the sergeant watching and shaking
head.

                                CUT TO:

100   JOHN flying toward Amiens, fast. Just before
he reaches the city he sees an ambulance on
the road, wobbling from side to side.

                                CUT TO:

101   THE AMBULANCE driven by drunken driver, rolls
off the road into ditch and stops.

                                CUT TO:

102   JOHN watching ambulance stop. He lands in
field beside road, gets out, takes drink from
his bottle, approaches ambulance. The driver
is slumped over the wheel. John tries to rouse
him but cannot. He pushes driver back into
ambulance, cranks engine, gets in and drives
on,fast.

                                     CUT TO:

103   JOHN driving ambulance, approaching Amiens,
passing refugee carts as city is being evacu-
ated. He enters deserted city, fast, drives
to estaminet, stops, springs out, wild, grim,
drinks from bottle, hurls empty bottle away,
goes to door. It is locked. He shakes door,
hurls himself against it. Further down the
street a French corporal stands in another
doorway, drinking wine from a bottle. The
corporal pauses and watches John hurl himself
against the locked door, which now gives and
John plunges into estaminet.

                                     CUT TO;

104   THE ESTAMINET. John on all fours where he has
fallen. He gets up, looks about. The room is
empty, the chairs and tables overturned, the
shelves behind the bar are empty of bottles.
He goes to bar, looks into the mirror behind
it and sees a bottle beneath bar and reaches
it out. He is a little drunk, he knocks bottle
neck off on edge of bar, fills glass and raises
it, facing himself in the mirror, wild, savage,
grim. As he stands so, a shell falls in the
city, the sound faint; from overhead a thin
stream of plaster dust falls down and a lean
cat leaps up from behind the bar and over it
and runs away, John looking after the cat. He
drinks, fills the glass and drinks again, swaying, holding himself up by the bar. His gaze
rests upon the closed door behind the bar, he
fills the glass, drinks, flings the glass down,
goes around the bar to the door and jerks it
open. It reveals a stairway mounting, with
sitting on the bottomstep the old woman. She
has her apron over her head and she is rocking back and forth. John stands above her,
swaying, holding himself up by the door.

                      John
Madame.
            (The old woman rocks back and forth.
            John leans and touches her shoulder)
Toinette. Ou est-elle Toinette?

         The old woman rocks back and forth. John looks
down at her, then he steps over her and mounts
the stairs, holding to the rail.   CUT TO

105   THE HEAD OF THE STAIRS, another door, John
facing it, swaying, grim. He opens the door
and enters.

CUT TO:

106   A LIVING ROOM. In the center a table, on the
table an officer's cap. John looks at the cap,
swaying; as he does so, the dog rises from beyond the table and they look at one another.
As they do so, the next shell falls, remote, the
curtains in the window blow in with the explosion. John circles the table, the dog circles
too, keeping the table between them. John
blunders into the table; he pauses, turns toward another door, listens.

                    Woman's Voice
                  (Beyond door)
      Maman?

John springs to door, kicks it, then he hurls
himself at it, bursts it in and plunges on.

CUT TO:

107   BEDROOM. John on all fours, the girl in her
underclothes just sprung out of the bed. She
screams, cringing. John gets up unsteadily,
looks at bed. The covers in a long ridge. He
looks about room while girl cringes, watching
him with terror. On a chair lies Spoomer's
uniform. While they stand so, the next shell
falls. John moves toward bed, the girl retreating, cringing, staring at him as he stops, swaying, his face wild and stupid, looking into the
bed. CLOCK to a long ridge of bedclothing
obviously concealing Spoomer. Antoinette stares
at John, her hand to her mouth, in terror. He
looks at her, dazed, moves toward her as she
shrings before him. He strikes her. She falls to
her knees, clutching his legs. He strikes her
again. She falls to the floor and lies there,
looking up at him quietly, a stain of blood at
her mouth. The next shell falls, the room
trembles a little. John picks Antoinette up,
carries her to the bed and drops her into it.
She lies again, watching him quietly as he sways,
looking about, trying to collect himself. He
turns, stumbling, goes to the chair and takes up
Spoomer's uniform, holds himself up along the
wall and exits.

CUT TO:

108 THE LIVING ROOM. John enters, swaying, holding himself up, looks about for the dog, stupidly. It is gone. He crosses room, takes up the cap from the table, goes on, lurching, out the next door.

CUT TO:

THE HEAD OF THE STAIRS -

John, carrying the uniform, holding himself
up by the rail, about to descend.

A Voice
Que faites-vous en haut?

John pauses, looks over stair rail.

CUT TO:

110   THE FRENCH CORPORAL -

Looking up at him. The Corporal jerks his arm.

Corporal
Descendez donc.

John looks down at him. Then he puts his hand
on the stair rail and vaults over it. The
Corporal springs aside. The old woman still
sits on the bottom step, her apron over her
head, rocking back and forth. John plunges
past the Corporal and falls against the wall,
gets to his feet and turns as the Corporal
kicks at him. John knocks the Corporal down.
The Corporal lies on his back, kicking at John
and tugging at something in his overcoat pocket.
He jerks out a pistol and fires at John. John
springs upon him, stamping the pistol hand.
The Corporal begins to scream, like a woman.
John lifts him and hits him on the chin and
knocks him out and drops him to the floor and
stands, swaying, looking about, wild and dazed.
The old woman rocks back and forth, her apron
over her head. John gathers up the uniform
and blunders out the door.

CUT TO:

111   THE BAR -

John, holding himself up against it, drinking
from the bottle, empties it and flings it to
the floor, looks about again, stumbles across
room toward street door.

CUT TO:

112   THE STREET -

The ambulance before the door. John goes to
it, dazed, stupid. He hauls the driver out and
puts the uniform on him and tumbles him back
into the ambulance again, swaying, trying to
collect himself. He turns and re-enters estaminet.

CUT TO:

113   INTERIOR ESTAMINET -

John at bar, goes around behind it, blundering, gets an ink bottle and a rusty pen. Hunts in his overall, draws out a bit of dirty paper, stares at it stupidly.

          CUT TO:

114   THE PAPER -

        WALKLEY
       Military Tailors
        The Strand
         London
           16 December, 1917

  To Lt. J. Sartoris

   1 Uniform, R.F.C.

         L 19.10

115   JOHN -

Turns paper over, writes on back:

          CUT TO:

116   JOHN'S HAND WRITING -

      Major C. Spoomer,
      ---th Squadron,
      Bertangles

         CUT TO:

117   JOHN -

Folding paper, clumsy, stupid, wild looking, leaves estaminet.

         CUT TO:

118   THE STREET -

John putting paper into tunic pocket on unconscious driver. Cranks ambulance, gets in, drives off.

       DOUBLE EXPOSURE DISSOLVE TO:

119   THE MEADOW -

A battalion of troops resting at roadside. John comes up, stops, gets out of ambulance, swaying, looks at troops.
        Continued -

324

                         John
          Here.

               The soldiers look at him. An officer comes up.

                         Officer
          Hullo. That your aeroplane there?

                         John
          Quite. Need four men. Hold wings. Tight field.

                         Officer
          Oh, quite.
                    (turns)
          Four men here.

               Four men come forward. They follow John to
               the ship.

                         John
                    (unsteadily)
          Hold wings.

                         Officer
                    (watching him)
          Look here. Hadn't you better leave it alone until
          you feel a bit better?

               John looks at him, walks unsteadily and with
               dignity to cockpit, sets throttle, Officer
               follows.

                         John
          Now. See? Gadget here? When I say contact, turn
          it. Like this. Shee?

                         Officer
          Quite. But, look here------

               John returns to prop, unsteadily. The men hold
               the wings, all watching John, the officer an-
               xiously. John pumps prop, sets it.

                         John
          Contact.

                         Officer
                    (turns switch)
          Right.

               John swings prop terrifically, engine catches,
               John sprawls onto the ground. The officer runs
               forward and helps him up.

                         Officer
          Look here, man! You can't-----

                                        - Continued -

John shakes him off, goes to cockpit, blunders
in. He leans out.

                        John
        Hold wings. Hard.

        The men brace themselves. John revs the engine,
        cuts it. Gestures men away, turns and taxis to
        end of the field. It is not much larger than a
        cottage yard. He turns again, beckons men to
        him. They approach gingerly.

                        John
        Hold wings. When I wave hand, let go. Better lie
        down, too.

        The men hold the wings gingerly. The Officer
        approaches cockpit, anxiously.

                        Officer
        Look here, Mister ---

        John opens throttle, Officer leans into back-
        wash, holding his cap.

                        Officer
        I say, Mister!

        John opens throttle, backwash sweeps Officer
        back. He shouts.

                        Officer
        The man in ambulance! What shall I do with him?

                        John
        Keep him! I don't give a damn!
                (opens throttle full, lifts his hand)

        The men at the wings sprawl as the ship shoots
        away, snaps upward at once at a crazy angle,
        the men on the ground and the Officer looking
        after it, their mouths open. They return to
        ambulance. The Officer looks at the driver,
        sees paper in his pocket, takes it out and
        opens it.

                        Officer
        Good gad. It's his commanding officer.
                (turns to men)
        Can any of you lads drive a motor?

                        Soldier
        Here, sir.

        SOUND of engine begins in,

                                        DISSOLVE TO:

120   THE AERODROME -

             the ambulance stopping at the mess. Adjutant
             emerges.

                              Officer
                       (on seat beside driver)
             Cheer-o. I've fetched your C.O. home. I say. Have
             you a drink about.

             Aeroplane engine in,

                                             DISSOLVE TO:

121   JOHN'S SHIP IN FLIGHT -

             crazily, fast, rushing low along trenches,
             firing.

                                             CUT TO:

122   GERMAN TROOPS -

             ducking and running, firing upward as ship
             zooms past.

                                             CUT TO:

123   SHIP -

             running into smoke of barrage, being tossed
             here and there. It emerges, below it trenches
             and men. John dives, firing.

                                             CUT TO:

124   BRITISH TROOPS -

             running, dodging, ducking, as ship zooms away,
             an officer shouting and shaking his fists at
             it.

                                             CUT TO:

125   JOHN -

             looking back and down, grim, savage, wild;
             produces an empty bottle from cockpit, hurls
             it down at trench.
                                             CUT TO:

126   SHIP -

straightening out and diminishing rapidly,
engine sinking.

DISSOLVE TO:

127   AERODROME. (ENGINE SOUND INCREASING)

Engine howls as three mechanics, passing between two hangars, look up with terror, run,
fall flat as ship dives over them by a few feet,
zooms on, mechanics look after it wildly. Ship
zooms, loops, dives at running mechanics, zooms,
spins upward, falls off on its back.

CUT TO:

128   JOHN -

in upside-down ship, looking down at dog grubbing in garbage can behind men's mess. Engine
cuts, splutters, cuts out, John in violent action.

CUT TO:

129   SHIP CRASHING -

mechanics beginning to run.

CUT TO:

130   THE CRASH -

John crawling dizzily out on hands and knees,
stops, vomits, as dog trots up and stands
looking at him. Dog comes up, sniffs at vomit,
John gets up unsteadily and kicks at dog, as
mechanics run up.

DISSOLVE TO:

131   A ROAD - A HORSE-DRAWN CART -

loaded with household goods, driven by a
peasant in a smock. On a chicken coop of hens
sits a woman with a shawl over her head. The
cart moves slowly.

DISSOLVE TO:

132   THE SQUADRON OFFICE.

A staff car stops, General and aide get out,
enter office.

                                        CUT TO:

133   OFFICE.

Adjutant rises, stands to attention as General
and aide enter.

                    General
Ah, Captain. Good day.

                    Adjutant
              (shows alarm, consternation)
G-good day, sir.

                    General
All flights out, eh? Major Spoomer himself went
out today, eh?

                    Adjutant
Ye-yes, sir.

                    General
Good. That's where a squadron commander should be
 these days. I tell you, Captain, things are
looking serious.

                    Adjutant
Ye-yes, sir. Quite, sir. Will you wait in the
mess, sir? Would you like a drink, sir?

                    General
Eh? No thanks. I'll sit here. But don't let me
interrupt you.

                    Adjutant
No, sir. I've a bit.... if you will excuse me for
a moment ---

                    General
              (sitting down, taking out pipe)
Quite. Carry on, Captain.

Adjutant exits, his face alarmed, almost wild.

                                        CUT TO:

154   THE MESS.

Adjutant enters swiftly, goes to bar.

                                        - Continued -

134   CONTINUED (2)

              Adjutant
            (in low, tense voice)
Smythe! Smythe!

              Orderly
            (enters hurriedly)
Yes, sir?

              Adjutant
Get me Hobbs. Quickly.

    Exit orderly. Adjutant registers nervousness,
    terror. Hobbs enters; Adjutant whirls on him.

              Adjutant
Go to town. Find the Major at once. The General's
here ---

              Hobbs
Gor, sir!

              Adjutant
Yes. Said he fancied that the Major was out with
the squadron this afternoon and I had to say yes.
Run.

              Hobbs
Right, sir.
      (exits running)

    With SOUND OF MOTORCYCLE,

                    CUT TO:

135   HOBBS -

    turning into road to town, going fast on
    motorcycle. He approaches the cart, passes
    it, glances up. An expression of shocked as-
    tonishment comes over his face, the motor-
    cycle darts from the road and overturns in a
    ditch. Hobbs sits up, looks back at cart
    with expression of shocked horror.

                 DISSOLVE TO:

136   The cart turning slowly onto aerodrome.

                                         CUT TO:

137   SQUADRON OFFICE

             The General smoking, the Adjutant at type-
             writer, tapping, glancing now and then at
             General in terror.

                                         CUT TO:

138   THE SHEET OF PAPER IN TYPEWRITER.

             A jumble of letters that make no sense at all
             as the Adjutant taps them out.

                                         CUT TO:

139   INTERIOR SCENE.

             General taps out his pipe, rises.

                              General
             Well. I shall walk about and watch for them to
             come in. They should be returning soon now.

                              Adjutant
             Y-yes, sir. Very soon, now, sir.

             General goes out, followed by aide.

                                         CUT TO:

140   Tarmac, General emerging from office, stops
             as cart reaches office, frowns.

                              General
             What the devil is this?

             The woman on the cart has not seen the general.

                              Woman
                         (in a man's voice)
             Par ici. Arretez.

             The cart stops. The woman descends, clumsy in
             her skirts. The General watches, swelling with
             outrage. Descends step, angrily, approaches
             cart as woman turns. They both stop dead still,

                                         CONTINUED:

140   CONTINUED (2)

        on the General's face an expression of outrage,
then puzzlement, then outrage again.

               General
Take off that shawl.

        The woman looks at him, then slowly removes the
shawl. It is Spoomer.

               General
Hah. Mrs. Spoomer. Good afternoon. Just back
from the front, eh?

                   DISSOLVE TO:

141   JOHN'S HANDWRITING IN DIARY:

        So that's that. Finished. I feel better.
The General himself was here when he got
down from the cart. But.they can't do
anything to him because his uncle or somebody is on the Staff in London. I don't
know what they will do to me, and I don't
care. It was worth it. Because I am
done now, finished, with her and with him.
My God, when have I known peace before.

                   DISSOLVE TO:

142   SQUADRON OFFICE.

        Spoomer and Adjutant behind table, John bare-
headed, facing table, surrounded by other officers at attention.

               Spoomer
            (reads from paper)
----For dereliction of duty. First Lieutenant
J. Sartoris did desert his post as Officer of the
Day. Did land in a forbidden zone with property
belonging to His Imperial Majesty and left it un-
guarded. First Lieutenant J. Sartoris is herewith
reduced to the rank of Second Lieutenant and is
transferred to --- th Squadron.

        A moment of silence, then Bayard moves
forward suddenly.

               Bayard
To what squadron?

                   Continued-

Spoomer continues to look at John, who has not moved.

Spoomer

You will prepare to transfer at once, Mr. Sartoris. Dismiss the court.

Exit John.   The group breaks, drifts away. Bayard approaches the table.

Bayard

You can't do that.

Spoomer looks at Bayard.

Spoomer

But I've done it.

Bayard
(trembling)

You can't send him up there on those rotten machines. Don't you know they are losing two or three men a week.   It will be murder.

Spoomer

But I've already done it, you see.

Bayard looks at him, trembling, regains control.

Bayard

Right.   Now, get this.   If anything happens to him.   If one of those goddamned rotten machines-----

Spoomer

I say.   Captain.   Will you ------

Adjutant rises, faces Bayard.

Adjutant

I say, Sartoris.   Come, now----
(Puts his hand on Bayard's shoulder. Bayard knocks the hand down, facing Spoomer.   They look at one another.)

Bayard

Remember, now.   If anything happens to him because of those rotten machines you have sent him to fly----

Spoomer

Do you intend to threaten me?

Bayard

Intend?   Hell, I've already done it.

He glares at Spoomer, leaning across the desk, laughs short and savage, exits.

DISSOLVE TO:

          John is packing, Bayard watching him.

                    Bayard
          By God, there must be something we can ----

                    John
                    (turns)
          Don't you worry about me, now.   I'll be all right....
          Kick those boots over here, will you?

                    Bayard
                    (shoves boots over with his foot,
                    his face troubled, musing, cold)
          But those rotten little machines.   Damn him!   Damn
          him!

                    John
                    (packing again)
          It is a joke, isn't it?   Sending me to a Camel
          Squadron, when I never could fly Camels.

                    Bayard
          By God, I'll see Colonel Blandings.   He's always
          been white to me.   By God, I'll----

                    John
                    (turning again)
          Steady.

                    Bayard
                    (violently)
          Steady, hell!   Am I to squat here and see him send
          you up to that suicide gang?   I'll see Blandings.
          By God, I'll go to Pershing with it------

                    John
          Whoa.   Back up.
                    (puts his hand on Bayard's shoulder,
                    his face bright, grave, calm)
          Don't you worry about me.   I'm all right now.   I
          feel fine now, that it's all over.   Done with.
          God, it was like I was bad sick a long time, and I
          took a good stiff dose of medicine and now I am well
          again.   Don't you worry about me.

          They look at one another for a moment.

                    Bayard
          Right.   But if anything happens to you up there-----

                    John
          I'll tell you what to do, then.

                    Bayard
          What?

                    John
          Watch your chance coming in, and the first time you
          catch that dog on the field, taxi over him.
                                             DISSOLVE TO:

334

A car halted at door. Orderly stowing John's
kit into the car. The door opens, John and
Bayard emerge, approach car, John turns, his
hand on the door.

                    John
Well?

                    Bayard
I'll ride to the gate with you.

They get in, car moves away. John looking
back.

                    John
Goodbye, you. A good squadron and a fine bunch of
men. But I have sure lost my taste for dogs.
Thank God I'll never even have to see that dog
again.

Bayard is sitting thoughtful, grave.

                    Bayard
                (suddenly)
John.

                    John
What?

                    Bayard
Beat it.

                    John
Beat it?
                (looks at Bayard)
Oh! You mean go A. W. L. Desert.

                    Bayard
Just hide out. Give me time to see Colonel Blandings. It will be fixed up then. It won't be
deserting, then.
                (John is watching him, bright, grave)
Not deserting. Blandings will understand how you
were forced to do it by that goddamned-----
                (His voice dies away, he does not look
                at John, who continues to watch him,
                bright, grave, almost smiling.)

                    John
No. You don't mean that. You don't want me to
do that. When you were the very guy that taught
me never to run from anything I ever did. Weren't
you?

                    Bayard
It won't be running. Goddamn it, can a man be
blamed for ducking around a corner from a murderer
with a gun?
                                    Continued-

                              John
          Look at me and tell me to hide, to run.
                    (After a moment Bayard looks at him)
          Now, say it.   Tell me to run.

                              Bayard
          It's not running.   It's just-----

                              John
          Ah.   You see?   You are telling me to do some-
          thing you wouldn't do yourself.   Aren't you?

                    The car has stopped at the gate.   John
                    and Bayard look at one another.

                              John
                         (grave, smiling)
          You see?   Buck up, now.   I'll be all right.   I
          guess I can outlast any damned little old squabble
          between huns and frogs.   You stop worrying about
          me and see that you don't let him write you off.
          You're the one to worry about him; not me.   I'm
          out of his reach, now, forever and ever.....
          Here's the gate.

                              Bayard
                         (rousing)
          Right.
                         (he gets out, turns)
          Well?

                              John
                         (extends his hand)
          Cheer-O.   And good luck.
                         (they shake; Bayard steps back)
          All right, Burke.
                         (the car moves; John leans out)
          Don't forget about that dog!

                    The car goes on, exits; Bayard looks after
                    it, worried, grave.   An orderly comes up
                    behind him.

                              Orderly
          Mr. Sartoris.
                         (Bayard does not hear him)
          Sir-----

                              Bayard
                         (turning)
          What?   What is it?

                              Orderly
          A lady to see you, sir.

                              Bayard
          A lady?   Me?

                                             Continued-

                         Orderly
A young French woman, sir.   She says it's quite
urgent, sir.

                         Bayard
Where is she?

                         Orderly
Waiting down there at that pub on the 'ighroad, sir.

                         Bayard
Are you sure it's me she wants?

                         Orderly
Yes, sir.   A-haxing for Mr. John Sartoris' brother
she was, sir.   In a fair state, too.

                         Bayard
Mr. John Sartoris' brother?.... Right.   Get me a
sidecar.

          Orderly salutes, hurries away, Bayard follow-
          ing.

          IN DISSOLVE motorcycle engine, to

145.   MOTORCYCLE LEAVING AERODROME.

                              DOUBLE EXPOSURE DISSOLVE TO:

146.   MOTORCYCLE STOPPING BEFORE CAFE.

          Bayard enters.

                                             CUT TO:

147.   INTERIOR   61.

        Mechanics and French people drinking, Pro-
        prietor bowing and scraping as he shows Bayard
        to a private room. Bayard enters, closes
        door.

                                        CUT TO:

148.   THE ROOM

        Bayard standing. Antoinette is crouching in
        a chair. She is distracted, white faced, almost
        cringing.

                        Bayard
        Je suis Sartoris. Vous desiriez, madame?

                        Antoinette
                    (moving quickly)
        Ah. Vous parlez! Jean m'en dirait!
                    (She approaches swiftly, anxious, distrait,
                        watching Bayard)
        Where is he? Where is he?

                        Bayard
        Ah. I see. You are the....

                        Antoinette
        Yes. I was wild, mad! He would not wait!
                    (Her hands flutter as though she is
                        about to touch Bayard, staring at him)
        Where is he?

                        Bayard
        Where? Where you have sent him, you and that man.

                        Antoinette
                    (falling back, staring at Bayard, her
                        voice faint)
        Sent him?

                        Bayard
        Yes. Where he can die quickly. Isn't that what
        the two of you want?

                        Antoinette
        Die? Die? Sent to die?
                    (She looks wildly about, snatches coat
                        from chair, is about to rush out)
        Where is he?

                        Bayard
                    (cold, grim, watching her)
        Do you think that you can prevent it, when I
        couldn't?
                                        Continued:

338

                                        Antoinette
Yes! Yes! Tell me.
                          (Bayard looks at her, grim, smiling a
                          little. She stares at him, rushes to
                          him, beating him on the breast with her fi
                          fist)
Tell me! Tell me!
                          (Bayard looks at her)
Ah, cold, cold! Is it this English uniform that
makes you as cold as they are?
                          (She is wild, distracted, staring at him,
                          She drops to her knees at his feet,
                          clutching his hand, kissing it)
Pity! Mercy! Ah, I was mad to do it! But it
began before I knew him, there was Tante; it was
bread for us, and protection. And then I knew
him, and he could speak no French and I could not
tell him. I intended to stop the other, but I was
alone against the two of them, him and Tante. But
I was going to stop it, go away, anywhere he wanted
me to go. And then he came in that day and I could
not tell him. And now they have sent him....
                          (She clings to Bayard's hand, looking
                          up at him)
You are his brother, his blood. If you say for me
to give him up, I will do it. But save him! Save
him! Tell! Tell me! Monsieur? Mercy! Pity!

                                        Bayard
Pity? Mercy?
                          (He looks down at her, grim, faintly
                          smiling. He strikes her on the mouth,
                          hurls her back, crouching, looking up
                          at him with expression of dazed astonish-
                          ment, touching her mouth dazedly.)

                                        Antoinette
Why......he struck me. He struck me too!
                          (Her face lights, an expression peaceful
                          and serene)
Ah, you're not cold! Oh, thank you! Thank you!
                          (She crawls to his feet, clutches his
                          knees)
You will tell then? You will let me do what I
can?

                                        Bayard
Yes. Get up.
                          (He helps her up. She catches up the
                          cloak)

                                        Antoinette
Quickly, then. So I can go, hurry, fly. There
are other wings than yours, monsieur. And other
armor than soldiers wear.

                                        Bayard
Wait. There is plenty of time. What will you do?
                                                      Continued:

                                        339

                    Antoinette
I will stay beside him and love him, monsieur.

                    Bayard
What good will that do? How can that make the
engine in his machine more powerful, and keep the
wings from coming off?

                    Antoinette
Ah, zut! You cold one! But, stay: you are cold
only in the mind, not in the heart. You have
never loved, have you?

                    Bayard
I don't know.

                    Antoinette
Then you have. not,. or you would know it. But
quickly; tell me and let me go.

                    Bayard
And you will stay with him. Suppose he will have
no more of you, after -----

                    Antoinette
Suppose, then.

                    Bayard
You mean, you will stay near him anyway?

                    Antoinette
But certainly. Don't you know that there is more
to love than ----- But how can you know, who have
never loved?

                    Bayard
Perhaps I do know. And you will stay near him,
where you can-----can ......
                    (His voice dies away. Antoinette watches
                     him)

                    Antoinette
My poor one. My poor one. You call yourself cold,
carry the vain pride of it like a mask before the
face, when this in here -----
                    (taps his left breast)
is breaking. Ha! Now I too can be a man, a
soldier.
                    (Puts her hands on his shoulders, looks
                     at him, her face serene, calm)
Do not be afraid.

                    Bayard
Afraid?

                    Antoinette
No, I tell you not to. Understood?
                                        Continued:

340

                    Bayard
Yes. And you will stay near him, and send me any
word if he ---- if he should.......

                    Antoinette
Yes.

                    Bayard
Thanks. And I am sorry I----that------sorry for---

                    Antoinette
                    (watching him)
Say it. Then you will not be frozen inside any
longer.

                    Bayard
Sorry I.....
                    (He looks down, takes her hand awkwardly,
                    is about to raise it to his lips. She
                    stops him, frees her hand)

                    Antoinette
Stay. We are brothers now, eh?

                    Bayard
Yes.

                    Antoinette
Good. Then as brothers do.
                    (Extends her hand. Bayard looks at it,
                    then takes it. Antoinette lays her other
                    hand on his shoulder)
So. Then. How does Jean say it? Cheer-O?

                    Bayard
Cheer-O.

                    Antoinette
Now, tell me.

                              DISSOLVE TO:

149.   JOHN'S HAND writing in diary:

           Apr. 1 ----. Well, here I am. April Fool.
           Only it's on Spoomer. This is a night flying
           squadron, the one that even R.E. and Fee
           guys call the Laundry because you are all
           washed up by Saturday night. They fly at
           night because everybody is in town until the
           bars close and they don't get back until
           midnight to fly them. And here I am in a night
           flying Camel squadron when I can't even fly
           Camels in the daytime. You have to land a
           Camel by setting the air valve and flying
           it into the ground. Then you count ten, and if
                                    Continued:

you have not crashed, you level off. And if
you can get up and walk away, you have made
a good landing. And if they can use the crate
again, you are an ace. But I've got the
night flying beat. Just not crash and have
the wing flares explode. I've got that beat.
I'll just stay up all night, pop the flares
and sit down after sunrise. So eat drink and
be merry, because it's not tomorrow they die
here, it's usually today.

>   DISSOLVE
>   WITH ENGINES
>   TO:

150.   A PATROL

taking off, passing over nearby village.
Clock to a house, the roof,

>   DISSOLVE THRU ROOF TO:

151.   ANTOINETTE

at a window, looking up as flight passes low
overhead and disappears. Antoinette turns from
window, swiftly, takes from beneath mattress
of bed a smock, a pair of trousers, a cap such
as peasants wear. She puts them on, pushing
her hair up under cap; she now looks like a
peasant boy. Takes up a basket and exits.

>   CUT TO:

152.   ANTOINETTE

passing along beside flying field, carrying
basket, she looks this way and that, turns
quickly in behind hangar, hurries on, watchful;
sees two mechanics, slows, her face a little
averted, goes on, they glance at her without
interest.

>   CUT TO:

153.   HUT

Sheet iron, lettered crudely B. Flight.
Antoinette appears around corner, watchful,
darts inside.

>   CUT TO:

342

Antoinette shutting door quickly, leaning
against it, looking this way and that, listening. She goes on, enters door.

                              CUT TO:

155.   ROOM

two bunks, kit about. Antoinette looks swiftly
about, exits.

                              CUT TO:

156.   ANTOINETTE

in corridor, going to next door, enters.

                              CUT TO:

157.   ROOM

Antoinette looking about. Beside bunk a kit
bag stenciled Lt. J. Sartoris ---th Squadron,
R.F.C. Antoinette goes to bag, touches it. A
garment half drawn from it, top of pajama
suit. Antoinette draws it out, holds it in
her hand, lays it to her face, puts it back,
sits on bunk in attitude almost crouching,
shrinking, still, as DISSOLVE begins.

158.   ENGINES in DISSOLVE TO flight returning, very
            apparent gap in the formation. They land on
            field, pilots get out. Patrol leader turns,
            concerned, angry.

                    Patrol Leader
            Where is Sartoris?

                    Pilot
            He broke formation just before we reached the
            lines and turned South.

                    Patrol Leader
            Confound him, what does he mean?

                    Pilot
            I don't know. Who's for a drink?

                Pilots go on. Patrol Leader looks into sky,
                angry, anxious. Turns and follows others.

                              CUT TO:

159.   ANTOINETTE

crouched on bunk, cringing almost, looking
toward door, her hand to her breast, as footsteps and voices pass it, die away. She sinks
back on bunk again still, alert, waiting.
Sound of engine begins, approaches, Antoinette's
face lights, she looks up as ship passes overhead in

DISSOLVE TO:

160.   JOHN

banking over field and landing, taxis up and
stops and gets out and moves toward hangar,
unfastening helmet as Patrol Leader emerges
and meets him.

                    Patrol Leader
Confound you, Sartoris, what do you mean?

                         John
               (at once innocent and belligerent)
What?

                    Patrol Leader
Leaving formation like that? Where have you been?

                         John
Hunting huns. That's what I was sent here for,
wasn't it?

                    Patrol Leader
But don't you know you stand no chance at all out
alone on one of these popguns we have?

                         John
Ah, go lay an egg, Skipper. The hun don't wear
pants that will get me. I've got too much
unfinished business to attend to. See you at
lunch, eh?

John goes on, Patrol Leader looking after him.
John enters hut.

CUT TO:

161.   PASSAGE

John, approaches his door, puts his hand on
knob.

CUT TO:

162   THE ROOM

Antoinette turned on the cot, watching door,
her hand lifted a little. Door opens, John
enters, pauses, looking at Antoinette. They
look at one another, then Antoinette lifts
her hand and removes the cap, her hair falls.

                    John
He.
                    (He enters, goes to her, puts his
                    hand on her shoulder. He is not
                    rough, yet he turns her a little,
                    his other hand lifted a little , as
                    if he would strike her. Ther he
                    desists, releases her with a little
                    flinging motion so that she sways
                    back against the wall, watching him)
Hell! What do I want to hit you again for? What
do you want?

                    Antoinette
Jean.

                    John
So he threw you out too, did he? Got rid of you
and me both, eh? He's a fast worker, that guy.
What do you want? Come on. Money?

                    Antoinette
Monee?

                    John
Money. Argent. Here --

        Puts his hand into his pocket, she watching.
        She rises suddenly.

                    Antoinette
Non! mon! non! Jean! Oh, if you only spoke French,
so I could talk to you!

                    John
What? A lot of jack? Big money?

        He approaches her, digging in his pocket.
        She shrinks back, her hands raised.

                    Antoinette
Non! non! non!

                    John
I'm not going to hit you. See? Here.
                    (Hauls a handful of money from his
                    pocket, holds it out. Antoinette
                    looks at it, begins to cry)
For Christ's sake!
                    (He looks at her, puzzled, softened)
Here. Stop crying, now. I'm not going to hurt you.
                                        CONTINUED

162   CONTINUED (2)

> Puts his arm about her shoulders, awkwardly;
> At once she leans to him, is about to throw
> her arms about him, desists, steps back,
> wipes her eyes, laughs hysterically.

                    Antoinette
     C'est rien. Nozzing. Pardon.

                    John
     Sure.   It's all right.   I've got plenty more.   Here.
               (Extends the money, takes her hand
               and puts the money in it)
     There.   All washed up.   Now, go.

                    Antoinette
     Go?

                    John
     Wee. Sure.

> Pushes her toward door, firmly, patting her
> back. Opens door, is about to shove her out,
> stops her, returns to bunk and gets cap,
> returns and puts it on her head. She ar-
> ranges her hair beneath it dumbly.

                    John
     Jesus, if they see you are a girl. Don't you know
     women are not allowed here? If they were to catch
     you here, don't you know you'd have to marry me to
     right my wrong? Beat it, now. Go home. Go to
     Paris. Go to Russia.

> Shoves her out the door, closes it, stands
> with his head bowed, his hand on the door.
> Turns suddenly, goes to kit bag, takes out
> bottle and drinks.

                    DISSOLVE TO

163   ANTOINETTE'S ROOM

> She enters, slowly, removes cap. Takes
> from her pocket the money he gave her,
> looks at it, goes to bureau, opens drawer,
> takes out small box, puts money in box, musing
> quiet, replaces box and closes drawer. Goes
> to window, stands there looking out.

                    DISSOLVE TO

164   TARMAC -

> Ships warming, pilots gathering. John comes
> up. Patrol leader turns upon him.

                              CONTINUED

164   CONTINUED (2)

                    Patrol leader
        Now, you stay in formation. If you break again,
        I'll have you paraded. Do you hear?

                    John
                 (sullenly)
            Yes. I hear.

            Ships take off, pass over village flying low
            and fast, vanish in mist.

                              DISSOLVE TO

165   ANTOINETTE AT WINDOW -

            looking after dying sound of them.

                    Antoinette
        Dieu! Dieu! Sauvez! Sauvez! Mère de Dieu,
        pleine de grâce...

                              DISSOLVE TO

166   JOHN'S HUT.

            Batman gathering up soiled clothes, goes to
            box table, takes from ashtray a few coins.
            FOCUS ON COINS. Batman puts them in his
            pocket, goes out.

                         DOUBLE EXPOSURE DISSOLVE TO

167   BATMAN WITH BUNDLE -

            walking down road in village. Antoinette
            emerges from doorway as he passes, stops
            him, touches bundle.

                    Antoinette
        Du lieutenant Sartoris, n'est-ce pas?

                    Batman
        Wee, Wee.

                    Antoinette
                 (pulling at bundle, indicating
                  café behind her)
        Venez. Venez.

                    Batman
                 (Clings to bundle)
        Ere, ere! I'm tyking them to the washerwoman. Leggo
                                        CONTINUED

167   CONTINUED (2)

Antoinette
(pulls at bundle)
Venez. Venez.

Jerks the bundle from him, runs into café.
Batman in outraged pursuit.

CUT TO

168   INTERIOR -

Antoinette beside proprietor as Baran enters.

Batman
Ere! Ere! Wot the bloody 'ell ---

Antoinette
Dites-lui, Monsieur.

Proprietor
(approaches batman, taps his
shoulder, puts both hands on
Batman's shoulders, who glares at
him in outraged suspicion)
Alors - Regardez. Mademoiselle - She wash for
monsieur le lieutenant. Good. Eh?

Batman
Good me foot. Wot'll I tell the old dame down the
road there?

Proprietor
(claps Batman on both shoulders)
Hah! Bravo! You english. No wonder -- how you
say, eh? Victorious always.
(Leans to Batman, his voice lowered,
winks)
Mademoiselle, she wash for love. Not -- how you
say again, eh? No Charge. No money. Eh, then?

Batman
No charge, eh?

Puts his hand into his pocket, Antoinette
watching him. CLOCK to Batman's hand
feeling the money in his pocket.

Batman
Is she a good washerwoman?

Proprietor
(kissing his hand)
Like angel. Good, eh?

CONTINUED

168   CONTINUED (2)

                    Batman
It better be good. Mind now, I won't 'ave Mr.
Sartoris coming down on me because ---

                    Proprietor
               (claps Batman on shoulders)
Have no alarm, brave English. Not one little alarm.
Return Fridcy; you will find them as though from
hand of angel.

                    Batman
Well, all right. But see to it, now.
               (He turns toward door)

                    Antoinette
               (watching him)
L'argent de monsieur le lieutenant. Il y en a.
Dites-lui revenir et lui y donner.

                    Proprietor
Alors, Monsieur le brave...
               (Batman turns)
Mademoioclle says, return to monsieur your patron
the money which he has given you for this little
affair.
                    Batman
Ah, go lay a hegg, will yer?
               (Exits)
                              DISSOLVE TO

169   ANTOINETTE'S ROOM.

               A line of washed garments. Antoinette mending
               a sock as noise of aeroplanes begin. She
               goes to window, looks up and out as flight
               passes overhead, again with a gap in the
               formation. She is anxious, holding the sock
               to her breast as the sound of engines dies
               away.

                              DISSOLVE TO

170   FLIGHT LANDING ON FIELD.

               Patrol leader jumps down. He is angry.
               Approaches Deputy, who is unfastening his
               helmet.
                    Patrol leader
Well?

                    Deputy
Same thing again.. As soon as we reached the
lines, he pulled out and headed south with his
throttle wide open.   CONTINUED

                      Patrol leader
Is he trying to commit suicide? By God, I'll
parade him. I'll have him grounded.

                      Deputy
                 (turns toward mess)
You'll have to catch him first.

        Patrol leader stands looking angrily and
        anxiously into sky.

        As he DISSOLVES, sound of engines begins to:

171   JOHN CRUISING -

           looking this way and that.

                              CUT TO

172   SPOOMER'S AERODROME -

           a flight on the line. Pilots come up,
           Spoomer leading, in flying clothes. He gets
           into his ship. FOCUS on markings on
           fuselage: Figure 1 and a woman's slipper
           upside down. Flight takes off, engines
           die away in
                              DISSOLVE

172 XY1   A SINGLE ENGINE -

           in RESOLVE to John cruising, looking about,
           sees flight far away, climbs, opens throttle.
           Spoomer's flight dives on two huns, John
           follows, his face grim, eager, looking at
           leading machine. FOCUS on number and slipper
           insignia. John dives.
                              CUT TO

173   Spoomer gets oh hun, firing at him. Suddenly
           John dives between him and hun, shoots hun
           down.
                              CUT TO

174   BAYARD ALARMED AND SURPRISED.
           Watches John follow hun until it takes fire,
           then zoom away, banks over Spoomer, his thumb
           at his nose.   CUT TO

175   SPOOMER ANGRY, ASTONISHED.   CUT TO

Angry, watching John bank over Spoomer,
thumbing his nose, then dart away. Bayard
pulls out to follow, but too late. John goes
swiftly on,

DISSOLVE TO:

177.   JOHN LANDING

He gets out, goes to mess, enters.

CUT TO:

178.   THE MESS

John goes to bar, pilots look at him.

                    Pilot
Where have you been?

                    John
Taking a ride.
          (to orderly)
Make it a double.
          (orderly pours drink, John takes it up)

                    Pilot
I say - Skipper's on the warpath.

                    John
That so? Hard on his blood pressure.
          (Goes to box on wall, takes out combat
          report sheet, goes to table, sits down,
          drinks, takes out stub of pencil and
          begins to write, pilots watching him.
          Enter orderly, approaches John - John
          looks up)
What?
                    Orderly
The Major wants you at once, sir, in the office.

                    John
All right.
          (Exit orderly. John writes, ceases,
          finishes drink, rises with paper in his
          hand, goes to office door, enters)
                                        CUT TO:

179.   OFFICE - MAJOR AND PATROL LEADER

John approaches desk.

                    Major
Black says you broke flight again. What's this,
Sartoris? Have you turned yellow, trying to force
me to ground you?
          (John lays combat report on desk. Major
          takes it up, reads)
                                        CUT TO:

179-XY1,   REPORT: 75.
                        COMBAT REPORT

              Pilot   J. Sartoris Flight B. Machine 5
              Duty   Single Reconnaisance Patrol
              Date   April 23, 1918. Time: 9:22 A.M.

              Encountered E.A. two seater 3 miles north
              of Roulers. E.A. took fire after one burst.
              Flight from---th squadron will confirm.

                                  F. Sartoris.
                                             CUT TO:

180.   MAJOR READING REPORT

                             Major
              H'm -- well --

                             John
              Am I grounded, sir?

                             Major
              Rat off. Clear out of here. But, look here.
              Can't you manage to stay in your flight from now on?

                             John
              I'll try.

                             Major
              Try the devil - do it! Cut along. I'll get this
              confirmed from----th. today.

                             John
              Right, sir.
                      (Exits)

                                             CUT TO:

181.   JOHN'S HANDWRITING IN DIARY:

              April 23------. Well, I did it at last. It
              took me three weeks, but this morning I took
              one right off of his nose. Before I'm through
              he's going to wish he'd sent me to Gallipoli
              or even Africa.
                                             CUT TO:

182.   JOHN READING WHAT HE HAS WRITTEN

              Grim, smiling. Batman enters, with bundle.
              John closes diary and looks around.

                             Batman
              Laundry, sir.
                             John
              All right. Did I leave the money for it?
                                             continued

352

                        Batman
    Yes, sir.
                    (Batman stows laundry away. John
                    looking at Diary, writes again.)
                                        CUT TO:

183.   JOHN'S HAND WRITING:

            "He's beat me at everything else, so far.
            But him and all hell, too, is not going to
            keep me from being an ace. I can beat him
            flying, and I'm going to beat him fighting.
            And he's going to be the one to confirm every
            hun I get."
                                        DISSOLVE TO:

184.   SQUADRON OFFICE

            Major at telephone.

                        Major
    Yes....hullo. Spoomer? I say - this is Kaye.
    One of my men just reported in, says he got a
    hun two-seater over Roulers this morning, and that
    a flight of yours was near enough to confirm.....
    yes. It was Sartoris, Yes......
                    (slowly Kaye's expression changes,
                    becomes grave, he leans nearer telephone)
    What? What's that?

                                DISSOLVE THROUGH TO:

185.   SPOOMER'S OFFICE

            Spoomer sitting easily back in his chair,
            holding phone.

                        Spoomer
    My dear man, there were two of my men on that hun.
    Yes - quite. I remember seeing your straggler
    hanging about. Fact, he dived in as the hun went
    down......Confirm? Ridiculous.......eh? I daresay
    he thought he did. But there were two of my men.....
    I had divided the hun between them, but I daresay
    they won't object to letting your chap in and
    taking a third each....yes, a third. And generous
    enough, it seems to me.....When are you coming up
    to see us?
                    (the line goes dead. Spoomer sits
                    holding telephone, smiling a little)
                                        CUT TO:

186.   KAYE PUTTING TELEPHONE DOWN

Stares forward. Adjutant watches him.

                    Adjutant
What now? Won't he confirm it?

                    Kaye
No. Says two of his men were on the hun, too.
He's giving Sartoris a third.

                    Adjutant
What?

                    Kaye
Confound him. Damn him!

                    Adjutant
No one likes him. Even his own men, I hear. If
it were not for that uncle of his, he'd be a
Quartermaster lieutenant, where he belongs. Well,
Can't be helped. I say - what will Sartoris do, d'ye
think?

                    Kaye
I don't know......damn him! Damn him!
                    (stares ahead, musing - rises suddenly,
                    takes up cap - adjutant watches him,
                    exit)
                                        CUT TO:

187.   THE MESS

Kaye enters, looks about, goes on, exits.

                                        CUT TO:

188.   KAYE CROSSING FIELD TOWARD HUTS

Puts hand on door.
                              DOUBLE EXPOSURE DISSOLVE TO:

189.   KAY ENTERING JOHN'S ROOM

John lying on bunk, a bottle and a glass on
box table beside him.

                    Kaye
Hullo.

                    John
Hullo.

Kay approaches table, takes up bottle.

                    Kaye
May I?
                                        continued

354

                         John
Help yourself.

                         Kaye
Thanks.
                    (fills glass)
Ought not to do this alone; do you know it?
                    (Drinks, sets down glass. John is
                    watching him. He does not look at John)
Just talked to Spoomer over the wire.

                         John
                    (quickly)
Wha--
                    (catches himself, still on bunk)
You did?

                         Kaye
                    (lighting cigarette)
He's giving you a third.

                         John
                    (perfectly still)
Giving me a.....
                    (he sits violently up)
What?

                         Kaye
Steady.

                         John
Steady, hell. By God, I -----
                    (Rises, violently. Kaye grips him,
                    holds him as he tries to jerk free)
Goddam it, let me go.

                         Kaye
Steady on. Stop it, Sartoris!

     John stops, glaring at Kaye; he subsides slowly.
     Begins to laugh.

                         John
God, God - a man. You can't beat him! Come on,
tell me -- I can take it.

                         Kaye
He said there were two of his fellows on the hun
when you dived in. He's giving each of you a third.

                         John
                    (laughing)
By God, he's magnificent. He can beat me even when
I'm forty miles away.
                    (He laughs, wildly, Kaye watching him)

                         Kaye
Steady, now - here.
                    (Pours drink, hands it to John who lifts
                    glass, pauses, sits on bunk, restraining
                    himself, breathing deep)
Go on, drink it.   (continued)

                              John
Right.
                    (Drinks, sets glass down)
God, Kaye, I got that hun, I know I did. I took
it right off his nose. He couldn't help but see it.
By God, I'll bet those other guys haven't even
claimed it.
                    (Springs up, violent)
Hell, I'm going up there. I -----

                              Kaye
                    (grips him again)
Steady! I know he's a rotter. Everyone knows it.
But he has a General for an uncle - you haven't..
What can you do about it?

                              John
I can go up there and make him eat his combat
report. That's what I can do. I don't want the
hun. To hell with the hun. Let his whole squadron
divide him. But I can----

                              Kaye
No.
                    (John pauses. They look at one another)
That's not what you can do.

                              John
    What can I do?

                              Kaye
Get another hun. Shoot down another aeroplane
that he can't steal from you.

                              John
Shoot down another....
                    (He looks at Kaye, his face quietens,
                    becomes speculative)
Shoot...yes, that's it. By God, I'll shoot down
one he will have to confirm.

                              Kaye
That's the spirit.

                              John
I'll go now. Can I go out now?

                              Kaye
Alone?
                    (John looks at him)
No. Wait until the flight goes. I can't risk it.
I have lost two men this week; you know that. I
can't risk it. There'll be huns out there then.
Right?
                              John
                    (Looking forward, quiet, his face secret)
Right.
                                        continued

                        Kaye
Good. Come on to the mess. I'll take this along
with me.
              (takes up bottle)

                        John
All right. I'll be along in a moment.
              (He watches Kaye exit. Then he begins
              swiftly to don his flying clothes)

                                        DISSOLVE TO:

190.   SPOOMER'S SQUADRON

              A hangar - mechanics attaching a camera to
              Bayard's machine. Sergeant watching as men
              step back.

                        Sergeant
All right?

                        Mechanic
All right, Sergeant.

              Sergeant gets into cockpit, mechanic goes to
              prop.
                        Sergeant
Off!

                        Mechanic
Off.
              (He primes engine, steps back)
Contact.

                        Sergeant
Contact.

              Mechanic swings prop, engine catches, Sergeant
              revolves it slowly. Suddenly a burst of
              smoke from engine, a clashing sound. Sergeant
              cuts switch as other mechanics spring forward
              with fire extinguishers and put out fire.
              Men stand about smoking engine.

                        Mechanic
There goes a new engine.

                        Sergeant
Don't stand around 'ere! Get that bonnet off!.

              Mechanics remove bonnet. Sergeant examines
              engine, steps down.

                                        continued

                        Mechanic
    What is it -- a valve?

                        Sergeant
    Get that camera off. Smartly, now.

        Exit Sergeant.

                                        DISSOLVE TO:

191.   THE OFFICE

            Spoomer behind desk with map, Bayard in
            flying clothes beside him. Spoomer points
            with pencil.

                        Spoomer
    The dump is just about here. I don't need to
    tell you to get in fast, get the photographs, and
    get back as fast as you can. Don't engage any
    enemy unless you have to. Now. You had best fly
    south to this point --

            Sergeant enters, salutes. They look up.

                        Sergeant
    Captain Sartoris' engine, sir --

                        Bayard
    What? The new engine?

                        Sergeant
    It chewed up a valve, sir, as soon as we cranked
    it.

                        Bayard
    Get me another bus ready.
            (to Spoomer)
    I'll take Mowbray's.

                        Spoomer
    No - take mine. Have the camera put on my machine,
    Sergeant. Smartly, now.

                        Sergeant
    Very good, sir.
            (Salutes exits - Spoomer and Bayard
            turn back to map)

                                        DISSOLVE TO:

192.   KAYE'S SQUADRON - a hangar

            John's machine inside hangar, facing door,
            the engine warming. John beside it.

                        Sergeant
            All right, men. Take hold 'ere now.

                        John
            No - wait.

                Men desist. They watch John as he goes to
                door and peers around it toward office. He
                returns, gets in.

                        Sergeant
            I say, sir. You're not going ---

                        John
            Why not? Get away.

                        Sergeant
            But the wind, sir ----

                John opens throttle suddenly. Men spring
                back as ship shoots out of hangar. They rush
                to door, looking out.

193.   SHIP TAKES OFF

            Dangerously crosswind. It vanishes swiftly.

                                    DISSOLVE TO:

194   JOHN'S COMPASS -

He is flying south, to tachometer and air
speed indicator. He is flying at top speed.

DISSOLVE TO:

195   BAYARD -

Taking off in Spoomer's ship.

CUT TO:

196   COCKPIT -

The map on Bayard's knee, as he flies his
course, looking down at landmarks. He looks
up, John dives across his nose, pulls up.
Bayard swings aside, angrily, looking up
as John rolls, shakes his hand at other machine,
not recognising John. Looks back, then forward again, flying on. Suddenly ship dives
again across his nose; he recognises John's
ship now, watches it zoom and Immelman again,
his face annoyed. A burst of tracer passes
him; he jerks his head up now, horrified,
zooms as tracer passes him again. He faces
John now, John flies straight toward him, his
guns flickering. Bayard zooms and rolls,
shaking his fist at John, his mouth open as
though he were shouting. John's face is cold,
grim, he turns and fires again, again Bayard
dodges, leaning out, jerks his goggles up,
pointing to his face. But John has banked,
zoomed, rolls again and almost gets in another
burst. Bayard pulls down his goggles, his
face grim. Raging. Crumples map into case and
gives all his attention to flying. Because of
his better machine he gets on John's tail.
John tries to escape, but he cannot. Bayard
without firing drives John lower and lower and
back. John turns, helpless, raging: Bayard
points downward, driving John down.

CUT TO:

197   A FIELD -

John lands, Bayard zooms over him and banks.
John stops, sits in machine, wild with helpless
rage. He does not look back as Bayard lands,
gets out, runs up.

                    Bayard
What in hell?

CONTINUED -

John turns. After a moment he recognises
Bayard. He stares at him stupidly, then he
swings at Bayard's head. Bayard stumbles back,
John gets up and sprawls out of cockpit,
striking at Bayard, who steps in and clinches
and holds John, who jerks and struggles.

>   John
>   (panting)
> Let me go! Let me go!

>   Bayard
>   (holding him)
> John! John!
>   (John ceases, panting)
> What in hell do you mean?

>   John
> You outflew me. Or you wouldn't have to ask.
> Lucky for you. But if it had been him, like I
> thought from the machine......

>   Bayard
> Don't you know that any S.E. could shoot you down
> on that popgun? Don't you know that?

>   John
> That's all right too. If it had been him and he
> had got me cold, I was going to turn and ram him.
> He would have confirmed that, all right.

>   Bayard
> John. John. Here.
>   (takes John's arm. John follows stupidly
>   as Bayard leads him to a broken wall)
> Sit down.
>   (John sits down, Bayard beside him, his
>   hand on John's arm)
> Suppose it had been him, and you had killed him.

>   John
> All right. Let's think about that. That's fine.
> I haven't thought about anything else since he
> stole my hun.

>   Bayard
> And a damned German is worth a court-martial and a
> firing squad? Think of Caroline.

>   John
> I don't have to think of her any more, you see.
> That's all finished. I have got to that place where
> you were always after me to get to. I have passed
> beyond the world of women. Forever and ever.
> Through. Even she, when she came down there, I
> didn't even hit her. I swear I didn't. I just
> gave her some jack and told her to beat it. I
> wasn't even mad. I wasn't anything. I'm not mad
> now. I don't even hate that guy back there any
> more. I'm just through, except for one little
> matter.

CONTINUED -

197   CONTINUED (3)

> Bayard

John. Are you going......Are you still going to
try.....

> John

It's no use talking. I haven't seen much of this
world, nor looked at that very long. But I haven't
seen anything yet that I want to hold on to. Except
one thing. No; two. I'm going to be an ace, and
then I'm.......
> > (he gazes forward, calm, resolute, Bayard
> > watching him)

> Bayard

Well, all right.   There's just one thing for me to
do. That's to report you to the General and have
you grounded.

> John
> > (looks at Bayard)

You're not going to do that. I know, you see.
Come on. Say you are.
> > (Bayard looks down)

You see?
> > (John rises)

Well, I've got to get on back. But take a little
advice yourself, first. Next time you borrow a
machine, don't take one with a slipper painted on
it.
> > (he looks at Bayard, who stands with
> > his face lowered, his hands gripped beside
> > him)

I'm sorry.
> > (John's voice softens, he puts his hand
> > on Bayard's shoulder)

You let me go on. I told you before that I would
never see home again. Well, I've got it stronger
than ever, after the way I have bitched up things
lately. But you will. After this mess is over,
you go back home. You make up for me. I mean----
mean---- We are twins, and you are the oldest twin;
I never was anything much but your shadow. So you
can go back and be the guy I never was and never
will be. So they will say, well those Sartoris boys
made one good man between them. See what I mean.
Well. I'm gone. Good-bye.
> > (he extends his hand)

> Bayard

Good-bye?

> John

Yes. Good-bye. I don't think I'll see you again.

> Bayard

See me again?

> John

Yes. After all, this is pretty good. Here we are,
alone, doing what we both wanted to do. You are a
> > > > Continued -

197   CONTINUED (4)

                    John (Cont'd.)
captain and you have a ribbon. I'll probably never
be a captain and I may not get the ribbon. But it
won't be because I didn't----didn't.......Anyway,
I'll know that you counted my huns right. That'll
be enough for me. So good-bye, fellow.

                    Bayard
               (takes John's hand. They shake, firm
               brief)
Get to hell on home, damn you. Damn you to hell.

                    John
     Right.
               (he goes on to his ship, Bayard watching
               him. He gets in, turns, takes off,
               banks back and passes Bayard, low, his
               hand lifted. Bayard responds, the ship
               goes rapidly on and dies away)

                                   DISSOLVE TO:

198   BATMAN -

             With bundle of soiled clothes approaching
             cafe. His cap is cocked, his attitude and
             gait indicate a kind of suppressed glee. He
             enters cafe.

                                   CUT TO:

199   INTERIOR -

             Batman swaggers in, looks about.

                    Batman
     Hi. M'soor. Double out 'ere-----
               (sees Antoinette entering)
     Oh. 'Ere you are yerself.
               (Antoinette approaches, takes bundle)
     Now, see yer do as nice a job this week as yer did
     last. I won't 'ave Mr. Sartoris coming down on
     me, mind.

             Antoinette has turned away. The Batman turns
             still swaggering, toward door. Antoinette
             pauses, looks back.

                    Antoinette
     English. Eef you please.

                    Batman
               (turning)
     Eh? What?
                                   CONTINUED -

199   CONTINUED (2)

                          Antoinette
                   (turns her face toward door, is about to
                   call when proprietor enters. She indi-
                   cates Batman)
          L'argent de monsieur le lieutenant.

                          Proprietor
          Eh, brave! The money of monsieur the lieutenant.
          Mademoiselle wishes to know, eh?

                          Batman
          Wot money?

                   Antoinette speaks to proprietor in a low
                   voice.

                          Proprietor
          Bon.
                   (to Batman)
          Mademoiselle says, take care.

                          Batman
                   (glares at them a moment)
          Ah, go lay two heggs.
                   (exits, swaggering. Antoinette looks
                   after him, follows with sudden decision)

                                   CUT TO:

200   BATMAN

             Turning into another cafe. He pauses, looks
             back, enters. Antoinette emerges from behind
             a wall, follows, enters.
                                   CUT TO:

201   INTERIOR -

             Batman at bar, his cap cocked, slaps down coins.

                          Batman
          Come, now; none of that. Yer must 'ave something
          a decent redblooded Henglishman can put down his
          bleeding throat.
                   (behind bar the owner shrugs, bows)
          Ayn't yer, eh?

                   Antoinette enters, goes to bar, sees coins,
                   takes them up.

                          Batman
          Wot the--------
                   (turns, sees Antoinette, ceases, looking
                   shocked and guilty. Antoinette stares at
                   him)

                                   CONTINUED -

                         Antoinette
          Thees is all?

                              Batman
                         (gulps)
               Yus.

                              Antoinette
                         (stares at him, cold, still)
               Animal. Cochon.
                         (turns, exits, Batman watching her,
                         slack-jawed)

                              Proprietor
                         (to Batman)
               Alors, monsieur. Monsieur voulait?

                              Batman
                         (glares at proprietor)
               Ahhhh. Go lay three heggs.
                         (shouting)
          Can you 'ear that? Go lay a 'ole blooming 'en!

                                        DISSOLVE TO:

          202   ANTOINETTE'S ROOM -

                       She enters, puts down bundle, goes to bureau,
                       takes out the box, adds the coins to the
                       money already there, puts the box away. As
                       she turns away, engines begin. She hurries
                       to window, looks out and up as flight passes,
                       John's place in the formation empty. The
                       engines die away as Antoinette turns, fills
                       tub from kettle on small heater, takes up
                       clothes and puts them in.

                                        DISSOLVE TO:

          203   THE ENTRANCE - THE STREET SEEN THROUGH THE
                       DOOR -

                       A car stops. Bayard gets out, enters.

                              Proprietor
               Pray to enter, my colonel.

                              Bayard
               Y a t-il Mademoiselle Gaussart?

                              Proprietor
               Vraiment, mon general. Montez au premier.
                         (conducts Bayard to door, opens it)

                                        CONTINUED -

203   CONTINUED (2)

                    Bayard
Merci.
                    (mounts stairs. The proprietor turns
                    back to the bar, old peasants, a French
                    soldier or two gathered)

                    Proprietor
These English. You cannot understand them, my
children. Do not try to. ·They have conquered the
world by corruption: regard: here is one of our
own women, a daughter of France, the friend of
generals and of lieutenants, who restores each
week the previous week's soiled wearing, for---mark
you---love.

                              DISSOLVE TO:

204   ANTOINETTE'S ROOM -

             Antoinette at ironing board, the garments
             about, Bayard facing her.

                    Bayard
So this is how you are saving him.

                    Antoinette
                    (looking down, faintly)
Yes. Yes. I came here believing that I-----that
he...... And instead, I wash his clothing by
subterfuge. I sit at that window and I see his
flight pass over, I have learned to know it now,
and his position in it. And I see them go out,
and they return and each time his position will
be empty, and I die, die, die.......
                    (sinks to her knees, her head in her arms
                    on the freshly ironed shirt. Bayard goes
                    to her, looks down at her, touches her,
                    his face cold, sober)

                    Bayard
Steady. See? You are spoiling the shirt.

             Antoinette raises her head quickly, takes the
             shirt up, smoothes it.

                    Bayard
And he doesn't know you do this?

                    Antoinette
                    (rises, dries her eyes)
See.
                    (she goes to bureau, takes out box of
                    money, opens it)
It is all here. For each week, and that which he
gave me when I------when he.......Zut! One would
think from me that no man had ever risked death
before. And I should be happy, now, since for two
days now he does not fly.
                              CONTINUED -

                        Bayard
Does not fly?

                        Antoinette
I learn from mechanics who come here, to whom the
patron talks. Three days ago he went off alone,
against orders, and when he returned, the major--
--how do you say it?

                        Bayard
Grounded him?

                        Antoinette
Yes.

                        Bayard
Oh......
              (looks at money in box)
Look here. How can you live on what he pays for
his laundry?

                        Antoinette
This? I? Spend this?

                        Bayard
What do you live on, then.

                        Antoinette
I live on terror and despair.
              (takes up box, holds it in both hands,
              laughing and crying hysterically)
Spend this. This. He thinks that I would spend
this.

                        Bayard
Steady, now.
              (puts his hand on hers holding the box)
How do you live?

                        Antoinette
Live? I------there are things I can do here, for
the patron, for lodging and food which I usually
cannot swallow anyway.

        Bayard looks at her; she looks down. He
        looks about the room. CLOCK to mops and pails
        in a corner.

                        Bayard
Ah. I see.
              (puts his hand into pocket, draws out
              money. Antoinette raises her hands,
              falls back)

                        Antoinette
No. No. No.
                                        CONTINUED -

204   CONTINUED (3)

                    Bayard
Yes.
          (takes her hand. She tries to wrench
          free. He opens her hand, putting the
          money into it)

                  Antoinette
No! No! Please! Please!
          (Bayard closes her hand on the money.
          Antoinette ceases to resist. She looks
          down at Bayard's hand on hers, with a
          sudden movement she lays her lips to
          Bayard's hand. He jerks his hand away)

                  Bayard
Here. Stop that.
          (steps back, Antoinette standing, her
          head bowed above her hands. Bayard
          takes up his cap and stick)
I must go. Get along.

                  Antoinette
You are going to the aerodrome?

                  Bayard
Yes.

                  Antoinette
You will.....see him?

                  Bayard
What? I don't know. No. No, I won't see him. Goodbye.
          (Exits, Antoinette watching him, her
          hands at her breast, her head bowed
          a little. Engines begin. She lifts
          her head as they roar overhead and die
          away, returning)

                        DISSOLVE TO:

205   KAYE'S OFFICE. KAYE AND BAYARD ARE SHAKING
           HANDS.

                  Kaye
I would have known you, but you don't look as much
like your brother as you would expect twins to look.
Sit down, won't you?

                  Bayard
No. We're not very much alike.
          (He sits down. Kaye takes out a bottle
          and two glasses)

                        continued

Kaye
Spot?

Bayard
Thanks.
(Kaye fills, they drink)

Kaye
Yes, I daresay there isn't anyone very much like
Sartoris -- your brother.
(He lights a cigarette, intently)
Look here. What's the matter with your brother?
Or did you come up here to ask me that?

Bayard
You've ground him, I hear.

Kaye
Yes. For deserting patrol. Not once, either.

Bayard
I know.

Kaye
(watching him)
Perhaps you know where he goes when he cuts away
alone.
(Bayard does not answer. He does not
look at Kaye)
You came here for something. What do you want?

Bayard
I......
(He looks at Kaye. They look at one
another)
Yes. To ask something. Keep him on the ground.

Kaye
All the time?
(Bayard looks at him)
You don't mean that. You see I can't. I'm running
a squadron. I can't turn it into a Chelsea board-
ing house, you see.

Bayard
Yes. I see
(Kaye watches him)

Kaye
What is this, Captain? What's going about here?

Bayard
(Not looking at him)
No. I see you can't do that. But will you do this?
When you put him back on duty, will you telephone
down to me at once?

continued-

                 Kaye
             (Watches him)
Yes. I can do that.

             Bayard
Thanks. Thanks.
             (Rises)
I must get along.

             Kaye
             (Watching him)
Don't go yet. Stop for lunch.

             Bayard
Thanks. I must get along.

             Kaye
             (Rises)
Well. If you must.
             (Looks at Bayard, who meets his gaze
             for a moment)
Is that all you will tell me about this Sartoris?

             Bayard
Yes. I promise you. If you will just let me know
at once, at once, when he goes back to flying duty,
I will-------

             Kaye
Will what?

             Bayard
I must get along.
          (Turns, salutes)
Thanks again.

             Kaye
             (offers hand)
Right.
             (they shake)
Come up again some time.

             Bayard
Thanks.
          (Exits. Kaye looks after him, musing,
          frowning)
               DISSOLVE TO:

206   JOHN'S HAND WRITING IN DIARY:

        May 4th----. Bayard was up here. He didn't
        even try to see me, as if I were already dead.
        It's funny, watching yourself getting gradually
        out of life while you are still alive, still
        breathe.
               DISSOLVE TO:

207   SPOOMER'S SQUADRON.

              A flight comes in, Bayard leading. He gets
              out and approaches office. Orderly emerges.

                         Orderly
                        (salutes)
              ---For you, sir.
                        (extends paper. Bayard takes it)
              Came through from ---th this afternoon.

                         Bayard
              Thanks

              Exit orderly. Bayard opens paper.

                                        CUT TO:

208   PAPER:

              Sartoris goes back to duty tomorrow
              morning.
                              Kaye.
                                        CUT TO:

209   BAYARD LOOKING AT MESSAGE -

              crumples it slowly, tears it into tiny
              pieces, watches them rain down.
                                        DISSOLVE TO:

210   BAYARD'S FLIGHT TAKING OFF.

              The cross lines, Bayard looking about
              constantly, his face grave. Sees something,
              watches it.
                                        CUT TO:

211   JOHN CRUISING ALONE -

              grim, deadly. Sees flight far ahead, turns
              and approaches, looking at the leading
              machine. Passes steadily on.
                                        CUT TO:

212   BAYARD WATCHING JOHN AS HE PASSES ON.

              Neither of them make any sign.
                                        DISSOLVE TO:

213   JOHN'S HAND WRITING IN DAIRY:

> May 9th ---. Washout. Saw Bayard. He
> didn't wave, and I didn't either. But we
> saw one another. Funny. Him sitting
> way up thére in a little flimsy crate of
> wire and wood, and me sitting way up
> there in a little flimsy crate of wire
> and wood, and neither of us could any
> more have touched or spoken to the other
> than I can't say fly.

                                     DISSOLVE TO:

214   HAND WRITING IN DAIRY:

> May 17th ---. Washout again. But he'll
> have to go up some day. I'm not worried.
> I played around with some clouds. The sun
> was right, and I could watch my own
> shadow scudding along. And after a while
> it would be like the shadow was still and
> the clouds were rushing past faster than
> light and not making any sound.

                                     DISSOLVE TO:

215   HAND WRITING IN DAIRY:

> June 4th ---. Washout. Didn't see any-
> body at all. I think I am going a little
> nuts. I get up there and then first
> thing I know, I find that I am not look-
> ing for anybody at all. That I have for-
> got to look for either him or Bayard. It
> would be a joke on me if I were to be
> upstairs some morning and wake up and
> find I was already dead and didn't know
> it.

                                     DISSOLVE TO:

216   HAND WRITING IN DIARY:

> June 27th ---. Washout. Getting to be
> monotonous. My hand writes that word
> almost before I know I have the book
> open. Didn't see anybody again. That's
> it, the loneliness. That's what gets
> you, I think. I don't think a pilot,
> even a ham, is ever outmanoeuvered and
> killed. Look how tyros shoot down the
> best ones now and then. I think the lone-
> liness just gets him one day. All of a
> sudden he will know that he had rather
> be with all the millions of comfortable &
> quiet dead, than to carry on.
>   DISSOLVE TO:

217   HANGAR

           Mechanics working over Spoomer's ship,
           rolling it out,

                                        CUT TO:

218   THE MESS -

           Spoomer and pilots in flying clothes.

                         Spoomer
           I will lead myself. I will take B and C flights.
           You will take the late patrol with your flight,
           Sartoris.

                         Bayard
           Right, sir.

                  Exit Spoomer and pilots. Bayard watches
                  them out.

                         Bayard
                    (calls orderly)
           Smythe.

                         Smythe
           Sir.

                         Bayard
                    (looking out window, tense, grim)
           Run down and tell Flight to get my bus out as soon
           as they get away.

                  Exit Smythe, Bayard looks out window,

                                        CUT TO:

219   FLIGHT TAKING OFF.

                  Bayard's ship rolled out. Bayard appears
                  quickly, with neither helmet nor goggles.
                  The ship warming up. He gets in, revs
                  engine, waves chocks away, takes off.
                                        DISSOLVE TO:

220   JOHN -

           cruising above lines, grim, looking about.
                                        DISSOLVE TO:

221   SPOOMER -

           leading flight over lines.
                                        DISSOLVE TO:

222   BAYARD –

           flying fast, also tense, grim.
                              DISSOLVE TO:

223   JOHN –

           crouching forward, looking off to left.
                              CUT TO:

224   FLIGHT IN DISTANCE, TINY.

           John swings toward them, opens throttle,
           glances aside, sees another single machine
           approaching him. Pays it no attention.
           Takes from cockpit a binocular, pushes up
           goggles, looks through glass.
                              CUT TO:

225   GLASS FOCUSED ON SPOOMER'S SHIP –

           with slipper and number. John flings binoc-
           ular overside, pulls down goggles.
                              CUT TO:

226   BAYARD APPROACHING JOHN,

           who is intent on Spoomer. Bayard dives behind
           John and beneath him.
                              CUT TO:

227   JOHN STARING FORWARD, GRIM.

           Suddenly Bayard's ship zooms up before him
           and half rolls, the guns flickering, the
           bullets passing to either side. John zooms
           and turns. Bayard heads him off again,
           shooting. John leans out, waving Bayard
           away. Bayard heads him off, driving him
           back and down.
                              DISSOLVE TO:

228   A FLIGHT OF GERMAN SHIPS –

           high above Bayard and John, the leader peer-
           ing down in astonishment at the two English-
           men apparently fighting one another. He looks
           back, signals, the flight dives.
                              CUT TO:

374

229 - 233   BAYARD STILL FORCING JOHN BACK.

The German flight dives upon them, firing.
Two of them engage John, four Bayard. The
German ships are superior to John's. Bayard,
fighting off his four, watches John anxiously.
Bayard shoots down one German, pulls away to
help John. A German is on John's tail. The
German's ship bears a skull smoking a pipe.
Bayard gets in a burst at him, has to whirl
to fight off the ones shooting at him. Evades
them again for a moment and looks back at
John. John's ship takes fire, the German
still on his tail. Bayard watches as John's
ship bursts into flame. John side slips,
Bayard follows, disregarding the Germans who
are firing at him. Sees John busy in cockpit.
John stands up, holding ship in side slip,
looks back at Bayard, makes a flippant salute
with his hand, jumps out. The body and the
ship fall together, the ship spinning. The
ship crashes, burning, a moment later a
German crashes almost beside it.

DISSOLVE WITH LOUD ENGINE TO:

234   BAYARD TRYING TO SHOOT THE MACHINE WITH THE
skull on it. The other three Germans dive
and zoom at him; he pays them no attention
save to dodge, as he tries to get on the
skull one. Suddenly the Germans pull away;
a flight of British machines dives upon them;
the Germans retreat, the skull one still
protected by the other four. Bayard turns
swiftly, returns home at top speed.

DISSOLVE TO:

235   SPOOMER'S PATROL LANDING.

Pilots get out and follow Spoomer to mess.
CUT TO:

236   BAYARD COMING IN FAST -

lands viciously, hurls his ship up to line,
jumps down before it stops, while mechanics
look after him in amazement, runs toward
his hut, enters.
CUT TO:

237   BAYARD'S ROOM.

          A pilot removing his flying clothes as Bayard
          runs in and jerks kit bag into middle of floor
          and hurls garments out. Pilot watches him,
          surprised.

                         Pilot
          What's up?

          Bayard doesn't answer. He takes from kit bag
          a pistol, flings kit bag down, whirls toward
          door, Pilot watching.

                         Pilot
          Here! What are you ---

          Bayard runs out. Pilot follows, alarmed.

                                        CUT TO:

238   BAYARD -

          running toward mess, Pilot behind him.

                         Pilot
          Sartoris!

          Pilot runs again, alarmed. Bayard flings open
          mess door, enters.

                                        CUT TO:

239   THE MESS.

          Spoomer sitting at table with drink, Adjutant
          at bar, other Pilots about, all turned toward
          door where Bayard stands, the pistol in his
          hand, looking about for Spoomer. Pilot enters
          behind Bayard, breathless.

                         Pilot
          Catch him! Catch ---

          Bayard sees Spoomer. moves toward him, grim,
          blazing.

                         Bayard
          Well. I told you. I warned you.

          At same time, the men move, two spring forward
          and grasp Bayard as he fires, jerking his arm
          up. The shot goes wild. Men swarm upon him,
          he struggles, fires twice more, the shots going
          wild as they hold him. Spoomer sits, his mouth
          open a little, staring at Bayard as he struggles
                                        - Continued -

376

CONTINUED (2)

    silently with the men who hold him.

                    Voice
Sartoris! Sartoris!

    Suddenly Bayard jerks his arm free, men grasp-
    at it wildly. He points pistol point blank at
    Spoomer, pulls trigger. The pistol clicks.
    Bayard hurls it at Spoomer. It strikes him on
    the side of the head. He falls to the floor
    beneath table. The men hold Bayard again.

                Adjutant
There. Hold him. Call the Corporal of the Guard!

                       DISSOLVE TO:

240   GUARD HOUSE -

    a small bare room, a cot, a door. Beyond the
    door the slow and regular tramp of a guard as
    he passes back and forth. Bayard sits on the
    cot, still, leaning back, his arms folded, his
    face still, cold, quiet. Beside him sits the
    General, leaning forward, looking at Bayard.

                General
I think I know how you feel. I lost my only son
two years ago, and for a time I felt as you do. I
wanted to behave as you did. But I had no immediate object to take vengeance upon. Then I realized
that there was no immediate object. That my son had
been murdered, not by the man who sent his battalion
in where it should never have been sent, but by the
war. And my only recourse, the only recourse of
any man who had lost son or brother, or who might
still lose son or brother, was to put an end to this
war. To kill and kill until the world would be so
sick of it that the voices of the very dead would
rise up and cry against it. Do you follow me?

                Bayard
              (not moving)
Yes, sir. I'm quite willing to take my medicine.
I told them that. I've no excuse to make.

                General
Medicine, nonsense. Your medicine is that of any
soldier, any man engaged in the profession of killing. That is, to continue to kill.

                Bayard
              (looks at him)
You mean ---- There will ---- won't be any court-
martial?

                     - Continued -

                         General
What worse sentence could a man receive than your
daily life has been since --- When did you come out?

                         Bayard
Gad, sir. You don't talk this to many soldiers, do
you?

                         General
Well. There are circumstances... Look here. This
is what I am going to do with you. You are to take
two weeks' leave in England, and then return. Not
here, of course. In fact, I think I will let you
chose what squadron you would ---

                         Bayard
Thanks. I -- I will.... But no leave, sir.

                         General
Yes. I think leave.

                         Bayard
No, sir. You have been damn white. I -- I am....
Thanks. Thank you, sir. Just let me go back to
duty. I'll be all right then. I'll promise.....

                         General
Well.
          (rises)
Of course, if you won't take leave.... What squadron
would you like?

                         Bayard
It doesn't matter. Just so it's not far from here.
And I can get back to duty soon.

                         General
Not far from here?
          (Bayard sits as before)
Look at me, Sartoris.

        Bayard looks up, rises.

                         Bayard
I beg pardon, sir. I was --

                         General
Sit down.
          (Bayard sits again, looks at General)
Not far?

                         Bayard
I know what you are thinking. Major Spoomer. But
that's all finished. I know that's no way to do it.
I guess I was crazy for a minute. But that's all
finished now. You can trust me, sir.

                                        - Continued -

                              General
                         (after a moment)
          Right. I'm going to, then. Very well, Captain.
          I'll have your transfer put through immediately.

                              Bayard
                         (rises, to attention)
          Thank you, sir.

                              General
                         (turns toward door)
          Carry on.

              Door opens, sentry at present with rifle.

                                          DISSOLVE TO:

241   AN R.F.C. IDENTIFICATION TAG, THE LETTERS::

                     Lt. J. Sartoris

                  Increase to tag nailed to a board, to board
                  nailed to section of broken propeller stuck
                  into earth at head of a mound, to a woman in
                  black lying upon the grave, to a pair of boots
                  standing beside the grave, to Bayard, erect,
                  his head bent, his face still, cold. Rain
                  falling.

                              Bayard
          Now. Get up. You'll take cold.

                  Antoinette does not move. Bayard stoops,
                  touches her, helps her up. They turn and go
                  away.

                                          DISSOLVE TO:

242   THE ROAD NEAR GATE TO AERODROME,

                  sentry walking back and forth. Antoinette
                  waiting. Batman enters, with bundle of
                  clothes, approaches Antoinette.

                              Batman
          'Ere you are, miss.

                  Antoinette takes bundle. Batman turns. At
                  that moment engines begin. Antoinette and
                  Batman look up as flight passes over, low,
                  gaining speed and climbing.

                                          - Continued -

       Batman
That's A. That's 'im.
     (turns to Antoinette, raises his voice,
     pointing to leading ship)
Captain. Captain Sartoris. Wee?

       Antoinette
     (watching flight as it goes on,
     her face grave, indomitable)
Yes. Yes.

       Batman
Kill. Bokoo 'uns, eh? Wee?

       Antoinette
Yes. Yes.

    She looks after flight as it disappears.
    Engines die away in,

          DISSOLVE TO:

243   AERODROME, TARMAC BEFORE HANGARS.

    Sergeant, hands on hips, looking toward hangar
    as two Mechanics enter, carrying Lewis drums
    and Vickers belts.

       Sergeant
     (points to his feet)
'Ere.

    Mechanics put ammunition on ground. Sergeant
    examines it.

       First Mechanic
We checked them as we loaded them, Flight.

       Sergeant
Tracer, two plain, buckingham, two plain, tracer?

       First Mechanic
Right. We checked them.

       Sergeant
You'd better 'ave. If I ever find ---

       Second Mechanic
I say. Wot's Captain Sartoris got against that 'un,
anyway? Spending arf 'is time leading 'is flight,
and the other arf out lone, 'unting one 'un out of
all the 'un air force?

       First Mechanic
Wot 'as 'e....

         - Continued -

CONTINUED (2)

                         First Mechanic (continued)
                    (looks at Second in scornful astonishment)
          The man that killed 'is own brother, and you arsk
          wot 'as 'e ---

                         Sergeant
          Nah then. Enough of that. You, Leake. Go to the
          captain's quarters and get 'is binocular and be
          ready. They'll be in soon now.

               First Mechanic exits. Sergeant stoops over
               ammunition.

                         Second Mechanic
          'Ere comes the petrol.

               Sergeant rises, looks toward approaching truck,
               beckons. The truck comes up, Sergeant indi-
               cates placing of truck. Leake returns with
               binocular, Sergeant takes it. Two other
               Mechanics enter; group stands by.

                                             DISSOLVE TO:

244   FLIGHT COMING IN, LANDING.

               Bayard taxies up to waiting group, jumps down.
               Mechanics come forward quickly.

                         Sergeant
          Machine all right, sir?

                         Bayard
                    (his face is grim, quiet)
          Yes.
                    (he goes on)

                         Sergeant
          All right, lads. Smartly, now.

               Mechanics swarm over machine.

                                             CUT TO:

245   MESS -

               Pilots at bar, talking. They look around as
               Bayard enters, goes to box, takes out combat
               form, goes to table, writes.

                         Pilot
                    (at bar)
          Drink, skipper?

                                        - Continued -

CONTINUED (2)

                         Bayard
No thanks.

          Fills out report, beckons orderly, who ap-
          proaches. Bayard hands him report, rises,
          exits, Pilots at bar watching him covertly.

                         Pilot
                       (suddenly)
          Good luck, skipper.
                       (Bayard has gone. Pilots look toward
                       door)
          I'm glad I don't take this war that hard.

                         Second
          You mean, you're glad you never had a brother in it.

                         First
          I daresay that's what I mean.

                                        DISSOLVE TO:

246   BAYARD'S SHIP.

          It is warming. Bayard enters, Sergeant hands
          him binocular. He gets in, Mechanics turn
          the ship. Bayard settles his goggles, begins
          to rev engine. Sergeant approaches, leans.

                         Sergeant
          Good luck, sir!

          Bayard nods, opens engine, ship moves, exits,
          engine increases, men look after sound as it
          dies away in,

                                        DISSOLVE TO:

247   THE EMPTY TARMAC.

          Engine begins, far away, increasing. Sergeant
          appears from hangar, looking toward sound as
          it grows louder.

                         Sergeant
                       (turns toward hangar)
          Double out 'ere!

          Mechanics emerge, all looking toward sound of
          landing ship as the engine cuts in and out.
          Ship taxies into view, stops. Bayard does not
          move, sitting with his head bent as crew runs
          up. Sergeant approaches.
                                        - Continued -

247   CONTINUED (2)

                    Sergeant
All right, sir?

                    Bayard
          (raises head, looks at Sergeant)
What? yes.
          (he climbs out, stiffly)

    Mechanics examine bullet holes; a burst near
    cockpit.

                Second Mechanic
Gor. Look at ----

                    Sergeant
JUMP to it! Jump to it!

    Mechanics spring into activity. Bayard moves
    away, Sergeant watching him anxiously.

                Second Mechanic
No luck, eh?

                First Mechanic
No luck?
          (indicates bullet holes near cockpit)
Do yer call that no luck?

                      DISSOLVE TO:

248   A TREE IN SUMMER FOLIAGE.

    Flight passes behind it from right to left,
    engines die away. Engine begins, a single
    ship passes behind tree from left to right,
    engine dies into,

                      DISSOLVE TO:

249   BAYARD CRUISING ALONE.

    He approaches a cloud as though it were a ren-
    dezvous. As he reaches cloud, ghost of John's
    ship resolves as though waiting him. John lifts
    his hand. Bayard points forward. John nods,
    the two ships go on together, Bayard looking
    this way and that through binocular. Steadies
    glass, turns, waggles his wings. John waggles
    back. Bayard indicates a flight of ships in
    distance. John nods. They turn and fly toward
    ships, Bayard watching them through glass.

                      CUT TO:

250   LENS OF BINOCULAR.

Flight increases in size, glasspicks up ships
one at a time, focuses on painted insigne on
fuselages. The pipe smoking skull is not a-
mong them. Bayard drops glass, points in another direction. John nods, they turn and go
on side by side. The engine dies away.

                                    DISSOLVE TO:

251   THE TREE.

The sky behind it darkens, sound of wind.
Tree begins to sway in wind, the rain begins,
tree tossing and swaying. The leaves begin
to blow from the branches, streaming at first,
then drifting down in the rain until the tree
is bare, the black branches stark against the
gray sky. With falling leaves,

                                    DISSOLVE TO:

252-to
260

LEAVES DRIFTING IN RAIN -

across a kaleidoscopic double exposure of:

Attacking troops running forward, field
guns fireing swiftly, aeroplanes zooming;

a climax of victorious armies;

peasants in hovels and gentle people in
chateaux to show a cross section of France
just before Nov. 11, 1918;

women and old men and maimed soldiers praying
in churches , in cafés --an air of waking joy,
of bewildered exultation, of not quite believing hope.   In the background are voices,
mingled, rising and falling.

                    The voices
Armistice!   Fini, la guerre!   They are whipped!
Armistice!...etc.

Voices in DISSOLVE become singing to tune
of Auld Lang Syne:

                    Voices
We're here because we're here because we're here
because we're here ---

RESOLVE a huge crudely lettered clock face,
the hand a broken propeller. Over the
number eleven on the clock face a long slash
of red paint. A man's hands in the act of
moving the propeller to nine o'clock. A
loud yell in men's voices in INCREASE TO

The mess, Pilots drinking, looking at clock
as they yell. Then the song begins again
as CAMERA CLOCKS to empty place at the
table, FOCUSES on it. DISSOLVE as singing
dies away and becomes sound of engine,
through chair to:

261

BAYARD ALONE FLYING.

His face is grim, it also registers
urgency, haste. He flies fast, flying
against time, goes swiftly on. His engine
dies through
                              DISSOLVE TO

262

ANTOINETTE'S ROOM.

She is kneeling before prie-dieu, her head
raised for the moment as sound of engine dies
                              CONTINUED

262   CONTINUED (2)

away. Washed garments hanging on a line
across the room. She rises, leaves room
hurriedly.

263   THE STREET.

Antoinette emerges from doorway, hurrying.
Soldiers about, with bottles of wine,
women and old men weeping and laughing,
dancing, embracing. An old woman stops
Antoinette, grasps her arm,

                    Old woman
Allors! Vite! Ton aviateur à toi. Tu peux lui
donner l'embrassade de gloire et de victoire.
Allez!

Pats Antoinette's back as Antoinette hurries
on. Old woman waves bottle of wine, dancing
on into crowd again.

264   GATE TO AERODROME, SENTRY BOX.

Antoinette hurries up, passes sentry box.
It is empty, save for the sentry's bayoneted
rifle leaning in box. Antoinette enters.

                              CUT TO

265   ANTOINETTE -

hurrying along before buildings. She
passes mess. As she approaches it, the
singing begins and increases, dies away
behind her as she hurries on toward hangars.

                              CUT TO:

266   A HANGAR.

Before it the petrol truck in position, but
without a driver. The sergeant standing,
looking toward hangar.

                    Sergeant
Nah then!   Nah then!

Two mechanics emerge from hangar, carrying
drums and belts. One of them is drunk;
he wavers and staggers up, dumps ammunition
on ground.   CONTINUED

                Mechanic
There yer are, me man. Goodbye. See yer in
Lunnon.
             (Turns and staggers away)

                Sergeant
You, Brown!

         Mechanic turns unsteadily.

                Brown
Eh?

                Sergeant
What did you say?

                Brown
Ah, rat off, yer bleeding blighter. The war's
over now. I'm tyking orders from no one but the
missus from now oh.

                Sergeant
You ain't, eh?

             Steps forward, knocks Brown down.
             Brown sprawls, sits up, rubbing his
             jaw.

                Brown
Ho. Striking a private soldier, hey? Well, I've
quit. I'm no longer one of yer bleeding puppets
to be hordered 'ere and hordered there just
because yer 'ave some bleeding little stripes on
yer arm --

             Gets to his feet, staggers forward, the
             other mechanic knocks him down again with
             a backhanded blow. Brown begins to weep.

                Brown
So that's the kind of cowards yer are, eh? Two
on one, hey?

                Sergeant
Get him up. Take him on back to his mess and let
him swill his head off if he will. See if you can
find another man sober enough to load a gun. The
captain will be in soon now.

                Mechanic
Right, Sergeant.
          (Jerks Brown roughly up)
Come on, now. Get up.

                Brown
Ho yus. Strike me, the both of yer. But I'll
'ave justice. I'll tell. 'Aig. I'll go to the
bleeding fushing Commander in Chief isself, s'welp
me.
                         CONTINUED

286   CONTINUED (3)

                              Mechanic
                         (leading Brown away)
          Ah, shut yer bleeding trap, will yer?

                    They exit. The sergeant stoops and begins
                    to examine the belts as Antoinette comes up,
                    hurrying. Sergeant rises.

                              Sergeant
          What the -- Here. What are you doing here? How
          did you ---

                              Antoinette
          Pitié, Monsieur, pitié! Le capitaine?

                              Sergeant
          Vous ne parlez pas anglais, eh?

                              Antoinette
          You speak French? Oh, thank God! Thank God!

                              Sergeant
          Don't thank Him for it, miss. Thank the four
          years I have been in this country. What are you
          doing here? How did you get in? Don't you know
          that women --

                              Antoinette
          Yes. Pity! Pity, Sergeant! Captain Sartoris?
          He is....
                         (She stares at him)
          Ah, you don't have to tell me. I know. I know.
          This morning, when I heard that it would stop
          today, I knelt before God. I believed that he
          would be safe now. that he would never go up
          again, hunting that man, that German. I believed
          that God Himself had said; Good. You have tried;
          it is well. Now I will take vengence to Myself.
          I Myself will assume your brother's blood along
          with the indictment of all the other ruthless
          and needless slain. Go, and grieve in peace.
          That's what I believed while I knelt there. And
          then suddenly....It was as if I had seen him get
          into his aeroplane and depart, as if I had heard
          the engine. He is gone? I know, but still there
          is something terrible in here ---
                         (Beats her breast)
          --that will not succumb and believe.

                              Sergeant
          Ay, gone. If you had watched him these three months
          since he came here as I have, if you had watched
          his face coming to look more and more like the
          face on a bronze man just out of the furnace, you
          would know that he is no man to let either God or
          General Staffs settle his scores or come between
          him and the man he wanted to be dead... Ay, gone.
          He's been out twice since dawn this morning.
                                             CONTINUED

388

                   Sergeant (cont'd)
He was sitting in his machine right here an hour
before it was light enough to see the field. Five
hours already he has been in the air today.

                   Antoinette
But not again! He won't go again! If he gets back
this time, he ---- Sergeant! God! Pity! Mercy!

                   Sergeant
Hmph. Do you see this?
          (Indicates the petrol truck, the
          ammunition)
Do you think this is all here by my authority alone?

       Antoinette looks at truck at ammunition, her
       hands pressed to her cheeks, her eyes wide
       with despair,

                   Sergeant
Come now. You've no business here. You can do
nothing. And don't worry about him. No one
flight of Germans will ever shoot him. Come, get
along, now.

                   Antoinette
Please, please. It's over! There was no sentry at
the gate, even. Nobody cares. Please. Please.

                   Sergeant
Well. But you'd best wait in the hangar yonder.

                   Antoinette
Yes. Anything. Thank you. Thank you.

       She turns, hurries on to hangar. Sergeant
       stoops again to drums. Enter two mechanics.
       One of them gets hose on truck ready, other
       arranges drums.
                      CUT TO

267   ENGINE BEGINS.

       Bayard coming in, lands, taxies up.

                     CUT TO

268   SERGEANT AND MECHANICS -

       waiting as Bayard taxies up. Antoinette
       runs from hangar, toward ship. Sergeant
       sees her, intercepts her. Bayard busy in
       cockpit. Mechanics prepare to service ship,
       working fast.
                    CONTINUED

                    Sergeant
Here, now. Here, now.

        Antoinette struggles free of sergeant, runs to
        cockpit, as Bayard raises his head.

                    Bayard
Hurry. Pass me those belts ---
            (Sees Antoinette)
Why, what are ----

                    Antoinette
No! No! No!

        Mechanics and sergeant are busy about ship,
        hurried. Bayard's face is strained, gaunt
        as bronze, hard.

                    Bayard
What? I can't hear you. Wait.
            (Unfastens helmet, pops his ears with his
            palms)
What is it?

                    Antoinette
Not again! Not again! Oh, God! Oh, God! Pity
him! Pity me!

                    Bayard
Not again? Confound it, can't you hear them?
            (His face is fretted, impatient)

                    Antoinette
            (watching him wildly, her hands
            to her face)
Hear them? What?

                    Bayard
Everywhere. Listen.

        Antoinette stares at him as if he were
        mad. Bayard's face is musing, detached,
        intent with listening.

                    The voices
Armistice! Finished! At eleven o'clock.

                    Bayard
See.?
            (Holds up his watch. It says
            eight minutes to ten)
Can't you hear?

                    Antoinette
No! I hear nothing. I thought I heard you say
that you are going up again, but that can't be
true. I cannot have heard that.
CONTINUED

268   CONTINUED (3)

                         Bayard
                    (as though rousing)
          You, men! Hurry! Smartly now. Belts, Sergeant!

                         Sergeant
          Right, sir. Here you are.
                    (Passes up belts)
          The top gun is loaded, sir.

                         Bayard
          Good. Help them with the petrol.

                         Sergeant
          Tank's about full, sir. You'll be away in half a
          moment.

                         Antoinette
          It will be murder now: don't you see? They have
          quit. Revenge for your brother is no longer yours.

                         Bayard
          No longer mine? Hah.

               He turns, looks up. FOLLOW him look to

268 XY1   THE GHOST OF JOHN'S MACHINE -

               overhead as though waiting.

                                        CUT TO

269   BAYARD LOOKING AT ANTOINETTE

                         Antoinette
          Bayard! Bayard!

                         Bayard
          Sergeant. Take this woman away.

               Sergeant comes, touches Antoinette's arm.

                         Sergeant
          Come, miss.

                         Antoinette
                    (clings to cockpit)
          No! No!

                         Bayard
          Take her away, Sergeant.

               Sergeant begins to draw Antoinette away,
               gently. She clings to cockpit.
                                        CONTINUED

269   CONTINUED (2)

                    Antoinette
No! NO! Please. Pity! Oh, God! Oh, God! Pity!
Pity!

          Bayard removes her fingers from cockpit,
          his face cold, grim. The sergeant draws her
          back as she struggles.

                    Antoinette
                 (now offstage)
Oh! Oh! Oh!

                    Mechanic
                 (at prop)
Contact, sir.

                    Bayard
                 (moves suddenly)
Contact.

          Engine starts, drowns Antoinette's
          screaming. DISSOLVE with engine to:

270   THE ROAD.

          Antoinette looking toward sound, desperate,
          wild of face, stumbling, panting.

271   SHIP PASSES OVERHEAD -
          fast, goes up, engine sinking.
                              DISSOLVE TO

272   BAYARD IN FLIGHT.

          Looks aside. John's ship there. John's
          face bright, peaceful. he lifts his hand.
          Bayard indicates direction, John nods, the
          ships turn and disappear side by side.

                              DISSOLVE TO

273   A CHURCH -

          empty, candles before Host. Antoinette
          lying on her face, motionless, before altar.
          In background a faint medly of sound, joyful,
          hysterical; bands, singing, voices. In
          DISSOLVE they become sound of engine, to:

274   A FLIGHT OF GERMAN SHIPS
          CLOCK to one bearing the pipe smoking skull.
                              CUT TO

275   BAYARD AND JOHN FLYING HIGH ABOVE GERMANS,

         Bayard looking down through glass. He raises
his head, also flings binocular overside,
turns to John, gestures downward. John nods,
bright, peaceful, lifts hand in salute. The
two ships dive, Bayard's engine roaring. In
long DISSOLVE the engine becomes very loud,
then begins to die away to:

276   AERODROME -

         Sergeant and two mechanics begin to run
suddenly.

                              CUT TO

277   BAYARD'S SHIP ON GROUND -

         motionless. Bayard in cockpit, his head
bent forward on his crossed arms. Sergeant
runs up.

                   Sergeant
Sir? Sir?

         Bayard raises his head slowly, looks at
sergeant. His face is grave, quiet, almost
peaceful.

                   BAYARD
Yes. Now I can sleep again, Flight.

                   Sergeant
Thank God, sir! Thank God, sir!

         Offstage, beginning faint, growing louder, the
voices in the mess, singing:

                   Voices
We're here because we're here because ---

         Bayard looks up. FOLLOW to John's ship
banking overhead turning to depart   John
looking down, bright, peaceful, raises his
hand to salute.

                   Voices
            (singing last half of verse)
--We're here because we're here because we're here
because we're here.

         John's ship fades slowly away into DISSOLVE
in which singing dies.

278   A LONG RESOLVE.

Faint shouting, bands playing snatches
of Marseillaise, God Save the King, Star
Spangled Banner, to give cross section of sound
on night of Nov. 11, to:

Throngs, women, soldiers, civilians, parad-
ing in streets, dancing, shouting.

                    DOUBLE EXPOSURE TO

279   LIGHTED FRONT OF CAFE.

                    DISSOLVE THROUGH TO

280   INTERIOR -

A table, Bayard and two flight commanders.
Bayard sitting still, moodily, his drink
untasted before him. First flight commander
watching him uneasily.
                    First
Sartoris.
           (Bayard looks at him)
You're out of formation, old chap.
           (Raises his glass)
To the future -- if any.

                    Second
No; to the dead. Gad, what do you suppose they
are thinking tonight?

                    First
           (hisses aside)
Stow it, you ass.
           (To Bayard)
No heel taps.

                    Bayard
           (after a moment, rousing)
Right.

     They drink. First turns.

                    Bayard
Garçon!

     FOLLOW TO old waiter, turning.

                    Waiter
Messieurs?

                         CUT TO

          First
        (looking at Bayard)
What are you going to do now, Sartoris? Going
back to the States, I suppose?

          Bayard
What? Yes. Yes. I'll go back home.

          Second
Gad, what can we do? Any of us? They taught us
to fly, and we taught ourselves to fight in order
to live, and now they are going to dump us back
into peace like a lot of pebbles from a lorry.

          First
Well, what are you going to do about it?

          Second
I'm going to have another drink. What, Sartoris?

          First
Right. So shall we all.
        (turns)
Gar ----- (his voice ceases, shows astonishment.)

            FOLLOW TO:

    THE WAITER, paused, facing door in attitude
    of astonishment. CLOCK to other people, French
    soldiers and civilians, all watching door in
    horrified astonishment.

          Voice
      (offstage, signing in drunken key)
---We're here because we're here beacause we're ---

    CLOCK toward door. Dorn and Artillery Officer
    enter, Dorn holding Officer up. Dorn's head
    is wrapped in a bandage, his face is sick look-
    ing. The Officer is quite drunk, singing.

          Officer
---- because we're here because we're here ---

    Crash offstage.
               CUT TO:

282   BAYARD - erect, leaning forward, his chair
    fallen backward. SWEEP about at horrified
    faces of French people, to Officer and Dorn
    as they waver across room. Officer's face
    lights as he sees three at table.

          Officer
Oh, there you are.
        (blunders toward them, Dorn holding him
        up)   Continued -

CONTINUED (2)

                          First
          Marley! What the devil ---

                          Marley
          Absh'lutely. Shhe what I have? Found him.

                          First
          You what?

                          Marley
          Quite. Belongs to me. No. That's backward.
          Belong to him. Ran over me with aeroplane. Fell
          on me with aeroplane.
                          (to Dorn)
          Nich wahr?

                          Dorn
                      (his face sick, strained, alert)
          -- Ja. Ja, Herr Leutnant.

                                              CUT TO:

BAYARD leaning forward across the table,
          glaring at Dorn. CLOCK across horrified
          French faces in background, still too astonish-
          ed to move, the Proprietress among them.

                          Marley
          Absh'lutely. Fell out of sky on me. Chose me to
          fall on out of entire allied forces. Was in ob-
          shervation post, minding own business, watching
          war stop with one eye and looking at watch with
          other, waiting for orderly to crawl up so I could
          borrow a cigarette of him (I had a match, myself)
          Hear noise; look up. Chap falling directly upon
          me. Jump out of hole, run, aeroplane in pursuit.
          Think for a moment I have it foiled, but no. No go.
          Completely enclosed and surrounded by aeroplane in
          violent state of beating itself to pieces on ground,
          I still holding match in my hand. Next thing I know,
          am lying on back, still holding match, with my
          breeks torn completely off -- never found one trace
          of them; aeroplane apparently having eaten them when
          it sprang upon me -- looking into face of this chap
          here hanging upside down. Said, 'I say. Good gad.
          Not hurt I hope. You don't happen to have a ciga-
          rette about you, do you?'

                                              CUT TO:

                              Bayard
Watching the war stop? What time was this?

                              Marley
Absh'lutely. Looking at watch when heard noise.
Watch said, eight minutes to eleven.

                              Bayard
Where?

                              Marley
Where?

                              Bayard
Where were you?

                              Marley
In obshervation post. Minding --

                              Bayard
Where, damn you to hell.

                              Marley
                         (patiently)
In obshervation post; where would I be? Hear noise;
look up. For moment all I can see is terrific skull
smoking pipe. Why remembered to ask for cigarette --

                              Bayard
A skull?
                         (looks at Dorn, furious)
Parlez-vous francais?

                              Dorn
Ja. Oui.

                              First
                         (puts hand on Bayard)
Sartoris --

                              Bayard
                         (glaring at Dorn, jerks
                         First's hand off)
Get away.
                         (to Dorn)
So you didn't die.

                              First
Here; Sartoris!

                              Bayard
You didn't die. But my brother died.

                              Dorn
                         (baffled, sick, strained)
Your brother, Captain?

                                        Continued -

CONTINUED (2)

                            Bayard
                     (in dead, quiet, level voice)
          Do you remember July the fifth? About nine o'clock?
          You brought your flight down on two of our machines,
          a Camel and a ---

                            Dorn
          Ah. The two Englishmen fighting one another. Yes.
                     (looks at Bayard, comprehends)
          You were the --

                            Bayard
          Yes. My brother was in that Camel. He jumped.

                            Dorn
          And it was you, the mad Englishman who dove upon
          me this morning. So.

                            Bayard
          Yes. Yes.
                     (his voice is cold, level, his face
                     completely dead. His hand goes inside
                     his tunic, slowly.)

                                            CUT TO:

285   THE FIRST watching him, puzzled, alarmed.
            Suddenly his face changes, he springs forward.

                                            CUT TO:

286   FIRST

                            First
            Sartoris!

            Bayard with pistol in his hand, his face
            deadly. First springs upon him, clutching
            at his arm. Bayard flings him back.

                            Bayard
            Back. Back. I have five bullets here.
                     (he holds pistol on Dorn)

                                            CUT TO:

287   DORN - looking into camera, facing pistol. He
            clicks his heels, salutes, holds it, looking
            at pistol, his face calm.

                                            CUT TO:

288   A COMMOTION in background, French
                people turning toward door. CLOCK to   122.
                SPOOMER as French people surround him,
                gesticulant. The Patronne shrieks at him.

                        Patronne
Voila, mon commandant! Boche'. Un boche chez la
maison Charlet! Une outrage affreuse a la France!

                        Spoomer
What? What?

                        Voices
                (the French clustered about him, waving
                their hands)
Allemand! Allemand, mon colonel!

                        Spoomer
                (to French Sergeant)
You, there. What ---

                        Sergeant
                (pointing)
Look, colonel.

                Spoomer looks, sees tableau of Bayard and
                Dorn and pistol. He moves forward, followed
                close by Sergeant and two soldiers, civilians
                behind them.

                        Spoomer
What the devil's this?
                (recognizes Bayard)
Ha. So you have decided belatedly to serve the
uniform which you wear, eh? Good, Captain; I'll
relieve you.
                (to Sergeant, pointing at Dorn)
Faites se charger cette prisonnier.

                Sergeant moves forward eagerly; behind Spoomer
                the people also have a leashed air, like barely
                restrained dogs. Bayard moves pistol to cover
                Sergeant.

                        Bayard
Arretez.

                Sergeant pauses, looks back at pistol.
                Spoomer looks on in astonishment.

                        Spoomer
Eh? What? What's this?

                        Bayard
Don't touch that man, He is mine.

                        Spoomer
What? What?

                              Continued -

                         Bayard
          I shot him down. Don't touch him.

               A long sigh goes up from people behind
               Spoomer. The pistol jerks toward them
               returns to Sergeant.

                         Bayard
          Ne bougez. Rien de personne.

                         Patronne
          Don't move? You men, if you are men, Frenchmen,
          if you are Frenchmen, soldiers if you so call
          yourselves, will you stand there and permit ---

               CLOCK to Patronne's wild, disheveled face
               as she screams. A French soldier grips her
               from behind.

                         Soldier
          Silence, woman!

               CLOCK to Bayard turning toward Patronne's
               voice, his face calm, deadly. Behind the
               Patronne two French soldiers crouch, looking
               at Bayard holding pistol on Sergeant. He
               looks away; at once the two soldiers creep
               behind the crowd, CLOCK to a bottle in the
               hand of one of them. CLOCK to Bayard facing
               Spoomer and Sergeant.

                         Spoomer
          This, to me? From you, with a damned captain's
          rank on your shoulders, and that only because I
          did not press against you a court martial for
          insubordination and deadly assault?

               CLOCK to Spoomer. His eye flicks aside for
               a moment.

                                             CUT TO:

289   THE TWO SOLDIERS creeping behind the crowd,
               approaching Bayard from rear

                                             CUT TO:

290   BAYARD facing SPOOMER

            Bayard

I see. You are now a colonel. I hadn't noticed.
Take these two, then.
         (with his free hand he jerks off his
         shoulder straps and flings them at
         Spoomer's face. They strike Spoomer
         upon the breast and fall to the floor.
         Again a concerted sigh goes up from the
         French people as they surge forward. Again
         the pistol lifts toward them, they halt,
         the pistol drops again.)
That's all over. Finished. As far as I am concerned, your rank and my rank vanished from the
face of the earth at eleven o'clock this morning.
As far as I am concerned, these little knobs on
your shoulders and mine too are as empty as last
year's acorns.

                  CUT TO:

291   SPOOMER'S glance again flicks sideways.

                  CUT TO:

292   SOLDIER rising behind Bayard, the bottle
           raised.

                  CUT TO:

293   FIRST FLIGHT COMMANDER springs forward and
           grasps soldier's arm as whole room breaks into
           uproar. French surge forward. Bayard whirls
           as First and Second knock down two soldiers,
           the three of them now struggling in mob.

                  CUT TO:

294.   Patronne struggling forward, men trying
to hold her. She strains, jerks, spits
at Bayard.

                     Patronne
                    (screaming)
--- Boche! Boche! Broken! Broken! Every cup,
plate, saucer, glass ---- all! all! Eight
months since the shell came have I kept them against
this day ---

                              CUT TO:

295.   BAYARD and two FLIGHT COMMANDERS AND DORN

struggling above the mob. Spoomer pointing at
Dorn.

                     Spoomer
Take that man!

              Bayard springs free, striking at the mob about
Dorn. Behind Bayard the Sergeant, crouching,
rises up with a bayonet in his hand. The FIRST
sees him.

                     First
Sartoris! Look out! Look out!

              First catches up a chair and springs forward.
At that moment Dorn frees himself and springs
toward Sergeant as he strikes. First swings
chair at light as Bayone falls. Darkness.
Furious sound of fighting dies away.

296.   RESOLVE
             .ANTOINETTE'S ROOM.

              Dorn lying on bed, three officers about bed.
Antoinette crouched at foot. Bayard giving
Dorn brandy. His wounded left arm where
bayonet struck. Dorn opens his eyes, moves
arm. First holds his arm still.

                     First
Steady.

                     Dorn
So. I haf voundt. Ja. I remember. Dot --- vat you
say? ---

                            CONTINUED-

CONTINUED (2)

> **First**
> Bayonet, eh? Yes. You took it. It didn't have
> your name on it, though. How do you feel, eh?
> Comment ca va?
>
> **Dorn**
> Ca va. Thanks.
>
> **Second**
> It was a confounded close thing for us all. Gad, .
> those French people were about up to tearing us all
> limb from limb.
>
> **First**
> Yes. I daresay we've not heard the last of it,
> either.
>
> **Second**
> Nonsense. They don't know one Englishman from
> another.
>
> **First**
> Have you forgot Spoomer?
>
> **Second**
> O. gad. O I say. I say. You don't think he ---
>
> **First**
> Can't say, of course. But we can hope that in the
> darkness someone got him confused with one of us.
>
> **Second**
> Yes. The one with the bayonet, preferably.
>
> **First**
> Oh, come. Perhaps he's not so bad as people think.
>
> **Second**
> I'm sure of that. He can't be. Well...
>
> **First**
>   (rising)
> Yes. We had better.
>   (to Bayard)
> Look here. I daresay the fastest way to get him
> to hospital would be to stop the first M.P. patrol
> we see, eh?
>
> **Bayard**
>   (moves toward door with them)
> Thanks. I'll attend to it. And thanks.
>
> **First**
> Right. See you tomorrow, then.
>   (Gestures second out door)
> Rat along, Mac.
>   (Second passes out door, First watches
>   him out, then turns to Bayard)
> I say. Not one to meddle. You know that. But....eh?
>   CONTINUED-

296.   CONTINUED (3)

                Bayard watches him, his face calm, grim.

                        First
You had that pistol out when ------ when.....eh?

                        Bayard
He killed my brother.

                        First
Oh, come. Your brother took his chance. And you
had your chance before eleven this morning. Had
your chance and took it.

                        Bayard
I'm the same man now I was before eleven this morning.
So is he. My brother didn't come back to life at
eleven this morning, like in a game for children.

                They look at one another, Bayard calm, grim,
                the First grave, speculative.

                        First
Right. I've always liked you, Sartoris. Know
you had rotten luck. But...well, when I see you
again -- or if -- just don't tell me about it.

                        Bayard
I won't.

                        First
Don't. Well.
                (Looks at Bayard, salutes)
Thanks.

                Turns swiftly away, exits, Bayard looks after
                him, turns back, approaches bed. At the foot
                of it Antoinette, crouching, watches him.
                Dorn also watches him. Bayard stands beside
                bed.

                        Dorn
Je parle francais plus

                QUICK DISSOLVE TO SAME, DORN STILL TALKING...

easier than English. But I know more English than
you think.

                        Bayard
Yes?

                        Dorn
Yes. I can almost tell you what you and the other
captain were talking about at the door there.

                        Bayard
Can you?
                                        CONTINUED-

404

296.   CONTINUED (4)

                            Dorn
Yes.
                    (He lies still for a moment, his eyes
                    closed. Antoinette crouches at foot of
                    bed, Bayard stands beside bed, beside
                    chair)
Will you ask mademoiselle to go out?

                            Bayard
Go out?

                            Dorn
Leave the room. Will you be so kind, mademoiselle?

        Antoinette half rises.

                            Bayard
No. Stay where you are.
                    (to Dorn)
You can tell me nothing that mademoiselle should
not hear.

                            Dorn
Ah. So.
                    (Lies silent for a moment, his eyes
                    closed. Antoinette watches him and then
                    Bayard, crouching at foot of bed. Bayard
                    looks down at Dorn, grim, waiting)
I have not told you about myself. My people are
little barons in Prussia, I the oldest son. In the
University I fell in love with the daughter of a
teacher of music, a peasant. I married her. When I
returned home and told my father, he ordered me
out of the house and fixed the succession on my
brother. My father did not live a year; they said
that my defection killed him. I do not know, because I was happy. But I will not bore you. What I
wish to tell is simply this: When the war came, my
brother, the baron, was killed in the first week of
1914, an officer of hussars in Belgium. My mother,
a princess in her own right, the daughter of a
prince, wrote to me that I am now baron; I cannot
help myself, and that all is forgiven. I wrote back
that I will not be baron; I am the husband of a
peasant woman, and the son which we are expecting
will be a peasant, too. I myself am away at war at
that time, fighting not for the little barons and
the kaisers, but for Germany, the fatherland, asking her to forgive me if she could, to forget me if
she would.
                    (He ceases, lies with his eyes closed)

                            Bayard
Well? Why are you telling me all this?

                                    CONTINUED-

                              Dorn
                   (raises his hand a little)
If you please. So I am waiting for my son to be
born; I have arranged my leave so. I go back home,
to Beyreuth, where we are living. My wife is gone.
They tell me that a fine lady, a princess, came and
fetched her away, where, they do not know, since
the lady was a princess. I never saw my wife again,
or my son; I do not know even if I have a son. I
only know that at the court martial-- I overstayed
my leave and was hunted down as a deserter by
armed soldiers--- a general who was a relation of
my mother's appeared at the court and whispered
something to them --- what, I do not know, since
I do not remember very much of that time--- and I
was permitted to choose another service. I chose
the air force; you will understand why, you who
have flown also. So, then.
                   (He ceases again. Bayard looks at him,
                   grim, puzzled)

                              Bayard
Well? What about it?

                              Dorn
                   (not moving)
Sit down. Please.
                   (Bayard sits down, puzzled. Dorn's good
                   hand comes out and touches Bayard, who
                   looks down at hand)

                              Bayard
Here.   What ----

                              Dorn
                   (again in that tone of courteous
                   command)
---Your pardon. Sit still please.
                   (Bayard obeys, watching the hand
                   fumble lightly at his tunic pocket.
                   It stops)
Ah. I thought I remembered seeing you, just be-
fore your friend broke the light...

                              Bayard
What are you getting at? What's the matter with
you?

                              Dorn
Still, please. Listen. I will try to tell you.
                   (At the foot of the bed, also unmoving,
                   Antoinette is puzzled, looking from one
                   to the other)
Listen, then. Your brother was slain. Jumped
from his burning machine and fell to death.
                   (CLOCK to Dorn's hand moving quietly
                   beneath the flap of Bayard's pocket)
Ha. He fell a long time, that morning, waiting to
die. Yes?

                                          CONTINUED-

296.   CONTINUED (6)

                    Bayard's Voice
                    (He draws a long shuddering
                    breath)
          Yes.

                    Dorn's Voice
                    (His hand is now inside the pocket
                    it can be seen to grasp something
                    inside the cloth)
          A long while, alone, looking back at the man who
          killed him and the brother who could not save him,
          waiting to die ---- so?

                    Bayard moves, his tunic pocket jerks away.
                    Dorn's hand moves too. It comes clear, holding
                    Bayard's pistol. Antoinette screams --

                                        CUT TO:

297.   BAYARD

                    standing crouched, tense, still, Dorn on the
                    bed, his eyes open, the pistol in his hand,
                    covering Bayard. Antoinette standing, her
                    hands to her face.

                    Dorn
          Do not move. And since that day you hunted the man
          who slew your brother. And when you found him, the
          man was not dead. The man lay on a bed and bored
          you with the history of his life. Do you know why?
                    (Bayard does not move nor speak)
          This is why. You have that man who did not die in
          your power and at your mercy. But unfortunately the
          circumstances in which that man became the slayer
          of your brother and the object of your vengeance have
          passed away, ceased. And worse than that, that man
          was enabled to do you a small service in the matter
          of an ill-directed bayonet. That man believed that
          perhaps this favor might counter balance his debt
          to you, thinking you were perhaps that sort of man.
          So he told you what he did in order to remove that
          counter balance, to free your hand.

                    Bayard
          Free my hand?

                    Dorn
          Free your hand.
                    (They look at one another. Suddenly Dorn
                    flips the pistol, catches it by the
                    barrel, the butt extended to Bayard)
          Here.

                                        CONTINUED-

                                                        407

                              Bayard
Here?

                              Dorn
Your pistol, Captain.

                    Bayard puts his hand out slowly. It touches
                    the pistol. They look at one another. Sud-
                    denly Bayard grasps the pistol, springs back.
                    Again Antoinette screams. Dorn looks at her.

                              Dorn
Perhaps mademoiselle would like to retire now?

                              Antoinette
Bayard!   Bayard!

                              Bayard
                         (crouching, glaring at Dorn)
To me?   To me?

                              Dorn
Yes. I thought you were the sort of man whom
that accidental favor of the bayonet might incom-
mode. But you are not that sort of man, are you?

                              Bayard
No.

                              Dorn
Then send mademoiselle from the room.

                              Antoinette
Bayard!   Bayard!
                         (Her hands to her face, she runs for-
                         ward a step, pauses again in horror.
                         They do not look at her)

                              Dorn
Well? Why do you wait? Your brother is slain,
but my country is slain; fallen from a greater
height than any Camel has ever reached. Shoot, Captain.

                    Antoinette watches Bayard, her hands to her
                    face, poised as though to run. Bayard looks
                    at Dorn, his face wrung, terrible. Slowly
                    the pistol rises, covers Dorn's chest, stead-
                    ies. They look at one another. Tableau.
                    Then Bayard flings pistol through window.
                    The fractured glass is in the shape of a star.
                    Antoinette runs forward, falls at Bayard's
                    feet, clutching his knees.

                              Antoinette
Thank God!   Thank God!

                                             CONTINUED-

CONTINUED (3)

Bayard stands, his head bent. As DISSOLVE
begins, the star shaped fracture in the glass
begins to glow faintly as daylight begins behind it. It is brightest at the instant of
complete dissolve, then it begins also to fade.
To:

298.   A PAGE OF THE DIARY

Caroline's hand holding it open, one of
Johnny's hands beside it:

> July 4th ---. And back home they will be
> popping firecrackers. And out here we are
> popping firecrackers too. That's all they
> are. There are no bullets in them. Not
> for me, that is. No bullet will ever kill
> me. I know that. Someday I will just get
> beyond all loving and hating, and I will
> just fly on away somewhere and vanish,
> like Guynemer did. Well, I have got beyond
> the loving and the hating. And so who
> knows? Maybe the next time I go up will
> be the time when I will fly on away into
> some sky without either air or gravity,
> where I will cruise on forever at about
> fourteen fifty, watching my shadow on the
> clouds and not even remembering how I
> got there.

Caroline's hand turns the page. The next page is
blank.

                    Caroline's voice
And that's all. His major sent it to me, with
his other things. And then Uncle Bayard came home,
bringing them with him, and I said, 'No! No!
Never!'

        DISSOLVE THROUGH BLANK PAGE TO:

299.   A BEDROOM

A baby's crib, a nurse beside it, Caroline
standing, facing Bayard.

        have   Caroline
You/brought them here, to live with me, in this
house? The woman with whom my husband betrayed
me, and the man who killed him? The man and woman
who between them killed your brother and this
child's father?

                            CONTINUED-

        She turns, runs to crib, crying, snatches up
child, putting shawl about it swiftly. Nurse
comes forward, tries to take child.

                    Nurse

Now, Miss Caroline!

        Caroline jerks child away, clasps child to her,
runs toward door, crying.

                  Caroline

Bring them, then! We will be gone; turn your
house into a mausoleum of your brother's infidelity
and a memorial to his murderer!

                  Bayard
            (moves forward, grasps her, holds her)

Caroline.
            (She struggles, crying)

Caroline. Stop it. They will go. They will not
come here. Do you hear me?

                  Caroline
            (wildly)

No, no! Bring them! I want them to come, to see
what they have done. Let me go! Let me go!

        Bayard holds her, takes the child from her
and carries it back to crib, NURSE hovering,
Caroline following. He lays child in crib,
Caroline kneels beside it, crying. Bayard goes
to door, turns, looks back, turns and exits.

                DISSOLVE TO:

300   THE BLANK PAGE, CAROLINE'S and JOHNNY'S Hand
           upon it.

                          Caroline's Voice
           So he found rooms for them somewhere. I didn't
           know where. I never asked and he never told me.
           But I knew that they were somewhere near, and I
           knew that they were seeing you when the nurse
           would take you out. Sometimes Uncle Bayard would
           take you alone, and I knew where he was taking you,
           but I never asked. I didn't want to know. Then
           the pony came. You were six then, and one day I
           realized that you and the nurse would go somewhere
           at the same time every day.

                                         DISSOLVE TO:

301   A STREET.
           Nurse and Johnny going along street, Johnny
           tugging on ahead, impatient, eager.

                                         CUT TO:

302   A CORNER, DORN and ANTOINETTE WAITING.

           Nurse and Johnny come up. Antoinette kneels,
           Johnny goes to her, she embraces him, Dorn
           watching. Johnny turns, looks up at Dorn,
           salutes. Dorn clicks his heels, salutes.

                          Dorn
           Salut, prinz!

                          Johnny
           Pony. Pony. Let's go see the pony.

                          Dorn
           Ja, Prinz.
                   (He stoops, Antoinette helps Johnny
                   onto his back, they go on up street)

                                         DISSOLVE TO:

303   A PASTURE. DORN and ANTOINETTE beside the
           fence. Dorn holding Johnny on fence. Inside
           pasture a spotted pony. Nurse approaches.

                          Nurse
           Now, Johnny. We must go home. You've seen the
           pony, and mama will be worried if we stay longer.

                          Johnny
           No. I want to look at the pony.

                                         continued -

303 CONTINUED (2) 135

                    Nurse
Come, now. Your uncle Bayard will buy you a pony
as soon as you are big enough.

          She lifts Johnny down from fence, Johnny
          looking back reluctant.

                    Nurse
Say goobye, now.

                    Johnny
Goodbye, Aunt Antoinette. Goodbye Uncle Lothar.
I'll come back tomorrow.

               Antoinette and Dorn
Goodbye. Goodbye, prinz.

                    Johnny
I wish you would come home with me. Why won't you
come home with me?

                    Nurse
                 (hurriedly)
Come, now. We'll come back tomorrow and see the
pony.

                    Johnny
But why can't they come home too? Why don't they
ever come home ----

                    Nurse
                 (leading him away)
Come, let's hurry. Let's see who can get home the
quickest.

          Exit Johnny and Nurse. .Antoinette and Dorn
          look after them. Then they look at one
          another. Dorn shrugs.

                    Dorn
It will take money. That I do not have.
                 (becomes grave- determined)
Money? Pah. I can work. I can earn it.

                    Antoinette
I have some. A little. I can earn also.

          They turn and look at pony.

                              DISSOLVE TO

304   ANTOINETTE'S ROOM. She takes from drawer the
               box of French money, counts it, puts it back,
               goes out,

                         DOUBLE EXPOSURE DISSOLVE TO:

412

305   ANTOINETTE approaching door of big house, rings, enters.

                    DOUBLE EXPOSURE DISSOLVE TO

306   LIBRARY. Antoinette standing, woman of house facing her.

                 Woman
You are a sempstress?

                Antoinette
Yes, madame. I have some skill with needle, if madame will permit me to try ---

                    DISSOLVE TO:

307   DORN mowing a lawn, clumsily, stops to straighten out mower and mop face. A man watching him from porch. Men approaches. Dorn looks about, straightens up.

                 Man
You are not accustomed to this kind of work, are you?

                 Dorn
As you see, sir. But any trade a man must learn. But I vill satisfaction give; that I -- how you say? - guarantee.

                 Man
I am sure of that. I just thought that perhaps there was something more in your line than manual labor.

                 Dorn
I thangk you. I vill learn.
             (takes up mower again, goes on, Man looking after him)

                    DISSOLVE TO:
308   ANOTHER LAWN, smoothly cut, Dorn using mower skillfully now.   DISSOLVE TO:

309   A SEWING ROOM. A girl trying on dress before mirror, Antoinette stooping with mouth full of pins. Enter woman, examines dress. Antoinette rises.

                    DISSOLVE TO:

310   LIBRARY. Antoinette standing, woman at desk, writing. Rises, hands Antoinette a check.
                    continued -

310   CONTINUED (2)

                    Antoinette
        Thank you, madame.
                (exits)

                                DISSOLVE TO:

311   DORN - waiting before boarding house.
       Antoinette approaches, swiftly. Dorn
       waves money.

                    Dorn
        Money! Much money!

                    Antoinette
        And I! And I! Wait for me.

        She runs on up to steps.

                                  CUT TO:

312   ANTOINEETE running upstairs toward door.
       Enters.

                                  CUT TO:

313   ANTOINETTE taking out box of French money,
       hurriedly, crams it into bag, exits.

                                  DISSOLVE TO:

314   Pony in pasture.

                        DISSOLVE THRU PONY TO:

315   A STREET. Antoinette and Dorn leading pony.
       Slowly RESOLVE JOHNNY on pony between them.

                                  DISSOLVE TO:

316   A BLANK PAGE. CAROLINE'S and JOHNNY'S HAND.

                  Caroline's Voice
       And that went on, and I didn't ask. I knew some-
       thing, felt something, but I didn't ask Bayard. We
       didn't even talk about them, until one day he--

                                  DISSOLVE TO:

317   ROOM, Caroline sewing. Bayard enters.

                        Bayard
Come, I want to show you something.

                        Caroline
What?

            Bayard down't answer. They look at one
            another.

                        Caroline
No. No. I don't want to see it. I know what it
is, but I don't want to see it. I won't see it.
I have kept from seeing all the time, even though
I knew there was something, that you were doing
something behind my back. But I won't see! I
won't! I.......

            Bayard approaches, takes the sewing
            from her hands, takes her hand and draws
            her up.

                        Bayard
Come.
            (she follows, watching him, as he
            leads her out.

                                DOUBLE EXPOSURE TO:

318   CAROLINE and BAYARD in a car, moving away.
           Caroline with a dazed air. The car stops on
           a hill, behind a screen of trees.

                        Bayard
Look yonder.

            Beyond the trees a lane - Antoinette and Dorn
            leading the pony, Johnny riding. . Caroline
            begins to pant.

                        Caroline
No. No. No.

                        Bayard
They bought it for him. Worked and earned the
money. I passed one day and saw him trying to run
a lawn mower. And she was sewing, doing needle
work from door to door.

                        Caroline
                        (weeping)
No, no, no.

                        Bayard
Yes. You can't help it. When we can't keep the
dead out of our lives, how can you hope to keep the
living? He calls them Aunt Antoinette and Uncle
Lothar. I didn't teach him that. Neither did they.
He did it himself.
                                        continued -

318   CONTINUED (2)

             Caroline weeps quietly.

                                        DISSOLVE TO:

319   ROOM. Caroline seated, Antoinette facing her,
             her head bent. In background Dorn at attention.
                          Caroline
             I ask you to forgive me. I don't --- don't hate...
             he is part of all three of us. Bayard says that in
             us he is not dead, in the three of us and Johnny.
             So I don't...just give me a little time to,....
                          (she buries her head in her hands,
                          Antoinette watches her, moves swiftly
                          forward, kneels and kisses her dress)
             It's because war with women doesn't stop with
             armistices and peace. So I ask you to forgive,....

             Antoinette catches her hand, draws it down
             to her lips. Caroline extends other hand
             blindly. Dorn comes foward, takes it , bends
             over it. Door opens, Johnny runs in, followed
             by Bayard. Johnny pauses, his face bright.

                          Johnny
             You've come home! You've come home!
                          (runs foward to Dorn, who turns.
                          Johnny salutes)
             Salut, Uncle Lothar!

                          Dorn
                          (clicks heels, salutes)
             Salut, prinz!

                                        ISSOLVE TO:

320   THE BEDROOM. Caroline and Johnny sitting on
             the bed, the open diary on Caroline's lap.
             She sits back now, looking at Johnny, who sits,
             bent forward, musing.

                          Caroline
                          (timidly)
             Johnny?
                          (He doesn't answer)
             Bayard said I must tell you someday. But I told
             him that when I told you, you would stop being my
             baby and would be a man, Johnny.
                          (She leans forward, anxiously, to put
                          her arms about him. He moves away)

                          Johnny
             It's all right. I'll get used to it in a minute.
             So that --that--he killed my father.
                                        continued -

416

320   CONTINUED (2)

                    Caroline
Who?

                    Johnny
You know.

                    Caroline
Who? Say his name.
          (Johnny stands before her, downlooking,
          musing)
Say it.

                    Johnny
No. Not ever again.

                    Caroline
Say it. Call his name.

                    Johnny
Uncle ----Uncle Loth ----
          (He falls at her feet, his head buried
          in her lap.
Mother! Mother!

          Caroline sits still, her hand stroking his
          head.

                    Johnny
And she --Aunt Antoinette, being his wife when you
were already that. Didn't he love you anymore? Was
that it?

                    Caroline
No. He still loved me. But she was there. And I
was busy doing for him what she could not. I was
giving him a son to bear his name. I left like
you do at first. I didn't see how he could still
love me and ----and -----but I know better now. I
know now that your uncle Bayard is right; that the
relations between man and woman are simple; it's
only the men and women who think they are complex.
They are so simple that even wars and all the other
disasters that men can invent don't even upset them.
Aunt Antoinette knows that. One day we were talking and she asked me if I were jealous of her and
I said 'Of course not'. And she watched me so,
looked at me so, that I began t cry; I couldn't
help it; she seemed to be looking right into my
heart. She said, 'So. You are jealous, then. That
is good. For a while I almost believed that you had
not ever loved him.' And we talked and she told me.
She said, 'I loved him too. So much so that I am
jealous of all three of you. I would be his wife,
his child and the man who killed him, and the earth
in which he is buried, all in one. And now your
Uncle Bayard has given me everything except the soil
where they buried him. I didn't see that at first.
But now I do. That's what he has given to us.
Don't you see?
                              continued -

              Johnny
Yes, I guess so.
           (He rises, avoids Caroline's eyes,
           turns away)

              Caroline
Where are you going?

              Johnny
Nowhere. Just down to the back porch, to wait for
Uncle Bayard.

              Caroline
Come here.
           (He turns toward her, still not looking
           at her. She sits still, her face lifted)
Closer.
           (He approaches, leans and kisses her,
           exits.)

     She looks after him, then she closes the diary
     quietly, her face is peaceful.

                 DISSOLVE TO:

321   THE HALL. Dorn's overcoat on rack. Johnny
     stands before it, looking at it, his face cold,
     grave, almost grim. He puts his hand out,
     pauses, his hand clenched. Then he touches the
     coat, becomes still, his face bent. His hand
     unclenches and he touches the coat quietly,
     stroking it, his face musing, not grim any
     longer, but quite grave. He goes on.

                 DISSOLVE TO:

322   THE BACK PORCH. The stable boy waiting for
     Bayard to return. Antoinette and Dorn standing
     beside lane, also waiting. Johnny sees them,
     stands for a moment looking at Dorn, then ap-
     proaches. It is sunset. Dorn hears him, turns,
     his face changes. He stands to attention as
     Johnny comes up, They look at one another a
     while. Antoinette turns, her hand rises, falls.

              Johnny
You did kill my father.

              Dorn
Yes.

              Johnny
Mother showed me the -- his diary. And what Uncle
Bayard said. There were seven of you, and just him
and Uncle Bayard. Do you call that fair?
                 continued -

                    Dorn
No. It wass not fair. It wass worse. It wass
cowardly. But war iss never fair. It iss not
supposed to be; else nobody would ever win. And
when a man iss about to kill another man, at that
moment, he iss always a coward.

                    Antoinette
                (faintly)
You have seen the book? Your mother has -----

                    Johnny
About you? Yes.
                (turns to Dorn, pausing, looks at
                Antoinette again,, who is watching
                him in terror almost. He goes to her,
                takes her hand)
That's all right. I'm not mad.

                    Antoinette
                (her hands fluttering to touch him,
                restrained, yearning, fearful)
Johnny. Johnny.

                    Johnny
No. It's all right. Here.
                (Takes her hand and kisses it before
                    she can protest)
That's how I have seen you do mother)
                (Drops hand, turns to Dorn, who is stiff,
                    still, watching him also with alert
                    anxiety)
So you killed my father. Well, if it hadn't been
you, it would have been another flyer, and at least
this way we haven't lost ----lost ----
                (His voice breaks; he regains control,
                blinking the tears quickly back while
                Antoinette yearns toward him, motionless,
                and Dorn stands as if facing a court
                martial)
You killed my father and then Uncle Bayard shot you
down and brought you back to me, and so we haven't
----haven't ----
                (erect, facing them, he begins to cry,
                hard, they watching him. Then Antoinette
                moves, swoops forward and puts her arms
                about him)

                    Antoinette
Johnny! Johnny!

            When she touches him, he recovers himself.
            He steps back, stops crying.

                                        continued -

322   CONTINUED (3)

                         Johnny
          I'm all right. It's all right.
                    (turns to Dorn, salutes)
          Salut.

                         Dorn
                    (Breaks, moves forward quickly, his
                         arms extended)
          Prinz! Prinz!

                    (Johnny does not more, holds salute,
                    his face firm again, Dorn stops,
                    clicks heels, salutes)
          Salut.

                         Johnny
          Look. Here comes Uncle Bayard. Come on; we'll
          miss seeing him jump the gate.
                    (They go on toward land. Johnny drops
                     behind, wipes his eyes hurriedly, then
                    rejoins them as they stand beside lane,
                    looking toward gate as Bayard's horse
                    soars over it and comes up the lane. As
                    he approaches, Johnny and Dorn stand at
                    salute, their backs to camera, Antoinette
                    beside them. Bayard looks down, slows
                    horse, salutes passing as SLOW DISSOLVE
                    BEGINS.

323   IN DISSOLVE there passes behind Bayard the
             ghost of John's ship, John looking down at
             them, his face bright, peaceful. The
             ship goes on in dissolve; sound of an
             engine dies away.

                    THE END.

420

7

Honor

Early in 1930, Faulkner wrote "Honor," a story about the postwar experience of Buck Monaghan (who had captured the German pilot in "Ad Astra") as a wing-walker and later as a car salesman, centering on his love affair with a married woman and his paradoxically honorable relationship with Rogers, her husband. The two men try to settle the question of who should have the woman, but Monaghan becomes impatient with her:

> ... like a woman, even when you love her, is a woman to you just a part of the time and the rest of the time she is just a person that dont look at things the same way a man has learned to. Dont have the same ideas about what is decent and what is not. So I went over and stood with my arms about her, thinking, "God damn it, if you'll just keep out of this for a little while! We're both trying our best to take care of you, so it wont hurt you."[1]

Rogers agrees to give her up. Later Buck and Rogers (there may well be a play here on the name Buck Rogers) perform a flying stunt that becomes a duel of nerves, with Rogers piloting and Buck wing-walking; Buck loses his footing and Rogers saves him. Not out of gratitude but because of the unsentimental clarity of the understanding between himself and Rogers, Buck pulls out of the love triangle and the act. The story appeared in the *American Mercury* later that year and was reprinted, with "Turn About," in *Doctor Martino and Other Stories* (1934) as well as the *Collected Stories* (1950).

MGM was interested in the story and tentatively approved a synopsis by Harry Behn. Behn's "Synopsis #2" was dated 13 January 1933; no others are in the file. This or the earlier one was sent to Faulkner by Howard Hawks (although Behn usually worked with King Vidor), and when Faulkner left Hollywood after completing the third draft of *Turn About*, it was understood that he was to do some work based on Behn's synopsis. His time was charged to *Honor* from 28 November 1932 to 20 February 1933, though it is clear that for much of that time Faulkner was writing *War Birds*. His payroll cards suggest that he was working by turns on both scripts (see Introduction) until 15 March, after which there are no references to *Honor*. One payroll memo (15 December 1932) bears a later, penciled note, "Not on 'Honor'" and the explanation, "When Faulkner left here he was to do 'Honor.' Plans changed and when he went on salary [i.e., 28 November] he was to do story which was a combination of his short stories 'All the Dead Pilots' and 'Ad Astra.'" Blotner records that Faulkner did work on *Honor*[2] but has told me that he based this statement on the payroll cards.

On 19 July 1933, Faulkner wrote to Marx, who had sent him contracts for the assignment of rights on his MGM scripts and the stories related to them:

> The contract forms received.
>
> All save the one for HONOR seem to be correct. Perhaps the HONOR one is correct too, though I have a question to ask about it. . . .
>
> I wrote the story HONOR previous to my association with the studio. Howard Hawks sent me a treatment by Behn, as I recall, to look over. I read it and returned it, though I did not change it or do any work on it at all, being at the time engaged on the WAR STORY. The two original stories in WAR STORY I did work on and adapt myself, and for this work I was paid in weekly salary.[3]

So we have Faulkner's word for it that he did not write or revise any of the scripts for *Honor*. The problem is that Behn's first full-length script, dated 24 January 1933, includes many alternate scenes dated from 28 January to 27 February (when Faulkner was supposedly working on the property) and that these pages conform to many of Faulkner's spelling habits (dont, cant, Mr, etc.). Furthermore, these interleaved pages, when read in sequence, almost compose an independent screenplay.

To a textual editor, Behn's first script might amount to a virtual nightmare. Its nearly three hundred pages involve four distinct kinds of manuscript: a single-spaced mimeograph produced by the Script Department; a double-spaced typescript, some on yellow paper and some on white (conforming to Faulkner's orthography, almost but not quite matching the typewriter on which *MLAK* was composed in Oxford, and substantially different from *MLAK* in format); many pages in a loose, round, penciled handwriting that bears no resemblance to Faulkner's; and superscriptions and crossouts in a different, much heavier, penciled handwriting that is also not Faulkner's. Beyond this, there are neat black pen superscriptions in a hand that could conceivably have been Faulkner's (amounting to a change of name here and there), and small penciled corrections (again, conceivably Faulkner's) that are mostly confined to changes in page numbering. The neater corrections do not reflect anything that could be called a revision. The thick pencil cross-outs correspond with changes that show up in the *following* script, dated 30 March (with changes to 10 May) and reliably attributed to Behn and Jules Furthman. It appears that Furthman made notes on Behn's first script while composing his revision, and it may be of some interest that Furthman (who later worked with Faulkner on *To Have and Have Not* and *The Big Sleep*) appears to have experimented in *Honor* with some of the themes and scenes he later incorporated into his script for Hawks's *Only Angels Have Wings* (1939). There is considerable business, for instance, about a two-headed coin and about a plane that crashes in the fog, killing the pilot (both of which are central to *Only Angels Have Wings*; the latter is of course highly reminiscent of *Flying the Mail*); some of these points of overlap could be taken to suggest that Faulkner did some work on the Furthman version, but it can be misleading to rely too heavily on scene content in these matters, and the fact is that the later script reads not at all like Faulkner and very much like Furthman. The next relevant detail is that the Furthman script is double-spaced on the same typewriter and in the same format as the double-spaced pages in Behn's first script, except that the spelling is conventional.

It is to the double-spaced pages in Behn's first script, then, that one must look for any evidence of Faulkner's contributions, and some of them do in fact sound like Faulkner. In this excerpt Mildred (formerly the wife), who has injured her ankle in a stunt, discusses her plans for the evening with Rogers and Lucky (formerly Buck).

> MILDRED: My Lord, a wing-walker! (to Rogers) Why couldn't you choose a friend we could invite out to dinner a week ahead—and not only count on his being there, but on his taking us out and spending his money on us.
> LUCKY: I'll take you now—
> MILDRED: That wasn't a hint. (she touches her ankle) I cant.

In the opening scene there is a mule on the fairground, and the crowd watching Mildred's act is in a "hush." One character has a "cold, furious" look. More to the point, Mildred's act bears much more resemblance to Laverne's in *Pylon* (1935) than to anything in "Honor," and Faulkner had met someone like her when he began taking flying lessons in February 1933.[4]

A close examination of the loosely handwritten pages provides the nearest thing to evidence that the double-spaced pages were in fact written by Behn. By an uncanny coincidence, the spelling in both is identical; whoever wrote the penciled manuscript consistently put "dont" and "cant," etc., just as Faulkner did. There is considerable overlap between the penciled and double-spaced texts, indicating that MGM had saved all of the materials that predated their clean-typed version. It seems utterly unlikely that Behn would have handwritten these sheets after receiving a typescript from Faulkner, let alone deliberately matched the spelling. For a given double-spaced scene, there are penciled pages that are word-for-word identical, as there are others with additional lines, and others with fewer lines. My conclusion, then, is that Behn worked first in pencil, then himself prepared the double-spaced version on a studio typewriter shared by Furthman, then revised in pencil and submitted his final pages to the Script Department for copying in the standard single-spaced format; this pattern repeats approximately every ten to fifteen scenes. Then the whole was turned over to Furthman for rewriting. All this textual evidence, despite the tantalizing similarity of much of *Honor* to Faulkner's other work, supports Faulkner's assertion that he did not contribute to this screenplay, and *Honor* has accordingly not been included in this volume.

There may be some interest, however, in examining the ways MGM attempted to adapt this Faulkner story to the screen. In his 3-page "Synopsis #2," Behn makes Rogers an impoverished commercial passenger pilot whose wife, Mildred, decides they should work in a flying circus. Rogers finds his old war buddy, Lucky, selling automobiles; Lucky had been a wing-walker, so the two go into partnership. Rogers flies to a fair, asking Lucky to drive Mildred there. Feeling "honor-bound because Rogers trusts him with her," Lucky resists his first impulse to seduce Mildred. Because he resists her, Mildred "becomes infatuated." Soon Rogers, misinterpreting the tension and distance between Mildred and Lucky, "throws them together" so they will become friends. Mildred's seductive behavior becomes "obvious," and Rogers becomes so jealous that he makes Lucky's stunt dangerous. "Lucky, rankling from unearned jealousy, decides to earn it," but by the time he and Mildred have become lovers, Rogers has apologized for his suspicions. When the truth comes out, Rogers and Lucky arrange a divorce. In the climactic stunt, Lucky is driven by his "conscience" to take wild risks, but Rogers saves him. "Then Lucky knows how sincere Rogers is—how much in love with Mildred he is. And when Rogers starts to bail out,

Lucky learns how much she is really in love with her husband." This synopsis, then, loosely follows the original story but "cleans up" the characters' motivations. It also makes Mildred the sexual aggressor.

In his 24 January screenplay (114 pages in the Script Department format), Behn told a more complex story. Here, Mildred is an accomplished parachutist; she and her manager, Harris, have seen pilots come and go. The script opens with her parachuting from the plane flown by her current lover, the former "war ace" Pusher Graham, and introduces Pusher's "heavy, stupid, good-natured" handyman, Willie. (Much of this is similar to *Pylon*, raising the remote possibility that the novel was influenced by Behn's script.) At the field, Harris meets Rogers and offers him a job, but Rogers has an offer to fly the mail in Utah. To show his scorn for Pusher's skill, Rogers loops around him during the next stunt; Mildred loses control and ends up parachuting into a woods. Rogers finds Mildred and takes her back to the hotel, where she invites him to meet Pusher. The two men recognize each other from Amiens ("Ad Astra") and quote the subadar to each other. Rogers tells Mildred "it makes a difference" that they were "buddies," resisting her sexual advances. Pusher invites Rogers to a poker game, loses to Rogers a diamond ring Mildred had given him, and later kills himself by deliberately nose-diving his plane. Because she loves him and needs his plane, Rogers decides to stay on with Mildred.

During the next two months Rogers becomes infatuated with Mildred, and they perfect a new act. Mildred, however, does not like men to depend on her affection and in fact prefers them to "despise" her; as Rogers warms up, she cools off. Their new stunt calls for Mildred to step from the plane's ladder onto a surfboard. Rogers, overcautious, misjudges the distance; Mildred falls into the ocean, hurting her ankle, and is pulled out by Lucky, a lifeguard who used to be a wing-walker and a "big shot in air pictures." Lucky and Rogers become friends. Harris, who blames Rogers for taking Pusher's woman, ring, and job, leaves to join the police force; before he goes he lectures Mildred.

> MILDRED (contemptuously): So the famous war ace ended it all! Why dont you blame me? I gave him the air. I was sick of him and told him so. I warned him that morning I was going to pick up the next guy who came along that could do me some good. Why dont you blame *me*!
> HARRIS: Nobody'd expect anything more from you anyway. Jack Rogers was Pusher's buddy in the war! That made it dirty, see. He should have kept hands off when he found that out. That's honor.
> MILDRED: A man's virtue—too much to expect of a woman!

Mildred is being ironic in that last line, of course, but Harris goes on to say much the same thing with no irony.

Lucky performs a brilliant jumping stunt (filling in for Mildred) and joins the act. Rogers leaves them alone overnight while he flies to Utah to confirm the mail job. Lucky, who likes Rogers and is intimidated by being trusted, accompanies Mildred and Harris to a party on a gambling ship. Arsonists burn the ship, and reporters at the scene spot the famous stunt flyers. The next morning Rogers returns; Mildred says she had an uneventful night. Rogers opens the paper to a story about the gambling ship and the flyers, realizes she has been lying, and becomes jealous of Lucky. In the stunt that day, Rogers flies recklessly, endangering Lucky. By the time Rogers decides that his suspicions have been unfounded, Lucky has decided to earn the jealousy and has given in to Mildred's seductiveness.

In the next scene Mildred kisses Lucky in front of Rogers, revealing all; her motive is to show Rogers she is not the wifely type and to force him to leave her. She is confused by Lucky's coldness and fears he doesn't love her; Lucky tells her to keep quiet and let the men settle things. Rogers gives Mildred up. The next day Lucky takes wild chances in their stunt, and Rogers saves him. Finally, Rogers sends Mildred the ring he had gotten from Pusher; she gives it to Lucky, then realizes what Rogers intends. The script ends with Rogers's killing himself by nose-diving his plane as Pusher had (at the last minute he decides to live, but cannot pull out of the spin).

This script includes a few scenes and details from "Honor," especially near the end, and works in the memories of Amiens in some dialogue between Pusher and Rogers. It builds loosely on the attitude toward male bonding implicit in the original story but loses the snappy bitterness of Monaghan's narration (similar to James M. Cain's) and the ironic, tense, ambivalent quality of the sense of honor that emerges between Buck and Rogers. The key to these changes is, of course, the character of Mildred. Perhaps to avoid censorship difficulties, the writers have no married couples in the script, and Mildred is presented as a destructive and sharp woman who is fatal to the men around her; Pusher is introduced to show the cyclical quality of Mildred's selfish relationships. It is clear both with Rogers and with Lucky that she has no sense of honor, and the script accordingly declines to leave her in anything like a stable marriage. What remains honorable—the code of male bonding—is likewise more conventional than what Faulkner presented in his story, and on the whole Honor is a fairly typical example of the ways Faulkner's

fiction was "cleaned up" and simplified by Hollywood profession-
als, a pattern that obtains from *The Story of Temple Drake* to *The
Tarnished Angels*.[5]

NOTES: INTRODUCTION TO *HONOR*

1. Faulkner, *Collected Stories*, 558.
2. Blotner, *Faulkner: A Biography*, 795.
3. Blotner, *Selected Letters*, 73.
4. Blotner, *Faulkner: A Biography*, 795–96.
5. See Kawin, *Faulkner and Film*, 14–68, for synopses and interpreta-
tions of the films made from Faulkner's fiction. In Furthman's revision of
Honor, Mildred fares better; she has the same motivations, but
Furthman—who wrote many of Marlene Dietrich's strongest roles—makes
it easier to understand her unsentimental perspective. "Willie," she says
once, "how'd you like somebody to think you're the sun and the moon with
a box of candy thrown in! I know what I am! I'm selfish and bad-tempered.
And somehow he [Rogers] makes me act like I was sweet and generous and
all that—as if I was sixteen and in love for the first time." Willie says,
"Maybe you are," and she snaps, "Don't kid yourself." On the whole,
Furthman's script is tougher and more adult; the question of honor is never
directly mentioned, and the plot is more economical. Some relevant
changes: Pusher beats Rogers in the poker game but deliberately crashes
his plane in a fog because he sees he is losing Mildred. Rogers is cold to
Mildred until she is hurt in the surfboard stunt; then he realizes how much
she means to him. Harris has wired Lucky, a famous stunt pilot, to join the
act; his motive is to "get even for Pusher." Lucky arrives in time to watch
the surfboard fiasco, but it is Willie who pulls Mildred out of the water.
Mildred resents Rogers's possessiveness, and when she finds out (through
Willie) that Rogers has a wife and child, she feels that she is "free" and
seduces Lucky. Rogers—who is in the middle of divorce proceedings
anyway—realizes that Mildred has just been looking for an excuse and
beats her. Lucky and Rogers have a confrontation, but they do not arrange
anything about Mildred. They perform their stunt, and after Rogers has
saved Lucky, Rogers simply flies away, leaving the couple to their own
devices. At the finish, Willie tosses a coin with two heads and says, "That's
life." It is not clear why this script was not approved for production.

The two-headed coin is a significant prop in *Only Angels Have Wings*,
written by Furthman for Hawks; the 1939 film also includes a line that
would recur in *To Have and Have Not*—"I'm hard to get: all you have to do
is ask"—which, along with numerous further points of overlap, suggests
that *Honor* was written for Hawks; that *Flying the Mail, Honor, Ceiling
Zero, Pylon, Only Angels Have Wings*, and *To Have and Have Not* are
closely interrelated (with Hawks the linking figure); and that Furthman
and Faulkner were brought together by Hawks long before they collabo-

rated on *To Have and Have Not* and *The Big Sleep*. In the last two films, by the way, they did not actually work together: Faulkner prepared the shooting script of *To Have and Have Not* after Furthman had finished several early drafts, and Furthman revised *The Big Sleep* during the shooting of Faulkner and Leigh Brackett's script.

Mythical Latin-American
Kingdom Story

Untitled and undated, Faulkner's last full-length screenplay for MGM was given the working title of *Mythical Latin-American Kingdom Story* and copied in the Script Department by 26 August 1933. A 110-page File Copy of that version exists, but the facsimile in this volume is of Faulkner's own 89-page typescript (93 pages, counting inserts). Although the typescript is full of typos, strike-outs, flying capitals, and penciled marginal notes (made by the Script Department in the course of copying), it has sufficient historical interest and curiosity value to compensate for these problems in legibility. Particularly since there is not much difficulty in reading the words Faulkner struck out with a /-mark, the typescript provides an opportunity to study some of his compositional practices at first hand.

Faulkner's salary was cut to $300 a week as of 18 March 1933, and MGM recorded $1,061.55 in "continuity costs" on *MLAK*, so it is likely that this script was written in less than a month, probably between mid-March and mid-April of that year. In a 22 June memo to F. L. Hendrickson, Sam Marx noted that Faulkner "at the time we took him off payroll [i.e., 13 May] was working on an untitled story which he has since delivered to us" and asked Hendrickson to authorize Faulkner's request "to novelize this story." Hendrickson complied on 27 June, agreeing with Marx that "the original story which he turned in is very unsatisfactory" and that "we may find a better basis for a motion picture in his novelization." Although Faulkner's request for these rights indicates that he felt *MLAK* had serious possibilities, there is no evidence that he actually began such a novel. On 24 August, Marx sent Faulkner a contract assigning MGM the rights to the *MLAK* screenplay and authorized the Script Department to copy the manuscript. All these memos, together with the tenuous state of Faulkner's employment, suggest a possible explanation for the unbalanced and unfinished quality of the script, which is carefully detailed and motivated at the start but whose conclusion suffers from many contradictions and loose ends. It is possible that Faulkner did most of the writing in March and early April, held on to the script for polishing and revision, and then hastily wrapped it up when he was fired—perhaps with the intention of working out the details and resolutions in a more complex fictional treatment.

To this day, Marx is certain that he was the only MGM executive to have read *MLAK* and that Faulkner was quite disappointed at the studio's lack of interest in the property. Despite the fact that Hawks was preparing a production of *Viva Villa* at the time (completed by Jack Conway), Marx recalls that "Back in my day they stayed away from revolution stories, Central American in particular. So I think that it had an onus on it at the time that it was written; they didn't want to make that kind of movie." Once Marx had decided that *MLAK* was better than it had at first appeared, he was unable to interest a producer in handling it: "Thalberg was ill and away almost the entire first half of 1933; he had a serious heart attack, then went to Europe for a tonsil operation. Irving might have been interested in something like that, but while he was away and Mayer was operating the studio, Mayer never read a script; he was more or less marking time until Thalberg came back. That period was almost a vacuum at the studio until David Selznick appeared—because without Thalberg to say 'I've read it and I think it'll make a good picture,' it was almost impossible to get a producer to read anything." The success of the Cuban revolution in the late 1950s rekindled Marx's enthusiasm for the script; in retrospect, he felt that the Chief bore "an uncanny resemblance to what many of us imagined Fidel Castro to be like, in those early days when he was just a shadowy figure of a rebel in a mountain lair."[1]

Faulkner's treatment of revolutionary politics in *MLAK* bears an interesting but coincidental resemblance to that of Hemingway. In the 1933–37 *To Have and Have Not*, Hemingway's Cuban terrorists justify robbing a bank in terms of ridding the country of American imperialism and big capitalist interests,[2] and his later *For Whom the Bell Tolls* features a hard-headed and assertive woman who sounds and acts very much like *MLAK*'s Maria Rojas. Since there is no possibility of Hemingway's having read *MLAK*, and the Spanish Civil War did not begin till 1936, it seems likely that both authors drew similar conclusions from their independent observations of the political unrest in Cuba between 1929 and 1933, when the Machado regime was embattled with terrorist and student groups. This situation was coming to a boil when Faulkner was writing *MLAK* and culminated in a general strike during August 1933—but the leader who emerged was Batista: hardly a Castro, let alone a possible model for Faulkner's gentlemanly Chief. What is particularly Faulknerian about the politics of *MLAK* is the emphasis on "chivalry" (see p. 28), a code to which the Chief subscribes and which Maria callously exploits in the "gringo" she manipulates (Bowden, the American pilot). This emphasis on honor and romantic idealism, which bears little or no resemblance to authentic left-wing priorities (a subject on which Hemingway is relatively better informed), finds expression in the rhetorically inflated dialogue and in the strained poses of many of the characters in *MLAK*. But it also tends to confirm that Faulkner had on his mind not only the Cuban upheavals but also Joseph Conrad's complex study of ethics and revolution in a "mythical Latin-American kingdom," *Nostromo: A Tale of the Seaboard* (1904).

While it would not be accurate to identify *MLAK* as an adaptation of *Nostromo*, there is considerable overlap between the two. Both fictitious countries include cities named Rincon (literally "corner" or "nook"). A minor figure in *MLAK* is named Guzman; Guzman Bento is a dictator in *Nostromo*. Toward the end of *MLAK* (p. 84), there is a joke to the effect that Bowden, the trusted pilot, "could just as easily fly away with the gold as to bring it in"—which is of course what the trusted and honorable Nostromo does with the silver shipment in Conrad's novel. Above all, there is the shared central importance of an American-controlled mine, one of whose regular bullion shipments could affect the course of an anti-imperialist revolution. Conrad is considerably more ironic than Faulkner about the relations between "material interest" and revolution, and the literary merit of *MLAK* is in no way comparable to that of *Nostromo*, but Conrad's influence here is distinct, not only in certain details but also in the general focus on ethics. Since Faulkner's interest in Conrad was profound and lifelong, these correspondences may lend *MLAK* special significance as a partial guide to his reading of his great precursor.

There is also some overlap between *MLAK* and a number of Faulkner's short stories and scripts. Two 1926 stories, "Black Music" and "Carcassonne," are set in Rincon, and a character in the 1940 "Pantaloon in Black" (later included in *Go Down, Moses*) is named Birdsong. Blotner has identified Otto Birdsong of *MLAK* as one model for Jiggs of *Pylon*, in that both are airplane mechanics who have deserted their families.[3] Birdsong himself represents a reworking of Das in *Manservant* (he has a doglike devotion to Bowden, who saved his life in France) and the Beery character in *Flying the Mail* (who had deserted his wife and daughter). Marion, Birdsong's daughter, is similarly modeled on the heroine of *Flying the Mail*, especially in her determination to seek out her wastrel father. And like most of Faulkner's MGM scripts, *MLAK* devotes considerable attention to World War I aviators.

One of the most interesting aspects of *MLAK* is its treatment of women. While Bowden's fiancée (Nancy) is a conventional feminine stereotype, the revolutionary Maria Rojas is forceful, experienced, and politically astute; her lack of sentimentality is presented not as a flaw but as an asset, just as her autonomy is not presented as being at the expense of her husband's masculinity (a significant difference between *MLAK* and *For Whom the Bell Tolls*). The character who is caught between these two paradigms of female behavior, Marion Birdsong, bears a certain similarity to Ann in *Turn About*. In the third draft of *Turn About*, Ann endures a lecture from the vicar to the effect that anatomy is destiny, both in love and in politics:

> ANN: Philosophies are not for women. You have told me so yourself.
> VICAR: But you have something else, something better, which nature has provided since you are a woman.
> ANN: What?
> VICAR: Marry. Have children. If you must be bereaved, be left a mother as well as a widow.
> ANN: Love? I? Love is as dead as grief, as hope.
> VICAR: There are times in the lives of women, even more than in those of men, when they must have a sublime and unreasoning faith in something even beyond hope, or perish.

Like Ann, Marion feels herself unable to love, and like Ann she rejects the priest's advice in favor of active political engagement—in the course of which she finds love. (*MLAK* includes several unresolved hints that Marion will become the Chief's wife; this image of the motherless child who wins the heart of the prince of a foreign land clearly owes much to fairy tales, which are of course rich in feminine stereotypes.) Here is the comparable scene in *MLAK*:

> GIRL: I dont grieve for her; I envy her.
> PRIEST: Come, come. This wont do. You cannot escape life, your appointed destiny, this way.
> GIRL: What is my appointed destiny?
> PRIEST: To be bereaved; to conquer death in turn by producing life.
> GIRL: I? Marry? Marry? I?
> PRIEST: God created woman to be the companion and the cherished of man.
> GIRL (Laughs wildly, bitterly): No, thanks. Not for me. I had a man for father once. [p. 8]

The dramatic energy in both these scenes is on the side of the women, who in any case have the best lines. Rejecting conventional marriage roles, Ann and Marion commit themselves to courses of revenge and action, achieving relative self-determination in their respective roles of ambulance worker and secret agent. But it cannot be ignored that both of them end up (taking hints in *MLAK* about the Chief at full value) in the arms of heroic men, almost as if the priests had been right. What Faulkner seems to be implying—and it is not at all clear whether he is being intentionally ironic about this—is that women should not accept conventional roles but instead discover them in the course of an independent adventure. There is a great deal of irony in the fact that the revolutionaries want Marion's role in their plot to be that of a feminine seductress; this leaves the impression that what is most untamed about Marion is not her rejection of any feminine stereotype but her anger toward men and particularly toward her father, an anger that apparently dissipates when she discovers that its object (Otto) is a pathetic drunk. The script's emphasis on chivalry, then, is not at odds with its relatively complex spectrum of female psychology: although Maria objects to the Chief's calling her "Doña" (p. 62), Marion is not far removed from the prototype of Cinderella or Snow White (particularly the latter, since toward the end of the script she becomes so passive).

An MGM reader who examined *MLAK* on 9 June 1933 (before it had been retyped) found it "A very ordinary story, with one or two characters that might have been very interesting if the author had taken the trouble to develop them." While it does not seem reasonable to call this story "ordinary," it is certainly true that Faulkner's development of both plot and character here is skimpy. While Marion's story is carefully developed from the time of her mother's search for Otto (which occasions an effective montage of newspaper headlines and items from the personals column—see pages 6–7) to the moment when she meets her father, the last third of the script hardly mentions her, and one is very much in the dark concerning her final attitudes toward the revolution, let alone her possible romance with the Chief. The ins and outs of Maria's plans to manipulate Bowden and Otto so that the gold in their plane can be stolen to aid the revolutionary cause are remarkably unclear, even when she explains them (as on p. 28). Since the gold had been unloaded (not to say confiscated) hours before the elaborate charade at Bowden's expense had begun, and since all the revolutionaries learned from Otto was that Bowden did not have the key that would indirectly render his plane operational, it is hard to see what the purpose of the charade might have been. There is clearly no need to fly the gold anywhere, and neither Bowden nor Otto is in a position to guard the shipment. Furthermore, the mine-owner takes the news of the loss of a ton of gold and the evidence of an overnight coup with incredible ease and good humor (pp. 85–86). The Chief is dropped from the story at the moment when he meets his long-lost sister and is about to take over the country. Otto never finds out who Marion is. Finally, the crucial scene between Bowden and Maria Rojas (pp. 79–81) hangs on an interchange of very obscure inferences that somehow convey the impression that Maria's plot has been successful without saying how; it seems important that Bowden be manipulated, out of chivalry, into offering to fly Marion out of the country, but it is not clear what that might have to do with the gold, which has in any case already been confiscated by the rebels. It must be that to control Bowden is to have access to future shipments.

Maria, the trickster, might, then, wish to extend her control of Bowden into the future, perhaps by counting on his compassion for the imprisoned Marion; in this light, Maria's insuring that Bowden remains in White's employ, but not bound in marriage to White's (via Nancy's) best interests, begins to make sense. She may even be trying to ward off some future counterrevolutionary gesture on Bowden's part; if this is true, then the conclusion of *MLAK* is less ragged than it at first appears, since it demonstrates the triumph of Maria's plans to control Bowden and rearrange his personal life. The trouble is that the evident focus of her plan is to seize the particular gold shipment Bowden has just flown into port; her control of Bowden is only a means to that end, and it is clearly established that the revolutionaries need only a single shipment's worth to finance their efforts. Another problem is that Maria is aware of the Chief's feelings for Marion. To have an intricate plot occupy the center of this story and then prove somehow irrelevant to the course of the revolution (unless I am simply missing some of the deeper workings of the plot) seems unfortunate, if not an indication of carelessness on Faulkner's part. Yet there must have been something about *MLAK* that prompted Faulkner's desire to turn it into a novel, and it is to be hoped that some evidence of that survives in this draft of the script.

For *MLAK* is baffling, and sticks with one, in much the way Faulkner's most involuted novels irritated their first readers. The unfathomable quality of Maria's plans may represent an authorial flourish rather than a failure, putting the audience in Bowden's position, as both learn simply that the balance of power has shifted and are equally unable to figure out how that happened (compare the confusing plot of *The Big Sleep*). *MLAK* is not just an inflated revolutionary fairy tale, but also a dark comedy, and it might be best described as a dialectical structure with those tones at its poles. In his previous scripts, Faulkner had demonstrated that he could do professionally linear work, but *The College Widow* and *Absolution* in particular attest that he did not abandon his characteristic interest in psychological complexity and deeply buried emotional conflict. It is in *MLAK* that the sense of underlying if not inaccessible conflict is most tantalizing, and here too that the diegetic presentation is most complex. What the tangles of this script suggest, then, is that in *MLAK* Faulkner experimented with nonlinearity and repression from much the same authorial vantage point that served him so well as a novelist, and that may well have been the reason he considered recasting it in fiction.

NOTES: INTRODUCTION TO *MYTHICAL LATIN-AMERICAN KINGDOM STORY*

1. Blotner, *Faulkner: A Biography*, 800. All other Marx quotes are from my interview with him in Los Angeles in 1980.
2. Ernest Hemingway, *To Have and Have Not* (New York: Scribner's, 1937), esp. 166–67. For a brief review of relevant Cuban history, see Kawin, ed., *To Have and Have Not*, 10; see 16–18 for the personal relationship between Hemingway and Faulkner.
3. Blotner, *Faulkner: A Biography*, 866. Also see 1795 for a possible connection between *MLAK* and *The Reivers*.

NOTES: SCRIPT OF *MYTHICAL LATIN-AMERICAN KINGDOM STORY*

P. 1 [margin]: At the top of the page Marx wrote "Untitled, by William Faulkner." Other hands wrote "Mythical"—a note toward the working title—and "3598," the file number. Throughout the script a typist wrote in scene numbers (1 through 78) and underscored words that were to be capitalized in their entirety. There are also several occurrences of "start" near hasty pencil strokes that undoubtedly marked points where the copying had been interrupted. None of these marks and numbers will be annotated, but they are useful in tracing the ways Faulkner's other manuscripts may have been converted into conventional script format. The Script Department version is almost identical with Faulkner's typescript, but the format is like that of *War Birds*. Because the final sheet of Faulkner's typescript is badly torn, the final page of the Script Department version is included as well; thus, the characteristic format changes can be examined first hand.

P. 1 [narrative], "as she thrusts through the crowd at a croner": Corner (typo).

P. 1 [narrative], "People in the crowd tu n to him": Turn (impression). Many of the letters in this script were faintly struck; only those that might prove confusing will be annotated. In the next line, for instance, "trying" seems sufficiently legible.

P. 1 [headline], "YANKS CAPTURE SAINT MIHIEL": On 12 Sept. 1918, the American army in France, in its first major offensive, overwhelmed the German fortifications at Saint-Mihiel.

P. 1 [Child], " ama, did it say where Pop is?": Mama (impression).

P. 1 [Newsboy], " ost your old man, eh?": Lost (impression).

P. 2 [Woman], "The folks that wri e them": Write (impression).

P. 2 [narrative], "RESOLVE": Come out of the dissolve to:

P. 2 [Sentry], " ooking for the old man": Looking (typo). The script is full of flying capitals. From now on, only those that might prove confusing (especially the Ls and Is that look like hyphens) will be annotated.

P. 2 [Sentry], "That guy—his name is O to—": Otto (impression).

P. 2 [Sentry], "He done a Steve Brodie into the army": I.e., took a flying leap. Brodie claimed to have jumped from the Brooklyn Bridge.

P. 4 [Captain], "His alotment has stopped comming": Allotment . . . coming (typos). Only misspellings that might prove confusing will be annotated. The captain's "to day," for instance—about 20 lines down from this one—can be easily understood as "today," while "eneters" (third line from the bottom of the page) seems to deserve a textual note: "enters."

P. 5 [Sergeant], "A.E.F.": Allied Expeditionary Forces, under the command of General Pershing.

P. 5 [Sergeant], "He probaly wouldn't know": Probably (typo).

P. 5 [Sergeant], "Not ing, mostly, I expect": Nothing (impression).

P. 6 [Sergeant, narrative], "holds paper, musi g, still)": Musing (impression). In the next direction, "put it into her hand" should read "puts" (typo).

P. 6 [narrative], "C–OCK": CLOCK, a camera direction calling for a pan or a dolly movement. See note to p. 26 [Avilas].

P. 6 [headline], "WILSON A LAUZANNE": "AT" (impression), "LAUSANNE" (typo). The next headlines should read "COSSACKS WIPE OUT WHITE VILLAGE" and "WARREN G. HARDING ELECTED." This sequence of headlines would by itself represent a conventional Hollywood montage, but with the intercut personals it more closely resembles parallel if not dialectical montage. Faulkner may have been influenced here by John Dos Passos's U.S.A., as Dos Passos was by Eisenstein.

P. 7 [headline], "PLURALITY A PROPHESY OF MILEN IUM OF ORLD PROSPERITY": "MILLENNIUM," "WORLD" (typo and impression).

P. 7 [headline], "NATIONS AGREE DISARMAMENT WILL BE CURE FOR WORLD BANKRUPTCY": Some of these words are obscured. These headlines cumulatively provide an ironic perspective on Wilson's "War to end war"—closing with notice of a Japanese invasion—and introduce the theme of the crisis of capitalism and its relation to the exercise of power ("HOOVER ORDERS TROOPS TO DISPERSE BONUS MOB OF UNEMPLOYED," etc.). Faulkner is laying careful ground work for a story of revolution, though it should be noted that *MLAK* will end with the restoration of a monarch rather than with a workers' state.

P. 7 [narrative], "He speaks to her in pantomine": Pantomime (typo). Two lines down, the obscured word is "kneeling." Four lines below that, the obscured word is "strained."

P. 8 [Priest], "[liv]ing acn not wait upon the dead": Can (typo).

P. 8 [Girl], "I dont grieve fo her": For (impression).

P. 8 [Priest], "to con uer death": Conquer (impression). His next speech begins with the word "God" (impression).

P. 8 [Woman], "—for rhem—": Them (typo). The obscured word four lines above this is "follow," and there are several flying capital Is.

P. 8 [narrative], "DISSOLVE to / A tenement street . . . look at one": These three lines, though marked as Scene 13, ought to have been deleted. They are a first draft of the beginning of the scene at the top of p. 9.

P. 9 [narrative], "Rear of store. A door": "A" is obscured.

P. 9 [narrative], "A room. A single portrait": "A" is obscured.

P. 10 [Chief], "which will sweep tyrrany and oppression—": Tyranny (typo). This speech is meant to indicate that the Chief will not be a conventional monarch, but a man of the people. He also exhibits an oddly patronizing view of women, arguing that his life might not mean more to God than Marion's grief, but that his death would mean more to his country than Marion's erratic behavior (or her grief).

P. 10 [Second], "Veritably, a wife. One in ten thousand": Nostromo is regularly referred to as "One in a thousand."

P. 11 [Rojas], "Were she tyrant president of our unhappy country instead of that accursed, an army of ten thousand beautiful women could not dislodge her": Some of these words are obscured, but so is the logic. Once a woman is imagined in power, it appears necessary to imagine her overthrown only by women who exceed her in beauty and numbers. Even granting that, the Third's "luckily for us" makes no sense, since they are not a band of women.

P. 11 [Chief], "Tres Hermanos": Literally, "Three Brothers"—a fictitious battle. In his next speech, the typo should read "old-fashioned."

P. 11 [Rojas], "since a nation, a country, is the mother of men": This is apparently the logic at the heart of the script, if not a convoluted metaphor for spanking the current dictator. Its intent is to justify women's role in politics.

P. 11 [Third], "Donna Maria": Doña (typo), a term of respect.

P. 12 [Maria], "Your li tle shop": Little (impression).

P. 12 [Pedro], "Manual": Manuel (typo); i.e., Rojas.

P. 12 [Maria], "on that dyy, I say": Day (strikeover); i.e., the battle at Tres Hermanos.

P. 13 [Maria], "since our mother land spawns only adolescents": This expands Rojas's metaphor (see p. 11). On p. 22 she speaks of her "fatherland."

P. 13 [Rojas], " ell, then?": Well (typo). In his next line, "What news?", the "W" is also high.

P. 13 [Chief], "Three hundred years age": Ago (typo). Note the shift to "fatherland," which suits his impatience with Maria. The obscured word five lines below is "bleeding."

P. 14 [narrative], "The othres look at him": Others (typo).

P. 14 [Chief], "Assasin's buttet!": Assassin's bullet (typos).

P. 16 [Maria], "Even thuogh him whom your tears indict": Though (typo).

P. 16 [Girl], "-es.": Yes (typo). The obscured phrases in this speech are "I dont have to cry" and "if I were only a man!" Marion's point is that she is crying not out of grief for her mother but in anger at her father.

P. 17 [Maria], "And there is yet one more an's act": Man's (impression). Six lines down, the parentheses close after "hypnotised."

P. 17 [Maria], "What partof": Part of (typo). In her next speech, "time if enclosed" should read "time it enclosed," "MAEION'S" should read "MARION'S," and "wruoght" should read "wrought" (typos).

P. 18 [Maria], "See By": See? (typo). Other obscured words are "(she turns" and "Here, in her father's blood."

P. 18 [Maria], "starts to remove glove) MARIA stops her": The parentheses should not close after "glove." Ten lines below: "Then foreigners began to enter our country." Six lines below that: "It is of one of these men I speak." Three lines below that: "regurgitated." Next line down: "I will not try to tell you all; I." Five lines below that: "He went unarmed." "Assassin" is usually misspelled. (Typos.) In this speech Maria performs the complex feat of convincing Marion that the Chief and his sister were orphaned, like Marion, by the actions of Otto Birdsong (a lie, of course; on p. 14 the assassin's death at the Chief's gloved hand was described). The civil war is presented as the work of money-hungry foreigners; this reinforces the theme of capitalist imperialism, while also giving "the old times" in Rincon the feeling of prelapsarian innocence. The old king's decision to meet his enemies unarmed echoes the death of Faulkner's great-grandfather, the prototype of Colonel John Sartoris, and may indicate some imaginative overlap between *MLAK* and *War Birds* in the genesis of "An Odor of Verbena."

P. 19 [Maria], "that I do not know": The "I" is high. Her next line should probably read: "But she is dead, and her daughter these five years . . ."

P. 19 [narrative], "MARION, who lo ks": Looks (impression).

P. 19 [Maria], "that man who fi ed that shot": Fired (impression).

P. 20 [Maria], "Next to MANuel": In directions, names are capitalized along with sound effects and camera movements. Faulkner often slips into this habit during dialogue passages; here he corrects himself in mid-word. These slips will not be annotated.

P. 20 [narrative], "his hands clasp before him": Clasped (typo).

P. 20 [Avilas], "She told us it w uld": Would (impression).

P. 21 [narrative], "ans MARIA and MARION are in the room": A typo for "and," though "as" is possible.

P. 23 [Maria], "And you restore their fatherland to these men. and you too will find a father": "And" should be capitalized (typo). Maria is manipulating Marion on many familial levels, first arousing her sympathy for the orphaned sister (prompting identification with her) while urging her to be free from male domination and to avenge her mother—then shifting the terms from sisterhood to patriarchy in this speech and arguing that Marion will soon find a spiritual father-figure. It becomes tempting here to read the script in Freudian terms, as if Marion were being led through an identification with femaleness to a maturity in which she can transfer her need for love to a male image—the basic Freudian model of female sexual development.

P. 23 [Rojas], "Just what hve you": Have (typo). In his next speech, the "I" in "I, who have been a husband" is high.

P. 23 [Maria], "— told her": I told her (flying capital).

P. 24 [narrative], "The tramping feet pace camera toa door": To a (typo). Two lines down the "T" in "They look" is high.

P. 24 [narrative], "MARIA again, cold, implicable": Implacable (typo).

P. 25 [Marion, direction], "breathing fast, rembling)": Trembling (impression).

P. 26 [Avilas, direction], "PAN to photo of BOWDEN": Some of these words are obscured. The correct use of the term PAN here suggests that Faulkner generally meant CLOCK to call for a track or dolly movement.

P. 27 [Avilas], "to be deliberatelt thrown": Deliberately (typo). Two lines below, the obscured word is "touching."

P. 27 [clipping], "the Trsx Hermanos mines": Tres (typo). The mine and the crucial battle are effectively interrelated by being set at the same location. The next direction should begin "PAN back" (typo).

P. 27 [Maria], "the body and the will?": Note the shift in terms that parallels a man's heart with a woman's body. Apparently Marion's heart, which might prompt her to fall in love with Bowden and thus make her a poor seductress, is not yet to be encouraged. What Maria wants from Marion is the use of her body.

P. 28 [Maria], "Would — have come this far": Would I (flying capital). Two lines down, Maria echoes the Chief's attitude toward the "vagaries" of young women (see p. 10). Two lines below that, "grongo" should be "gringo" (typo), i.e., an English-speaking foreigner. Three lines below that, "princilpe" should be "principle." Apparently, Maria's intricate plan is to seduce not Bowden's body but his sense of right and wrong, to arouse his compassion for a captive "compatriot."

P. 28 [Maria], "And if by doing so he can put her in o the arms of another": Into (impression). It is possible that "another" is the Chief, unless this is simply an observation on the American chivalrous mentality.

P. 28 [Avilas], "That is starnge": Strange (typo).

P. 28 [Maria], "It is moer than that. It is embecile": More . . . imbicile (typos). In the last line of this speech, "as" is obscured.

P. 28A [Chief], "And if she should not fa l in love": Fall (impression).

P. 28A [Chief], "a road fro which there can": From (impression). Three lines below, "words;" should read "words,"—and in the final line, "Then what?" is partially obscured.

P. 28A [Maria], "Then let her father protect her": Some of these words are obscured. This seems to set up an expectation Otto Birdsong is incapable of fulfilling, perhaps motivating the need for the Chief to protect Marion later.

P. 28A [Avilas], "-xcellency": Excellency (flying capital).

P. 29 [narrative], "-e stands almost proudly": He (flying capital).

P. 29 [Maria], " hat is true": That (impression). Five lines down, the obscured words are "mountains, I." The final line reads, "He chose the obscure and foreign girl." Note that Maria can manipulate even her king, who is coming to resemble Prince Charming.

P. 29 [Maria], "she will continue as she ahs acst her lot": Has cast (typos).

P. 29 [narrative], "-e bows his head": He (flying capital).

P. 30 [Chief], "I am bot much you senior": Not much your (typos). Four lines below, "I say to you know" should probably read "I say to you now."

P. 30 [Marion], "What si this?" Is (typo).

P. 30 [Maria], "Brother? father": In such lines Marx found evidence that Faulkner meant to suggest the Chief as a "Christlike figure."

P. 31 [margin]: Opposite "29" the typist wrote "Back to scene," indicating that the camera should not rest on Maria's face during the Chief's line and exit. In the following direction, "begin, grown louder" should read "begins, grows louder" (typos).

P. 32 [Soldier], "duros in gold; we, four copper pestas": A duro is a Spanish gold dollar (short for "peso duro" or "hard money"); a peseta (typo) is a smaller unit of Spanish currency, originally one-fourth of a "piece of eight."

P. 33 [narrative], "looking at approaching hord": Horde (typo). A peon is an unskilled or feudal laborer; a burro is a small donkey used as a pack animal.

P. 34 [Bowden], "Eddie Cantor": A famous vaudeville, radio, and Hollywood comedian. This baffling reference could be to his high-toned voice, to his popular song "Making Whoopee," or to his 1932 hit, *The Kid from Spain*. A more likely possibility: Cantor used to pop and roll his eyes, which in this context might be a dangerous way for Otto and Bowden to react to the odors. Cantor was also known for performing in blackface (i.e., the Americans are out of their racial element here).

P. 34 [Lieutenant], "The bags, senores": Some of these words are obscured. "Señores" means "gentlemen."

P. 35 [Lieutenant], "who no longer is please": Pleased (impression). By the end of the script, this lieutenant has done a political turnaround—though it is remotely possible that he is only pretending to oppose the malcontents and is somehow involved in the disappearance of the gold.

P. 36 [Lieutenant], "These dissatisfied people returned here from": Some of these words are obscured. The first word in his next speech is "Where."

P. 36 [Otto], "the spanner": An adjustable wrench.

P. 36 [Lieutenant], "They wil- be sent on to the hotel": Will (impression). Bowden's response begins, "So do I" (impression).

P. 36 [narrative], "they look at one aonther": Another (typo).

P. 36 [Bowden], "Get him the magneto": A small AC generator from the plane's ignition system. Apparently this procedure has been going on regularly, except that Bowden has usually been allowed to keep the key to the box. Now the plane is out of his control entirely. It seems the army wants to be sure that Bowden cannot fly off until the gold has been unloaded; it is also possible that the lieutenant is a revolutionary, but if that were so, the later business about the key would be unnecessary.

P. 37 [Otto], "these Spiks": Derogatory term for Spaniards and Spanish-Americans.

P. 37 [Otto], "I aint got a skirt waiting for me": "Skirt" is obscured (strikeover); the reference is to Nancy.

P. 38 [Otto], "Dont, chief": The use of "Chief' suggests that Faulkner is establishing a parallel buddy-structure between Bowden and Otto, and the Chief and Avilas (see p. 72).

P. 38 [Bowden], "mozos": Porters and errand-boys.

P. 38 [Bowden], "No spika": Pidgin for "I don't speak the language."

P. 39 [narrative], "sound ot engine begins. Men peer out tiward sound": Of . . . toward (typos).

P. 39 [Bowden], "Stay away from cantinas": Taverns.

P. 39 [Bowden], "and then b at it back here": Beat (impression).

P. 40 [Otto], "Howdy, amigos": Friends. His use of Spanish here indicates his unreliability, though the fact that Otto already knows some of these men ought to rule out the "No spika" tactic; thus, the fact that he goes on to try to take refuge in that ploy indicates further his lack of intelligence.

P. 40 [First], "our little drink together, as usial": Usual (typo).

P. 40B [narrative], "-an lowers paper": Man (flying capital). The typist marked this page "A" above "40-B"; apparently, Faulkner once had three pages between pp. 40 and 41, then condensed 40A and 40B into these few lines and neglected to renumber this and the C page.

P. 40C [Manager], "as usial": Usual (typo). His last line should read, "As soon as he reached the hotel."

P. 40C [narrative], "TRUCK to NANCY at phone": "Truck" is another term for a track or dolly shot. In this case the camera pivots horizontally (pans) to Carlota's face, then moves (trucks) back and over to show Nancy at the phone.

P. 41 [narrative], "PAN to CARLOTA'S face watching NANCY": This is an efficient visual means of indicating that Carlota is involved in the plot and the false message.

P. 41 [George], "I't all right": Probably a typo for "It's," though "I'm" is a possibility. Faulkner is not consistent in identifying speakers by a single name; here Bowden becomes George, as later on Rojas will become Manuel (see p. 54).

P. 42 [Nancy], "el capitan—Nonesence. Listen at me. . . . I would like why you said that": Nonsense (typo). "El capitan" (the captain) indicates that most of this conversation is going on in English. "Listen at me," since it is followed by a laugh, is probably not a typo. Her last line should probably be, "I would like to know why you said that." Her next speech, which is partially obscured, begins, "Nothing. You didn't say anything; that is true."

P. 43 [Carlota], "And now what shall - do?": Shall I do (flying capital).

P. 43 [narrative], "telephone booth, thou htful": Thoughtful (impression).

P. 43 [Bowden], "-t doesn't matter": It (flying capital).

P. 43 [Manager], "magnanimosity": Magnanimity or magnanimousness. This may not be a typo, since it could function both as a joke on the manager's English and as a pun on "animosity."

P. 44 [narrative], "BOWDEN pauses, hou htful alert": Thoughtful, alert (impression and typo).

P. 45 [narrative], "CARLOTA eneters": Enters (typo). The "CLOCK" at the head of this paragraph (bottom of p. 44) is not a camera direction but a prop.

P. 45 [Nancy, direction], "9restraining herself)": (restraining herself) (flying capital). It is remarkable how many of the young women in Faulkner's scripts suffer from hysterics, and how few in his fiction.

P. 46 [Nancy], "Trying to decieve me! What si it?" Deceive ... is (typos). Four lines above, the obscured word is "find."

P. 47 [Otto], "That's all - am": I (flying capital). Two lines down, "serted" is short for "deserted." "Unfortuniate" is probably a typo rather than an indication of drunkenness.

P. 48 [First], "To hell with that man, senors!": Señores (typo). This is not false logic but a turnaround to keep Otto happy.

P. 48A [First], "the best pilot in the wotld!": World (typo). The same typo appears in Otto's speech at the bottom of p. 49.

P. 53 [Avilas], "- have not forgot it": I (flying capital).

P. 53 [narrative], "She looks at AVILAS, col, still": A typo for "cold" or "cool."

P. 54 [narrative], "Again MARION galnces up": Glances (typo). Apparently, Marion is not playing the seductress but is unwittingly being used to embarrass Bowden in front of Nancy and to arouse Bowden's chivalry for a compatriot. At this point the role of the key to the magneto box is unclear.

P. 56 [Nancy, direction], "(cling to him": Clings (typo).

P. 57 [Nancy], "Tell me - dont understand": I (flying capital).

P. 57 [Marion, direction], "(with wild, azed air)": Dazed (impression). Like the Chief, Marion quickly puts away political considerations in the interest of a woman's feelings. Throughout the script, the choice seems to be between politics and sentiments, a choice reflected structurally in the centrality of this scene.

P. 57 [Nancy], "And thsi! ... 'I'm tired of yoy": This ... you (typos).

P. 58 [Bowden], "I dont know what is is, myself. - just": It is ... I just (strikeover and flying capital). In the next line, "come on to you" is colloquial for "come on over to you."

P. 58 [Bowden], "Well- You took that trick too": It is unclear what punctuation mark should have followed "Well." The "trick" metaphor is from card games: Maria has won the hand and picked up the cards.

P. 58 [Marion], "I wante to help": Wanted (impression). Three lines down, the typo should read "brother." Nancy and Bowden are not married yet, but nothing has been said to correct Marion's impression. It is possible that Maria's plan includes Marion's distress: that the main objective was not to break up Bowden's engagement but to arouse further his sympathy toward Marion.

P. 59 [Maria], "out of thsi room": This (typo).

P. 59 [Manuel], "That is ture, senor": True (typo). Manuel is Rojas (see note to p. 41).

P. 59 [Maria, direction], "she ooks at him": Looks (impression). Two lines down, "doyou" should read "do you." Note Maria's abrupt way of silencing her husband.

P. 60 [Maria], "jeopardised by he recalcitrance": The (impression).

P. 60 [Bowden, direction], "watching them with quiet, daze air": Dazed (impression).

P. 60 [Maria], "quitnow? Do you regret the life you use to": Quit now . . . used (typo and impression).

P. 60 [Bowden], "But - have watched": I (flying capital). Two lines down, the obscured phrase is "do you mind telling me just what."

P. 61 [Otto, direction], "She stands shriking": Shrinking (typo). Four and five lines above, "gorl" is a typo for "girl."

P. 61 [Manuel], " oftly, senor": Softly (impression).

P. 61 [Marion], "Have I got to wait here until": Some of these words are obscured.

P. 61 [Marion, direction], "(Goes int wild laughter": Into (typo). This father/daughter encounter is the emotional climax of the script. One can assume that if Marion were naked under the negligee, Faulkner would have mentioned it, but the implicit sexuality of the scene is still obvious.

P. 61 [Maria, direction], "(MANUEL eneters with cloak; they put around MARION": Enters . . . put it around (typos).

P. 62 [narrative], "as centry goes to door": Sentry (typo).

P. 62 [Chief], "- trust you": I (flying capital).

P. 62 [Chief], "What do you think, gentlemne?": Gentlemen (typo).

P. 62 [Chief], "They are here, then": Some of these words are obscured, and there should be a period after "then."

P. 62 [Chief], "True, he must remain in the employ of the mine, since he no longer has the key to the aeroplane. But why do you say free him now, Donna?": This question suggests another reading of Maria's original plot: to break up Bowden's engagement and discredit him with Nancy's father, on the assumption that Mr. White would fire Bowden. At that point, Bowden might have been willing to turn against his former employer and use the key to fly the plane to the mine, conceivably to steal another gold shipment for the benefit of the rebels, who might be counting on his and Otto's sympathy for Marion, their hostage. But all this is only a guess. At this point it seems they need Bowden to remain employed. "Donna" should read "Doña."

P. 63 [Maria], "She did that which I expected her to do": Some of these words are obscured. As usual, Maria has anticipated every turn of the plot—but compare her lines on p. 27.

P. 63 [Chief], "She saw thiw man": This (typo). In the Chief's previous speech, "qiuetly" is a typo for "quietly"; in his next, "qiuckly" should read "quickly."

P. 64 [Maria], "Not at o ce": Once (impression).

P. 64 [Avilas], "The Donna Maria . . . And she has not failed yet": Some of these words are obscured.

P. 64 [Chief], "-et them be taken. -ut do not harm him": Let . . . But (flying capitals).

P. 65 [Chief], "Five years and athousand miles of sea seperated us": A thousand . . . separated (typos). This offers a clue to Rincon's location. The Chief and Asuncion (p. 75) are another example of Faulkner's vision of intense brother-sister devotion.

P. 65 [Chief], "But three will escape where a dozen would": Some of these words are obscured.

P. 65 [Chief], "in particular - leave this girl": I (flying capital). Other obscured or mistyped passages in this speech: "She has put herself" (one line below); "but leave her as she is now" (three lines below that); "These hands which hold" (two below that); "hair of this girl's head" (six below that); "quiet dignity" (next line down); "How can I hope to father a people when I cannot brother one orphan girl?" (next three lines down); "But she was merely a foreigner" (four lines below); "listened to a child" (five lines below that); and "if I live to give a thousand others and you live to receive them" (next lines down).

P. 66 [Avilas], "To Las Vegas": Literally, a fertile lowland or plain.

P. 66 [narrative], "-e then.lo ks at MARION": He then looks (impression and paper flaw).

P. 66 [Bowden], "-e watches her) Visiting here with your people, - suppose?": He watches her). Visiting here with your people, I suppose? (typos).

P. 67 [Marion], "they . . . . die ?": Died? (impression). In the direction above, the obscured word is "looks."

P. 67 [narrative], "She sits quite still, shrinking, as he watches her. His ironical tone changes": Some of these words are obscured.

P. 68 [Marion], "Will they kill e too?": Me (impression).

P. 68 [Bowden], "Oh. - see": I (flying capital). At this point, Bowden's interpretation of the plot is that the rebels still need him to steal the plane; see note to p. 62.

P. 69 [Marion], "I can make her believe. - can": I (flying capital). The reference is to Nancy. Marion's strongest ties are consistently with other women (her mother, Nancy, and the image of Asuncion); in this scene, Faulkner seems to be implying that this is related to her sexual immaturity.

P. 69 [Marion], "I can. - know I can . . . some ing?": I . . . something (flying capital and impression).

P. 69 [narrative], "She falls back, her ahnds raised": Hands (typo).

P. 70 [Bowden], "-ll right": All (flying capital). In the last line of this speech, the obscured word is "couldn't."

P. 70 [Bowden, direction], "sits deside her)": Beside (typo).

P. 70 [narrative], "She closes ger eyes": Her (strikeover).

P. 71 [Otto, direction], "shamed air; quietw again)": Quiets (typo). The crosscutting of Otto's unknowingly incestuous impulses with the scene of Marion's asexual night in captivity gives further plausibility to a Freudian reading of Marion's sexual psychology. For Faulkner's interest in Freud, see Carvel Collins's introduction to Faulkner's *Mayday* (Notre Dame: Univ. of Notre Dame Press, 1980), 33–36. Appropriately, the element of marriage (in the relatively passive if not asexual prospect of Marion's being chosen by Prince Charming) is presented in the following scene, where the Chief declares his intentions. It seems reasonable to treat these three scenes as deliberately interrelated: a Gestalt—if not a dialectical montage—of Marion's sexual alternatives.

P. 71 [narrative], "Mountian trail, dawn breaking . . . b eathes a deep breath": Mountain . . . breathes (typo and impression).

P. 71 [Chief], "But now - am again a King": I (flying capital). The patriarchal element is very strong in this speech and reinforces the connection (undoubtedly at the heart of the logic of *MLAK*'s structure) between the well-run government and the stable family. At the negative extreme, Faulkner presents Otto's desertion of wife and daughter and Rincon's corrupt government (so that at least on the symbolic level, Maria's lie that Birdsong is responsible for assassinating the old monarch is not far wrong); on the positive side, he presents the Chief's vision of the patriarchal line and his love for Marion. The current of Marion's sexual psychology—and perhaps Faulkner's ambivalent view of postwar history—runs between these poles, and it is this hidden structure that gives *MLAK* some degree of coherence and relevance, despite its obvious flaws and loose ends.

P. 72 [Chief], "We were boys together": This pattern recurs in Faulkner's contributions to Hawks's *Land of the Pharaohs* (1955) and is another example of the recurring "buddy" theme in his MGM scripts. Four lines down, the mistyped line is "and I yours when we sang our first serenade."

P. 72 [Avilas], "Estabin": Esteban (typo). Faulkner continually attempts to balance inflated political rhetoric with a sense of personal intimacy.

P. 72 [Chief], "-o. I am not a king yet": No (flying capital). This almost contradicts his speech on p. 71, and Avilas catches the hint.

P. 73 [Avilas], "It is becaus - do not know": Because I (typo and flying capital).

P. 73 [Chief], "But I do know thsi": This (typo).

P. 74 [Chief], "Supposed my father's blood avenged, the tyrant's yoke lifted": Suppose (typo).

P. 75 [Guzman], "Madre de Dios!" Mother of God!

P. 75 [narrative], " DISSOLCE to / The cell, morning": DISSOLVE TO (typo). Again the intercutting is significant: the meeting of brother and sister is juxtaposed with the innocent embrace of Bowden and Marion. "Puzzical" is a coinage, on the model of "quizzical."

P. 75 [narrative], "then recognizes sistuation": Situation (typo). The reference is to Bowden's arm around her. Marion's extreme reaction goes beyond questions of propriety and suggests that she unconsciously desires Bowden.

P. 76 [Manuel], "in the vaudiville": Vaudeville (typo). On p. 82, White makes a comparable reference to "a stage scene," but these do not amount to a reflexive structure.

P. 77 [Bowden], "Suppose - dont want to go": I (flying capital).

P. 77 [Manuel], "Do y speak perchance of my wife": You (impression).

P. 78 [Manuel], "perhaps now we can l t this istol rest": Let this pistol (impression).

P. 78 [Bowden], "It I do, doubt ess you will be here": If . . . doubtless (typo and impression).

P. 79 [Bowden], "Gte out your pop gun": Get (typo). Obscured phrases in this speech: "tell me that this girl could," "Tell me that."

P. 79 [Bowden], " ery well. I'll take that dare and give you on in return. I dare you to": Very . . . one (impression).

P. 79 [Bowden], "I t o ght so": Thought (impression).

P. 80 [Manuel], "–hat I do not know": That (impression).

P. 80 [Manuel], "What shall – say to him (MARION muses)": I (flying capital).

P. 80 [Marion], "Say t is to him, MAnuel": This (impression). It should be noted that this is Marion's final scene. Although little information has been given about her plans for the future or her sense of her current situation, it is clear that she has reached a point where she is capable both of this selfless gesture (telling Bowden to forget her) and of "childlike" passivity. Her situation closely resembles that of the sequestered Sleeping Beauty.

P. 81 [margin]: The typist wrote "FIRST ROOM" opposite "70" to indicate a return to the previous setting.

P. 81 [Bowden], "- know when I am beat": I (flying capital). It is not at all clear how Marion's answer represents a victory for Maria, unless the implication is that Bowden will have to cooperate with Maria to secure Marion's release. On p. 85, it becomes clear that the gold has already fallen into rebel hands ("over night").

P. 81 [Maria], "Man proposes; circumstance disposes": The original saying is "Man proposes, God disposes." This change is appropriate for Maria and is also in line with period stereotyping of the revolutionary impulse as anticlerical.

P. 82 [Maria], "There will not be room for all": Some of these words are obscured.

P. 82 [Maria], "Fotever": Forever (typo).

P. 82 [Bowden], "That si true": Is (typo).

P. 82 [Bowden], "Then I will say goodbye": Some of these words are obscured.

P. 82 [narrative], "Fiacre drives up": A small hackney coach.

P. 82 [Bowden], "I guess you ahve heard": Have (typo). The reference is to his fight with Nancy.

P. 83 [White], "You're not trying to tell me that you were innocent":

Some of these words are obscured. Other obscured phrases: "the woman before," "understand a young," and "get mixed up."

P. 83 [narrative], "looking down, stobborn": Stubborn (typo).

P. 84 [White], "see her for a mo ent": Moment (impression). Other obscured phrases: "as fond of you," "can be, I suppose," "Thank God," and "They get over it."

P. 84 [servant], "-he is not well this morning": She (flying capital).

P. 84 [Bowden], "- guess I'm fired": I (flying capital).

P. 84 [White], "Did say you were?": Did I say (impression).

P. 84 [White], "both ring Nancy. I ahve your word": Bothering . . . have (impression and typo).

P. 84 [Bowden], "you'd bet er fire me": Better (impression). Bowden is probably thinking of Maria's hold over him.

P. 84 [White], "Do you w nt to quit?" Want (impression).

P. 84 [White], "get eve because Nancy—": Even (impression).

P. 84 [White], "what did you mean while ago": Awhile (typo). The first line of this speech should read, "Meaning that you could just as easily fly away with the gold as to bring it in?"

P. 84 [Bowden], "-ust do like I ask you": Just (flying capital).

P. 85 [narrative], "WHITE taps on desk, t oughtful": Thoughtful (impression).

P. 85 [McPherson], "I didn' say it left no trace": Didn't (impression). It seems odd that White would not have mentioned any of this to Bowden, since it is clear that McPherson is updating a situation with which White is already familiar. In the line below, "prade" is a typo for "parade."

P. 85 [White], "we ahve been expecting this. As you say, this country has been good to long": Have . . . too (typos). The final word of his unrealistically congenial speech should be "confiscation." Note the implicit comparison between this country and a child ("been good"), which is absent from McPherson's remark ("been peaceful").

P. 86 [narrative], "the negligee clutched in his ahnd": Hand (typo). Faulkner continues to emphasize the incestuous subtext via this negligee, though the negligee is equally important as an emblem of Maria's machinations.

P. 86 [Bowden], , "Come,on.Mop yourself off": Come on. Mop (paper flaw).

P. 86 [narrative], "where he aprawls, looking up as BOW EN": Sprawls . . . BOWDEN (typo and impression).

P. 87 [Otto], "You brpught her here": Brought (typo).

P. 87 [Otto], "even going to get the kimona": His version of "kimono," or robe; the reference is to the negligee, which Bowden lets him keep. There is considerable irony in making Otto's folding the negligee the conclusion of his relationship with the woman he does not realize is his daughter, but there is also an unfortunate impression of authorial haste: too much is left out.

P. 87 [narrative], "flivver": An old, cheap car. Faulkner had a beat-up Ford.

P. 87 [Otto], "What a head": Otto's hangover and Bowden's controlling nurturance are similar to aspects of the relationship between Morgan and Eddy in Faulkner's version of *To Have and Have Not*.

P. 88 [Bowden], "You didn't even know I intended": The pilots usually spend more than one night in town, so it is surprising to find the plane ready for their departure. Bowden first wonders whether Otto might have told them of their plans for a short visit, then dismisses that and suggests here that he might have "intended" to steal the plane. The fact that the plane is ready, and the lieutenant's attitude, suggest that the army is in league with the rebels, or at least knows all that has transpired.

P. 88 [Bowden], "Yes. I see that now": In this exchange, Bowden appears to accept that the situation is and will remain out of his control. Both he and the gold shipments will henceforth be subject to domestic (doubtless revolutionary) manipulation.

P. 88 [Lieutenant], "Permir me, senor": Permit (typo).

P. 89 [Otto], "take a littl   hop in our own ship, huh?": Little (typo).

P. 89 [Lieutenant], "It seems that you did not need them last night": This clinches the lieutenant's involvement in the plot.

P. 89 [Otto], "Sure I';; get set with it": I'll (typo).

P. 89 [Bowden], "I hope it will se safe. anyway": Be safe anyway (typos).

P. 89 [bottom]: The torn lines read: "Engine catches. Otto enters ship, engine increases and carries through DISSOLVE to SHIP—TAKING OFF. Diminishes above pass, sound dies away."

3598

VAULT COPY

original

MYTHICAL LATIN-AMERICAN KINGDOM
STORY

8-26-33

449

Untitled
by William Faulkner

A city street, the people mostly women er old men, to
establish the summer of 1918. A woman, poor, in a shabby
dress, a shawl over her head, leading a girl of about
ten by the hand. The woman has a tired, anxious face
as she thrusts through the crowd at a croner, where a man
standing on a box is making a liberty loan speech.

       SPEAKER----Our boys, our sons in the trenches
       of France, dying to make the world safe------

The woman tries to pass, being pushed this way and that,
the child looking about, wide eyed, sober. A NEWSBOY
enters, his voice heard as he enters.

       NEWSBOY----Extra! Extra! All about the new
       offensive!

People in the crowd turn to him, buying his papers. The
old woman pauses, thrusts up, trying to see his papers.
he turns to her, whips paper toward her.

       NEWSBOY----Latest from the American front!
       Yanks capture Choiman prisoners!

He is busy making change, selling his papers, keeping
his eye on the woman, who is looking at the paper. She
is looking at it hurriedly. PAN to headline:

       YANKS CAPTURE SAINT MIHIEL

PAN to woman's face. It is fearful, baffled, hurried,
the girl looking too, soberly.

       CHILD----Does it tell about pop, mama? Does
       it tell where Pop is?

       NEWSBOY---Well, come on. Are you going to buy
       it, or are you just renting it?

The woman hands paper back to NEWSBOY, who looks at her
in disgust.

       NEWSBOY----Well, I'll be------

       CHILD----Mama, did it say where Pop is?

       NEWSBOY---Lost your old man, eh? Come on, buy
       the paper. He's worth three cents to you,
       aint he?

       1.

WOMAN (takes child's hands, moves on, Speaks
in bitter voice)-----You come on. He wont
be in no paper. The folks that write them
aint got time to look behind every tree in
France.

She goes in, in laughter from people nearby. The SPEAK-
ER'S voice again in DISSOLVE.

          SPEAKERS---Drive forever from the world the
          Apocalyptic beast of blood and destruction---

2

RESOLVE

Another street, a recruiting office, posters, a sentry.
The WOMAN and CHILD approach. Sentry starts, recognises
them, turns as though about to depart, pauses, turns
toward them as they come up.

          SENTRY---Morning, Mrs Birdsong. No news from
          the old man yet, huh? (BIRDSONG looks at him
          with her baffled, weary, patient air)

          BIRDSONG---No. I aint heard yet. I look in
          the paper every morning, but he aint there.

          SENTRY---Do you look in the evening papers too?
          (BIRDSONG looks at him) Maybe he's on the day
          shift and dont do no fighting for the morning
          papers. (BIRDSONG looks at him dumbly. Another
          soldier comes up, stops. BIRDSONG turns toward
          doorway, leading child) You go on in and make
          them tell you where he is. They know. He's
          just changed his name. Maybe he's this guy
          Pershing the papers mention now and then. Ask
          them.(BIRDSONG and the CHILD go on. The two
          soldiers laugh)

          SOLDIER---Who is she looking for?

          SENTRY---Looking for the old man. He run out
          on her. Been about a year now. One day he
          come running in here with his collar tore open
          and a couple of dozen finger marks on his
          face, and just after he ducked inside the door,
          here she come in sight, running too, holding
          that shawl over her head and dragging that kid
          behing by the hand. (He laughs) But she was
          too late. That guy---his name is Otto---didn't
          enlist. He done a Steve Brodie into the army.
          I guess he was hunting a place where it would
          be quiet. And now she turns up here with that
          kid every Monday morning, trying to find out

2.

where he's at.

SOLDIER---Hoping he's dead, so she can collect the insurance, huh?

SENTRY---Sure. Wondering why it's taking them Germans so long, I guess.

They laugh in DISSOLVE through doorway to interior, to CAPTAIN'S office. CAPTAIN writing at desk. SERGEANT enters. CAPTAIN looks up.

CAPTAIN --Well?

SERGEANT---It's that old dame again, sir. Mrs Birdsong.

CAPTAIN---Well, dont bring her in here. I havent got her husband. Here; didn't we get that information about him last week? Give it to her and tell her not to come back here anymore. Tell her to go back home and knit him a sweater or something.

SERGEANT---Yes, sir. I did. But.......

CAPTAIN----What? But what?

SERGEANT---Hopkins out in front told her some bull about how he changed his name.

CAPTAIN---Well, what about that? I can't hepp that. All we can tell her is where Private Otto Birdsong is. If that's not her husband, we cant help that.

SERGEANT---Hopkins told her that he had changed his name to Pershing.

CAPTAIN---To what? Changed his name to what?

SERGEANT---Yes, sir. That's what she said.

CAPTAIN---Dash dash flash to dash. Send her in here. Then send that blankety blank Hopkins to me.

SERGEANT---Yes, sir. (Exits. CAPTAIN watches the door, fuming. Enter SERGEANT, with BIRD- SONG and CHILD. SERGEANT exits. BIRDSONG and CHILD stand in door)

CAPTAIN---Come in. Dont stand there. (BIRD- SONG and CHILD approach) Dont you know better

3.

452

than to believe anything a confounded enlisted
man tells you?

BIRDSONG---He said they had changed his name
to Pershing. And I saw the papers how there
was a soldier named Pershing in the army.

CAPTAIN (shouts)---Sergeant! Get Hopkins in
here at once!

SERGEANT'S VOICE without---Yes, sir.

CAPTAIN---What's the matter, anyway? He came in
here and said you were trying to murder him,
and yet you cant rest.......(He ceases. BIRD-
SONG stands stolidly. His face clears) I see.
His alotment has stopped comming to you. That's
the trouble, eh? Well, I will-----

BIRDSONG---No. I still get the checks.

CAPTAIN (stares at her)---Then what is the
trouble? You ran him out of the house and got
him ónto the army, where he cant bother you
anymore, and each month you get his alotment
check. Do you mean to tell me it's him
you are anxious about?

BIRDSONG (stolidly)×--He is my husband. He's
Otto. If I could just see him, tell him I
didn't-------never meant, that day........

CAPTAIN---Well. I give up. (Rises; his actions
and voice quite gentle now as he takes her
arm and leads her toward the door, the CHILD
following) You go home. Wait for him there.
This world is full of women doing that to day.
Sergeant Mayhew will give you his address. You
write him and tell him that you aren't mad at
him anymore. (Opens the door, they pass out)
Here. (He takes a coin from his pocket, gives
it to the CHILD) Buy yourself something. A
doll. Candy. And you. You go home and wait for
him. Write him. And dont come back here. You
hear me?

BIRDSONG doesn't answer. She goes on, passes SERGEANT
and sentry at door.

CAPTAIN---You, Hopkins. Come in here. (HOP-
KINS eneters office, door closes. CAPTAIN'S
voice beyond door) What the blankety blank
hell do you mean-- ------

4.

BIRDSONG, leading CHILD, follows SERGEANT to his desk.
Two other soldiers at typewriters nearby. SERGEANT
takes paper from desk.

> SERGEANT----Here you are. Do you know that
> they had to stop this whole war for about
> twenty four hours to find out where your hus-
> band is? But here he is, see? Otto Birdsong,
> private, second class, aviation Section, Sig-
> nal Corps, A.E.F., attached 113 Squadron. See?

> BIRDSONG (stares at paper)---Aviation?

> SERGEANT---Sure, like the birds. (Flaps his
> arms. BIRDSONG stares at paper; her hands be-
> gin to tremble)

> BIRDSONG (whispers)----Flying. Flying. Otto.
> Otto!

> SERGEANT---Yep. That's him. You already had
> him flying when he come in here that day.....
> Here! What§s the matter?

BIRDSONG holds paper, looking at it, tears rolling slowly and quietly down her cheeks. The CHILD looks at her
and also begins to cry, loudly.

> BIRDSONG---Otto! Otto! Flying! Them generals
> have killed you!

> SERGEANT---Here! Here! (To CHILD) Stop it!
> Stop it! (to BIRDSONG) He aint in danger! He's
> a mechanic or something.

> BIRDSONG---You mean,he dont go up in the air?

> SERGEANT---Him fly? That fellow? He probaly
> wouldn't know which end of the aeroplane went
> up first even.

> BIRDSONG (still,holding paper; to CHILD)---
> Hush. (CHILD hushes. She speaks in musing
> tone) H'mmm. He dont fly, then. What does he do?

> SERGEANT---Nothing, mostly, I expect. Sleeps
> and eats his three a day, maybe tightens a nut
> now and then. Dont you worry about him.

> BIRDSONG---Sleeps and eats and tightens a nut
> now and then. And them other boys getting shot
> and killed. I might have knowed it. The lazy
> son of a b--------

5.

454

SERGEANT---Here! Here! (BIRDSONG stops,
holds paper, musi g, still) Aint you ashamed,
cursing before these young soldiers here?
Here, you know where he is, now. You go on
home and stop worrying about him. Stop worrying us about him, anyway. (Puts paper in envelope and put it into her hand. She takes
CHILD'S hand and goes out, SERGEANT and Soldiers watching)

CLOCK to them walking on. They walk through DOUBLE EX-
POSURE of news paper headlines;

VICTORY IN ARGONNE

GERMANS RETREATING

ARMISTICE

A beat of martial music increases. BIRDSONG and CHILD
in crowd cheering at curb, flags etc., as returning
troops pass, BIRDSONG looking at each passing face until
last one is gone. She and CHILD stand as crowd disper-
ses and they are alone, BIRDSONG with her weary, patient air. The two figures fade into headlines, which
DISSOLVES to

3
        WILSON AT LAUZANNE
        'WAR TO END WAR'

Pages of paper turn to personal column, FOCUS on

        Otto. Come home. All is forgiven. Maggie.

Pages turn to headline

        COSSACKS WIPE OUT WHITE VILLAGE

DISSOLVE to

4   WAR EN G. HARDING ELECTED

DISSOLVE to

5   FIGHTING IN RIFF
        FRENCH TROOPS CAPTURE

Pages turn to personals: FOCUS on

        Otto. Come home. All is forgiven. M.

Pages turn on to headlines:

                6.

```
                              HOOVER ELECTED BY GREATEST POPULAR
                              LANDSLIDE IN HISTORY
                              PLURALITY A PROPHESY OF MILEN.IUM
                              OF WORLD PROSPERITY

        DISSOLVE to

                          6   WORLD LEADERS SAY DEPRESSION WILL
                              TURN CORNER BY XMAS

        DISSOLVE to

                          7   HOOVER ORDERS TROOPS TO DISPERSE
                              BONUS MOB OF UNEMPLOYED

        DISSOLVE through to personal:

                          8  Otto. Where are you? I am sick. M.

        DISSOLVE through to headlines:

                          9   NATIONS AGREE DISARMAMENT WILL BE
                              CURE FOR WORLD BANKRUPTCY

        DISSOLVE to

                         10  JAPANESE TROOPS ENTER GREAT WALL

        DISSOLVE through to personal:

                       11   You dont need to hide anymore. She died last
                            night.

        DISSOLVE to

     12  A poor cemetary. It is raining. A fresh grave,a few
         poor flowers, a woman kneeling beside grave. A few
         mourners in background, a priest looking at kneel-
         ing woman with commiseration. The mourners are foreign
         looking, mostly women. They talk among themselves, anx-
         iously, watching the priest and the kneeling woman. The
         priest turns, beckons, a woman approaches. He speaks to
         her in pantomine, indicates the kneeling woman. The
         woman shrugs. The priest approaches the kneeling woman,
         whose face is still hidden, touches her shoulder.
                 PRIEST---Come, daughter.

         The woman looks up at him. She is young, her face cold
         and strained with grief.

                 WOMAN---Go away. Let me alone.

                 PRIEST (gently but firmly raising her)---Come.
         I do not ask you not to grieve. But the liv-
```

ing acn not wait upon the dead.

GIRL---Then dont wait on me. When have I lived?
Look. (Opens shabby coat, shows shabby worn
dress, flings out her hands. FOCUS on work
roughened hands. FOCUS on GIRL'S bitter face)
Let me alone. I dont grieve for her; I envy her.

PRIEST---Come, come. This wont do. You cannot
escape life, your appointed destiny, this way.

GIRL---What is my appointed destiny?

PRIEST---To be bereaved; to conquer death in
turn by producing life.

GIRL---I? Marry? Marry? I?

PRIEST---God created woman to be the companion
and the cherished of man.

GIRL (Laughs wildly, bitterly)---no, thanks.
Not for me. I had a man for father once. (Turns
away, fast. PRIEST watches her anxiously. The
mourners also watch as the GIRL passes them
swiftly)

PRIEST (gestures)---Go with her.

WOMAN (To her companions)---Go. I will follow
in a moment. (The others, two women and two men
follow GIRL. The WOMAN turns to the PRIEST) Do
not fear, padre. I will see to her, I. I do
not need to remind you who it is/ was who cared
for her---for rhem---through this. /Idb/hét
(Indicates the grave)

PRIEST---True. God will reward you for it.

WOMAN---I do it for no reward from God or man,
my father. Here is my reward. (Slaps her bosom
lightly)

PRIEST---Then you will be doubly blessed by
Him who giveth all to them who ask for nothing.

WOMAN--- We will see. Bless me, my father.

PRIEST blesses her. She exits, follows others.

DISSOLVE to
13 A tenement street, a door. The GIRL enters, followed by
the two women. The two men halt at the door, look at one

8.

DISSOLVE to

14 A tenement street. GIRL walks along, bowed in grief,
the two women follow, followed in turn by the two men.
GIRL enters a doorway beside a foreign looking store.
The women pause, glance back. One of the men orders the
women to follow with a hidden gesture. The women enter.
The men pause, men pause at door, glance swiftly up and down
the street, then at one another.

    FIRST---Well, then?

    ROJAS----Wait here on Maria.

    FIRST (quickly)---The/ you think perhaps that
    she-----

    ROJAS---You know her too, Maria my wife. It
    might be better said of her that she is a
    giver of grief rather than a victim of it.

    FIRST---That is true. You think, then----

    ROJAS---I do not know. But I do know my wife.
    Remain until she arrives. I go.

    FIRST---With God, then.

ROJAS turns and enters store. DISSOLVE to

15 Interior. ROJAS glances about, goes on toward rear.
CLERK looks at him. ROJAS makes hidden signal, goes on
CUT to

16 Rear of store. A door. ROJAS looks back, taps lightly.
Door opens, he enters, door closes. CUT to

17 A dim stairway. ROJAS descends to cell/ a cellar filled
with barrels and boxes. He approaches a box, tugs at it.
It swings back like a door. ROJAS enters, box closes
again. CUT to

18 A room. A single portrait on wall, of a foreign man in
uniform, draped with a flag. Five men sitting about room,
the chief in the center, all watching the door as ROJAS
enters. He approaches, the chief extends his hand. ROJAS
kisses it, the men watching him, eagerly.

    FIRST---Well?

    ROJAS---It is over. She has returned.

    FIRST---In grief?

       9.

458

ROJAS---In grief.

FIRST (with gesture of despair)---Then our
plans, the labor of a whole year----(snaps
fingers, shrugs) Like that. Women. In love and
in grief. It is as though to them no one had
ever loved before or ever died.

SECOND---And yet upon whom the incalculable
behavior of whom we must risk not only our
lives, but this sacred life here-----

CHIEF---Silence, dear friend. My life is nothing. Before God certainly it is of no more
weight than the grief of a young girl. But
surely, in the restoration of our unhappy country my death will be of more weight than
the vagaries of a woman. Look! (he rises,
indicates the draped portrait) He died; his
spilled blood cries yet aloud to us in the
voices of our oppressed people. Who knows but
what my own spilled blood may be the tide
which will sweep tyrany and oppression----

The others rise, electrified, save ROJAS, who wears
still his thoughtful air.

All---Viva! Viva!

CHIEF (looks about)---Come, then. This is an
affair for men and courage, not women and
words. Let us trust in God and in honest bul-
lets with constant hearts to direct them. (To
ROJAS) Eh, my friend?

The others look at ROJAS, excited. His attitude has
not changed. At once the excitement cools a little.

ROJAS---Perhaps. But in this affair of ours
I myself had rather have one woman than a
hundred cannon. I have a wife, you know.

FIRST---Eh, he has.

SECOND---Veritably, a wife. One in ten thous-
and.

THIRD---In ten million. (Their airs are now
almost despondent) What a captain of troops
she would have made.

FIRST---A colonel, you mean.

10.

459

ROJAS---A general. I, her husband, say it.
General? Were she tyrant president of our
unhappy country instead of that accursed, an
army of ten thousand beautiful women could
not dislodge her. I, her husband, say it.

THIRD---And I, the friend of her husband, agree.
But luckily for us, she is not. And so now
we have lost our battery of one woman, eh?
What shall we do?

CHIEF---Ah, Avilas! This, from the man of
Tres Hermanos, who fought at my side when
right and justice were slain at Rincon?

THIRD (shrugs, downlooking)---As I will fight
again, as them who know me, know.

CHIEF (quietly, touches him on shoulder)---So
I do know it, my friend. (To ROJAS)---Come,
then since my simple belief that injustice is
to be conquered only by hearts which are
not afraid to die is oldfashoined and out
of date.

ROJAS (downlooking)---I do not say that. I
only say that since a nation, a country, is
the mother of men, that an evil child of it
can quickest be punished by.......eh, then.
a female hand, if you must have it.

The CHIEF bows his head. The others watch him covertly.

CHIEF (after a moment)---So be it, then. But
you say that this woman, this young girl-----

ROJAS----I did not say so, my prince. I only
said that this young girl has returned from
the funeral of her mother in grief. And that
I have not yet seen my wife.

THIRD (quickly)---You think then that the
Donna Maria------?

ROJAS---That too I have not said. But I know
my wife. I know that if she believes this
girl to be God's instrument in the freeing of
our unhappy country, God's instrument this
girl will be, grief or no grief------

Three spaced taps sound from the wall. All turn toward
sound, then they all face the door. FOCUS on door, DIS-
SOLVE through to stairway, to ROJAS'S companion
descending. DISSOLVE through PEDRO to

II.

460

Street before the door. PEDRO waiting as MARIA comes up.
PEDRO watches her with a kind of respectful alarm.

MARIA---Eh, then. Your li tle shop. It conducts itself, eh?

PEDRO---I was just going, Donna Maria. It was
Manual who----

MARIA---Ah. And what commands did my husband
leave for me?

PEDRO---We thought that now, perhaps, after
this unfortunate........(gestures toward door.
MARIA watches him)

MARIA---So. You thought. And then what?

PEDRO---That our plans now, after this unfortunate.........

MARIA---You thought, eh? Look you. Five years
ago, on that day when justice and truth fell
at Rincon; on that day, I say, when we were
driven by this accursed monster from our native soil, you and my husband were not among
the least of them who saved the life of our
prince. How did you do it?

PEDRO---We did what lay in the power of mortal man. Let no man say-------

MARIA---But not with thinking. You did; you
asked not whence nor why. Did you?

PEDRO---No. But let no man----

MARIA---Then continue to do so, so that again
you will not be among the least when the day
arrives for which we pray and labor.

PEDRO(quickly)---Then you also think that----

MARIA----Think? I do not think; I do. Go, and
fetch me the glove.

PEDRO---The glove? The glove, Donna?

MARIA---Yes. Why not?

PEDRO---The sacred relic of our martyred king?
Entrusted to------

12.

461

MARIA---Then what? Entrusted to-----?(PEDRO
looks down. MARIA watches him) To a woman, eh?
(She laughs, quietly, coldly, without mirth)
Men, men. It is no wonder there is no stability
in our country, since our mother land spawns
only adolescents. Go; fetch me the glove. Tell
them that Maria Rojas desires it.

PEDRO---And the signal?

MARIA---It will be four blows; that too will
not be long away, tell. Go.

PEDRO departs swiftly. DISSOLVE to PEDRO descending
the stairs, to

The men in the room watching the door as it opens and
PEDRO enters, goes to CHIEF and kisses hie hand.

ROJAS---"ell, then? You have seen her?

PEDRO---But now.

ROJAS---Good. "hat news?

PEDRO seems to be too terrified to speak. He looks about
at them, beseechingly at ROJAS while the CHIEF watches
him.

AVILAS---Come, out with it. We are men; we
can bear bad news.

ROJAS---It is not bad news. My wife has no
traffic with bad news. That is known. (Claps
PEDRO on shoulder) Did she not say so herself?

PEDRO---Yes. Yes. She said she/ the news would
be good news, that she would make the signal soon
a signal of four blows. And so she......

THEY watch him as he stands before them, again terrified,
looking about beseechingly. The CHIEF watches him. Suddenly the CHIEF turns to the portrait, raises his Arms.

CHIEF---My king and father! Three hundred years
age, when thy ancestor and the forefathers of
us who stand here today crossed the sea to
carve from the wilderness a fatherland for
their children, they moved at the direction of
a hero, behind iron armor; now when their de-
scendents return to wrest our bleed ng country
from the grasp of a tyrant, we must move at
the direction of a woman, behind a silken petticoat.

13

462

ROJAS---If you are speaking of my wife, her petticoat is not of silk, my prince.

CHIEF---That is true, good friend. I ask your pardon, and that of the Donna......(to PEDRO, quietly) Eh, then. What does this lady patriot want now?

PEDRO looks about, terrified. They watch him.

ROJAS---Well, then? Out with it.

PEDRO (with a kind of sudden desperation)--- She wants the glove.

There is a movement among them, almost of horror. The CHIEF alone has not moved, looking at PEDRO. The othres look at him, motionless. PEDRO stands before him like a culprit. The CHIEF seems to be in deep thought. Slowly he moves, takes from inside his coat an elegant gauntlet, opens it reverently, the others looking on, reverent, hushed, still in a kind of horrified suprise. Opened, the glove has a bullet hole through the palm, and it is stained with dried blood.

CHIEF (quietly)---And now this. And now this. (Turns slowly toward portrait, his head bowed above the glove. Raises his head, lifts glove suddenly toward portrait, raises his voice) This! This! Which enclosed that martyred hand which thou raised between thy heart and the assassin's buttet!

AVILAS---And which enclosed thine own living hand when it tore the life from that assassin's throat, O prince! Do not forget that.

CHIEF (Quietly)---I have not forgot. (He turns, lays glove on table before him, makes a gesture, stands with head bowed)

ROJAS (half whispers to PEDRO)---Take it and be gone.

PEDRO---He has not told me to.

They all look at the CHIEF. He looks up.

CHIEF---Well? Is this poor object perhaps not enough for her? Why do you not take it?

AVILAS---You have not yet commanded him to, prince.

14.

CHIEF (looks about, bitterly)---Is this too
reserved for me? Must I, with my own mouth
......What are your commands, gentlemen?

They do not meet his eyes. They look aside from one another, uncomfortably.

AVILAS (suddenly)---Take the glove.

CHIEF---Ah, Avilas!

They look at one another. The chief is the one who looks
away. He sits slowly in his chair, bows his head on his
hands.

AVILAS---Take the glove, and go.

ROJAS (hissing)---Quickly, brute.

PEDRO takes up glove, gingerly, terrified, turns.

AVILAS---Stay. (PEDRO halts) With this glove
she will be successful? She said so?

PEDRO---Yes, general. These were her living
words when I said to her, 'And the signal
of four blows, Donna?' She said, 'That too
will not be long away. Let them wait.'

AVILAS---Good. Go.

Exit PEDRO. The CHIEF sits, his head bowed. The others
stand looking toward the door as PEDRO exits.

DISSOLVE to
A poor tenement room. The GIRL sits at a table, her air
dazed. Her garments drip with rain as she gazes before
her, motionless. In the background the two women move
about at a stove, building up the fire, setting a coffee
pot on it. The door opens. MARIA enters. The women look
at her, indicate the GIRL, shrug, watch her as she
approaches. MARIA goes to the GIRL, touches the shawl
which the GIRL wears over her head.

MARIA---Eh, you are soaking. (Removes the
shawl, the GIRL stirs dully, resisting. MARIA
wrings water from the shawl before the GIRL'S
eyes) See? You have not even any need for tears.

GIRL---I cant cry. I tried, but I cant.

MARIA---What? Not even that one woman's weapon
in this misrun world of men? Tears are a woman's heavy artillery, as a glance of the eye
is her single neat thrust of the dagger. Try,

15.

464

then; come. Will you be forever more a helpless
victim of man?

GIRL (Looks at MARIA)---Of a man. Of man.
(She begins to cry)

MARIA---Good. (She turns toward watching women)
Eh, then, you two. What are you doing, then?

WOMAN---We are making coffee for her, Donna.
We thought-----

MARIA---That is well. The stove burns, the pot
is on the stove; the coffee will now make itself. Go down to the store, tell Escamille to
give you a bottle of wine. Of my wine.

The women glance at one another, hesitating.

FIRST---I will go.

SECOND----No;I will go.

MARIA---Let you both go; the air will do you
good. And look. (The women halt) Do not hurry.

FIRST---Not hurry, Donna?

MARIA---The stairs are long and steep; you are
no longer young. (The women exit. MARIA turns
back to the GIRL, who is crying) Good; weep.
Even thuogh him whom your tears indict will
never even know that you wept.

GIRL (wildly)---Yes. Yes. Never to even know
it! I'm not crying for grief; she knows that
I dont have to cry to grieve for her. (Rises,
wildly, passionately) Oh, if I were only a
man! Just for a little while. This whole world
would not be big enough to hide him from me.

MARIA---So?

GIRL (walks up and down the room, wild, MARIA
watching her, still, cold)---Yes. A slave she
was. You know, you know---slaving to keep a
roof over our heads and bread in our mouths
until I was big enough to help. Denying herself food to have a few pennies to advertise
for him in the papers, knowing that he would
not anwser. Then when she lay sick she begged
me to try once more, and I told her we had
not the money now, for even that. And I left
her with money to pay for her medicine when it
came, and the next day I saw in the paper,
Otto. I am dying. Come home to Marion or

16.

God will curse you! For me she did it; for
me, for me! And now all 1 can do is cry. If
1 were only a man! Just for one month. A
month? A day, and hour!

MARIA---So? What would you do?

GIRL (whirls upon her)---Do? Do? (she stares
at MARIA. Suddenly she holds out her hands)
Look. Look at my hands.

Her hands clench slowly as though gripping a throat.
MARIA watches them.

MARIA---One would scarce call them ~~hands~~/ the
hands of a woman even now.

MARION (laughs bitterly, wildly)---Why should
they be? Since 1 was fifteen, they have done
the work of a man's hands.

MARIA---And there is yet one more man's act
which they would like to perform, eh? (MARIA
now looks full at MARION. MARION'S face grows
still. She stares at MARIA. MARIA speaks in
a quiet tone, as though talking to herself.
MARION watches her like one being hypnotised)
They look quite capable of performing the act
of any man. Eh, let us see.

From beneath her apron she draws the glove, puts it on
MARION'S hand. MARION watches, turns her hand in the
glove.

MARION---It almost fits.

MARIA---Why should it not? What was your hand
thinking of when that glove enclosed it?
(They look at one another, MARION fascinated)
Come, What partof a man's body was your hand
thinking of at that moment?

MARION---Of the throat.

MARIA---Good. So was this glove, on the last
time if enclosed a human hand. Look at it.
(She takes MARION'S gloved hand and surports it
MARION'S hand goes lax and immediately the
glove assumes the faintly curved shape that
any used glove will. MARION is too wruoght up

17.

think of this) See? By its very shape it cries
to high heaven against the assasin whose bullet
it could not stay. And look----(she turns the
palm up, points to the bloodstain) Here, in
her father's blood the voice of an orphaned
child cries against the murderer of her father
and mother.

MARION---Murderer of her-----

MARIA---Of her mother also. Yes. Sit down. I
will tell you a story. (Pushes MARION into
a chair. MARION stares at her, unconsciously
starts to remove glove) MARIA stops her quickly) No, No; keep it on. And listen. This was
five years ago, in the old times which for so
long we believed would never return, in my
country in the south, which, when I think of
it, I too would weep. We were a small nation
but happy, with a king in turn son of son of
son of a king. We were happy; we knew little of
the world and cared less. Our king was our father and our brother; his children were our
cousins were our nephews and our nieces. Then foreigners began to enter our country, men without
country, men of violence and blood, seeking
gold and silver among us who knew little of either
being content with our flocks and herds, until
soon there was no more peace among us. It is
of one of these men I speak. He too came from
nowhere, fleeing; you knew that. Looking at his
/his/ face you said, 'Here is a man whom that
land which bore him has regurtitated. But
I will not try to tell you all; I will tell
only of that day upon which the civil war
which these foreigners had instigated tore our
country apart, of that day when our martyred
told his wife and daughter goodbye, and went
to his death. He went unarmed, to make one
last plea to them who had severed his people;
he wore this glove upon that right hand
which he lifted between the assasin's bullet
and his heart.

MARION (hushed, wide eyed)---And his wife and
daughter?

MARIA---And his son. Our prince, who was at his
father's side and who snatched this glove from
his father s dead hand to strangle that assasin
with and was prevented by my Manuel and others
who thus saved his life. But you asked of the
wife and daughter. This wife is also dead; how,

18.

467

none whom ~~knew~~ we know can say. Some say it
was also by a bullet, but perhaps not. Perhaps
it would be wrong to accuse these foreigners
of killing women; that ⊥ do not know. But
she is ~~not~~ dead, and daughter these~~s~~ five
years has lived in the hovel of a peasant in
the mountains, where she is safe to grieve.
She will be about your age.

MARIA watches MARION, who lo ks at the glove, wide eyed,
still.

      MARION---And the assasin?

      MARIA---Eh, he flourishes. Why not? Surely a
      man does not make orphan a son or a daughter
      without gaining by it.

      MARION (rouses)---In a peasant's hovel in the
      mountains. Well, she has a brother, which is
      more than some have.

      MARIA---She has a brother.

      MARION---Why doesn't he go to her, then? Or are
      all men alike, even brothers?

      MARIA---Listen. For five years he has dreamed
      nothing else, thought nothing else, but of the
      day when he can return and with this glove tear
      the life from that man who fired that shot.

      MARION---And the daughter?

      MARIA----Will be ~~sptinceses//with/power/to/~~
      a princess, with power to right such wrongs
      as she has suffered, be they the wrongs of
      her own countrywomen or of northern women,
      of white women or of------

      MARION~~///~~ (rises quickly)---But what is this
      to me? She can no more right my wrongs than ⊥
      can right hers, since you say that even her
      own brother, a man, can do nothing but dream
      for five years.......Let us pray to God, she
      and ⊥; He alone can---------

MARIA grips her arm; they stare at one another; again
MARION subsides.

      MARIA---This brother no longer only dreams.
      Look; who among us here have been most kind
      to you and her who is dead? I will not say---

MARION---Yes; say it. I am grateful. You have done everything---- -

MARIA---Who, then? Next to MANuel and myself?

MARION (staring at her)---The---That young man, whom even Manuel calls Mister Steve.

MARIA---Mister Steve. So. He is that prince.

MARION ---He is.......?

MARIA---Now he no longer dreams.

MARION----You mean he is going back there----

MARIA---He, and Manuel, and others.

MARION---They will be killed!

MARIA---It' is better to die on the soil that bore you than to live on a foreign one.

MARION (stares at MARIA, who looks steadily back at her)---But what is this to me? Do you want me to pray for their success?

MARIA---You can do more than that.

They look at one another.

MARION---I?

MARIA---You. That assassin------

MARION---That assassin!

MARIA---Listen well. His name is Otto Birdsong.

DISSOLVE to
Underground room, the men at table, The CHIEF in the center, his head bowed, his hands clasp before him. ROJAS stands, watching covertly, with an air of one respectful and defiant. The other men also watch the CHIEF covertly, or rather, they are quiet, as though he were a mourner at a funeral. They talk among themselves with gestures and shrugs.

AVILAS (suddenly, looking at ROJAS)---You Manuel. She told us it would not be long, didn't she?

ROJAS---Pedro told you that she said to him it would not be long, my general.

AVILAS---Pedro said that she said, then.

20.

ROJAS---Pedro said that she said, my general.

He moves, to a box in the corner. A few of the men watch
him, though the CHIEF does not move. He takes from the
box a wicker covered flask and some glasses, approaches
the table. AVILAS waves him off.

AVILAS---This is no time for that , my friend.

ROJAS calmly sets flask and glasses on table, prepares to
pour.

ROJAS---In battle, your gesture has ever been
our command. Eh, my general?

AVILAS---You were not the least of them who
fought under my sword. Have I not always said
so? And what then?

ROJAS (pouring)---You are still our general.
I merely load the guns.

They watch ROJAS. Then as one they turn and look toward
the wall, then at ROJAS again.

AVILAS---You think then that Pedro----

ROJAS---I do not have to think, my general. I
know my wife-------

He ceases as first knock sounds from wall. They turn a-
gain, electrified, motionless as the four spaced knocks
sound and cease. VOICES---The signal!

ROJAS---Did I not tell you? Give the command
to fire, general.

AVILAS rises, takes up his glass. A wave of excitement
passes through the room, all rise save the CHIEF, though
he too rouses. All raise glasses.

AVILAS---To the day! As Rojas says, fire!

DISSOLVE to
Same, men in same attitudes, though CHIEF now stands also
ans MARIA and MARION are in the room.

ROJAS---Eh, my wife. I told them.

MARIA---Silence, you. They also know me. (She
stands beside MARION, almost protectingly.
MARION in suppressed excitement, a little fearful)Now, then. She is one of us. (Turns to
MARION) Eh, my dove? You tremble? Come. They

21.

too are orphans. You have lost a mother; there
are some here who have lost both father and
mother, as well as fatherland. And there is
one here who does not even know ~~he~~ where lies
his mother's grave. Eh, my prince?

ROJAS---That is so. I, Manuel, tell you.

MARIA---Silence, you. (To MARION) eh, then?

MARION (nervous, trembling, looking at the
CHIEF)---I want to----to-----your sister
in the-------

MARIA---Good. You have heard, gentlemen?

AVILAS---We have heard.

MARIA---Good. Then tell her what you want her
to do.

The men watch quietly. AVILAS glances at the **CHIEF**, who
makes a sign. AVILAS faces MARION.

AVILAS---You have heard, doubtless, of the
situation of our unhappy-----

MARIA---I have told her that, general. Begin
with the mine.

AVILAS---Good. Then. There is a mine, as the
Donna Rojas has told you. From this mine gold
is taken. This gold is put into an aeroplane
and carried to the coast, to the ships. We
must have this gold to buy guns with. Even one
load of it may save our country and our people--

MARIA---One load, mind. Think. One little load
of gold, and an orphan girl hiding like a
beast in the mountains may return to the grave
of her mother, which she has never seen.

They look at MARION, none moving.

MARION---But how can I......

MARIA---Eh? Do you not see? This aeroplane full
of gold is conducted by a man, an American.

MARION---An American? An aviator? (They watch
her. A fierce exultation passes over her face.
It fades) No, no; how can I------

MARIA---Eh? You ask that? (To the others) You
see? Can you imagine/~~what/a/life/this~~/ now
what a life this

22.

girl's has been? (to MARION) You ask how? You
have never then looked into a mirror? I, with
the face of a horse, could steal an aeroplane
full of gold; you with your face could steal
a mountain of it.

MARION (her face waking again)---An aviator.
(To the CHIEF) and then your sister----

MARIA---Will find a brother. And you restore
their fatherland to these men. and you too
will find a father. (To the CHIEF) have I not
said it?

All look at CHIEF, who rises.

CHIEF---Yes. I swear.

ALL---Viva! Viva!

MARIA---EH, then! Your cups! Pour Manuel!

ROJAS---I have already poured.

All stand with lifted cups, excited.

AVILAS---Death to tryants and assassins!

MARION (excited, almost hysterical)---Death!
Death!

All drink. ROJAS looks at MARION, then at MARIA, specu-
latively, shrugs, drinks too.

DISSOLVE to
All departing, MARION among them, led out by CHIEF. MARIA
last, ROJAS hanging back until others exit. The sound of
their feet still heard, tramping up stairs like the
march of soldiers. ROJAS touches MARIA, who turns.

ROJAS---Just what hve you told this girl,
my wife?

MARIA---What?

ROJAS---I watched her face as that toast was
drunk. I only hope that no woman ever has such
a look on her face when drinking to me. I, who
have been a husband for fifteen years, say it.
Come, what did you tell her?

MARIA---I told her what was necessary for her
to be told.

ROJAS---Come. You gave her to believe that it

23.

472

was that animal BIRDSong---a stupid brute
whose intelligence goes no further than a
doglike devotion to his compatriot who conducts the aeroplane, and to begging~~s/further~~
a further wine credit from the keepers of
cantinas----- who fired the shot which slew
our king. Come, is that not true?

MARIA---And then what?

They look at one another. ROJAS looks away, shrugs.

ROJAS--- Nothing.

MARIA---Good. (Turns, halts again) And on the
subject of stupid brutes: I have known stupid
animals to do a good service on occasion; I,
who have been a wife for fifteen years, say it.
But they did it by being stupid brutes. Do you
mark me, my husband?

ROJAS---I mark you, my wife.

MARIA----Good. Come, then.

They exit. The tramping of feet continues through DISS LVE
to.

A ship's corridor, on the wall a life belt. The tramping
feet pace camera toa door, where it halts upon the door.
The tramping increases; AVILAS and CHIEF enter, pause at
door. Their air is conspiratorial, alert. They look at
both ways as sound of tramping goes on, dies away as
AVILAS opens door, which reveals a mirror. In the mirror
MARION stands, in a dress of deliberate seductive lines,
standing as though some one were speaking to her. DISS
SOLVE through mirror to stateroom, MARION facing MARIA
as CHIEF and AVILAS enter quietly, unheard, and pause
in background.

MARIA---So. That is how you would invite a
lover, eh? (MARION stands, her head bowed)
Eh, then, watch me.

MARIA seems to change completely, to become another woman. With measured and seductive stride she crosses to
sofa, half reclines, swirls her dress to expose her
shape and looks back over her shoulder with a voluptuous
air, holds tableau, rises, becomes MARIA again, cold,
implicable.

MARIA---Like that. AGAIN, now.

24.

473

MARION---No. No. I cant.

MARIA---Why?

MARION---I cant. I shouldn't have come. Let
me go back home. Let me........(She ceases.
They look at one another. MARION looks down,
breathing fast, trembling)

MARIA---So.¥ỏ¥ You would return home. Good.
Then you will not need this new dress.

MARION looks down at herself. Her hands begin to fumble
at dress, to remove it.

MARION (whispers)⁂--No. No. I wont need it.
I wont.......

MARIA----Good, remove it. I will ǵiⱡⱡ get your
old one.

MARIA turns. She sees CHIEF and AVILAS, pauses for a
second, goes on without making them any sign. Disappears
behind screen. MARION fumbles at dress, her head bowed.
MARIA reappears, carrying MARION'S old shabby dress, returns, extends it to MARION.

MARIA---You are wise; this is not for you. We
were mistaken. What you desire is not revenge,
but poverty and obscurity in which to grieve
for your murdered mother. No; revenge is not
for you, since you are not a man.

MARION takes the old dress. A packet of papers falls from
it; MARION stoops for them, MARIA watching her, cold.
With hand extended, MARION pauses, picks up papers.
FOCUS on clippings:

Otto. Come home. All is forgiven. Maggie.

Otto. Where are you. Answer me. M.

Otto. I am sick. Come to Marion. M.

You needent hide anymore. She died last
night.

PAN to MARION holding clippings, MARIA watching her.
Suddenly MARION flings away clippings, begins hurriedly
to pull up dress again.

MARIA---Eh? You will not change now?

25.

474

        MARION (wildly, almost hysterical, fumbling at
        dress)---Tell me again how to do. Hurry! Hurry!

MARIA doesn't answer. She steps back, watching MARION,
who with her hysterical air apes MARIA'S recent pantomime of crossing the room to sofa and reclining upon it,
bettering MARIA even in her hysterical passion, holds
tableau. In background AVILAS claps his hands.

        AVILAS---Bravo! Bravo!

MARJON springs up, glances wildly at CHIEF and AVILAS,
runs from room. AVILAS and CHIEF approach. MARIA bows to
CHIEF, without servility.

        AVILAS---She learns, eh? Under your tutelage,
        Donna, she cannot but conquer him,

        MARIA---No woman needs to be taught how to se-
        duce a man, my general. I teach her to seduce
        herself.

        AVILAS---Ah. That is well. She will need that.
        I too have news this morning.

        CHIEF---yes. And have I not always said-----

        MARIA---Your pardon, my prince. (to AVILAS)
        You have recieved news this morning.

        AVILAS---By the best of fortune. In time for us to
        get someone else to do that which I now see
        this girl cannot perform.

        MARIA---And what is this that another woman can
        do that this girl cannot?

        CHIEF---We have not said another woman,
        Donna. Ha, have I not said from the first that
        the stout hearts of men will-----

        MARIA----My prince! (to AVILAS) What do you fear?

        AVILAS---This. (Takes from pocket papers, ex-
        tends one to MARIA. PAN to photo of BOWDEN,
        PAN back) You see? If this were merely the
        picture of a pistol or a bomb-------

        MARIA---And if she of whom you have fears were
        a man? I see.

        AVILAS---But she is not. She is------

        MARIA----A woman who has never been a girl, who

                        26.

                                                475

has been all her life a thing, a brute animal,
slave to a mother slowly dying of poverty and
helpless rage.

AVILAS---Yes. And now this face----(strikes
picture lightly)---to be deliberatelt thrown
at him, who has never known a young man, who
who knows not even a brief ouching of hands
through an iron grille-----

MARIA---that this simpering likeness of a handsome face of whose kind the world is full, will
be a knife thrust to her heart.

AVILAS---Yes. (He muses upon the paper picture ,
MARIA watching him coldly) And this is the
instrument with which we had hoped to conquer
a man who is already in love. Because look.
(Produces another paper. PAN to newspaper
clipping, photographs of BOWDEN and NANCY:

        Engaged
        Engaged. Miss Nancy White. Captain
        George BOwden. Miss white is the
        daughter of Carter White, owner of
        the Trsx Hermanos mines operated un-
        der the/goverment supervision here.
        Captain Bowden, late of the Air Corps
        A.E.F., is a pilot in the employ of
        Mr White.

PAN bac. AVILAS muses upon picture, MARIA watching him.

CHIEF (suddenly; they look at him)---and this
is he whom you hope to seduce with a woman
who will fall in love with him at sight.

MARIA---Look you, my prince. What is the difference between one man and another? What is
there that one man can do that another man cannot, provided he have one thing-----

CHIEF----The heart and the will; yes.

MARIA----The heart and the will. So what is
there that one woman can do that another cannot
provided that other have the body and the will?
(They look at her) And she has the body; that
you have seen.

AVILAS---And the will?

MARIA---I have that.

27.

476

AVILAS---Bravo. And your will alone can keep
a young girl from falling in love? Can even the
Donna Maria Rojas do this?

MARIA---No.

AVILAS---So. And then?

They look at ~~no~~ one another.

MARIA---And then, my general?

AVILAS---What shall we do?

MARIA---Nothing. I am counting on that.

AVILAS---Counting on-------?

MARIA---Would I have come this far, put my
head into this noose, in blind dependence on
the unpredictable vagaries of a young girl?
Have you forgot that we have to do with a
grongo, not a Latin who will risk death and
dishonor for the glance of a woman's eye? Gringoes do not do that. GRIngoes risk death and
dishonor for a princilpe, not for a small fragment of delicate flesh. It is chivalry, not
love, for which we play this game.

AVILAS---You mean-------?

MARIA----Loving her, he would sacrifice her to
his prônciples without batting an eye. Pitying
her, a compatriot in the toils of unscrupulous
brigands, as he will consider us, he will sacrifice honor and perhaps life too, to save her.
And if by doing so he can put her into the arms
of another, he will do it only the more eagerly.

AVILAS---That is starnge.

MARIA---It is moer than that. It is embecile.
But gringoes are like that, and it is unfortunately a gringo with whom we have to deal----
a people not only who cannot be corrupted with
promises of honor and glory, but who are even
impervious to promises of money. So do not
be alarmed, my general. If, at any time later,
other aspects of theß situation occur to you
to give you unease, say to yourself, 'My/Has
'Maria has already thought of this.' My neck
is in this also, as this gringo would say.

AVILAS---Yes. Well---------(Puts papers back into

28.

his pocket slowly. Again the CHIEF speaks
suddenly)

CHIEF---And if she should not fall in love
with him. If he should not be moved to protect
her, and she should prove herself no help to
us?

MARIA looks at him. They look at one another steadily.

MARIA---Then what, my prince?

CHIEF---We are taking this weak girl into a
sick country whose ill must be washed away in
blood. And we, her only protectors, are entering upon a road from which there can be no
return, whose end must be /victory/of/ either
victory or death. And you admit that possibly
she cannot help us. So I repeat your words;
my good friend. Then what?

MARIA---Then let her father protect her. She
has a father there.

AVILAS---And look, Excellency. As Donna Maria
says, we do not know that she will fail us;
it is only that we are forewarned in time to----

28 A.

478

CHIEF---And thank God for it. Call her. We will
send her back home, as she requested herself.
Thank God, we are not yet so little of men
that we must march to a throne over the tender
flesh and heart ofa young girl.

They look at him. He stands almost proudly, commanding.

AVILAS---Is that your command, my prince?

CHIEF---It is, good friend. Come; are we not
men yet? It is not hard to die. It is much
easier to die than to live in glory but with
out honor.

MARIA---That is true. We are but men and women;
It is not hard to die. It is not even very hard
to live under oppression or in exile. Even the
daughter and sister of kings can become used
after a while to living in a peasant's hovel
in mou tains, I dare say. (The CHIEF winces;
his face is torn; MARIA and AVILAS watch him
as he struggles with himself) Man can leave
but execration or glory behind him. But he
will be dead then; the voices cannot trouble
him. What will it matter to him that they say,
'This man put in the balance, on the one side
an obscure girl of a foreign people; on the
other side an oppressed people, an orphaned
sister, a glorious birthright. He chose the
obscure and foreign girl.

They look at the CHIEF; his face shows his struggle.

CHIEF(with gesture)---No. No. I cannot. (looks
about at them) Cannot? I will not. Call her.

AVILAS---But, Excellency. Let her choose. Will
you do that?

MARIA---Come, my prince. Do as our general
says. Let her choose, if she will return or if
she will continue as she ahs acst her lot.
Let her too choose between obscurity and glory.

They look at him. He bows his head. After a moment he
makes a gesture of acquiesence with his hand.

AVILAS (to MARIA)---Call her in.

CHIEF---Stay. (MARIA stops)---If it be but
one little word or sign or shadow-------

29.

MARIA---To her poverty and obscurity she shall
return. That is understood.

CHIEF---Good. Call her in.

They watch MARIA go to the door, open it, beckon. Enter
MARION. She and MARIA approach. CHIEF meets them takes
MARION'S hand. She looks at him with diffident, almost
shy curiosity and respect.

    CHIEF---My child----Eh, I can call you so.
    I am bot much you senior in years, but in the
    last five yeers I have lived a century. When
    I ~~entered~~/ entered this room, before you knew
    that I was here, I heard you say, 'Let me re-
    turn home'. I say to you know, 'You are free.
    Return home.'

    MARION---Return home? (Looks at CHIEF, wide
    eyed, looks at others, astonished) You mean
    I cant-----That you are sending me----that
    you wont let me......(looks at MARIA, wildly)
    Maria! You promised me-------(MARIA shrugs.
    MARION looks at AVILAS and CHIEF) What si this?
    Do you think that I cannot help you? That I am
    ~~too/weak/or/afraid/(Becomes/thoughtful)~~/
    too weak to, or afraid? (Becomes thoughtful,
    looks from one to another) Oh. I see. For a
    minute I thought.......I see now. It's because
    we may all be killed. Is that it? (She looks
    at CHIEF)

    AVILAS (Watching her)---Yes.

    MARION---I am not afraid to die.

    MARIA----Think well. You can return home, and
    live in safety; you can go with us, and per-
    haps die in a foreign land.

    MARION---A foreign land? What land can be more
    foreign to me than the place where you aren't?
    You, the only friends I have, the only living
    people who have seen my mother's grave to know
    it was here? You, and Manuel, and......(she
    looks at CHIEF, her wildness goes, she is
    almost shy) You see, I dont even know what to
    call you now. (To MARIA) Am I still to call
    him Mister Steve, like I----------

    MARIA---Call him brother. Brother father.
    Father of a fatherless people; brother to
    every orphan who will come to him.

30.

MARION (ecstatic)---Yes. Yes. (Turns to CHIEF,
grips his arm) If you are to die, then let
me die with you. I can do what you want me to
do. I can learn. Maria will teach me.

CHIEF---That is your choice?

MARION---Yes. Yes.

CHIEF (to MARIA)---You have beaten me.

MARIA---I have conquered a throne for you.

CHIEF---As you will. But mark my words......
(He looks at them, then at MARION'S ecstatic
face. His face softens, becomes gentle, almost
sad) Eh, then. So I have been conquered by a
woman. Let us hope that this is an augury for
our.......But talk is idle. Perhaps already
there has been among us too much of it. (He
looks at MARION, who watches him, shining. He
lays his hand gently on her head) By this hand
I swear it. No harm shall come to thee.

28   CLOCK to MARIA'S cold watchful face as CHIEF turns away.

29   Back to Scene   CHIEF---Come, Avilas.

They exit as DISSOLVE begins. Sound of tramping feet be-
gin, grown louder a̶s̶/̶M̶A̶R̶I̶O̶N̶/̶w̶a̶l̶k̶s̶/̶a̶g̶a̶i̶n̶/̶t̶o̶/̶s̶o̶f̶a̶/
gradually as MARION walks again to sofa in voulptuous
pantomine asDISSOLVE becomes complete.

          MARIA'S voice----That is better. Now. Again.

The tramping feet are very loud, measured, implacable
30 . and portentous. Slow RESOLVE a flag flying in a stiff
breeze. It is of three parallel stripes. The tramp of
feet dies i̶n̶t̶o̶/̶t̶h̶e̶/̶i̶n̶c̶r̶e̶a̶s̶i̶n̶g̶/̶s̶o̶u̶n̶d̶/̶o̶f̶/̶a̶e̶r̶o̶p̶l̶ slowly
into the increasing sound of aeroplane. Out of Flag
31 . RESOLVE aeroplane in flight. Flag fades, leaves aeroplane flying above mountains, tiny with distance.

32   RESOLVE an Indian seated beside small fire. Engine increases, Indian looks in that direction, rises, takes
up a bundle of fuel and places it on fire, which begins to
smoke. Indian removes blanket and prepares to signal as
engine grows very loud and ship roars past overhead.
Indian continues to signal as engine dies in DISSOLVE to

33   A sentry box, in background mountain range. Before box,
dozing, a soldier. A bayoneted rifle beside him, he
wears many bandoliers. His appearance fantastic and
deadly of Latin-American soldiers, gaudy, sloven, and
armed to the teeth. He rouses, stretches, takes out to-
bacco and is about to roll cigarette, when he apparent-

          31.

481

ly remembers his duty. Takes up clumsy brass telescope, points it toward mountain pass for a moment, lowers it and rolls and lights cigarette. Then again as though prompted to his indolent duty, he takes up glass and looks toward pass. This time he starts, halts, looks thruogh glass. DISSOLVE to

34 Moutain pass, smoke column framed by glass. DISSOLVE to

35 Sentry lowers glass, takes up rifle, points it straight into camera, fires. DISSOLVE through flash, explosion, to

36 An iron wall, splashed with bullet marks. Another bullet strikes it. DISSOLVE through wall to

37 Interior of a hut, a barracks. Soldiers about, equipment, etc. SOLDIERS in various attitudes of indolence, looking at wall as another bullet clangs against it on outside. Enter CORPORAL.

> CORPORAL--On your feet men! On your feet! Dont you hear the signal?

He gestures toward wall as another bullet clangs against it. The soldiers stir, rise, indolently take up arms.

> SOLDIER---We didn't know, since it is Tomaso who is on post today.

> CORPORAL---And what has that to do with it?

> SOLDIER---We didn't know that Tomaso could hit a house with his rifle.

> CORPORAL---Your backside is not much smaller than a house, but neither is my foot Tomaso. Fall in!

Enter a LIEUTENANT, who stops at door. CORPORAL sees him, becomes very officious.

> CORPORAL---Fall in, I say! The aeroplane is coming.

> SOLDIER---Let it wait.

> CORPORAL---Eh? What was that?

> SOLDIERS (in lowered tone)----t cannot expect us to keep up with it. It is worth a million duros in gold; we, four copper pestas a day.

> CORPORAL (springs forward)---That was that, animal?

32.

                    LIEUT (to CORPORAL)---Animal yourself. Get the
                    men out.

          CORPORAL pauses, looks back toward LIEUT.

                    SOLDIER (in undertone)---Animal yourself.

          CORPORAL whirls.

                    CORPORAL---Who said that?

                    SOLDIER---Nobody, Corporal. It was the echo.

          CORPORAL glares at soldiers. LIEUT watching him.

                    LIEUT---Well? Are you going to march the men
                    out, or am I going to appoint a new corporal?

                    CORPORAL (to LIEUT)---Very good, senor lieuten-
                    ant. (to men)---Fall in. Smartly, now. (Hisses,
                    glares at them) Animals! Insects! Just wait!

                    LIEUT(turning turning away)---Get the box for
                    the fire machine.

          CORPORAL takes up a lock box. Men march out as another
          bullet clangs against the wall. CORPORAL shakes his fist
          at sound. DISSOLVE to

     38   Flying field surrounded by mountains, bordered by iron
          buildings with faintly military air. Sound of engine
          far away. SOLDIERS marching, peons with burros hurrying
          from barracks, excitement. Engine increases as camera
          picks up ship. It increases, lands, rolls up and stops,
          soldiers, peons, burros, all hurrying toward it. BOWDEN
          gets out, stands, hands on hips, looking at approaching
          hord with a kind of sardonic contempt. OTTO in cockpit
          looks out.

                    BOWDEN---Here comes nursie.

                    OTTO---He's got the whole national guard,
                    this time.

                    BOWDEN---Yeah. You can cut it.

          Engines stop. OTTO descends. SOldiers arrive.

                    CORPORAL---Halt!

          SOLDIERS halt, slovenly, surrounding ship, curious.

                         33.

                                                            483

Peons and burros come up, surround BOWDEN, pandemonimn,
BOWDEN registers bad odor.

        BOWDEN---It's not the national guard ⊥ mind,
        so much as the national air.

        OTTO---Maybe we ought to carry a couple of
        clothes pins.

        BOWDEN---Yeah. Maybe we ought to have a couple
        of bullets in us for playing Eddie Cantor down
        here without an encore.

LIEUT appreaches, bows, salutes.

        LIEUT---Senor.

        BOWDEN---Senor.

        LIEUT (Looks at BOWDEN and OTTO)---You said?

        BOWDEN---I said the air is ƒ/n/e//h/e/r/e fine here.
        Makes me home sick. (LIEUT watches him) I used
        to live near the gasworks. One is now permitted
        to depart, my lieutenant?

        LIEUT---Why not, senor? Doubtless the aero-
        plane is also tired.

        BOWDEN---Doubtless. (Turns to OTTO) Get the
        bags ahd lets go.

OttO reenters ship, LIEUT watching, emerges with two
kit bags, they are about to move on when the LIEUT interposes. They pause, Tableau.

        BOWDEN---Well? What's wrong?

        LIEUT---The bags, senores. They will be sent
        on to your hotel.

        BOWDEN---Thanks. We'll carry them, though.

LIEUT makes gesture, two soldiers lower bayonets.
Tableau again.

        BOWDEN---Come on. What is this?

        LIEUT---The senor aviators are guests of our
        country. We cannot see them carry their own
        baggage like peons.

        BOWDEN (looks at LIEUT; they look at one anoth-
        er)---You've been watching us carry these
        bags in to the hotel every time before, without

suffering.

LIEUT---Perhaps you have noticed something else different about this time.

BOWDEN---Yes. You have more soldiers here this time. I noticed that.

LIEUT---And you wondered. Naturally.

BOWDEN---But I did not ask, naturally too.

LIEUT---Nevertheless, I will tell you; that will show you that we have confidence, eh?

BOWDEN---Confidence in me? Have I asked you for that?

LIEUT---Confidence in ourselves, senor.

They look at one another.

BOWDEN---I see. So now you are afraid of us. (Indicates OTTO)

LIEUT---Do not say, afraid, senor.

BOWDEN---All right. Not afraid, then. So what is it?

LIEUT---Nothing. Less than nothing. It is merely that, since you were here before, certain dissatified people have come here.

BOWDEN---Dissatisfied people?

LIEUT---They lived here at one time. Then they found that they did not like our country any longer, and they departed. That was well and good; we force no one to remain here, who no longer is pleased with our country. Even yourself, for instance, senor.

BOWDEN---And now they have come back?

LIEUT---On a ship.

BOWDEN---Then why do you think that they are still dissatisfied?

LIEUT---Because they came back in secret.

BOWDEN---In secret? Then how do you know-----

35.

LIEUT---Is it not amusing, eh?

OTTO---What is it? Does he think we've got some of the gold in our grips?

BOWDEN---Well, what is all this to me?

LIEUT---These dissatisfied people returned here from your country, senor.

BOWDEN---From my country?

LIEUT---Where they have lived for five years ----also in secret. Is that not amusing?

OTTO---Well, if you cant do anything with him, ~~I can~~/ I can. Keep him talking to ~~you~~ you a minute longer, until I can get back into the ship and get hold of the spanner------

BOWDEN---Be quiet. (To LIEUT) Very amusing. The moral being that secrecy doesn't get very far in this country, eh?

LIEUT---Not one little inch. You would be surprised, senor.

BOW EN---Not me. I fly this aeroplane when and where I am told to. What you people do or dont do is not skin off my back. (To OTTO) Give him the bags.

OTTO---Let them have them?

BOWDEN---Yes.

LIEU----They will be sent on to the hotel to you, senor----I hope, undisturbed.

BOWDEN---So do I. (Turns away) Come on.

LIEUT---There is one more little thing, senor.

BOWDEN turns; they look at one aonther.

LIEUT---The machine which makes the fire.

BOWDEN---Oh. (To OTTO) Get him the magneto.

OTTO reenters the ship, emerges with magneto, jams it at LIEUT. the CORPORAL opens lock box and holds it out. LIEUT puts magneto on box, closes and locks it, removes key. BOWDEN extends hand for key.

LIEUT (putting key in ~~pocket~~ his pocket)---- Again I will not trouble you, senor.

36.

OTTO(glowering)---Are you going to let him
get away with that too?

BOWDEN (Turns away)---Come on.

They walk on. The LIEUT looks after them, makes sign,
peons swarm about ship, beginning to unload the gold.
DISSOLVE to

39 BOWDEN and OTTᵛ getting into battered Ford.

OTTO---Now, what do you make of that?

BOWDEN (Starts Ford)---Nothing.

OTTO---We have been flying out from the mine
with a load of bullion once a month for a̶ ̶y̶e̶a̶r̶
a year, with these Spiks not even caring
whether we ever got to a hotel or not. And now
all of a sudden we get to be too good to carry
our own grips. (The car moves on, BOWDEN driving) And every time we come in, I have to
take the mag off so they can lock it up in that
little box and give you the key. That was goo-
fy enough. But this time they dont even give
you the key. Why is that?

BOWDEN---I dont know.

OTTO---What do you think,then?

BOWDEN---I dont think anything. And listen.
Dont you think anything, either.

OTTO---Dont?-----(Looks at BOWDEN. BOWDEN
glances at him)

BOWDEN---Dont think anything. And dont say
anything. See?

OTTO (Looks at him suprised)---Why, I......
(Sees that BOWDEN is serious) ----Sure. O.K.

BOWDEN---And lay off the booze.

OTTO---Ah, I dont hit it much. Besides, what's
a guy to do when he comes to town? I aint like
you. I aint got a skirt waiting for me.

BOWDEN---Yeah. I'd noticed that. You dont have
that trouble.

OTTO (looks away, his face suddenly grave)---no

37.

I aint got that trouble.

BOWDEN glances at him, sees his averted face, looks at him.

> BOWDEN---Well, dont cry about it. Wasn't it
> just last month I had to get you out of the
> jug for celebrating over that newspaper clip---

> OTTO---Dont, CHief.

> BOWDEN---Right. I'm sorry. But remember what I ßáŻ
> said. Lay off the booze. Until I find out
> just what is going on.

> OTTO---Going on?

> BOWDEN---Up to today, they have had about a
> dozen soldiers there to meet us, and they
> took their time about unloading the ship. To-
> day there must have been a hundred there, and
> the whole field háßŻ/háŻŻ was full of mozos
> and mules.

> OTTO---That's right. What do you think is up?

> BOWDEN---I dont know. But this country has been
> quiet for five years,now. Since they ran the
> king out. That's too long for people down here
> to behave.

> OTTO---Jeez. And you think----

> BOWDEN---I'm not thinking. And dont you think
> any, either. And if you do think, dont tell
> anybody. Get me?

> OTTO---Dont tell anybody what?

> BOWDEN---Dont tell anybody anything. Let them
> run their country like they want to. If they
> want to spend a holiday shooting each other,
> let them. And if anybody asks you what you
> think about it, say, No spika. Get that?

> OTTO---O.K.

> BOWDEN---Right, then.

38.

40 DISSOLVE to hotel entrance. Tramp of feet in distance.
Three men lounging beside entrance with watchful airs.
As feet increase, they move back behind a column as soldiers pass, watching them. Feet die away, sound ot engine begins. Men peer out tiward sound, withdraw again
as car drives up. Men watch as BOWDEN gets out and OTTO
takes wheel.

        BOWDEN---I want to find you here and in bed
        when I come in tonight. We'll leave early in the
        morning.

        OTTO---What the hell? You mean, we're only
        going to stay in town one night? After a month
        o̶u̶t̶/t̶h̶e̶r̶/w̶i̶t̶h̶/n̶o̶t̶h̶i̶n̶g̶/t̶o̶/l̶o̶o̶k̶/a̶t̶/b̶u̶t̶/
        out there with nothing to look at but scenery?

        BOWDEN---Yes.

        OTTO---Ah, come on, chief. (BOWDEN looks at
        him) Well, you're boss. But hell, I.......
        (Looks aside, his air is fasle) O.K., then.
        I'll just listen around, and if anything breaks
        tonight I'll get in touch with you at the
        boss's house--------

        BOWDEN---With every Spik detective in town
        listening in?

        OTTO---Who, me? They haven't got anything on
        me.

        BOWDEN---Until we get out of town again, we
        probably wont even be alone when we bathe.

        OTTO (Looks at BOWDEN in alarm)---The hell you
        say. What is this, c̶h̶i̶e̶f̶ anyway, chief?

        BOWDEN---I dont know and I dont care. You just
        do like I tell you. Get some dinner and come
        straight back here. Stay away from cantinas.
        And if anybody asks you how you like your
        soup or what time it is or anything else, you
        say No spika. Do you hear me?

        OTTO---I hear you.

        BOWDEN---Get along, then. Put the car in the
        garage and get something to eat and then beat
        it back here.

39.

OTTO drives away. While BOWDEN lokks after him, the three
men quit column and move away. BOWDEN turns to enter;
tramping feet increase; BOWDEN pauses as another squad
of soldiers passes, looks after them as their feet carry
into DISSOLVE.

41

With sound of engine RESOLVE entrance to garage as OTTO
drives in. Enter three men, who pause at door. OTTO e-
merges, men move forward.

      FIRST---Well, well. It is Senor Otto.

(He takes OTTO's hand before OTTO can resist, shakes it)

      OTTO---Howdy, amigos.

OTTO tries to withdraw hand, as though remembering BOW-
DEN'S injunction. FIRST continues to shake it.

      FIRST---And here is Roderigo, whom you know.

RODERIGO and OTTO shake, OTTO quite wary.

      FIRST---And this is Senor Ortega, who has just
      returned from your country.

      ORTEGA (bows)---Good day, Senor.

      OTTO (looks about at them, wary)---How are you.
      What are you guys up to?

      FIRST---Eh, we have come to greet you. To have
      our little drink together, as usial. (Locks his
      arm in OTTO'S, who holds back) Come. To the
      cantina! Forward!

      OTTO (Holding back)---No, no, I cant------

      FIRST (leading OTTO on)---Eh, Ortega! Is he
      not amusing? Did I not tell you? This Americano
      will make you laugh before the evening is over.

      OTTO(holding back vainly)---No, no, I cant
      I tell you! I got to------(they lead him on)
      No spika! I tell you! No spika!

      FIRST (Pauses, looks at OTTO)---Eh? You insult
      us, then? You insult Senor Ortega, who has
      come all the way from North America to drink with
      you?

      OTTO---Well......But just one now.

      FIRST---Hah! Did I not warn.you, Ortega? Is he

not the funniest man in America? (Locks arms
and leads OTTO on again) Forward!

They exit. DISSOLVE to

42   The hotel. BOWDEN enters, passes a man seated behind
a newspaper. —an lowers paper; it is AVILAS. MANAGER
comes forward, greets BOWDEN effusively.

MANAGER---Ah, senor! Welcome. A good trip, eh?

BOWDEN---Thanks. Any mail for me? (Looks ø toward desk. When he does so, MANAGER makes signal to AVILAS)

40-B.

MANAGER---It is in the Senor's room, as usial.
Also there is a message, doubtless of more
importance. (His air is knowing. BOWDEN looks
at him, coldly. MANAGER resumes ordinary tone)
From Miss White. She asked that the captain
telephone her at onee. As soon as he reached
the hotel.

BOWDEN---Thanks. (Turns, approaches telephone
booth. AVILAS rises, goes to stairs, mounts.
MANAGER watches BOWDEN in booth.

PAN to BOWDEN in booth.

BOWDEN---Hello. That you, Carlota? Miss Nancy,
please.... ...yes. This is el capitan.

43   DISSOLVE through instrument to another on feminine dressing table, a hand putting it down. PAN to CARLOTA'S face
as she turns away. It is something like MARIA'S, cold ,
still, inscrutable.

NANCY (offstage)---Who is it, Carlota?

CARLOTA---It is el capitan, senorita.

NANCY---Heavens, el capitan must be in love,
telephoning me when he is supposed to be here
-----(enters, takes telephone from CARLOTA. She
wears negligee) What time is it now?

CARLOTA withdraws, stands, looks at NANCY, cold, still.

CARLOTA---Ten minutes to six, senorita.

PAN to CARLOTA'S face, TRUCK to NANCY at phone.

NANCY----George? This is nice. To what do I owe
this honor, kind sir?

GEORGE (after a moment)---Did I surprise you?

NANCY---Most pleasantly. Knowing how you
adore to telephone in Spanish, I hadn't heped
to hear from you until I see you this evening.

GEORGE (After a moment)---Oh. You didn't leave a
message for me to call you?

NANCY (surprised)---Why, no. Who told you I did?

40-C.

492

PAN to CARLOTA'S face watching NANCY.

>GEORGE (off stage)---Nothing. I'll see you
>tonight, then?

>NANCY (offstage)---Did they tell you at the
>hotel that I left a message for you to call?

>GEORGE (offstage)---It was a mistake, I guess.
>I'll see you tonight, then. Right?

>NANCY (offstage)---At dinner, mind. It was
>funny they told you I had left------

>GEORGE (offstage)---It dosen't matter. Do I
>have to dress up?

PAN to NANCY at telephone.

>NANCY---I'm afraid so. We're having some peo-
>ple in later---very high and diplomatic. Do
>you mind? Of course you do, my poor darling.

>GEORGE---Damn. I mean, no I dont mind. Until
>then, then.

>NANCY---Until then, then.... .George.

>GEORGE----What?

>NANCY----That was funny about that m------

>GEORGE---It all right. I'll see you soon.

>NANCY---Right. Soon. Come early.

Puts down telephone, turns to CARLOTA.

>NANCY---Did you send word to the hotel for el
>capitan to call me?

>CARDOTA---No, senorita.

>NANCY---That's funny. Somebody did.

>CARLOTA---Perhaps there was no message. Perhaps
>el capitan merely wanted to see if you were
>at home.

NANCY pauses, looks at CARLOTA, who looks steadily back
at her.

>NANCY---Why should el capitan want to know if
>I am home?

CARLOTA---I do not know, senorita. I only said that perhaps that was why he called.

NANCY---And besides, why should he need an excuse to call me? What do you mean, Carlota?

CARLOTA---I? Nothing, senorita. I did not mean to alarm you.

NANCY---Alarm me? I am not alarmed. You do mean something. What is it? Is there something about el capitan-----Nonesense. Listen at me. (Laughs nervously, gestures, ceases) I would like why you said that.

CARLOTA---Said what, senorita?

NANCY---Nothing. You didn't say anything; that is true. Besides, he will be here in.....what time is it?

CARLOTA---Five minutes past six, senorita. You can ask him then.

NANCY---Yes, I can ask h̶i̶m̶/-------(ceases, nervous, catches herself) What am I saying? You've got me all......(catches herself again) I'm going to rest for a while. You may go. Come back in twenty-five minutes.

CARLOTA---Very good, senorita. That is all?

NANCY (restraining herself)---Yes. Go. Go.

CARLOTA goes toward door. NANCY makes movement toward telephone, restrains herself, waiting for CARLOTA to exit. CARLOTA passes through door, closes it to a crack, stands so. NANCY goes to phone, takes it up, pauses again in i̶n̶d̶i̶c̶a̶t̶i̶o̶n̶ indecision, nervous, decides, puts phone down, turns away. CARLOTA closes door, goes on.

TRUCK with CARLOTA to her room in servants' quarters. She opens door, enters. MARIA sits in chair. It can now be seen that they are sisters.

MARIA---He has called?

CARLOTA---Yes.

MARIA---And she?

CARLOTA---Is worried. Of what, she does not know. But she is ready to believe anything. Did I do well, my sister?

42.

Maria---You did well, my sister.

CARLOTA---And now what shall ᴵ do?

MARIA (Rises, puts on shawl)---Wait. Can you
also do that?

CARLOTA---Why not? Have ᴵ not waited for five
years?

MARIA exits. DISSOLVE to

4 4 Hotel. BOWDEN outside telephone booth, thoughtful. MAN-
AGER behind desk, apparently busy. BOWDEN looks at him,
approaches.

BOWDEN---Just what time did this message come
for me to call Miss White? Can you tell me?

MANAGER---Of a certainty, senor. Ɪ̸ẋ̸/ẉ̸ẋ̸ṡ̸/Ɑ̸ṅ̸ḍ̸ṙ̸ḛ̸ọ̸/
(claps his hands. PAGE enters. To PAGE) At
what hour did the message arrive for ṡ̸ḛ̸ṅ̸ the
captain to telephone Miss White?

PAGE---ᴵ do not know, senor. ᴵt was Andreo
who told me of the message.

MANAGER---Why did you not say so at first, im-
becile? (PAGE shrugs) Call Andreo. (Exit PAGE;
reenters with ANDREO. To ANDREO) You, then.
At what hour did the message arrive for el capitan?

ANDREO---ᴵ do not know, senor. ᴵt was Carlos
who--------

MANAGER---Animal! Insect! Species of a mule!
Will you tell me next that it was the cook
who took the message? Send me Carlos, then.

PAGE turns away.

BOWDEN---wait. (PAGE halts; they look at him)
Never mind. ᴵt doesn't matter.

MANAGER (To PAGES)---Begone, then. And thank
the magnanimosity of the senor that ᴵ do not
lay a strap to your backs. Begone! (Exit PAGES)
You see? They are children. ᴵf there has been
a mistake, ᴵ shall be desolate, senor.

BOWDEN---There was no mistake. ᴵt's all right.

He turns away, MANAGER watches him mount stair.

43.

TRUCK to corridor. BOWDEN pauses, thoughtful alert,
watchful, listening, goes on to his door, pauses again,
thoughtful; then as though dismissing thought, he opens
his door and is about to enter, pauses again. Open door
/r̶e̶v̶e̶a̶l̶s̶/m̶i̶r̶r̶o̶r̶/ reveals a mirror. In the mirror door in
opposite side of room can be seen to close hurriedly,
as though interloper were suprised. BOWDEN springs
into room, runs to other door, jerks it open, falls
back as door reveals MANUEL with pistol. BOWDEN looks
about, his glance pauses, widens, narrows. CLOCK to

45   MARION lying on sofa, in attitude of shipboard pratice,
in negligee. CUT to

46   BOWDEN watching her while MANUEL holds pistol on him.

            BOWDEN (suddenly)---Otto! Otto!

DISSOLVE to
47   Cantina. Otto and three men, drinking.

            OTTO---Just one more. Then, no spika, See?

            FIRST (pouring)---But certainly. (Shoves glass
            to OTTO, they raise them.) My heroes! No spika!

OTTO drinks, the other three empty their drinks on the
floor.

DISSOLVE to
48   BOWDENS room, tableau, MANUEL, BOWDEN, MARION.

            MANUEL---Louder, senior. Louder.

DISSOLVE t̶o̶/o̶/ over sound of tramping feet to

49   Stairway, a footman mounting. TRUCK withFOOTMAN to door.
He knocks. Door opens, it is CARLOTA.

            FOOTMAN---The master wishes to know why the
            senorita does not come down. Dinner has been
            announced.

            CARLOTA---Tell the master that the senorita
            has been taken with a violent headache and
            asks to be excused until after dinner.

FOOTMAN turns away. Door closes, tramp of FOOTMAN'S feet
dies away in DISSOLVE to

50   CLOCK on NANCY'S dressing table, at a minute past eight.

44.

NANCY before it, turned toward door, her face wild, disheveled. She is still in negligee. CARLOTA eneters.

                NANCY---Yes? Was that-----

                CARLOTA---It was the footman again. Wanting to
                know why the senorita has not come down to
                dinner.

NANCY turns back to the clock with a wild gesture, her
hands to her face.

                NANCY---A half hour. The messenger has been
                gone half/ a half hour. (Whirls upon CARLOTA,
                grips her shoulders)You are lying to me. You
                dian't/send even send a messenger.

                CARLOTA---I sent him. The senorita knows that.

                NANCY---Then why hasn't he come back? A half
                hour.A half hour! Just to the hotel and back.
                Telephone again,

                CARLOTA ---If the senorita wishes. (Approaches
                phone) And does not object to the hotel people
                knowing that she is jealous of her young man like
                any peon girl.

                NANCY--True. True. (stops CARDOTA with a ges-
                ture, clasps her head in her hands, pauses
                again) Jealous? You said jealous! I, jealous?
                Of what? (Whirls grips CARLOTA again)You know
                something. You have been trying all evening
                to hint sonething to me. What is it? (CARLOTA
                shrugs, indicates patient indifference. NANCY
                clasps her head again) I shall go wild, wild!

                CARLOTA---Why doesn't the senorita lie down and
                compose herself? The messenger------

                NANCY---Lie down? Compose myself? (laughs, wild
                and hysterical) Compose myself? I----(ceases.
                a knock at the door. NANCY almost glares toward
                sound) There! Quickly! see!

CARLOTA goes to door, opens it, enter COACHMAN.

                NANCY (restraining herself)---Well?

                COACHMAN---I went to the hotel, as the senor-
                ita commanded. The senor has been there.

                NANCY---I know that. Been there? You mean, he is
                not---------

                COACHMAN---He was not seen to leave.

                        43.

                                                        497

NANCY---Idiot! Do you mean that you did not
even go to his room?

COACHMAN----I did. The door was locked.

NANCY---Locked?

COACHMAN---Locked, senorita. And the manager----

NANCY---Well? (begins to lose control) are
you trying to drive me mad?

COACHMAN (shrugs)---He would not open the door.
He said it was none of his affair.

NANCY makes wild gesture, begins to laugh hysterically,
strives to control herself.

NANCY---First he telephones me saying something about a message which was never sent
and then you---(to CARLOTA, fiercely)---begin
to hint around about this and that, and then
he does not come and I can find out nothing,
nothing! The manager of his hotel says that
it is none of his affair. (looks at them,
trembling, losing control) You are all lying
to me! Trying to decieve me! What si it? (
(Grasps COACHMANS shoulder) I will know! I
will know!

COACHMAN--- I know nothing, senorita.

NANCY---NOthing? Nothing! That's what is driving
me mad! (thought strikes her; claps her hands
in agony for having wasted time) Otto! He will
know. (Turns to COACHMAN) Is suppose you will
tell me now that Otto also cannot be found.

COACHMAN---I do not know that, senorita. The
companion who flies with el capitan is in a
cantina, drinking.

NANCY---In a cantina, drinking. (To CARLOTA)
get my cloak.

CARLOTA---Your cloak, senorita?

NANCY---Cloak! Cloak! Do you think I am going
to sit here holding my hands and going quietly
insane?

46.

498

CARLOTA---Very good, senorita. But what will
the master-----

start
NANCY---Will you get my cloak and stop driving
me crazy?

CARLOTA---Very good, senorita.

CARLOTA exits. NANCY turns to COACHMAN.

NANCY---Have the carriage at the side door.
Hurry.

COACHMAN exits. CARLOTA returs with cloak. NANCY puts
it on hurriedly.

NANCY---Come. (They exit. DISSOLVE to

51   Side entrance, carriage waiting, NANCY and CARLOTA enter
hurriedly, enter carriage, it drives away. Sound of
hooves die into tramp of soldiers.DISSOLVE

52   RESOLVE newspaper clippings, worn and creased with time.
They are seen at random.

Otto. Where are you.

Otto. Come home to.

The last one entire:

You dont need to hide any longer.
She died last night.

PAN slowly back to take in table top, glasses and bottles, OTTO'S hand fumbling at clippings in a drunken
way.

OTTO (offstage)--- Boss said no booze. But how
in hell can a man forget grief if he dont
drink?

FIRST (offstage)----Bravo. Come, then; let
us forget our grief.

Enter FIRST'S hand, filling glasses during PAN back to
take in scene at table, OTTO staring at clipping in
drunken way, FIRST filling glasses, other two watching
OTTO quietly)

OTTO---Brave, hell. I'm not brave. Just a poor
bum. That's all ‹ am. (looks at clippings,
tearful, his hand fumbling at his glass) Jush
poor bum that serted,.......serted....... .
(begins to cry) just a poor unfortuniate son of

47.

a bitch. That's all I am.

FIRST leans, claps OTTO on shoulder.

      FIRST---You? A brave aviator like you? Eh?

      OTTO (looks at him glassily, ceases to cry)
      ---Huh? You say I aint poor son of a bitch?
      Come on.Say it.

      FIRST---Not in ten thousand years.

OTTO makes drunken movement, strikes table, glares at
them, swaying.

      OTTO---Man that says I aint....aint.....says
      I dont have grief-------

      FIRST---To hell with that man, senors! Have
      I not said it? Eh, then. (raises his glass,
      others follow) To grief!

      OTTO(Fumbling)---To hell with grief. To hell
      with everything. (Drinks,again others do not
      drink. OTTO sets his glass down)

      FIRST---Eh, senors! You, Ortega. You do not know
      what this brave senor does every day of his life.

OTTO stares at FIRST, trying to focus his eyes.

      ORTEGA---That is true.

      FIRST---And he will not tell you, not he; not
      this hero. (Claps OTTO on shoulder) Eh, Otto?

      OTTO---Not every day. Onesh a month.

      FIRST---What is the difference? Once a day,
      once a month, once ayear. Does it matter how
      often er how seldom a hero performs his deed
      of heroism? I ask you, senors; as a friend, I
      ask you.

      RODERIGO----No.

      FIRST---Not in ten thousand years. Ten thous-
      and years? A million years! Look, then. This
      senor, with another to help him, conducts the
      aeroplane each across/the/mountains/ month
      across the mountains. Alone, mind you, save for
      one little companion to keep him company in his
      gallant risk of death.

                48.

OTTO (staring at FIRST)---What do you mean,
little? Best pilot in the world, shee? Chief
best damn pilot in........(stares at them stupidly) Who says Chief aint just poor son of
a.......(ceases, begins to cry again) Jush
poor son of a bitch, that's all I am. (Fumbles at clippings. Speaks in tearful voice)
Saved my life in France. That's what he did.
Saved life of me, nothing but poor son of
bitch that.....serted....serted wife and
baby--------(pulls himself up, stares at them,
swaying, crumbling the clippings) What the
hell you trying to do, huh? Come on. Say it.
Finest man in the world. Man that says different I'll-----(reaches for glass as though it
were a weapon. FIRST leans forward quickly
with bottle)

FIRST---Bravo. (Fills OTTO'S glass, who ceases,
watches stupidly. FIRST fills other glasses,
lifts his) COme, senors. To El Capitan Bowden,
the best pilot in the wotld! Drink!

OTTO---By God, I'll drink that. Drink that
hundred times. Because chief said so.. Said take
just one more. Then---No spika. shee? (drinks
sloppily, sets glass down) Saved my life. I
would die for him. Shee?

FIRST---Bravo! (Fills OTTO'S glass for him again,
lifts his own) Again! To a grateful man as
well as a hero, senors! To Otto! (They drink;
OTTO bows drunkenly) But let me tell you, senors,
how heros are treated. Once each month these
brave men risk their lives to conduct the aeroplane across the mountains. And then, when
they reach here, what do you think they are
compelled to do?

48-A.

RODERIGO---I for one cannot guess.

FIRST---You cannot, senors. Soldiers with bayonets force them to take from the m̸a̸c̸h̸i̸n̸e̸/
aeroplane the fire machine which makes it go,
and lock it up in a box which the soldiers keep.
(to OTTO) Is t̸h̸i̸s̸/ not that true?

OTTO---You're damned right it is.

FIRST---But stay; that is not all. That is
injury, but this is insult. What do you think they
do with the key to the box?

RODERIGO---That too, I for one cannot guess.

OTTO now watches FIRST.

FIRST---They make el capitan keep the key. Is
not that insult?

RODERIGO---No! I cannot believe it, senor.

FIRST---It is true. (they w̸a̸t̸c̸h̸ are watching
OTTO, who rouses, drunken)

OTTO---You're wrong there.

FIRST---It is----eh? (They look at OTTO) you
mean, el capitan no longer has the key to the
m̸a̸c̸h̸i̸n̸e̸ fire machine?

OTTO (tries to pull up; cunning)---No spika.
Attemps to get up) Got to go. Been here too
-------(Almost falls to floor. **FIRST** catches
him up)

FIRST---Good! We will all go. But first, one
little one. (fills glasses, passes them. OTTO
pushes his away)

OTTO---No. Dont want more. Got to go.

FIRST---Eh? You will not drink again to el
capitan, the pilot of magnificence?

OTTO (takes his glass, fumbling)---Sure.
Drink all day to man saved my life. (loudly)
to best damned pilot in world. (Drinks, unawares that the others have paused, looking at
door. OTTO drinks, looks puzzled, sways forward onto table as COACHMAN enters) RODERIGO
examines OTTO, nods to first)

FIRST (to COACHMAN)---Well?

49.

502

COACHMAN---She is outside now. We go to the
hotel?

FIRST---Yes. But first get this message to
him whom you know. Listen carefully. The message is, 'He does not have the key.' Repeat.

COACHMAN----I am to get this message first to
him whom I know:'He does not have the key'.

FIRST---Good. Go now. And take this ---(indicates OTTO)----with you. (To RODERIGO) Go
with him.

RODERIGO and COACHMAN raise OTTO and carry him out. DIS*
SOLVE to

53   Hotel entrance. Carriage stops, COACHMAN gets down, o-
     pens door, NANCY gets out hurriedly, CARLOTA and RODER-
     IGO follow . NANCY runs toward door.

CARLOTA (gestures to COACHMAN) ---Go. Quickly.

COACHMAN follows NANCY.

RODERIGO (indicates carriage)---Shall I bring him
too?

CARLOTA--- No. Keep him here. Wait. (She
follows. DISSOLVE to

54   Hotel lounge, NANCY and COACHMAN entering, NANCY distract-
     ed, catching herself up. MANAGER comes forward; his air
     is alert, as though waiting for his cue. CARLOTA enters.
     MANAGER glances at her, then back at NANCY, his air
     properly obsequious.

MANAGER ---Good evening, senorita.

NANCY(distracted)---I have come....CARLOTA...

CARLOTA---We wish to see Captain Bowden, senor.
He is here?

MANAGER---He is here, senora.

NANCY***-Then why didn't you-----

CARLOTA (touching her)---Senorita. (to MANA-
GER)---Then why have we not been able to reach
him? I telephoned twice, and then sent a

50.

messenger in person.

MANAGER@--Quite. But I did not tell you that
he was not here, senora.

CARLOTA---That is true. But we couldn't-----

MANAGER---He is a guest of the hotel. It is
my duty to carry out his wishes; not to question them.

NANCY---You mean, he told you to tell me that
he.....me? Tell me?

CARLOTA(Grips NANCY again)---Senorita. (to
MANAGER) Will your duties as manager permit
you to tell him now that a lady wishes to
speak with him?

MANAGER---Certainly, senora. Will you wait
here?

NANCY---Wait? I wont wait. There's something
queer about this. (To CARLOTA) You have been
hinting and hinting, and I have not been permitted for some reason to.......(looks from one
to the other, panting)

CARLOTA---To what, senorita? (NANCY looks at
them, wildly. CARLOTA stand, cold, still. MAN-
AGER shrugs. To MANAGER) Go. Tell Captain Bowden that Miss White is here. (To COACHMAN) go
with him.

MANAGER pauses, glances at COACHMAN, shrugs, goes on.

MANAGER---Come, then.

Exit MANAGER and COACHMAN up the stairs. NANCY looks
after them, panting, CARLOTA touches her.

CARLOTA---It will be all right now. Compose
yourself. There are people watching.

NANCY---Yes. Yes. (restrains herself, sits.
CARLOTA stands beside her) DISSOLVE to

5 S̄ Upper corridor. MANAGER enters from stair, pauses, his
manner changes as COACHMAN enters.

MANAGER---Well?

COACHMAN---There is a message. It is, 'He no
longer has the key.'

MANAGER---Good. Wait here.

51.

504

TRUCK with MANAGER down corridor, to ¢¢¢ a door. He
taps, door opens, he enters. DISSOLVE to

56 Room, MARIA, and AVILAS, MANAGER facing them.

MARIA---She is here?

MANAGER---Yes.

AVILAS---Good. And have you heard from----

MANAGER---Yes, general. He does not have the
key.

AVILAS---So.

MARIA---So they suspect something, then. Good;
now we can begin to-----

AVILAS---Perhaps it is not that bad. Perhaps
they only know. With an enemy who knows, I can
deal. It is the one who suspects, whom I fear.

MARIA---That is true. And now we can begin to act.
I have brought this situation about; it is
now your turn.

AVILAS---He must remain in the employ of this
gringo who owns the aeroplane; that is obvious.

MARIA---Good.

AVILAS---Therefore, ¢¢¢ this griggo's daughter cannot find ¢¢¢ what we have planned for
her to find.

MARIA---Why not?

They look at one another.

AVILAS---Eh?

MARIA---Look. In my conduct of this affair, in
my handling of these two young women, have I
yet made a false move?

AVILAS---That is true.

MARIA---Then depend on me.

They look at one another, MARIA cold, AVILAS trying to
read her thought.

52.

AVILAS (after a moment)---Good. (turns to MAN-
AGER, is about to speak, turns back to MARIA)
What do you intend to do?

MARIA looks at him steadily.

MARIA---In what way, my general?

AVILAS---What do you intend to do next with
this girl?

MARIA---Which girl? There are two of them.

AVILAS---You know which one I mean. Marion.

MARIA---That I cannot tell you. Ask that of
need and circumstance; not of me.

AVILASS--Ha. And that is what I.....(ceases,
looks at her, who meets his look steadily)

MARIA---Fear? Is that the word you were about
to use?

AVILAS---We have much at stake; a kingdom,
honor, the privilege of dwelling on the soil
from which we sprung------

MARIA---And life too. Do not forget that.

AVILAS---I have not forgot it. And I have not
forgot this. Our prince said to you, 'No harm
must come to her'. Have you forgot that?

MARIA---No. And I have not forgot what I said
to him in turn. (They look at one another) I
said, 'Then let her father shield her; she
has a father there'.

She looks at AVILAS, col, still. After a moment AVILAS
looks down. MARIA turns to MANAGER.
MARIA/(quietly)/---Take/her/to/the/room.

MARIA(quietly)---Take her to the room.

MANAGER exits. MARIA rises and follows. Tramp of feet
begins, rises and carries through DISSOLVE to

5 7   BOWDEN'S room. BOWDEN sits in attitude of patient resignation. MANUEL at ease, with pistol. MARION sits now
with negligee wrapped closely about her; she is
almost cringing; she is worried. Tramp of feet die away
as soldiers pass on.

53.

506

                    MAROIN---What time is it now, Manuel?

MANUEL looks at his watch.

                    MANUEL ---Twenty minutes of nine, senorita.

                    MARION---And we have been here since before
                    six oclock. I dont understand this.

                    MANUEL---Do not try. They will come soon. Then
                    you can ask.

                    MARION---I want to help. But how can I help this
                    ----

MANUEL gives her a meaning look, indicates BOWDEN. MA-
RION ceases, looks at BOWDEN with kind of shy alarm.

                    BOWDEN---Go on. I'm in no position to tell
                    your secrets, even if I knew them. (To MANHEL)
                    Isn't that right?

                    MANUEL---That is so, senor.

                    BOWDEN (to MARION)---I wish you'd tell me one
                    thing, though. (MARION gazes at him, cringing
                    into her negligee, her legs curled under her)
                    You're an American. What are you doing mixed
                    up in this?

MARION looks at him, terrified, glances at MANUEL, who
is watchful, grim, looks at BOWDEN, then away.

                    BOWDEN---Come on. Tell me. Aren't you an Amer-
                    ican?

Again MARION galnces up in cringing alarm, meets MANUEL'S
look, forces herself to look at BOWDEn.

                    MARION---No. I'm not an American.

                    BOWDEN---I see. Of course not. You are a native,
                    of course. With that hair and that accent, how
                    could I have been mistaken.

MARION glances at him, nervous. MANUEL watches.

                    MANUEL---The senorita's nationality does not
                    matter, senor. The important thing is that
                    she is a woman.

BOWDEN turns slowly and looks at MANUEL.

                    BOWDEN---So. And just what does that mean,
                    senor?

                    54.

                                                       507

Door in back opens; they turn as MARIA enters. MANUEL
and BOWDEN do not change position. MARION half springs
up.

>MARION---Maria! I thought----was afraid......

>MARIA (to MANUEL)---Be ready. (To MARION)---
>Quick. the sofa.

>MARION (pausing, staring at MARIA)---The sofa?

MANUEL moves swiftly across to a screen. MARIA approaches
MARION as BOWDEN watches in curiosity. MARIA pushes MA-
RION toward sofa.

>MARIA---Quickly.

She thrusts MARION down. MARION automatically arranges
herself in pratice attitude , looking at MARIA.

>MARION---But I dont understand. What-----

BOWDEN sits forward, watching, becoming angry. A knock at
the door; all turn toward it.

>MARIA---Go. (to BOWDEN) You, senor.

>BOWDEN---Me? I'm not boss here any longer, it
>seems, Look here------

>MARION---Who is it, Maria? (Tries to rise,
>MARIA holds her down) You're hurting me!

BOWDEN springs up.

>BOWDEN---Let her go.

MARIA holds MARION down, MARION looks up at her, terrified.

>MARIA---You speak loudly, senor, not to know who
>it-is who---------

A commotion beyond door, then NANCY'S voice is heard.

>NANCY----I will! I will! I heard him! George!

BOWDEN and MARIA look at door, BOWDEN turns.

>BOWDEN---So. I see now. So this is the game,
>eh?

>MARIA---Will you go, or shall I?

55.

508

BOWDEN (glares at MARIA)---Right. This is
your trick. But dont forget: This game is not
----(Turns to door, opens it. MARIA and MANUEL
step behind screen. MARION is ⌀⫽⫽ half risen
from sofa. TRUCK to BOWDEN at door, NANCY facing
him as he blocks view of room. Behind her CAR-
LOTA and MANAGER)

NANCY---George! George! (Flings her arms around
him, wild, hysterical) Are you all right?

BOWDEN---Of course I'm all right.

NANCY---You phoned me,that queer message, and
you didn't come and I tried to get you and I
couldn't and I got worrieder and worrieder---
(clings to him, laughing and crying)

MARION starts up from sofa with expression of dawning
comprehension on her face. BOWDEN sees her movement,
moves again to hide her from NANCY.

BOWDEN---Sure I'm all right. (Holds NANCY, with
his other hand he gestures MARION back. MARION
continues to approach, the negligee slipping
from her shoulder, she pulling it back, the
comprehension solidifying in her face) It was
just some business I had------

NANCY---I was a fool! But I didn't know,
couldn't imagine-----(cling to him, laughing
and crying, regaining control) But now it's
all right. I'm all right now. (Wipes her eyes,
regains control, laughing now at her own fears.
MARION approaches staring, pulling the negligee
up, BOWDEN trying to interpose himself) But
why didn't you let me know? (Feels BOWDEN'S ⫽⌀⫽⌀⫽
movement, looks at him, surprised) Why, what
is it? What are you trying------

MARION (her air as wild as NANCY'S)---Wait. Let
me. Are you his wife?

NANCY looks past BOWDEN, who now with ⫽⌀⫽⌀⫽⫽/⫽⌀⌀/ air
of savage resignation steps aside, turns. NANCY stares at ⫽
MARION who faces her wildly, tugging up the slipping
negligee.

NANCY (staring, still)---Oh. Oh. Oh.

MARION---They didn't tell me this, that he had
a wife. I promised to help them, but I didn't
know that I--------

NANCY (staring, in her quiet tone)---I dont

56.

understand. (Stares at MARION, dazed, raises
her hand in a childlike gesture, touches BOW-
DEN, seems surprised to find him there)George!
I dont understand, George! Tell me - dont understand.

MARION---I can tell you. Listen----Oh, I dont
even know what your name is, what his name is
--------- --

NANCY watches her in quiet horror. Suddenly CARLOTA
moves, touches NANCY-

CARLOTA---Come, senorita. The senor capitan is
engaged. Let us go.

NANCY (turning to CARLOTA)---Go?

CARLOTA---Yes. Let us go home.

NANCY (in dazed tone)---Home? (Suddenly she be-
gins to laugh, restraining at first) Home?
Home? (Louder; turns to BOWDEN) George! George!
You didn't need to fool me! I'm too easy fooled
It's not fair! It's not fair!

CARLOTA (touching her again)---Senorita------

NANCY flings off CARLOTA'S hand. To MARION, furiously.

NANCY---Explain? What do you have to explain?

MARION (with wild, dazed air)---They didn't
tell me. I wanted to help them. But they didn't
tell me that he had a--------

NANCY---Ah. He fooled you too, did he? He
neglected to tell you that he had a wife, and
he neglected to tell me that he had a-------

BOWDEN (grips her)----Nancy!

NANCY (trying to jerk free)----Oh! 'Oh! Oh! To
fool me when I couldn't see, I could forgive
that. But to keep on trying to fool me when I
can see with my own eyes......George! GEorge!
And thsi! You didn't have to do this, George.
Let me come up here and find.....you could
have sent me word. You could have done that,
George! Could have sent me a message! 'I'm tired
of yoy. I have another girl. Goodbye.' You
could have done that, George!

BOWDEN---Will you listen for one minute?

57.

510

NANCY---Listen? Have I done anything else except wait and listen since six oclock, until I came here and saw? Well?

BOWDEN---It's like she is trying to tell you. I dont know what it is, myself. I just came up to my room to dress to come on to you and when I walked in------

NANCY---a strange woman was waiting here half naked. And she kept you prisoner here since six oclock---you, a strong man.......(jerks free, makes wild gesture, tugs at her ring finger, panting) Captain George Bowden, the war ace, the matchless and brave pilot, but what a liar. If you flew like you *fly* lie, you would not be here and I would not have to do this----this.....(tugs ring off, steps back and flings it at his face. PAN to BOWDEN'S face a small bleeding cut from ring)

CARLOTA (offstage----Come , senorita.

NANCY (Offstage)---Yes. Home. Home!

PAN back to BOWDEN watching them down corridor. He turns, looks at MARION who stands, pulling dully at negligee, her face dazed. MARIA and MANUEL emerge from behind screen.

BOWDEN (to MARIA)---Well? You took that trick too, didn't you?

MARIA (looking at MARION)----I took that trick too, senor.

MARION turns, looks at MARIA, brushes her hand across her eyes.

MARION (beginning to pant)---Oh. Oh. Oh.

MARIA---You did well. Mister Steve will be *p* pleased with you.

MARION (looks at MARIA, dazed, whispers)---Did well? I did well. (Louder, wildly) What have you made me do? (MARIA watches her coldly. MA*RION is wild, distracted, her hair loose, her hands to her face, the negligee falling away). I came to help. I wanted to help. To help Mister Steve's sister because she is a girl like me, and they killed her father and mother and drove her borther from the country. And the first thing I must do us make another girl like me think that her husband and I-----and me-----her husband is.... ..(moves, wildly) My coat. Quickly. I must go, catch her and

58.

                    tell her-------

MARIA moves swiftly, grips MARION, stops her.

                    MARIA---No.

                    MARION (tugging vainly at MARIA, wild, dazed)
                    ----Yes. I will. I must.

MARIA whirls MARION, thrusts her roughly onto sofa. BOW-
DEN moves forward angrily. MANUEL produces pistol, BOW-
DEN halts.

                    MANUEL---Softly, senor.

BOWDEN glares at MANUEL, pauses, shrugs, relaxes. But he
still watches MARIA. MARION, flung down on sofa, also
watches MARIA with a kind of quiet horror.

                    MARIA---Listen well, my girl. One little step
                    out of thsi room, one little step beyond my
                    will---- ------

                    BOWDEN---And what will you do?

                    MARIA----I? Nothing.

                    BOWDEN---Come on. Come clean. Just what is
                    your ~~threat~~ threat?

                    MARIA---I do not bhreaten; I do; Them who know
                    me well will tell you that.

                    MANUEL---That is ture, senor.

                    MARIA (aside to MANUEL)---Silence, you. (To
                    BOWDEN; she looks at him for a moment, with
                    calculation) Come; let us be frank for a mo-
                    ment. What doyou think of these recent happen-
                    ings in which you have had a part, senor?

                    MANUEL (With a slight movement)----My wife----

                    MARIA (without turning)---Silence, my husband.
                    (To BOWDEN) Come. What do you think?

                    BOWDEN (thoughtful, watching MARIA)---I think
                    there is more going on here than I know about.

                    MARIA---Underneath, let us put it. As a pot
                    begins to boil. Eh?

                    BOWDEN---Yes.

                    MARIA---Let us call it a brew, then. A brew
                    which is being brewed by people who are risk-
                                59.

512

ing everything to make the drink: honor, the
happiness of a people, even life.

BOWDEN---And then what?

MARIA---That is all.That is enough. Anyway,
it is so much that the brewing of it cannot
be jeopardised by the recalcitrance of
one man who knows too much. Or one woman.

BOWDEN---Or one woman. Oh. I see. (he looks at
MARION on sofa. MARION is more composed now,
sitting in her former attitude of shrinking,
watching them with quiet, dazed air) Send her
home, back where she came from.

MARIA shrugs slightly, looks at MARION.

MARIA---Have I not just said that it is now
too late? Besides, perhaps she does not want
to go. EH, my daughter. Do you wish to quit
quitnow? Do you regret the life you used to
lead, eh? When you had quiet in which to grieve?

MARION (whispering)----No. No. I......(looks
quickly at BOWDEN, rousing, then away; louder)
----No. I dont want to quit now. I promised
Mister Steve that.

MARIA (To BOWDEN)--- You see? Now, what?

BOWDEN---Nothing. But I have watched you work;
all I say is, God help her. And speaking of
myself, do you mind telling me just what----

They all turn toward door; sound of slow dragging feet
without, a knock.

MARIA---Enter.

Door opens, RODERIGO enters, supporting OTTO, who looks
about with drunken air, rousing, sees BOWDEN.

OTTO---Ah. There you are. Look everywhere for
you, one cantina after nother. Took jush one
more; That's all. (He sways into room; they
watch him, MARION with mounting disgust) Ha.
Company, I shee. Get out bottle, have jush one
more, eh? (Sways, blinks, sees MARION. His face
changes) Well, well, look who's here. Pretty
girl making shelf at home in chief's room. (To
BOWDEN) Ah there. You sly dog, you. Best pilo$
in world; have lots of girls; bring one home to
old Otto, eh? (Approaches MARION, wavering, his

60.

face grimacing, placative. BOWDEN starts forward, angrily, watching, as MARION retreats in alarmed disgust. Otto approaches, reaches his hand) Pretty gorl waiting for old Otto. Old Otto cant get lots pretty gorls like chief, so Chief bring one home to old Otto -----(reaches forward, stumbles, falls, clutches MARION'S negligee as he falls and jerks it from her. She stands shriking as BOWDEN springs angrily forward until MANUEL interposes pistol)

MANUEL---Softly, senor.

BOWDEN---Damned drunken------

MARION(laughs wildly)---Another one? Have I got to wait here until his wife comes and/ in and thinks------

MARIA---There is no danger of that. Luckily for him, he has no wife. (To MANUEL) Get her cloak, quickly.

MANUEL exits, they stand looking down at Otto, who begins to snore, the negligee crumpled in his hand. MARION shrinks, repressing hysteria. MARIA watches her.

MARIA---Do you know what his name is?

MARION---His name?

MARIA---His name name is Otto Birdsong.

MARION looks at MARIA.

MARION (whispers)---Birdsong? Otto Bird------ (she begins to laugh, wildly, trying to repress it) Birdsong. Otto Bird----Bird...... (Goes int wild laughter. MARIA moves swiftly and grips her, but MARION cannot stop) Birdsong! Birdsong! (she looks down at Otto as MARIA shakes her, laughing and laughing)

MARIA---Hush! Hush. (MANUEL eneters with cloak; they put around MARION, who still laughs wildly. They lead her toward door. BOWDEN still looking on in astonishment until MANUEL prods him with pistol)

MANUEL---You too, senor.

They move towards door while MARION continues to laugh into DISSOLVE during PAN to OTTO lying on floor, clutch-

58

6I.

ing negligee, as DISSOLVE completes PAN to <u>watch</u> on his wrist at Twelve minutes past nine. Tramp of feet begin and rise and die away.

RESOLVE a room something like the cellar in New York, the same men about a table, with several new faces, the CHIEF in the center, all watching as centry goes to door, pauses beside it.

SENTRY---Who goes?

He listens a moment, opens door, enter MARIA and MANUEL. CHIEF leans eagerly forward as MARIA approaches table and salutes him, her air proud, calm, without servility.

CHIEF---Ah, Donna? Yes?

MARIA---They are here, my prince.

CHIEF---Uninjured?

MARIA (shrugs faintly)---I have not hurt this girl, excellency.

CHIEF---I know that, Donna. Better still, I believe. You I do not command; I trust you. Gentlemen, a chair for the Donna Maria.

MARIA (with gesture)---I will stand. It will not take long.

CHIEF---As you will----eh, shall I not say, General? What do you think, gentlemne?

MARIA---I am Maria, Excellency. Maria Rojas. Let me remain so.

CHEEF---Again, as you will. They are here, then And now what?

MARIA---Free him.

The men glance at one another, at MARIA, at the CHIEF.

ONE---Free him? When we have just got him?

MARIA stands, cold, still almost contemptuous, waiting. The CHIEF looks at her.

CHIEF---True, he must remain in the employ of the mine, since he no longer has the key to the aeroplane. But why do you say free him now, Donna? Why do you think that he will not go away, that we will not lose all that we have gained? Come.

SPEAKER---Does the Donna Maria mean to tell us

62.

that this cold gringo, this man of the north
who is already in love with the daughter of
his employer (or what passes with these people
for love) is now ready to sacrifice himself
and his fiancee and his employer too for a
woman whom he saw for the first time three
hours ago?

The CHIEF looks quietly at SPEAKER.

CHIEF---Why should he not have fallen in love
with her? What is so strange in that?

They all look at the CHIEF. MARIA watches him with a
cold, speculative look. AVILAS also examines him, then
AVILAS looks at MARIA, his eyebrows raised, an expression
of dawning thought on his face. MARIA meets AVILAS'S
look then looks at CHIEF again.

CHIEF (to MARIA, quietly)---So. She has confounded us after all, by doing that which we
did not believe her capable of.

MARIA---Yes. She did that which I expected her
to do.

The CHIEF looks at MARIA; now his expression becomes
quite grave, intent.

CHIEF (sharply)---Eh? (more qiuetly) What do
you mean?

AVILASS---The Donna told us on the ship, Excellency. She has fallen in love with him.

The CHIEF looks at MARIA. The others do not look at him,
standing quietly, not moving. The CHIEF looks down, his
face grave, quiet. His tone is quiet.

CHIEF---Is this so, Donna? She saw thiw man
one time, and fell in love with him?

MARIA---No.

CHIEF (qiuckly)---Ah!

MARIA---She was in love with him before she
ever saw him.

Again the CHIEF looks down, again they watch him
covertly.

CHIEF (quietly)---Ah. In love with him. She
has fallen.......(becomes aware that they are
watching him curiously, raises his head) And
now you say that we can free him?

63.

MARIA---Not at once. Tomorrow

CHIEF---They are together now?

MARIA---With a jailer. Let them have this night
together, prisoners together, believing themselves both prisoners. Then as they say in
his country, in the north, I will guarantee
them.

Again they watch the CHIEF covertly as he stands, his
head lowered, apparently watching his hands as it
clenches slowly.

AVILAS (quietly)---The Donna Maria says truly,
Excellency. And she has not failed yet.

CHIEF (looks up suddenly)--- Be it so, then.
But if, after this, if he should----if he....

MARIA---Then will be the time for men to act,
not for me.

AVILAS---And there are precautions for that.

CHIEF---Let them be taken. But do not harm him.

AVILAS---Do not harm him?

CHIEF looks at AVILAS.

CHIEF---No. Bring him to me. To me. Do you
hear ?

AVILAS---Bring him to you---unharmed. It shall
be done, Excellency.

CHIEF---Good. (He looks about, then quietly)
And now I shall ride.

ONE----Ride, Excellency?

CHIEF---To the mountains. Yes.

SPEAKER---When they already know that you are
here? When there is already a price on your
head? Listen.

They pause, listen. Tramp of soldiers, muffled; they follow sound as it passes and dies away.

64.

CHIEF---I go to my sister, gentlemen. Five
years and athousand miles of sea seperated us
but let it not be said that a mere tramping of
feet on the stone of my grandfather's city
kept us asunder. That sound? That sound is
going to carry us to a throne.

SPEAKER---Good. Come, gentlemen; let us ride.

CHIEF---No. I thank you. But three ¢¢¢¢/ will
escape where a dozen would not pass the first
civil guard unchallenged. I will take AVILAS
and Pedro.

He leaves table. AVILAS and PEDRO prepare to follow.
CHIEF pauses, turns.

CHIEF---Gentlemen, and you Donna----(he looks
about at them, then at MARIA) In your hands
in particular + leave this girl. She is an
orphan, a foreigner in a strange land. She
has put herself unreservedly in our hands, to
assist us toward an end whose very success can
but leave her as she is now: An orphan in a
land which is not hers, no matter how grateful or how kind. These ha nds which hold her
security must not falter. They must not. If we
are victorious, let it not be said that we
moved to victory across her brief life; if we
fail, let it not be said that we drew her into
the maelstrom. A victory at the price of one
hair of thia girl's head can be no victory.
(Looks about him with proud and uiet dignity and
simplicity) Look you, gentlemen. How can I
hope to fathe a people when I cannot brother
one orphan girl? How can I look my own orphaned sister in the face and say to her, 'I
have repurchased your birthright with the happiness of another fatherless and brotherless
girl. But she was merelya foreigner, and the
price was not dear'. (He looks quietly about
from face to face. The men look down; only
MARIA meets his gaze, her face still, cold,
with a kind of weary patience, as though she
listened to a child) That was my first command; if I live to give athousand others and
you live to recieve them, that will also be
my last. Come, Avilas,

Exit CHIEF, AVILAS and PEDRO , the others look after
them.

SPEAKER---Eh, it is no gringo who has fallen
in love with this girl.

65.

518

61   DISSOLVE with sound of hooves to a shadowy courtyard,
      CHIEF, AVILAS and PEDRO mounting. AVILAS in lead. As
      they are about to emerge into street, AVILAS reins
      suddenly back at sound of tramping feet. They draw
      into shadow as soldiers enter.

            CORLORAL---Halt!

      Soldiers halt. CORPORAL flashes pocket torch. CHIEF keeps
      his face hidden behind AVILAS, who faces light boldly.

            AVILAS---Well, senor?

            CORPORAL---You ride late, senors.

            AVILAS---As you see.

            CORPORAL---Might one ask where to?

            AVILAS---One may, senor. To Las Vegas.

      Tableau for a moment, AVILAS facing light.

            CORPORAL---You depart late, senors.

            AVILAS---It will be later still when we arrive.

            CORPORAL---That is true. (Light goes off) For-
            ward.

      The soldiers move on, the riders depart, hooves die into
      tramp of feet in DISSOLVE to

62   A corridor, a sentry pacing slowly, his shadow pacing
      him on wall, to a barred door. His shadow falls upon
      door, DISSOLVE through with his shadow to

63   A cell, MARION and BOWDEN sitting on a stone bench, the
      soldier's shadow with his rifle falling upon MARION,
      who sits still, almost childlike, wrapped closely in her
      cloak. BOWDEN is watching the soldier's shadow as it
      moves on and disappears. He then looks at MARION. His
      expression is grave and thoughtful

            BOWDEN---So you are an American, after all.
            (MARION doesn't answer nor move. He watches
            her) visting here with your people, I suppose?

            MARION (she doesn't look at him, still)---No.

            BOWDEN---I see. Your people are back home. In
            the states. (She doesn't answer) I have no
            people, myself.

                        66.

                                                      519

She lo.ks at him, her glance diffident.

        MARION---You mean, they.......died?

        BOWDEN---When I was a kid. Yes. (He watches
        her) And so did yours. Didn't they?

She looks away, quickly; again she sits still. He watches
her. BOWDEN speaks now with irony.

        BOWDEN---Well. All right. You have lots of peo-
        ple. You just came down here on a vacation.
        Doing this just for fun.

He watches her. She glances at him again, her glance
fluttering up, diffident, shrinking, meets his and falls
away again.

        BOWDEN---Helping these people just for fun.
        Because they are good people, only they just
        happen to need an aeroplane full of gold. Isn't
        that right?

She sits quite sti l, shrinking, as he watches her. His
ironical tone ¢¼¼¼¢¢¢/ changes.

        BOWDEN---But the plan went sour somehow, and
        they forgot to tell you. And so now we're both
        ....(He watches her. She does not move)
        His tone and air now very serious) Aren't you
        afraid? (she looks at him)

        MARION---Afraid?

        BOW EN---Listen.

Tramp of sentry increases as they turn to face barred
door. His shadow crosses bars and again falls upon
MARION and rests upon her as the sentry halts for a
moment.

        BOWDEN---Look here. Look at yourself now.
        sitting in the shadow of one of them with a
        rifle on his shoulder. One of your friends.
        And you are not afraid?

        MARION---No. He---Mister Steve said that no
        harm should--------

        BOWDEN---He? He said? It's no man you have to
        be afraid of. It's that woman. Dont you know
        that? (She sits still, looking down, her hands
        on her lap. He watches her. Suddenly he leans
        forward and grasps her arm) Listen. If I get
        you out of this, will you leave here? Leave
        this country by the first ship or the first

        67.

train or the first moving anything that will
take you,and never come back?

She looks down at his hand grasping hers.

MARION---Would you get me out of this?

BOWDEN---Yes. Will you go away then?

She looks at him, still, grave, quiet.

MARION---It doesn't matter what happens to me.

BOWDEN----Doesn't matter? Doesn't life matter,
to you?

MARION---Will they kill me too?

BOWDEN---Too? Who else do.......(pauses, looks
at her) Oh. I see. Hell, they're not going to
hurt me: who else can steal that aeroplane
except me? Until that's done,I'm more important than your Mister Steve, even. But you.
Either you failed to do what they wanted you
to, or you have already done it. If you hadn't
why have they got you locked up here?

MARION---And you think they are going to kill
me now?

BOWDEN---I dont know. It's that woman. She will
do anything.

She looks down again, still, musing, quiet.

MARION---Kill.......me. That's funny.

BOWDEN----Funny.

MARION----That they should need to. Because I
lived such a short time. Not long enough to
do anyone any good or any......(she ceases.
He musing air goes. She sits quite still.
Then she looks at him) And they wont kill you?
You know that?

BOWDEN---Not as long as they need that ship
load of gold and I'm the only man who can get
it for them.

MARION---And after that?

BOWDEN---After that? Hell, they'll probably
make me prime minister then.

She looks at him.

68.

                    MARION---I will. I'll go away. Can you get me
                    out?

                    BOWDEN---Yes. If you will do like I-----

MARION stares past him, her face determined, dreamy,
fixed.

                    MARION---Yes. I will go to her, make her lis-
                    ten to me, make her believe---------

                    BOWDEN---Her?

                    MARION---Yes. She is young too, like me. When
                    I looked up and saw her face in the door.....
                    (she looks at him tense) I can make her be-
                    lieve. I can. Dont you believe I can?

BOWDEN watches her in astonishment, comprehends, makes
gesture of exasperation.

                    BOWDEN---That. That's all right, I tell you.
                    I can fix that. She'll be all right. Is that
                    what you are worrying about? Are you sitting
                    there worrying about that,while-------(he
                    turns his head toward door as tramp of sentry
                    increases again and shadow falls upon them/
                    MARION. She sits guite still, musing, serene
                    again, looking down. He watches her)

                    MARION---Yes. I can. I know I can......will
                    you let me ask you something?

                    BOWDEN---Well? What?

                    MARION---Do you love her very much?

                    BOWDEN (fretted, impatient)---Yes. I guess so.
                    Sure I do. What------

She sits looking down. His hand still holds her arm,
After a moment she looks up.

                    MARION----How does it feel to be in love?

He looks at her, astonished.

                    BOWDEN---How does it......Haven't you ever
                    -----You mean, you never have----(she watches
                    him) You mean, you haven't got any people or
                    a sweetheart or anybody but these----(jerks
                    his hand savagely as shadow of sentry passes
                    again) You poor kid. You poor, damned------

He releases her arm and moves suddenly and instinctively
as if to embrace a child. She falls back, her ahnds

                               69

        522

raised, her face terrified.

     MARION (whispering)---No! No!

     BOWDEN---Poor, damned-------(he ceases, watch-
     ing her, astonished. She continues to shrink
     before him, retreating) Here. All right. all
     right. I wasn't going to...(she stops,her
     terror ebbs. He watches her) Good Lord, you
     didn't think I was going to......(she is quiet
     now, watching him. He looks at his watch) Look
     here. It's after midnight. What ever they are
     going to do with us, they wont do it it until
     morning now. So we might as well get some rest.
     (He extends his hand. She does not retreat, He
     takes her arm and leads her to the bench)
     They could have at least given us a blanket to
     lie on, couldn't they?

     MARION---No, I'll-------

She sits on bench, her cloak wrapped about her.

     BOWDEN---Come on. Lie down. You ought to get
     some sleep. Here; my jacket will do for a pil-
     low. (Begins to remove jacket. She stops him,
     quickly, shrinking)

     MARION---Please. I wont take it. I will be all
     right.

     BOWDEN (Pauses, replaces jacket, sits deside
     her)---Right, then. And you thought I was go-
     ing to......I wouldn't hurt you, either. If a
     damned yellow bellied spik promised you that no
     hurt would come to you, dont you know that I
     ....(He looks at her as she sits, small,
     still, closely wrapped in her cloak)

     MARION---I know it. I didn't mean;...I'm sorry.

     BOWDEN---Sure. Well, lets try to get some
     sleep; shall we?

     MARIOM---Yes;

     BOWDEN---Goodnight, then.

     MARION---- Goodnight.

She settles back against wall. BO WDEN leans back too,
folds his arms, watches her. She closes her eyes.

     BOWDEN (quietly)---Good Lord.

Folds his arms again, settles himself. PAN to watch on

     70.

            523

his wrist at half past one. DISSOLVE through watch to

64 Watch on Otto's wrist, PAN back to Otto as he stirs, raises his head, looks stupidly about, raises his hand and looks at negligee which $\not{b}\not{h}\not{e}/\not{b}/$ he still clutches. He feels the soft silk, fondling it, examining his rough dirty hand, smells the silk, looks up with quiet, drunken air.

> OTTO (muttering)---Pretty little girl come see old Otto. Eh? (looks about for MARION) Hello. You. Pretty girl. Where you hiding?Just old Otto. Old Otto's a good guy. He wont hurt you. (Gets to his feet, swaying, staggering) Come, pretty little girl. (makes chirping sound, like calling a canary, listens, swaying. Looks at neglige, touching it, stroking it,looks about with covert air, raises negligee/ to his face, his eyes closed, looks quickly about again with shamed air; quietw again) Come on, pretty little girl. Chief got plenty others. (moves forward slowly, his hand extended) You wouldn't hide from old Otto, would you? From poor old Otto? (blunders into sofa, grunts, tries to catch himself, sprawls upon it, tries to rise again with stupid and blundering air, fighting off sleep, drawing negligee toward him as if it still contained MARION, falls forward again in slumber, his last movement drawing negligee beneath his face)

65 DISSOLVE to
Mountian trail, dawn breaking. CHIEF, AVILAS and PEDRO mounting. CHIEF halts his horse and looks back, others stop also. CHIEF looks $\not{o}\not{v}\not{e}\not{r}/$ out over panorama, b.eathes a deep breath.

> CHIEF---Ah,Avilas! (Extends his arm) Look One of my first memories of my father is of being held here in his arms. He brought me here, an infant, and held me aloft, so, and said: 'This is your country, beautiful and smiling as a wife, beautiful and jealous as a mistress. To it you must be both lover and husband in one. Love it well, and you will be its master; betray or defile it, and you will be your own base born slave'. (He looks quietly about, breathing deep) For five years I have not seen it. But now ⁻ am again a King, Avilas.

> AVILAS---You have always been a king, Excellency.

> CHIEF---No. For five years I was just a man.

71.

AVILAS---Have I not also heard your father say to you, 'Be first man among men; among beggars and the basely born, any knave can be king'.

CHIEF---True. Ah, Avilas! If he has but left me the wisdom to make of myself both the man and the king that he was.

AVILAS---He has done that, Excellency.

CHIEF---You think so? Well, I hope that I am that man. But I am not that king yet. And so I do not like his Excellency, good friend.

AVILAS---Not like--------? What do you mean, Excellency?

CHIEF (looks at AVILAS, smiling faintly, tranquilly)---There again. We were boys together, you and I; eh! have we not both felt my father's and your father's hand in displeasure? We were youths and young men together; you carried my mandolin and I yours when we sang our first serinade beneath a balcony----- where, by the way, you sang better than I. (He looks at AVILAS'S puzzled face, smiling) You did not call me Excellency then, Ramon.

AVILAS---That is true, Ex...........

He ceases. They look at one another.

CHIEF---Come; say it.

AVILAS---Estabin.

CHIEF----Good. Was that hard to say?

AVILAS---On the contrary. So much so that I am afraid that when you are king........

CHIEF rouses, turns.

CHIEF---That time is not yet. Let it take care of itself. (Looks out across plain, then he looks at AVILAS) No. I am not a king yet. I have been only a man for five years; you cannot change five years in a day. (He looks at AVILAS, who looks at him, puzzled) Perhaps you can never change it.

AVILAS---What do you mean, Excellency?

CHIEF---Hah. You have forgot already.

72.

AVILAS---I have not forgot. It is becaus I
do not know whom I am talking to.

CHIEF---And now, what do you mean, Ramon?

AVILAS---Am I talking to my prince, or to my
..........to Estaban?

CHIEF---To both of them. They are one. What
sort of a king I shall be, I do not know. But I
do know thsi: I have a Prince's heart, since
it is big enough to also contain Estaban's.

AVILAS---So do I know that.

He continues to watch the CHIEF, his expression curious,
thoughtful. The CHIEF is serene, grave. He looks down;
 seems to examine a twig in his hand, turning it.

CHIEF---Yes. I have been a man for five years
now. I hope a good one.

AVILAS---Has any man said-------(CHIEF stops
him with a gesture)

CHIEF (Still watching the twig)---I mean, as
men go. (AVILAS watches him, puzzled) In the
eyes of women. As a woman might choose between
two men.

He seems to be preoccupied with the twig. The puzzlement leaves AVILAS' face; he looks at the CHIEF intently.
Suddenly the CHIEF drops the twig and faces AVILAS. He
speaks now simply, frankly.

CHIEF---Ihave not the tall light colored
beauty of gringo men; I am not even handsome
among men of my own race. But tell me this,
Ramon--------

He ceases, looks down. AVILAS watches him.

AVILAS---Yes. What would you know?

CHIEF---Is it not barely possible that------
Is the idea utterly ludicrous that between a
Northern man and a man of my race---eh, myself,
say---a northern woman would even be aware
that a choice had been offered her?

They look at one another.

AVILAS---So. Before I answer that, let me ask
a question myself.

CHIEF---A thousand, if you wish.

73.

526

AVILAS---I will ask only two. Are you in love
with this girl?

CHIEF---Yes.

AVILAS---Now, my second. Is it my prince who
asks this question, or is it Estaban?

CHIEF---Supose I say it is your prince?

AVILAS---Then I will answer thus: Is it the
love of a foreign and anonymous woman that you
have come all this distance to discuss with
the unavenged and bloody spirit of you murdered father?

CHIEF looks down, quiet, grave. AVILAS watches him.

CHIEF---But, suppose---------

AVILAS---What?

CHIEF----Supposed my father's blood avenged, the
tyrant's yoke lifted from my people---all
by means of this girl. Suppose that; that I
then took this girl's hand in mine and led her
before my father's spirit and said, 'Look,
father; this is the hand that struck fetters
from your people and assisted your son back
to your throne'. What then?

AVILAS---In other words, it is Estaban who
now asks.

CHIEF (looking down, still)---Yes. What would
you say then?

AVILAS---I would say, may you be happy in your
love, Estaban.

CHIEF reaches his hand.

CHIEF---Thanks, Ramon. (they clasp hands, the
CHIEF turns, spurs his horse on) Come; let
us ride on.

66   DISSOLVE through hooves to mountain hovel, CHIEF, AVI-
LAS and PEDRO ride up. Old peasant emerges, looks
at them, alertly as they halt.

AVILAS---Eh, Guzman, man, dont you know who
this is?

GUZMAN looks at CHIEF, puzzled. Slowly his face wakes.

74.

527

He flings his hands up.

> GUZMAN---Prince! Prince! Madre de Dios! (Turns
> and shout toward hovel)Woman! Ramona! The
> little princess! (Turns and runs forward as
> CHIEF dismounts, falls at his feet as CHIEF
> catches him and raises him. RAMONA and ASUN-
> CION emerge from the hovel. ASUNCION looks at
> CHIEF, falls back, raises her hand to her mouth
> as RAMONA catches her)

> ASUNCION---Estaban! (louder) Estaban!

CHIEF frees himself of GUZZMAN and approaches, halts;
they look at one another. Suddenly ASUNCION runs forward into his arms, crying.

> ASUNCION---Estaban! My brother! My brother!

> CHIEF---Asuncion my sister.

DISSOLCE to

67

The cell, morning. BOWDEN and MARION asleep on the bench.
MARION asleep on BOWDENS shoulder, childlike, his arm
about her. Tramp of sentry, his shadow crosses door, the
door opens, enter MANUEL. He approaches, stands, looks
down at the sleepers, his face grimly puzzical. BOWDEN
wakes, looks about, puzzled, becomes aware of MARION
looks down at her, recognizing situation, moves his arm
a little to make her a little more comfortable. MANUEL
coughs. BOWDEN whirls, looks up.

> BOWDEN---You again? I didn't recognize you
> right away, half dressed like that. Where is
> it? Did somebody borrow it to wear to church
> maybe?

> MANUEL---Borrow what, senor?

> BOWDEN-----The pistol. You look half naked with-
> out it.

> MANUEL---Have your joke, senor.

> BOWDEN---Thanks. If this is a joke, I've had
> plenty. I've------

MARION wakes, looks about quietly too, then
puzzled, then recognizes situation, touches BOWDEN,
looks up at him, springs suddenly away.

> MARION (wildly)---I have-----I didn't know...
> You'll have to forgive----forgive........

75.

528

BOWDEN---Forgive what? Waking you up? That wasn't me; that was this kind senor here----- (turns to MANUEL) you realy must be suffering without that pistol.

MANUEL (shrugs)---The senor is too comical. He should be on the stage in the vaudiville.

BOWDEN---I wish he was---provided the stage is somewhere beside here. (Turns to MARION)You got a little sleep,didn't you? Feel better?

MARION (trembling, distracted)---Yes. I--- I .....I'm sorry. I didn't-------

MANUEL---It is early yet. You can finish your sleep in there, senorita. (points toward a second door in end of room. MARION pauses, looks from MANUEL to the door, then back to MANUEL. BOWDEN looks at MANUEL, hard)

BOWDEN---You mean,she must go in there, whether she sleeps any more or not?

MANUEL (Shrugs, looks down)---Perhaps she can sleep though, senor. (Looks up again) Eh, senor. I do as I am told to do. As she must and as you-----(Pauses, they look at one another)

BOWDEN----Must? (MANUEL shrugs. BOWDEN turns to MARION) Must seems to be right. Maybe he's right about you getting some more sleep, too. You'd better go, I guess.

MARION---Yes. (restrains herself, looks at him and away) And you will be........

MANUEL---Perfectly, senorita. If the aeroplane does not kill him, he will be a grandfather surely.

MARION---Do you promise that, Manuel?

MANUEL---But certainly. Who could have anything but admiration for this brave senor who daily consorts with eagles? Tempered of course with just a little envy, eh, senor?

BOWDEN---Sure. I'll be all right. You run along now. I'll be seeing you soon.

MARION---Yes. And then I will tell her, make her believe-------

BOWDEN (Quickly)----Sure. Sure. Run along now.

76.

529

MARION---Yes. And I didn't mean, last night....
I was asleep, and I-----

BOWDEN---Sure. Get along with you.

MARION goes toward the barred door, the men watching her.

MANUEL---Not that door, senorita. The other one
is for you. (Points. MARION turns, approaches
smaller øñé/ door, exits. MANUEL looks back
at BOWDEN) And now this one for you. (indicates barred door)

BOWDEN----For me? You mean, I am free?

MANJEL---As air, senor.

They look at one another, MANUEL inscrutable, quizzical,
BOWDEN grave, frowning, intent.

BOWDEN---Suppose ⊥ dont want to go.

With a sudden movement MANUEL produces pistol. BOWDEN
looks at it, then at MANUEL.

BOWDEN---So. You use this pistol one time to
put me in here, and the next time to put me
out, eh?

MANUEL---Yes. But this pistol is like neither
the senor nor myself: it does not joke.

BOWDEN looks at pistol, shrugs.

BOWDEN---Well. It seems to be the boss. But
look here. ⊥ want to speak to that woman who
was in my room with us yesterday.

MANUEL---Do you speak perchance of my wife,
senor?

BOWDEN---Is she your wife?

MANUEL---So she has been telling me for firteen years, senor.

BOWDEN---Then let me congratulate you. You
have a wife as well as a pistol who does not
joke.

MANUEL---That I have known for firteen years
without having to be told, senor. And youɣ
wish to talk with her?

BOWDEN---If that can be done; yes.

77.

MANUEL---Why not? Let us go; eh, perhaps now
we can let this pistol rest.

BOWDEN---Yes. I will not undertake to cope with
both a pistol who cannot joke and a wife who
does not joke too.

MANUEL (pockets pistol)---Good. Forward, then.

They exit. Door opens, closes, DISSOLVE with tramp of
feet to

68   A room. BOWDEN faces MARIA, MANUEL a little behind BOWDEN
listening and watching.

BOWDEN---So I am free now. I can go.

MARIA---You can go now.

BOWDEN----Supose I do not want to go now.

MARIA (shrugs)---Then stay. You are your own
master.

BOWDEN---And this girl, this American Girl?

MARIA---And this girl?

BOWDEN---Is she also her own mistress?

MARIA---That is another affair. This girl is
my responsibility. She put herself in my hands,
of her own will, back home in the States, in
her country. My responsibility ends when I
return her there.

BOWDEN---When? Do you mean if, perhaps?

MARIA---Is this your affair, senor?

BOWDEN---Yes. I dont believe you. You are-----

MANUEL----Senor.

BOWDEN pauses, looks at MARIA, who waits, cold, still.
MANUEL waits also, still, alert.

BOWDEN---That's right. The pistol does not
know how to joke also; I forgot.

MANUEL---Do not forget again, senor.

BOWDEN---It I do, doubtless you will be here
to remind me.

78.

531

MANUEL---That I do not know, since you are
now free to go.

BOWDEN---Yes. I am free----suddenly.

MARIA---You mean that you have suddenly found
that you are free. (BOWDEN looks at her) You
did not try last night to see if you were free
then.

BOWDEN---You mean, I could have------Senora,
you are lying.

MANUEL---Senor.

BOWDEN (not turning, still facing MARIA)---
All right. Gte out your pop gun. You are lying,
senora. Come; tell me that t is girl could
have departed last night also. Tell me that
she is here of her own will.

MARIA---Did you ask her if she was not? (BOWDEN
looks at her, he glares at her and at MANUEL,
baffled)

BOWDEN---I see. You locked us up together to
dare me to ask her if she wished to leave. I
see. Very well. I'll take that dare and give
you one in return. I dare you to let me ask
her now.

MARIA---I accept.

BOWDEN (Turning)---Good. Where----

MARIA (Lifts her hand)---Stay. (BOWDEN pauses,
looks at her)

BOWDEN---I thought so. You wont let me, eh?

MARIA---Perhaps she will not want to see you.

BOWDEN glares at her. She faces him steadily.

BOWDEN---Is that a dare also?

MARIA---Call it what you will. I will send
word to her that you wish to see her. I will
let her choose whether she will or not. Will
that satisfy you ?

BOWDEN---What word will you send?

MARIA (To MANUEL) ---Go. Say to her that Captain BOWDEN wishes to speak to her, Say only

79.

that.

    MANUEL---I shall say only that. Good. Shall
    I answer questions, if she should ask them?

MARIA looks at BOWDEN, her eyebrows raised interrogative-
ly. BOWDEN looks at her, makes gesture to MANUEL.

    BOWDEN---Yes.

    MARIA---Go. We will wait.

Exit MANUEL in DISSOLVE to
A small room, MARION turning as MANUEL enters. She looks
at him.

    MANUEL---This gringo wishes to speak with you
    again, senorita.

    MARION---Again? (she sits slowly on bed) Is
    he....Are they going ....

    MANUEL---He? He is free.

    MARION---Free. (Looks down her attitude still
    childlike) What does he want with me, Manuel?

    MANUEL---That I do not know, senorita.

    MARION---Is he....,where------

    MANUEL---He is with Maria.

    MARION (Quietly)---With Maria. (she looks
    down at her clasped hands, her face still,
    quiet) He is free now, you say? He can go?

    MANUEL---Yes. As air is free, senorita. (She
    sits still, musing, MANUEL watches her) What
    shall I say to him? (MARION muses) Come, seno-
    rita.

    MARION (rouses, looks at MANUEL) ---Say this to
    him, Manuel: Go, and do not think of me. Tell
    him to forget the harm that I have done, if it
    be harm and can be forgotten.

She looks down,still, MANUEL watches her.

    MANUEL---That is all, senorita?

    MARION---Yes.

MANUEL exits into DISSOLVE to

        80.

FIRST ROOM

BOWDEN and MARIA watching ~~55~~/ door as MANUEL enters.

      BOWDEN---Well? Say it.

MANUEL glance at MARIA, his eyebrows raised.

      MARIA---Tell him.

      MANUEL---She said to tell you this, senor:
      'Go, and do not think of me. Tell him to forget
      the harm that I have done, if it be harm and
      can be forgotten.'

BOWDEN looks at MANUEL. They watch him. He looks down,
shrugs.

      BOWDEN---So. Well, that is that. (Muses, MA-
      RIA watching him, looks up) I'll hand it to
      you. I dont know how you did it. But you're
      hard to beat. Can I ask you something? I mean,
      on the up and up. I know when I am beat.

      MANUEL---Ask ten, senor. Air is still free.

      BOWDEN---Right. (to MARIA) We all know what
      the other wants. So that's out of the way now.
      Suppose you get what you want? Then what? You
      know what I mean; about the girl.

      MARIA---Even a gorged lion betrays what might
      well pass for gratitude---for a while, until
      he feels hunger again. And we are not beasts,
      senor.

      BOWDEN---In other words, you will have no
      further use for this girl, and she can-----

      MARIA---Return to where she came from, if that
      is her desire.

      BOWDEN---Will that be your desire too?

      MARIA---Why not?

      BOWDEN---And if you fail to get what you want?

      MARIA---Ah. There is a saying, senor: Man pro-
      poses; circumstance disposes. We are playing no
      game for children. We have laid a train of pow-
      der and we have struck the spark. Not I and not
      you can stop that explosion now. All we can do
      is ride it. And........

      BOWDEN---And?-------

              81.

MARIA---There will not be room for all.

BOWDEN---I see. Well, there had better be room
for-----(ceases, MARIA watching him) Well. So
I am free. Until when?

MARIA---Fotever. I do not wish to see you again
anymore than you wish to see me, senor.

BOWDEN---That si true, senora. In this case,
since both man and woman b̶o̶t̶h̶/propose so, let us
hope that circumstance too will dispose.

MARIA---Let us hope so, senor.

BOWDEN---Good. Then ⋆ will say goodbye. (turns,
looks at MANUEL) And you, senor. If there be
further dealings between us, permit me to hope
that your pistol will this time be my principal
opponent. It will be more pleasant.

MANUEL---Doubtless. My pistol has no wife,
senor.

71   Exit BOWDEN in DISSOLVE to
Street— BOWDEN emerges, looks/a̶t̶/h̶o̶u̶s̶e̶,̶/t̶h̶o̶u̶g̶h̶t̶f̶u̶l̶/
back at house, thoughtful. Tramp of feet as soldiers
pass. BOWDEN goes on, pauses, signals. Fiacre drives
up, he enters. DISSOLVE with sound of hooves to

72   NANCY'S home. Fiacre stops, BOWDEN gets out, approaches
patio gate, pulls bell rope. Gate opens, he enters. DIS-
SOLVE with sound of his feet to

73   Library. BOWDEN and Mr WHITE facing one another. WHITE
sits, indicates chair.

WHITE---Sit down, George.

BOWDEN---Sit down?

WHITE---Damn it, sit down. You dont expect me
to make p̶s̶ a stage scene out of this, do you?

BOWDEN sits down stiffly. WHITE offers box of cigars.

WHITE---Smoke?

BOWDEN---No thanks. (WHITE lights cigar, BOWDEN
watching him) Well, I guess you ahve heard. I
guess there's not much I can tell-----

WHITE---Heard? I haven't been able to hear anything else for twelve hours. Why the devil did
you do it? Why couldn't you have told her like

82.

535

a man, instead of------(puffs his cigar furiously) I'm no heavy father, and Nancy is a
modern young woman. But it's coming it pretty
thick to let her come to your room and find
you and the other woman together.

BOWDEN---So you believe it too, do you?

WHITE---What else would you have us believe?

BOWDEN---Yes. That's so. (Looks down) Well.
But I thought maybe Nancy----that I could tell
her that it was a mistake-------

WHITE---I'm sure it was a mistake. I'm sure
Nancy knows that too. I'm sure the last thing
in the world you wanted was for her to catch
you redhanded at it.

BOWDEN---That's not the sort of mistake I meant.

WHITE looks at him.

WHITE---Oh, come. You're not trying to tell me
that you were innocent? That you never saw the
woman before. I can understand a young man's
weakness that would let him get mixed up with
two women at one time. But I dont think very
much of him when he tries to rat off on both
of them.

BOWDEN---You mean, you wont let me see her?

WHITE shrugs, puffs his cigar.

WHITE---I wont stop you. Do you want to see
her now?

BOWDEN---Well, I dont see any reason to wait.

WHITE---Wait a while. Give her a little time to
recover from the shock. Then, perhaps.....

BOWDEN sits still, looking down, stobborn.

BOWDEN---I guess I'll try it now.

WHITE---All right. (puts his hand out to
bell, pauses) Wait. Lets have this understood.
I wont have her bothered. This is to be final.
What ever she does, forgives you or
refuses to forgive you or refuses to see you,
it must be final. Right?

BOWDEN (After a moment)---Right.

83.

536

WHITE---Good. (Rings bell. Servant enters)
Tell Miss Nancy that Captain Bowden wishes to
see her for a moment. (Servant exits, WHITE
lights his cigar again) I like you, George.
And Nancy is as fond of you as a young girl
can be, I suppose. But I'll be damned if I
can see why........Well. She's young. Thank
God young girls cannot fall very deeply in
love. They get over it------(Reenter servant)
Yes?

SERVANT----Miss Nancy asks to be excused. She
is not well this morning.

WHITE---That's all. (Exit servant. White looks
at BOWDEN) Well?

BOWDEN rises.

BOWDEN---Well. That's that. I guess I'm fired
too, am I?

WHITE---Did I say you were?

BOWDEN looks at him quickly.

WHITE (quickly)---But that doesn't mean that
I am going back on the bargain we made about
both ring Nancy. I ahve your word for that?

BOWDEN---Yes. (Muses, thoughtful) I guess you'd
better fire me.

WHITE---Do you want to quit?

BOWDEN---You'd better fire me.

WHITE leans forward, watching him.

WHITE---Sit down. (BOWDEN doesn't move) What
do you mean? Who'd fly the ships? Birdsong
cant do it. Are you going to let me down to
get even because Nancy---------?

BOWDEN---You wont trust Nancy to me, but you
will trust me with a ship full of gold bullion.

WHITE (Watching him)----Meaning that you could
just as easly fly away with the gold as to
bring it in? Sit down. (BOWDEN doesn't move.
WHITE watches him, thoughtful, intent) Just
what did you mean while ago when you were
trying to tell me that this is all a mistake?

BOWDEN---Nothing. Just do like I ask you. Fire

84.

537

me.

WHITE---No.

BOWDEN---Not even when you are trusting your
gold to a guy who has ratted off on your daughter?

WHITE (watching him)---No.

BOWDEN (Still, musing; he raises his head)---
Well. I guess I'll get on, then. Goodbye, sir.
And---thanks.

WHITE---Goodbye, George.

BOWDEN exits, WHITE looking after him, thoughtful. He
rings bell. Enter SERVANT.

WHITE---Is Senor McPherson here yet?

SERVANT---He waits, senor, as you directed.

WHITE---I'll see him now.

Exit SERVANT. WHITE taps on desk, thoughtful. Enter Mc-
PHERSON, in riding clothes.

WHITE---Well, Mac?

McPherson---No trace of it since it was taken
from the aeroplane yesterday afternoon. I met
with the utmost courtesy, of course. It was
like trying to penetrate a wall of perfumed
cotton batting. There is something going on
here, underneath; it is like a mine about to be
exploded. It's in the air, the earth; everywhere. But I have said for a year that this
country has been peaceful too long.

WHITE---I'd say that something had already
happened, when two thousand pounds of gold
bullion can disappear over night and leave no
trace.

McPHERSON---I didn' say it left no trace.
Traces? With the flying field like a prade
ground, and the streets themselves.. ..listen
now. (They listen as tramp of feet increasees
and passes and dies away)

WHITE---Well, at least we ahve been expectibg
this. As you say, this country has been good
to long. America north of the equator would be
a wilderness yet if man had not invented plows

85.

538

and axes. But where would this country be if
he had not invented confistication?

DISSOLVE to
Hotel entrance. BOWDEN enters swiftly. TRUCK with him
into lobby, MANAGER looking up from desk as BOWDEN
goes on and mounts stairs. TRUCK with him to corridor
as he reaches his door opens it and enters.

DISSOLVE with snoring to OTTO on sofa, the negligee
clutched in his ahnd. BOWDEN approaches and looks down
at him.

       BOWDEN---Otto.

OTTO doesn't stir. BOWDEN shakes him.

       BOWDEN---Otto!

He lifts OTTO'S head, shakes him, drops him, looks a-
bout, crosses to screen, emerges with pitcher of water
returns and dashes it upon OTTO'S head. OTTO jerks up,
spluttering.

       OTTO---What the----(stumbles erect, swaying,
       splu.tering) Say, who the-----(raises negli-
       gee to wipe his face, sees what it is, desists.
       BOWDEN watches him)

       BOWDEN---Come on.Mop yourself off with the rag.
       We've got to get out of here.

       OTTO (turns, bleary eyed, blinking, dripping)
       That you, Chief? Say, what happened last night,
       anyway? Jees, what a head!

       BOWDEN---Come on. Wipe yourself off with the rag.

Again OTTO is about to use the negligee, pauses.

       OTTO---This? This aint no rag. See?

He opens the negligee, BOWDEN glances at it, pauses and
looks closer.

       OTTO---Come off a pretty girl, see? I dont re-
       member much about last night, but I remember I
       took it off her. And now I'm going to put
       it back on her-----

BOWDEN catches him by the shoulder, whirls him,
glaring at him, savage, cold, thrusts him down on sofa,
where he sprawls, looking up as BOWDEN snatches the
negligee from him.

       86.

OTTO---Well, for Christ's sake. (He looks at
BOWDEN; a puzzled look comes into his face)
Hell. You brpught her here. You brought her to
me, didn't you? Well, what the-----

BOWDEN---Shut your rank mouth.

OTTO ceases. They look at one another.

OTTO--- Oh. Excuse me. I thought you brought
her to me, seeing that you already-----

BOWDEN--- Will you shut up?

BOWDEN glares at OTTO. He gets up, shakily, still drunk.

OTTO---Jeez. what a head. I'm sorry, chief.
I didn't know she was your girl. I didn't....
I ought to knowed it was a mistake. Here I am,
thinking I'm going to get a girl when I aint
even going to get the kimona.

He sways, looks drunkenly about. BOWDEN looks at the
negligee, grins, musing; suddenly he flings it to OTTO.

BOWDEN---Here. Take it, then. Come on, now.
We're going.

OTTO catches the negligee.

OTTO--- Going?

BOWDEN---Back to the mine. Snap out of it now.

He turns away and gathers up his jacket. OTTO holds the
negligee, stupidly,folds it and puts it inside his
shirt. Goes to corner and fills glass of water and drinks
it, fills again. BOWDEN watches him, ready to depart.

BOWDEN--- Come on, come on.

OTTO (drinking, filling glass again)---Water,
water. Jeez, I dreamed last night they had
stopped making it.

76 DISSOLVE with sound of engine to BOWDEN and OTTO in
flivver, leaving hotel.

77 DISSOLVE with engine to flivver stopping at field, BOW-
DEN and OTTO get out.

OTTO--- What a head. What a head.

BOWDEN---Why did you keep on drinking it then?
Didn't I tell you not to?

87.

540

OTTO--- I didn't think you meant it then. Jeez
what a -----

BOWDEN---Come on.

He turns, halts. PAN to BOWDEN'S view of the ship alread
on the line, squad of soldiers about it. PAN to BOWDEN'S
face, grave.

BOWDEN--- They've got the ship out.

OTTO---Oh, what a------ Huh?

BOWDEN---Did you send word out here that we
were-----Hell. You couldn't have. You didn't
even know I intended......

OTTO---What's the matter? You guess they are
not going to----

BOWDEN (turns on)--- Come on.

TRUCK on to ship, soldiers about it, the LIEUTENANT
turning, recognises BOWDEN, his expression becomes suave
and alert.

LIEUTENANT---Senor, good morning.

BOWDEN---Morning. (Glances about, watchful)
All ready for us, I see.

LIEUTENANT--- When have we not been ready for
you, senor? And when will we not always be?

BOWDEN---Yes. I see that now.

LIEUTENANT---Meaning that for a time you did
not know it?

BOWDEN---No. Not at all. (Looks about, grave,
alert, then at LIEUTENANT) Well?-----

LIEUTENANT---You wish to depart now?

BOWDEN---I don't know. Do I? You seem to know
more about my actions than I do.

LIEUTENANT---Ah. This little affair. (Produces
key, offers it with an air) Permir me, senor.

(BOWDEN takes key; LIEUTENANT turns to CORPORAL)
You, there. The box which contains the fire
machine.

CORPORAL takes box from a soldier, presents it. BOWDEN
looks at LIEUTENANT, who watches him, shrugs, opens box,
jerks his head at OTTO.

88.

541

                    BPWDEN--- Put it on.

                    OTTO (takes magneto)---They're going to let us
                    use it, are they? Going to let us take a littl
                    hop in our own ship, huh?

                    BOWDEN--- Come on. Get it on the ship.

OTTO climbs aboard. LIEUTENANT is watching BOWDEN.

                    LIEUT---Your bags are already aboard, senor.

                    BOWDEN--- Thanks. Good of you.

                    LIEUT---It seems that you did not need them
                    last night, anyway.

                    BOWDEN---Are you asking me? (to OTTO)
                    Want any help?

                    OTTO---No. (He emerges carrying crank) O.K.
                    What do we do now?

                    BOWDEN--- Get set with the crank.

                    OTTO---Sure I';; get set with it. You just
                    keep him looking at you a minute longer. 1'll
                    get it set into him and take a couple of turns

                    BOWDEN--- Get set there. (To LIEUTENANT) One
                    may depart, senor?

                    LIEUT--- Why not, senor?

BOWDEN approaches, mounts, OTTO sets the crank.

                    LIEUT--- A pleasant journey.

                    BOWDEN---Thanks. (To OTTO) Clear. (OTTO begins
                    to turn crank. The LIEUT watches BOWDEN)

                    LIEUT---And a safe and quick return.

                    BOWDEN---Thanks.I hope it will se safe. any-
                    way.

                    LIEUT---It will be, if it is also quick.

                      es.oOTTO enters ship, engine increases and
                      gh DISSOLVE to

                        diminishes above pass, sound dies away.

                      89

         542

Bowden
Get set with the crank.

Otto
Sure I'll get set with it. You just keep him looking at you a minute longer. I'll get it set into
him and take a couple of turns...

Bowden
Get set there.
          (to Lieutenant)
One may depart, senor?

Lieutenant
Why not, senor?

Bowden approaches, mounts. Otto sets the
crank.

Lieutenant
A pleasant journey.

Bowden
Thanks.
          (to Otto)
Clear.
          (Otto begins to turn crank. The
          Lieutenant watches Bowden)

Lieutenant
And a safe and quick return.

Bowden
Thanks. I hope it will be safe, anyway.

Lieutenant
It will be, if it is also quick.

Engine catches. Otto enters ship, engine increases and carries through

DISSOLVE TO:

78.   SHIP - TAKING OFF.

Diminishes above pass, sound dies away.

T H E   E N D

On the set of *Lazy River* (1933). The man sitting on the right with script and pipe may be Faulkner. (c) MGM. From the Library of the Academy of Motion Picture Arts and Sciences.

Louisiana Lou / Lazy River

Between late April and mid-May of 1933, Faulkner wrote a 62-page script for Tod Browning's *Louisiana Lou*. The first half of the script has apparently disappeared, and the second half has not been released for publication. It may still be of interest, however, to learn something about the material he was adapting and the picture that, under the direction of George B. Seitz, was released on 7 March 1934 as *Lazy River*.

The original property was Lea David Freeman's play *Ruby* (also known as *Dance Hall Daisy*). It is the story of Bill Lawton, who falls from his rich father's graces when he marries Ruby, a dance hall hostess. Convinced that Ruby is of good character and that he will someday be a famous writer, Bill takes his wife to a shrimping camp in the bayou country, where he plans to research a book. The camp is run by Miss Minnie (a part tailored for Marie Dressler, one reader observed; Ruby was considered a good part for Jean Harlow), a Yankee who advises Ruby to leave Bill for her own good; in the intervening three years since he left his family, Bill has deteriorated into an adulterer—he is currently having an affair with Delphine, a young Cajun—and a self-pitying nonwriter. The Cajun Dr. Titeaux discovers the affair and warns Bill that the Cajun men have a tradition of killing anyone who seduces one of their own. Although he had promised to take Delphine to New Orleans to buy her some new clothes, Bill decides instead to break it off with her, but she has stolen Bill's gun and threatens him with it, which leads to a struggle in which Delphine is accidentally killed. Bill leaves her body on "Suicide Bench," as if she had killed herself for love, then confesses the whole thing to Ruby, who forgives him and tries to arrange for them to leave that same night on a boat run by Chinese Sam (who smuggles aliens at $1,000 a head—very much like Mr. Sing in Hemingway's *To Have and Have Not*). But Minnie's partner, Captain McTavish, scares off Chinese Sam and forces Ruby to agree to sleep with him if he takes them away in *his* boat. Bill, who has discovered his integrity in the course of the evening, starts a fight with McTavish; Minnie intervenes, telling the couple to escape in her boat while she holds off a band of Cajuns (who have come to avenge Delphine) with Bill's gun.

The two pages of *Louisiana Lou* (34 and 62) I have been able to examine suggest that Faulkner worked from the basic outline provided by *Ruby*, changing Bill's name to Ed, Chinese Sam's to Sam Kee, and Ruby's to Dolly. One page has Dolly discover that Delphine expects to go with Ed to New Orleans for some clothes. The final page is difficult to sort out, but it appears that Faulkner had Minnie be Dolly's mother. Minnie tells Ed that he should escape on a small boat and promises to get Dolly to Sam Kee's "in time." Ed reminds her that if she fails, he will surely be murdered. Minnie goes to Dolly and tells her to unpack her bags; then they hear shots. There is a dissolve to Delphine's body hanging from "Suicide Oak," then a shot of Minnie's playing a carillon in the church belfry. The script closes with a shot of Dolly "in Evangeline pose"; she is being watched through the window by Armand. This suggests at the very least that Faulkner gave the story an unhappy ending, making Minnie partly responsible for Ed's death.

The earliest surviving script in the MGM files is a Dialogue Continuity from Chandler Sprague and Harry Hervey, dated 19 June 1933 and covering the first half of the story. It seems very likely that this script was partly based on Faulkner's, since it includes "Suicide Oak" rather than "Suicide Bench" and since it introduces the figure of Armand and the theme of "Evangeline." In this version, Minnie is Ed's mother, and Ed's wife is named Helen. Delphine is afraid of the "Avenging Angels," who trace on the doors of wayward girls' cabins a mysterious circle, the sign of "the wedding ring she didn't wait for." Armand is a young Cajun who falls in love with Helen; both of them confess a mutual childhood fascination with the story of Gabriel and Evangeline, and Armand points out the oak tree where, according to legend, they used to meet. Armand used to imagine he could see Evangeline in its branches; what he does not say is that he has found in Helen the image of that romantic ideal. Toward the end of the script, Helen is preparing to dress as Evangeline for the "Fete," the party during which Delphine was killed in *Ruby*. It seems reasonable to project some of these details onto Faulkner's script.

A much longer script—whose details are not relevant to this discussion—was prepared by Jules Furthman between August and September of 1933. By early January 1934, the producer Lucien Hubbard had prepared his own script after replacing Browning with Seitz. (Other writers listed in the legal file on *Lazy River* include Erskine Caldwell, Ray Schrock, Arthur Caesar, Leon Gordon, John

Colton, George B. Seitz, and those listed previously: Faulkner, Sprague, and Hervey). In Hubbard's version—substantially the same as the film—the hero is Bill Drexel, a newly released convict who goes to the bayou to blackmail Minnie (whose son, Armand, died in the prison). Bill discovers that Minnie is not rich, in fact that she is about to lose her shrimping property to Sam Kee; then he falls in love with Minnie's daughter, Sarah, and decides to help them. Gabby and Tiny, his prison buddies, show up at this point and help Bill frustrate Sam Kee's plot, stealing Kee's money and using it to outbid him for Minnie's property at auction and then even pickpocketing Kee afterward; Bill uses this money to become Minnie's partner. Bill then confesses to Sarah that he has "a worthless wife, Ruby." Ruby arrives that day, hoping to share in any loot. Soon afterward, a mysterious northerner appears; he turns out to be Bill's father, who welcomes Bill back into the family after seeing how well he has turned out and who reveals that Ruby secretly divorced Bill while he was in prison. Bill and Sarah marry, and Gabby and Tiny together win the affections of "Fat Suzanne," Minnie's cook.

Hubbard's script was entitled *Louisiana Lou*, but in early January 1934, Frederick Donaghey wrote to MGM inquiring whether they were adapting his play of that title. Hubbard replied that his picture was "entirely original," that he had "inherited this production after it had been shelved," and that some previous work had been done toward making a film of *Ruby*. "Our present scenario, however, bears no relation whatever to anything which went before," he continued, "even having a completely new set of characters. The title LOUISIANA LOU does not fit it and we are, for the time being at least, calling it IN OLD LOUISIANA."[1] That title was shortly changed to *Lazy River*, and legal negotiations began for the rights to the title of the (unrelated) popular song.

When the picture was previewed in New York in late February, Frank Whitbeck cabled MGM his impression of the audience's response: "Divided preview opinion *Lazy River*. Picture is hokum quicky entertainment class what you would expect from average studio. Is not big in any respect except laughter. Question in minds some executives whether we are right in using superlative and extraordinary world premiere campaign on picture insignificant as *Lazy River*." Two days later he wired that "Preview cards *Lazy River* good. Mister Mannix satisfied to world premiere picture New Orleans providing you understand it is not outstanding production." The *New York Times* found *Lazy River* a "dawdling" picture with an "exceptionally well done" bayou atmosphere and "extraordinarily good" cinematography by Gregg Toland. Jean Parker (Sarah), Robert Young (Bill), C. Henry Gordon (Sam Kee), and especially Ted Healy (Gabby) and Nat Pendleton (Tiny) were praised for their performances; still, the review could not be called a rave.

When *Lazy River* was shown in Oxford, as Blotner recounts, "some Oxonians had gone to see it under the impression that it was a Faulkner screenplay," and at least one of them observed in surprise, "Bedogged if it wasn't good!"[2] But *Lazy River*, as released, was not at all the type of material Faulkner had been writing for MGM, and even *Today We Live* fails to give an adequate impression of the often complex, intense, at times personal and even—as in *MLAK*—baffling and intriguingly involuted work he had done in his first year in Hollywood. It is only with the publication of this volume that it has become possible for Faulkner enthusiasts to examine and evaluate the screenplays themselves, and it is to be hoped that much of this work, whether in part or on the whole, will prove worthy of a better-informed "Bedogged if it wasn't good!"

NOTES: INTRODUCTION TO *LOUISIANA LOU / LAZY RIVER*

1. The letter is dated 12 Jan. 1934.
2. Blotner, *Faulkner: A Biography*, 845.

Selected Bibliography
Faulkner's Film Career

ARTICLES AND BOOKS

Blotner, Joseph. "Faulkner in Hollywood." In W.R. Robinson, ed., *Man and the Movies*. Baltimore: Penguin, 1969.

———. *Faulkner: A Biography*. New York: Random, 1974.

Cowley, Malcolm. *The Faulkner-Cowley File: Letters and Memories, 1944–1962*. New York: Viking, 1966.

Dardis, Tom. *Some Time in the Sun*. New York: Penguin, 1981.

Eames, John Douglas. *The MGM Story*. New York: Crown, 1976.

Fadiman, Regina K. *Faulkner's "Intruder in the Dust": Novel into Film*. Knoxville: Univ. of Tennessee Press, 1977.

Harrington, Evans, and Ann J. Abadie, eds. *Faulkner, Modernism, and Film: Faulkner and Yoknapatawpha, 1978*. Jackson: Univ. Press of Mississippi, 1979.

Kawin, Bruce. "A Faulkner Filmography." *Film Quarterly* 30, no. 4 (Summer 1977): 12–21.

———. *Faulkner and Film*. New York: Frederick Ungar, 1977.

———. "William Faulkner." *Dictionary of Literary Biography: American Screenwriters*. Detroit: Gale Research, in press.

Marx, Samuel. *Mayer and Thalberg: The Make-Believe Saints*. New York: Random, 1975.

Mississippi Quarterly: Special Issue / William Faulkner 30, no. 3 (Summer 1977).

Sidney, George. "Faulkner in Hollywood: A Study of his Career as a Scenarist." Unpubl. Ph.D. diss., Univ. of New Mexico, 1959.

Wilde, Meta (Doherty) Carpenter, and Orin Borstin. *A Loving Gentleman: The Love Story of William Faulkner and Meta Carpenter*. New York: Simon and Schuster, 1976.

Wood, Robin. *Howard Hawks*. Garden City, N.Y.: Doubleday, 1968.

OTHER PUBLISHED FAULKNER SCREENPLAYS

Bruccoli, Matthew J., ed. *The Road to Glory*, by Joel Sayre and William Faulkner. Carbondale: Southern Illinois Univ. Press, 1981. (Afterword by George Garrett.)

Garrett, George, O.B. Hardison, Jr., and Jane R. Gelfman, eds. *Film Scripts One*. New York: Appleton-Century-Crofts, 1971; now available through Irvington Publishers. (Includes the Faulkner and Brackett script for *The Big Sleep*, though it is identified as the Furthman revision.)

Gassner, John, and Dudley Nichols, eds. *Best Film Plays—1945*. New York: Crown, 1946. (Includes Renoir's script for *The Southerner*, much of which may have been written by Faulkner.)

Kawin, Bruce, ed. *To Have and Have Not*. Madison: Univ. of Wisconsin Press, 1980.

TREATMENTS, SCREENPLAYS, "DOCTORINGS," AND TELEPLAYS BY FAULKNER

(*after a produced film indicates some on-screen evidence of Faulkner's contribution.)

Manservant (MGM, 1932, unproduced).

The College Widow (MGM, 1932, unproduced).

Absolution (MGM, 1932, unproduced).

Flying the Mail (MGM, 1932, unproduced).

Turn About (MGM, 1932; released as *Today We Live*, 1933, dir. Howard Hawks; screen credit for original story and dialogue).*

War Birds / A Ghost Story (MGM, 1932–33, unproduced).

Mythical Latin-American Kingdom Story (MGM, 1933, unproduced).

Louisiana Lou (MGM, 1933; released as *Lazy River*, 1934, dir. George B. Seitz).

Sutter's Gold (Universal, 1934; released 1936, dir. James Cruze).

The Road to Glory (Fox, 1935–36; released 1936, dir. Howard Hawks; screen credit with Joel Sayre for screenplay).*

Banjo on my Knee (Fox, 1936; released 1936, dir. John Cromwell).

Gunga Din (RKO, 1936; released 1939, dir. George Stevens).

The Last Slaver (Fox, 1936; released as *Slave Ship*, 1937, dir. Tay Garnett; screen credit for story and additional dialogue).*

Four Men and a Prayer (Fox, 1936; released 1938, dir. John Ford).

Splinter Fleet (Fox, 1936; released as *Submarine Patrol*, 1938, dir. John Ford).

Dance Hall (Fox, 1937; released 1941, dir. Irving Pichel).

Drums Along the Mohawk (Fox, 1937; released 1939, dir. John Ford).*

The De Gaulle Story (Warner Brothers, 1942, unproduced).

Air Force (Warner Brothers, 1942; released 1943, dir. Howard Hawks).*

Revolt in the Earth (Warner Brothers, 1942, unproduced).

Background to Danger (Warner Brothers, 1942; released 1943, dir. Raoul Walsh).

The Life and Death of a Bomber / Liberator Story (Warner Brothers, 1942–43, unproduced).

Five Thousand Trojan Horses (Warner Brothers, 1943; released as *Northern Pursuit*, 1943, dir. Raoul Walsh).*

Deep Valley (Warner Brothers, 1943; released 1947, dir. Jean Negulesco).*

Country Lawyer (Warner Brothers, 1943, unproduced).

Dreadful Hollow (c. 1943, for Howard Hawks, unproduced).

Battle Cry (Warner Brothers, 1943, unproduced).

Who? (Warner Brothers, 1943, unproduced).

To Have and Have Not (Warner Brothers, 1944; released 1944, dir. Howard Hawks; screen credit with Jules Furthman for screenplay).*

God Is My Co-Pilot (Warner Brothers, 1944; released 1945, dir. Robert Florey).

The Damned Don't Cry (Warner Brothers, 1944; released 1950, dir. Vincent Sherman).

The Adventures of Don Juan (Warner Brothers, 1944; released 1945, dir. Vincent Sherman).*

Fog Over London (Warner Brothers, 1944, unproduced).

Strangers in our Midst (Warner Brothers, 1944; released as *Escape in the Desert*, 1945, dir. Edward A. Blatt).

The Southerner (Producing Artists, 1944; released by United Artists, 1945, dir. Jean Renoir).*

The Big Sleep (Warner Brothers, 1944–45; released 1946, dir. Howard Hawks; screen credit with Jules Furthman and Leigh Brackett for screenplay).*

Mildred Pierce (Warner Brothers, 1944; released 1945, dir. Michael Curtiz).*

Barn Burning (1945, independent, unproduced).

Stallion Road (Warner Brothers, 1945; released 1947, dir. James V. Kern).

Continuous Performance (1946, independent, unproduced).

One Way to Catch a Horse (no date, independent, unproduced).

Untitled science-fiction scenario (no date, independent, unproduced; Alderman Library).

Untitled script (no date, independent, unproduced; Alderman Library).

Intruder in the Dust (MGM, 1949; released 1949, dir. Clarence Brown).*

The Left Hand of God (Warner Brothers, 1951; released by Fox, 1955, dir. Edward Dmytryk).

The Brooch (CBS TV, 1953; broadcast 1953).*

Shall Not Perish (CBS TV, 1953; broadcast 1954).*

Old Man (1953, independent teleplay, unproduced).

Untitled television series (no date, independent, unproduced; Alderman Library).

Land of the Pharaohs (Warner Brothers, 1953–54; released 1955, dir. Howard Hawks; screen credit with Harry Kurnitz and Harold Jack Bloom for screenplay).*

The Graduation Dress (CBS TV, no date; broadcast 1960).*

Index

(The facsimiles in this book have not been indexed.)

Index

Faulkner's MGM Screenplays has been set into type on Mergenthaler Variable Input Phototypesetter in 10-pt Melior with 2-pt spacing between the lines. Broadway Engraved type was selected for display. The book was designed by Jim Billingsley, composed by Computer Composition, Inc., Nashville, Tennessee, printed by Thomson-Shore, Inc., Dexter, Michigan, and bound by John H. Dekker & Sons, Grand Rapids, Michigan. The paper on which the book is printed bears the watermark of S.D.Warren and is designed for an effective life of at least 300 years.

THE UNIVERSITY OF TENNESSEE PRESS : KNOXVILLE